Brooklands Books

CW01660475

BMW M3 Ultimate Portfolio 1986-2006

Compiled by R M Clarke

ISBN 185520 7508

BROOKLANDS BOOKS LTD.
P.O. BOX 146, COBHAM,
SURREY, KT11 1LG. UK
sales@brooklands-books.com

A-BM3UP

www.brooklands-books.com

Printed in China

Brooklands Books

Acknowledgements

Regular readers of Brooklands books will know that books like this one are an attempt to create a living archive and to make available to todays enthusiasts material about their cars which has become hard to find. In putting such books together, we depend on the generosity and understanding of those who originally published the copyright stories we reproduce. For material in the present volume, our thanks go to the publishers of *Autocar, Automobile, Autosport, BMW Car, Car, Car and Driver, Car Australia, Car South Africa, EVO, Max Power, Motor, Motor Australia, Motor Sport, Motor Trend, Performance Car, Road & Track, Road & Track Specials, Sports Car International, Sports Car Monthly* and *What Car?*

R.M. Clarke

One of the most iconic cars out of Germany is undoubtedly the BMW M3. Based as it is on the prosaic 3 Series family sedan, it has taken the term "sports sedan" to spectacular heights over the past two decades. In fact, it has redefined it.

As with many developments from BMW, racing played a big part in the evolution of the M3. Remember the M1 with its sonorous 24-valve 3.5-litre DOHC six-cylinder engine? Well, in creating the first M3 those clever engineers at M GmbH removed two cylinders from the six to make a 2.3-litre DOHC four that produced 200bhp, gave it a top speed of 140mph and ran from 0-60mph in 6.8 seconds; add in flared wheel arches and take some of the luxury items out and voila! they had a race winner straight out of the blocks.

There were several iterations of the M3 including two EVO versions, and a convertible. By 1990 there was the Sports Evolution version that had a 2.5-litre DOHC four-cylinder engine that raised the bar even further. Think in terms of 238bhp at 7000rpm(!), a near 155 top speed and 0-60mph in 6.0 seconds. That was quick by any standards, let alone for a compact family sedan.

BMW shocked the world with the release of the E36 M3 in 1993. Using the stylish coupe body M GmbH designed and produced a new DOHC 24-valve in-line six-cylinder engine with 3.0-litres capacity. It has gone down in motoring history as one of the most magnificent engines of all time and deservedly so. It pumped out a stunning 286bhp at 7000rpm! Maximum speed was now an electronically limited 155mph (a few early cars had no restriction and a top speed of 162mph) and the classic 0-60mph sprint took just 5.4 seconds. Not only was the new M3 quick but the international media went ballistic in its praise for the German hotrod. Everybody who was anybody simply had to be seen in one.

Development continued with a convertible being available from 1993 and a four-door sedan the following year. A GT was built for Le Mans homologation in 1995 with 295bhp and an EVO edition came the same year with a larger 3.2-litre engine and VANOS camshaft timing, power now being 321bhp at 7400rpm. At the end, in 1998, BMW built just 50 of the M3 GT2 that had larger spoilers and polished alloy wheels.

In 2000, BMW released the much anticipated E46 M3 that, while only fractionally faster in acceleration (0-60mph in 5.0 seconds), boasted a thoroughly revised engine that was a mere 45cc larger in capacity but now produced 343bhp at an amazing 7900rpm. It was a much more refined car to drive. In some of the darker colours available it looked drop-dead gorgeous. A convertible came in 2001, the much talked about M3 CSL with it carbon fibre roof in 2003 and the M3 CS in 2005.

In the opinion of the world's media the E46 BMW M3 was a simply brilliant package that had absolutely no peers unless you considered the true exoticars. It was a genuine sales success all over the world.

Gavin Farmer

Brooklands Books

Contents

Evolution of the M3

It's 21 years since BMW first unleashed the brilliant M3. **Ben Barry** celebrates its coming of age

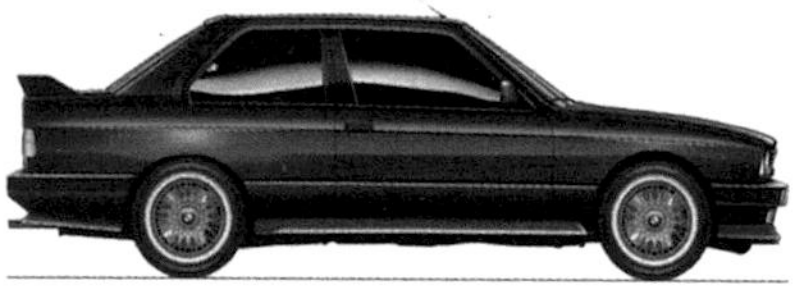

E30 M3 EVO 1 (1987)
Slightly more aggressive front lip spoiler, extra blade under rear spoiler and no foglights differentiate this model. Retains the original's 15in wheels. **Engine:** 2302cc 16V in-line four, 200bhp @ 6750rpm, 176lb ft @ 4750rpm **Stats:** 6.8sec 0-60mph, 143mph **Price 1987:** £22,750 **Price now:** £8-11k

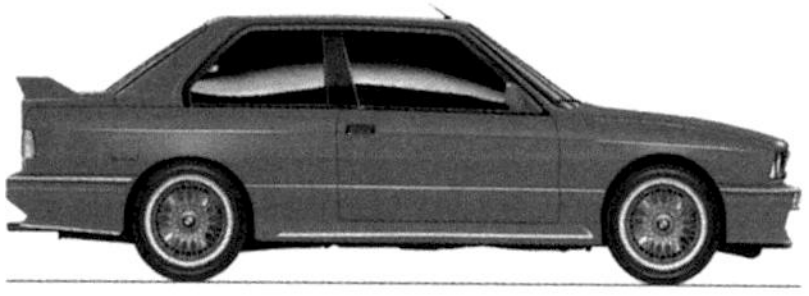

E30 M3 EVO II (1988)
Wheels now 16in, engine gets new pistons, cams, increased compression ratio and re-map. Body colours limited to blue, silver, red. Engine detailed in white. **Engine:** 2302cc 16V in-line four, 220bhp @ 6750rpm, 181lb ft @ 4750rpm **Stats:** 6.6sec 0-60mph, 148mph **Price 1988:** £26,960 **Price now:** £9-13k

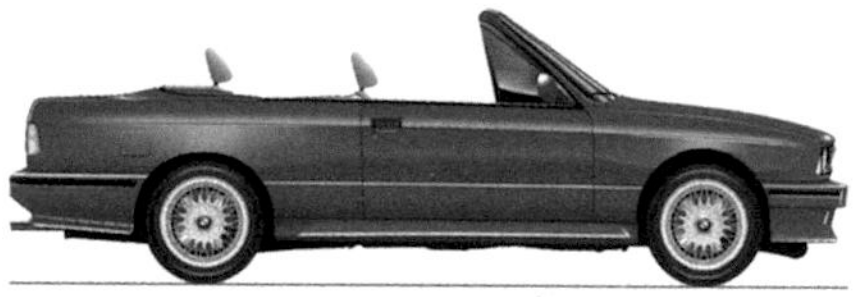

E30 M3 CABRIOLET (1988-1991)
Only 786 hand-assembled at BMW's Garching Motorsport plant. Outputs were 195bhp, 200bhp and 215bhp, all got leather. Boot lid shared with 325i. **Engine:** 2302cc 16V in-line four, 215bhp @ 6750rpm, 170lb ft @ 4750rpm **Stats:** 6.8sec 0-60mph, 146mph **Price 1989:** £37,250 **Price now:** £9-12k

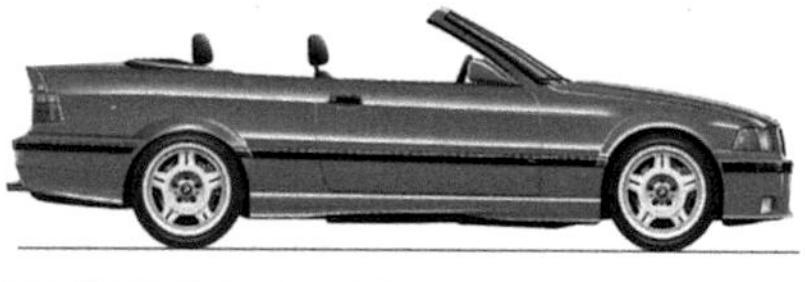

E36 M3 CONVERTIBLE (1993-1999)
Structural bracing adds 80kg, bodyshell less rigid. Hood is electric, seats comfort-spec, coupé's optional five-spoke alloys standard, though polished. **Engine:** 2990cc 24V straight six, 286bhp @ 7000rpm, 236lb ft @ 3600rpm **Stats:** 5.7sec 0-60mph, 155mph **Price 1994:** £38,210 **Price now:** £6-9k

E36 M3 SALOON (1994-1998)
First saloons feature softer suspension, Evo cars revert to coupé spec. All get nasty wood trim, Nappa leather and comfort-spec seats. 1114 built in RHD **Engine:** 2990cc 24V straight six, 286bhp @ 7000rpm, 236lb ft @ 3600rpm **Stats:** 5.5sec 0-60mph, 156mph **Price 1994:** £32,450 **Price now:** £6-9k

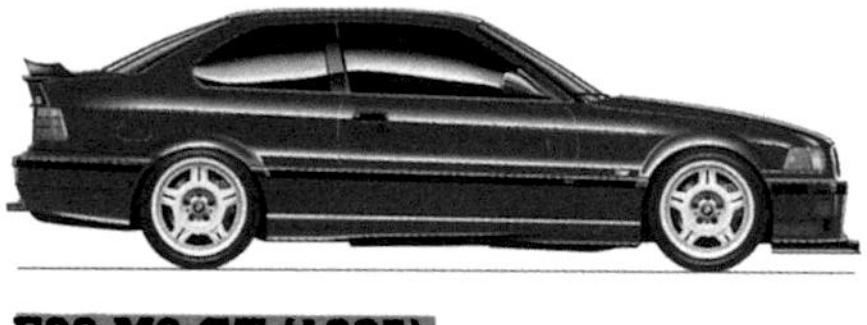

E36 M3 GT (1995)
Built to comply with Le Mans regs, just 356 LHD and 50 RHD were made. All green with larger spoilers and upgraded 3.0-litre. UK cars get wood, as it were. **Engine:** 2990cc 24V straight six, 295bhp @ 7000rpm, 238lb ft @ 3900rpm **Stats:** 5.4sec 0-60mph, 155mph **Price 1995:** £39,000 **Price now:** £9-12k

E46 M3 CONVERTIBLE (2001-2006)
More convincing than the E36 drop-top, but still missing the point. Plenty of people disagree, mind. **Engine:** 3246cc 24V straight six, 343bhp @ 7900rpm, 269lb ft @ 4900rpm **Stats:** 5.3sec 0-60mph, 155mph **Price 2001:** £41,950 **Price now:** £20-25k

E46 M3 CSL (2003)
Carbon roof, buckets, SMG and *that* noise create ultimate track-day special. Expensive then, cheap now. **Engine:** 3246cc 24V straight six, 360bhp @ 7900rpm, 273lb ft @ 4900rpm **Stats:** 4.7sec 0-60mph, 155mph **Price 2003:** £58,455 **Price now:** £30-35k

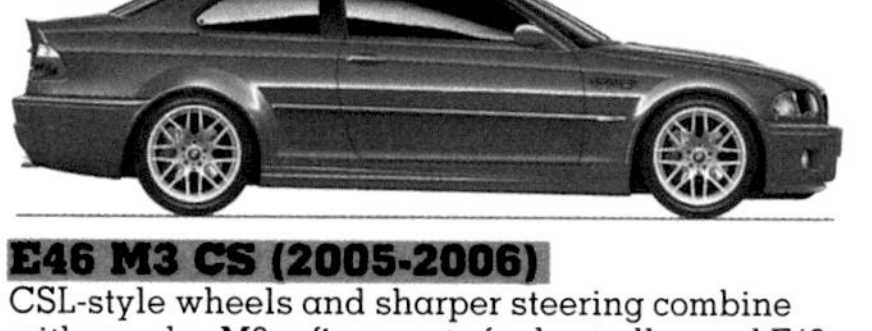

E46 M3 CS (2005-2006)
CSL-style wheels and sharper steering combine with regular M3 refinements for best all-round E46. Brilliant. **Engine:** 3246cc 24V straight six, 343bhp @ 7900rpm, 269lb ft @ 4900rpm **Stats:** 5.0sec 0-60mph, 155mph **Price 2005:** £43,555 **Price now:** £35-38k

Illustrations Archimede

E30 BMW M3 (1986-1990)

Homologated to compete in Group A touring car races, the first M3 is the only generation to have genuine motorsport origins and to be LHD only. Based on 1982's two-door E30 shell, it was nonetheless very different – blistered arches allowed for larger race rims, while a higher boot lid and more steeply raked windscreen helped aero and visually set it apart. Four-pot prototypes were famously created by removing two cylinders from an M635 cylinder head. Despite being a motorsport special, demand was so high that 17,184 cars were made. **Engine:** 2302cc 16V in-line four, 200bhp @ 6750rpm, 176lb ft @ 4750rpm **Stats:** 6.8sec 0-60mph, 143mph **Price 1987:** £22,750 **Price now:** £8-11k

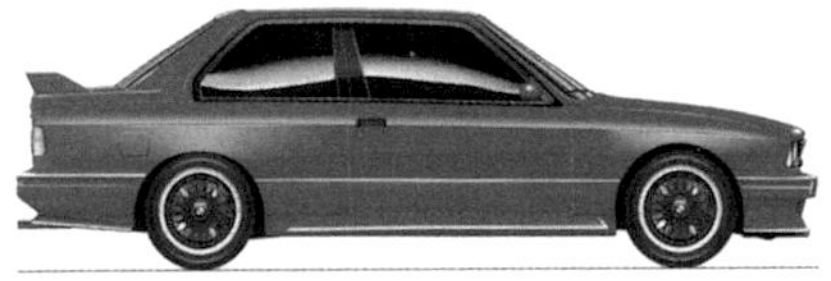

E30 M3 RAVAGLIA (1989)

UK limited edition in Misano Red only with half-leather seats. Near identical but far rarer than Euro-only Cecotto which came with Nogaro Silver paint. **Engine:** 2302cc 16V in-line four, 215bhp @ 6750rpm, 170lb ft @ 4750rpm **Stats:** 6.8sec 0-60mph, 148mph **Price 1988:** £26,960 **Price now:** £9-13k

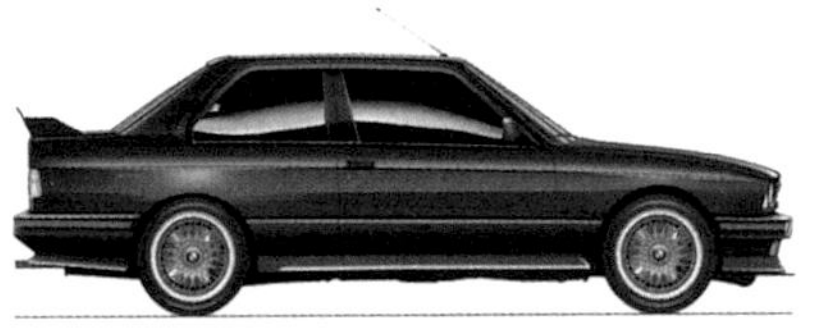

E30 M3 SPORT EVO (1989-1990)

Red with black stripes or vice versa and featuring adjustable front and rear spoilers. Bore and stroke increase took four-pot to its limit. Just 51 came to UK. **Engine:** 2467cc 16V in-line four, 238bhp @ 7000rpm, 177lb ft @ 4750rpm **Stats:** 6.0sec 0-60mph, 154mph **Price 1988:** £34,500 **Price now:** £14-20k

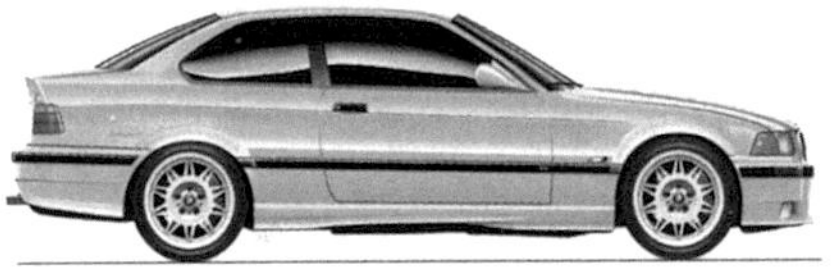

E36 M3 (1992-1995)

Unrecognisable as E30 offspring, E36 was more understated, more refined and boasted a brilliantly fizzy straight six. 54,500 sold. First cars unrestricted. **Engine:** 2990cc 24V straight six, 286bhp @ 7000rpm, 236lb ft @ 3600rpm **Stats:** 5.4sec 0-60mph, 162mph **Price 1993:** £32,450 **Price now:** £6-9k

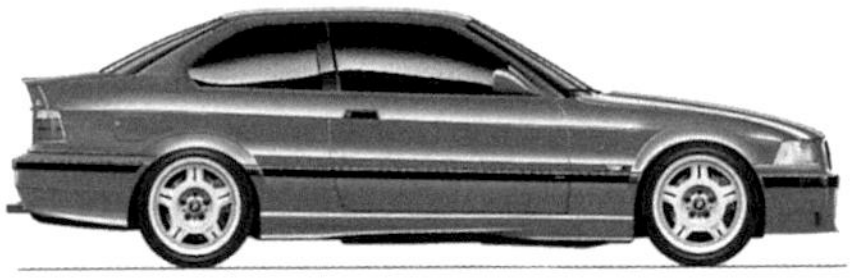

E36 M3 EVO (1995-1999)

Makeover includes extra capacity, six speed 'box, M5 brakes, new suspension, new colours… and faulty VANOS units. Convertible and saloon still sold. **Engine:** 3201cc 24V straight six, 321bhp @ 7400rpm, 258lb ft @ 3250rpm **Stats:** 5.3sec 0-60mph, 155mph **Price 1996:** £36,550 **Price now:** £8-14k

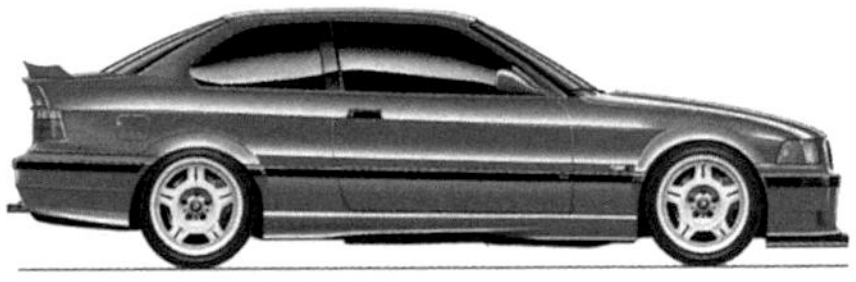

E36 M3 GT2 (1998)

Just 50 built to mark end of E36 production. Cosmetic tweaks only, including larger spoilers and convertible-syle polished alloys. High spec. **Engine:** 3201cc 24V straight six, 321bhp @ 7400rpm, 258lb ft @ 3250rpm **Stats:** 5.3sec 0-60mph, 155mph **Price 1998:** £43,995 **Price now:** £10-13k

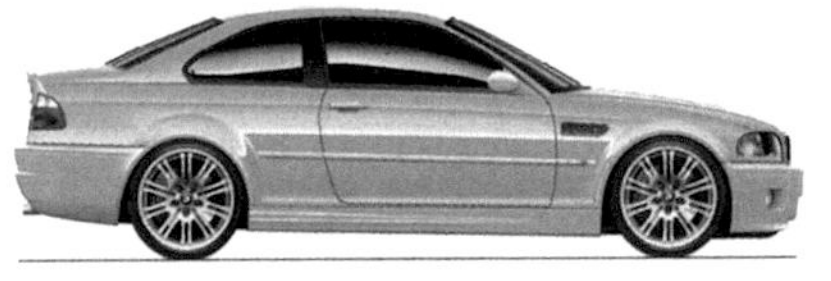

E46 M3 (2000-2006)

The luxury of the E36 coupled with a modern-day interpretation of E30 dynamics. Not hugely faster than an E36 but so much better to drive. **Engine:** 3246cc 24V straight six, 343bhp @ 7900rpm, 269lb ft @ 4900rpm **Stats:** 5.0sec 0-60mph, 155mph **Price 2000:** £38,500 **Price now:** £17-20k

THE E46 M3 IS NOT HUGELY FASTER THAN AN E36, BUT IT'S SO MUCH BETTER TO DRIVE

BORN THREE

It's been a long time in the making but BMW's 150 mph M3 is ready to take on Ford's Sierra Cosworth and Mercedes' 2.3-16. And win. David Vivian has driven it

Dieter Quester turned in and there was understeer. It scrubbed off some speed but not much; the chassis was still finding plenty of bite from tyres that had taken a fearsome hammering. More importantly, the understeer settled the car in preparation for the ensuing bootful of power. With it, Quester instinctively wound off half a turn of lock and the M3 drifted, all-of-a-piece, towards the exit, balanced easily and undramatically on the throttle. With the straight fast approaching, the tail drifted gently out of line but Quester didn't lift, preferring to hold the slide with the steering and straighten it at the last moment by nudging the outer kerb with the M3's rear tyre.

"The feel is different," said BMW's articulate racer. "More safe." *More safe* for Quester was turning in early and pressing the lightweight trainer on his right foot into the carpet so hard it left the imprint of its sole there. What we were turning into was the Mugello racing circuit's famously long and demanding right-hander – a bend that in one neck-straining sweep takes you back in the direction from which you have just come.

What Quester was saying, in the politest possible way, was this: in a regular BMW 325i, we would have been pointing in the opposite direction long before the end of the bend – probably upside down as well. In the M3, however, not only was there every chance of completing the manoeuvre with the rear wheels following the front, but of completing it in some style and with respectable pace. For here, at last, was a 3-Series BMW with a seriously well-balanced

chassis.

A German racing car in road-going trim on an Italian racing track set among the olive groves of Tuscany was our venue. We had driven to the latter in the former to be enlightened by a man who made his mark driving the M3's only true ancestor, the M1. The mid-engined M1 was conceived to meet and beat the might of Porsche in Group 4 but, as a fast and beautifully-engineered alternative to the fragile Modenese exotics, the Giugiaro-styled, 24-valve missile was little short of a miracle.

Unlike the Motorsport products that directly succeeded the M1 – the M635 CSi and the M5, both of which are on sale in the UK – the M3 exactly shares the M1's design objective: to succeed in the toughest arena of all – motorsport. More specifically, it will be campaigned in Group A, the touring car class in which the machines are closest to standard road trim. As such, a minimum of 5000 M3s have to be built within 12 successive months but, since the M3 is to be made alongside other BMWs on the production line (rather than hand-built like the M1), BMW's aim is to sell a total of 13,000. It thus joins Mercedes' 190E 2.3-16 and Ford's just-launched Sierra RS Cosworth as a desirable "off-the-peg" racer boasting supercar performance from an exclusive four-seater package. But don't reach for your cheque book yet. BMW say they have no plans to make the M3 in right-hand drive. To do so, the excuse goes, would involve fabricating a smaller and less efficient exhaust manifold, knocking the claimed power output down from 200 bhp to around 185 bhp. Not very BMW.

It is tempting to regard the M3 as an expedient ticket back into the sport, a once-over-lightly homologation special conveniently based on the top 3-Series model – a car which, as the 325i, boasts a healthy power/weight ratio. But it is easy to be deceived. The neat, tightly-dimensioned shape is unmistakable but look more closely, and you discover that only the bonnet and the doors are original. Fatter body-colour bumpers, bulging wheel arches, deep chin-spoiler and side skirts, raised polyurethane bootlid topped off with prominent ski-blade spoiler, steeper rear screen and C-posts: it all adds up to more than your average side-street conversion. But the cosmetics are only the start.

More likely to quicken the pulse is what lurks under the skin. The four-cylinder 2.3-litre engine that powers the M3 is, logically enough, a chopped-down version of the 3.5-litre straight-six, twin-cam powerplant from the M6/M5 and, in slightly de-tuned form, the legendary M1. The four-valves-per-cylinder head naturally loses eight valves but, in respect of cam profiles and combustion-chamber design, little has been changed. The latter are pent-shaped and there are lips on the piston crowns to promote "squish". Fuel supply and engine management are looked after by Bosch's computerised ML Motronic system and an oil cooler comes as standard. On a compression ratio of 10.5:1, maximum outputs are 200 bhp at 6750 rpm and 175 lb ft of torque at 4750 rpm. For comparison, the 2.3-litre 16-valve "four" developed with the help of Cosworth for the MB 2.3-16

delivers 185 bhp and 173 lb ft while the turbocharged 2-litre of the Sierra Cosworth matches its 201 bhp with 200 lb ft. But let's not forget the 325i's turbine-smooth sohc 2.5-litre straight-six which develops 175 bhp – not bad for a "cooking" unit.

Chassis improvements are extensive, as they need to be if the M3 is to be regarded as a serious racer. Changes include increased castor for better stability and steering response, with revised steering knuckles and meatier wheel bearings to cope with the greater cornering forces. At the rear, a stiffer anti-

Right: M3 boasts BMW's usual high standards of instrumentation and ergonomics. Left: Great looking 16-valver delivers what feels like an honest 200 bhp

roll bar is linked to the struts via connecting bars instead of being attached directly to the suspension arms. Both the rates of the coil springs and the gas-filled dampers have been up-rated for quicker response at the helm, while wide 15 in diameter five-stud alloys by BBS wearing fat 205/55 VR15 tyres guarantee more grip. The brakes have also received attention. There are bigger discs front and rear and heavy-duty calipers to work with them. The master cylinder has been recalibrated for swifter pedal response. Also more direct is the steering which boasts a 19.6:1 rack against the 325i's 21.4:1.

The standard equipment list for Germany (where the car costs 58,000 DM or £17,600) is unusually fat and includes ABS anti-lock braking, electrically-adjusted and heated door mirrors, fog lamps front and rear, Recaro bucket seats, a close-ratio five-speed gearbox, a limited-slip differential, power steering and a long-range (15.5-gallon) fuel tank.

Inside, the M3 isn't unnecessarily macho. But for its thicker leather rim, the steering wheel is the familiar BMW three-spoke design through which the four-dial instrument display can be clearly seen. There is no drilled accelerator pedal (it *is* ideally placed for heel and toe downshifts), no expanses of matt-black plastic. Instead, the cabin looks and feels rather more plush than usual, with the seats and door panels trimmed in pleasant-to-touch pepita cloth and the switchgear, as ever a pleasure to use. The driving position is as near perfect as makes no difference and seats offer real support.

On the other hand, there is no way a 325i driver can fire-up the M3 and not be disappointed. If he has just chopped-in his sweet-revving paragon for this broad-shouldered street-racer, he will be tempted to switch it off again. It's no use being coy about this: at tickover and cruising around town, the M3 sounds every bit as terrible as the 190 E 2.3-16 – clattery, thrummy, horrible. No BMW salesman would try to sell this car on the basis of a "spin round the block" But then the M3 doesn't try to be all things to all men. What it tries to be is fast, and if a claimed top speed of 147 mph and 0-100 kph (62 mph) in 6.7 sec isn't fast, Ronald Reagan's face is smoother than a baby's bottom. It puts the Bavarian bomber a rung above Merc's rival 2.3-16 (137 mph and 0-60 mph in 7.4 sec as tested by *Motor*) and BMW's own 325i (135 mph, 7.4 sec). Take the M3 to the limit in the lower gears, and you don't feel inclined to disbelieve the figures.

Blasting on to the Bologna *autostrada*, the M3 delivered a devastating kick in second and third, revving furiously to the 7000 rpm ignition cut out and sounding not unlike an M-powered F3 car belting out of the Silverstone pit-lane. Over the final 1500 revs, the engine's disappointing boominess disappears and is replaced by a hard, crisp bark only high-performance "fours" can make. There's plenty of push in fourth, too, but in fifth (directly geared, take note, and not an overdrive) the pace slackens noticeably: you sense the engine's relatively meagre torque and a reduced margin of superiority over other fast traffic. The M3 certainly isn't the 150 mph car the Sierra Cosworth is and anything over 140 mph is likely to be hard won. It feels as if it has the legs of the pricier Merc, though and, for BMW, that's the important thing.

Whether it has the better chassis is much harder to decide. The ride comfort contest is closer than anyone would have expected – quite simply, because the 2.3-16 is so unreasonably good. If the BMW gives anything away to the Merc it is at low speed: it doesn't filter out the small bumps quite so well and there's a trace more bump thump. For overall damping control and composure, however, it's a dead heat. Both cars feel tremendously level and stable at speed.

In the handling stakes, it's even better news for the BMW. The 2.3-16 – judged by many to have the finest chassis of any front-engined/rear-driven production car in the world – has finally met its match. For on-the-limit poise, the Merc still holds a small advantage, but when it comes to steering response and feel, neutrality and grip the M3 has it What is so remarkable is that all this ability has been extracted from a chassis that, over the years, has become one of the most criticised in the business. Most of the tail-happy tendencies have, thankfully, been eradicated from the 325i and its less powerful stablemates. But, be in no doubt, the M3 operates in a different dimension. After the M1's, it has the most impressive chassis to emerge from BMW Motorsport.

We found out at Mugello. Chasing Quester round the track, he was neat, I was spectacular. Any car that can make a great driver look ordinary and an ordinary driver look good can't be at all bad.

PRICE £22,750, **TOP SPEED** 139mph, **0-60mph** 7.1secs, **MPG** 20.3

FOR Performance, handling, stability **AGAINST** Rear accommodation

WINNING COMBINATION

For an homologation special, BMW's M3 offers a remarkable combination of performance, refinement and practicality. Its price tag may seem high but, as our test team discovered, it is certainly a lot of car for the money

The launch of the BMW M3 marks an historic moment for the Bavarian manufacturer, since this is the first BMW to be developed by the motor sports division and produced by BMW AG.

The M3 is seen as a successor to the legendary M1 — a competitions inspired machine — but the M3 is much more than a production racer. BMW has made every attempt to make the car as civilised as possible for everyday driving. It may have all the latest innovations in its make up to ensure highly competitive track performance, but BMW has deliberately not compromised comfort or equipment levels.

The 2.3-litre, 16-valve engine, developing no fewer than 200bhp at 6750rpm, easily puts the M3 at the top

TIM ANDREW

of the 3-Series performance league.

The general exterior specification, which includes distinctive wheelarch flares (designed to accommodate up to 10ins wheels in full race trim), extended sills, front and rear air dams, plus light alloy wheels and low-profile tyres, ensures a further degree of exclusivity. In addition, BMW has carefully raked the rear screen to give a coupé appearance to the two-door shell. The boot is now slightly shorter and the lid higher.

Under the steel shell and composite body add-ons, BMW has paid ▶

Raked rear screen *gives distinctive coupé appearance*
Hard cornering *(right) produces balanced and progressive understeer*

TECHNICAL FOCUS

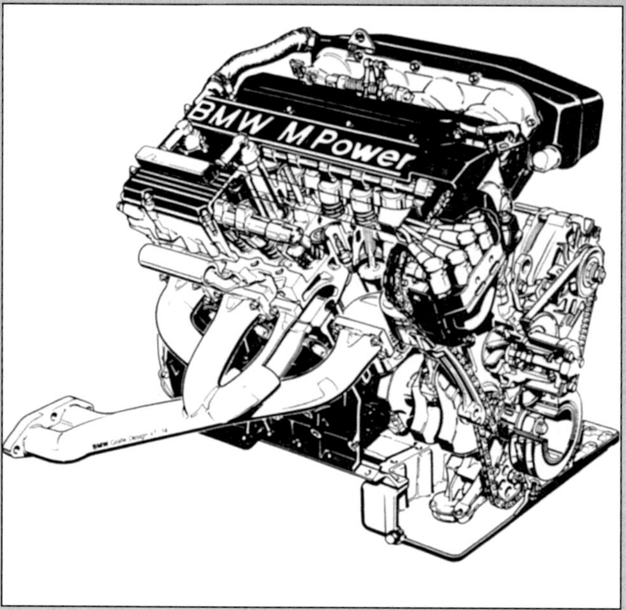

Having decided in 1981 to end production of the mid-engined, two-seater, M1 coupé, BMW initiated development for a Group A production-racing successor.

It was decided to base the new sports car on the 3-Series (introduced in 1982). Five years of intensive development later, we have the result in the shape of the M3 — albeit in left-hand-drive form only.

The heart of the M3 is the 2.3-litre, 16-valve engine — chosen because of its compact size and the reduced torsional vibration resulting from the short-throw crankshaft. The power unit is also happy to rev far higher than a straight six engine, for example.

The M3's block is based on the four-cylinder unit which first entered production in the 1960s with the BMW 1500. This is a cast-iron unit with its cylinder bore increased to 93.4mm. As a result of this larger bore, the individual cylinder liners in the middle of the block had to be cast together — a design feature already adopted by BMW for its large six-cylinder engine. The forged crankshaft running in five main bearings has a stroke of 84mm, giving decidedly over-square dimensions.

A special cast light-alloy sump with baffle plates and oil ducts improves oil supply while a separate oil cooler is also fitted, behind the front spoiler.

The dimensions of the combustion chamber correspond largely to the four-valve-per-cylinder head of BMW's six-cylinder unit, featured in the M1, M635CSi and M5. The twin-overhead camshafts are driven via a duplex chain while the valves are operated by cup tappets.

The 37mm inlet valves are inclined at an angle of 18deg and the 32mm dia exhaust valves cut at an angle of 20deg. The spark plug for each cylinder is arranged centrally between the valves.

Fuel is supplied by the Bosch BMW Digital Motor Electronics (Motronic) fuel-injection with air volume metering. The fuel/air mixture is fed into the combustion chamber via four separate intake manifolds, each featuring an independent throttle butterfly. The exhaust manifold is a tubular, four-branch one.

Meticulous engine assembly, with great attention being paid to high efficiency, results in a power output of 200bhp in road trim, and almost 300bhp in full-blooded, Group A specification for the racetrack.

◀ particular attention to good directional stability. Wheel castor is increased threefold, the anti-roll bars are a larger diameter and the steering modified to give increased feel.

Apart from the tuned shock absorbers and rear springs, the rear axle assembly is the same as other 3-Series BMWs. The brake system, however, is not. Both front and rear discs are bigger and thicker with reinforced calipers. Larger 5-Series-size wheel bearings are incorporated on special front stub axles for increased durability.

Inside, equipment levels are high with central locking, electric windows, door mirrors and slide and tilt steel sunroof as standard. There's also a leather-rimmed steering wheel and gearknob, hide-trimmed seats front and rear, plus a Blaupunkt radio/cassette player with four speakers and electric aerial.

Standard safety items include ABS anti-lock brakes and a limited slip differential, designed to operate with 25 per cent locking action.

BMW does not offer any extras with the M3 (although metallic paint is a no-cost option). The high standard spec goes some way to justifying the £22,750 price tag, £5000 more than the next most expensive model in the 3-Series, the 325iX four-door.

PERFORMANCE

With 200bhp to play with in a car weighing under 25cwt, performance is naturally one of the M3's strong suits. Our mean maximum speed of 139mph was achieved in driving rain on a very wet track, and there would certainly be another couple of mph to come in ideal conditions — BMW in fact claims 146mph. At the best one-way speed of 140mph the engine is spinning at 6600rpm, just 150rpm below the power peak which demonstrates near-ideal gearing.

The Bosch Motronic management system incorporates a rev limiter set at an indicated 7300rpm, coinciding with the start of the solid red sector although the broken red line starts at 7000rpm. We took 7000rpm as the limit for our in-gear figures, and this equates to maximum speeds in the gears of 40, 62, 84 and 118mph.

Standing starts were conducted on a still-damp track and yielded a mean 0-60mph time of 7.1secs. 0-30mph still came up in 2.8secs though, with perhaps only another 0.3secs to come off that on a perfectly dry surface. This compares well with BMW's quoted 6.7secs to 62mph and shows the superior traction of rear-wheel drive in the wet — a powerful front-wheel-drive car would have been lucky to get within a second of its potential in such conditions.

The close-ratio Getrag five-speed gearbox has a dog-leg first, and the gearchange is sprung to the centre 2nd/3rd gear plane. The gate is rather vague and it was all too easy to find fourth instead of second when going for a quick ratio swap. Obviously the box was designed with competition use in mind, where first is used only on the starting grid, but for normal road use it does require some care.

The M3's 200bhp from a 2.3-litre normally aspirated engine might seem like the recipe for a very peaky power delivery, but this is far from the case. The 16-valve unit is in fact extremely flexible, and will pull without hesitation from well below 1000rpm.

Its mid-range punch is very impressive indeed, as a glance at the in-gear acceleration figures will confirm, and the power is, of course, delivered without any troublesome turbo-lag. In third gear for example, the M3 will accelerate from 50-70mph in 4.1secs, and in top gear each 20mph increment from 20-90mph takes less than 10 seconds.

ECONOMY

For a car offering this sort of performance, an overall fuel consumption figure of over 20mpg is very good indeed. Our figure of 20.3mpg includes the speed-testing sessions and is a tribute to the efficiency of the 16-valve engine and its Bosch management system. The average owner could certainly expect over 22mpg, giving a range of 300 miles from the 15.4-gallon tank.

REFINEMENT

Given that the M3 is an homologation car, on sale to ensure the BMW's inclusion in Group A saloon car racing, you might expect it to have a few rough edges. But as 5000 examples have to be produced BMW obviously needed to make the M3 an acceptable road car to avoid a huge financial loss on the project. As a result the car has been built to provide the standards of luxury that a BMW owner expects, and that includes the levels of refinement.

The engine, although it can't match the smoothness of BMW's six-cylinder units, is still remarkably civilised. There is the characteristic rasp that many sporting 16-valve powerplants produce, but the noise levels in the cabin are very well controlled — when accelerating hard there is just enough noise to get the adrenalin pumping.

On the motorway both wind and tyre noise are very subdued, so that the dominant noise is from the engine. The motor is turning over at almost 4000rpm at 80mph, but that's the price for the sporting nature of the overall gearing. In fact because fifth gear is where fourth would normally be, there is a great temptation to change up another gear to a non-existent sixth.

Although tyre noise is well suppressed, the suspension is definitely on the sporting side of firm. At high speeds the ride is very good, even on very badly surfaced corners, but at lower speeds most surface irregularities are transmitted to the interior. The very comfortable seats and driving position more than make up for this thorough, and the M3 is a suprisingly relaxing high-speed cruiser.

ROAD BEHAVIOUR

The true benefits of the substantially uprated and refined chassis are best exploited on the track. In such an environment a driver cannot fail to be impressed by the M3.

Handling is very predictable in both wet and dry conditions with mild understeer generated at moderate cornering speeds with a very gradual transition through to mild oversteer on a suddenly closed throttle. The overall feel is of a very well-balanced car, one which can be turned through corners deceptively quickly and one which also feels very safe at the limit of adhesion.

The uprated steering and revised front suspension geometry allows a driver to feel precisely what the wheels are doing and though the rack is still a little low geared for a true competition machine (with 3.6 turns lock to lock) it received universal praise for both response and feel. The

Rear spoiler *helps produce impressive straight-line stability*

The M3 *is available only in left-hand-drive format*

power-assisted system is well weighted especially at speed and not excessively heavy round town.

High speed cornering is accompanied by minimal body roll and in the dry the M3 hugs the road surface, generating very high forces in the process. Also worthy of note is the M3's ability to run arrow straight, even in very windy weather. This particular aspect was experienced when circulating the high-speed banked track at maximum speed in the wet, where the M3 tracked perfectly straight and was unfussed by the less than perfect road surface and side winds. BMW's attention to aerodynamic refinements has obviously paid off.

Of the homologation specials that have passed through our hands recently, and the list includes the Mercedes-Benz 190 2.3-16 and Ford Sierra Cosworth, the BMW M3 is without a doubt the most well mannered from a handling point of view. There are no quirks to take into consideration, nor is there any tendency for the car to move about on uneven road surfaces or tramline in the ruts often found on well-used motorway sections.

You might expect something of a compromise in terms of ride quality and though the suspension is uprated all round, and the M3 rolls on low-profile 55-series rubber with their low shoulders, the sacrifice in ride comfort is marginal. At speed the car feels well composed and is able to soak up even quite severe irregularities without complaint. It is only when negotiating road imperfections at low speeds that a driver begins to notice the increased stiffness, though to be fair, the ride quality is no less competent than that of most current sports cars.

The much improved, servo-assisted, four-wheel disc braking system (ventilated up front), provides a reassuring degree of stopping power with a progressive and well-weighted pedal action. The M3 came through the fade tests unscathed — there was a slight and predictable rise in pedal pressures through the 10 high-speed stops.

The standard equipment ABS system came into operation with a 50lb effort during retardation tests,

Boot opening: *limited*

thereby limiting the deceleration figures to a maximum of 0.80g. This figure is not outstanding for a car of this type, but when you consider the figures were taken in the wet, it doesn't look bad at all.

AT THE WHEEL

The driver is greeted by a predominantly black interior layout. The facia, doors and surrounding areas are all moulded in a black grain plastic finish. The leather-trimmed seats are stitched in a similar shade, while the carpet material is a charcoal colour. The test car with its pristine interior certainly looked the part but we would imagine that it could look quite grubby in a very short space of time unless looked after.

The driver sits in a sports seat with plenty of lateral support and good location. The front squab is adjustable in length while the seat itself has a tilt facility and separate rake control. There is no adjustable lumbar support but the seat does not suffer for the lack of this; you sit in, rather than on, the seat and this adds to the overall feeling of being 'at one' with the car.

A leather-bound three-spoke wheel is provided, through which a driver can easily read the large 160mph speedometer and matching rev counter with its red line marked from 7000rpm. Set into the rev counter is an additional oil pressure gauge occupying the spot normally filled by the economy gauge in lesser BMWs. In all other respects the ▶

Leather trimmed *seats are unique to the M3*

Oil temperature *gauge replaces the usual economy indicator*

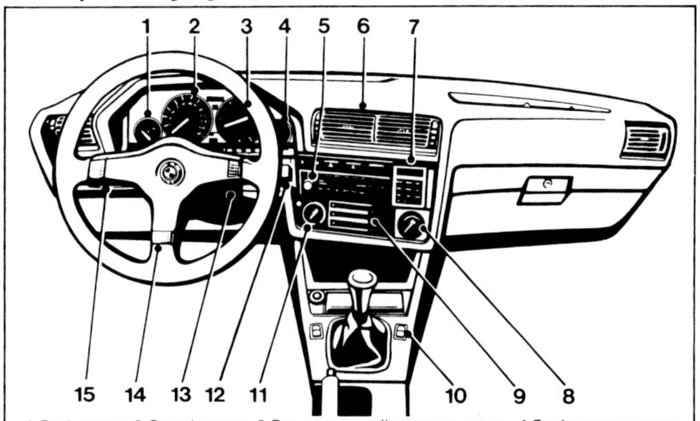

1 Fuel gauge, 2 Speedometer, 3 Rev counter, oil pressure gauge, 4 Engine temperature gauge, 5 Radio/cassette, 6 Ventilation outlets, 7 Trip computer, 8 Fan control, 9 Heat/air direction controls, 10 Electric windows switches, 11 Temperature control, 12 Washers/wipers stalk, 13 Ignition switch, 14 Horn pad, 15 Indicators and high/low beam stalk

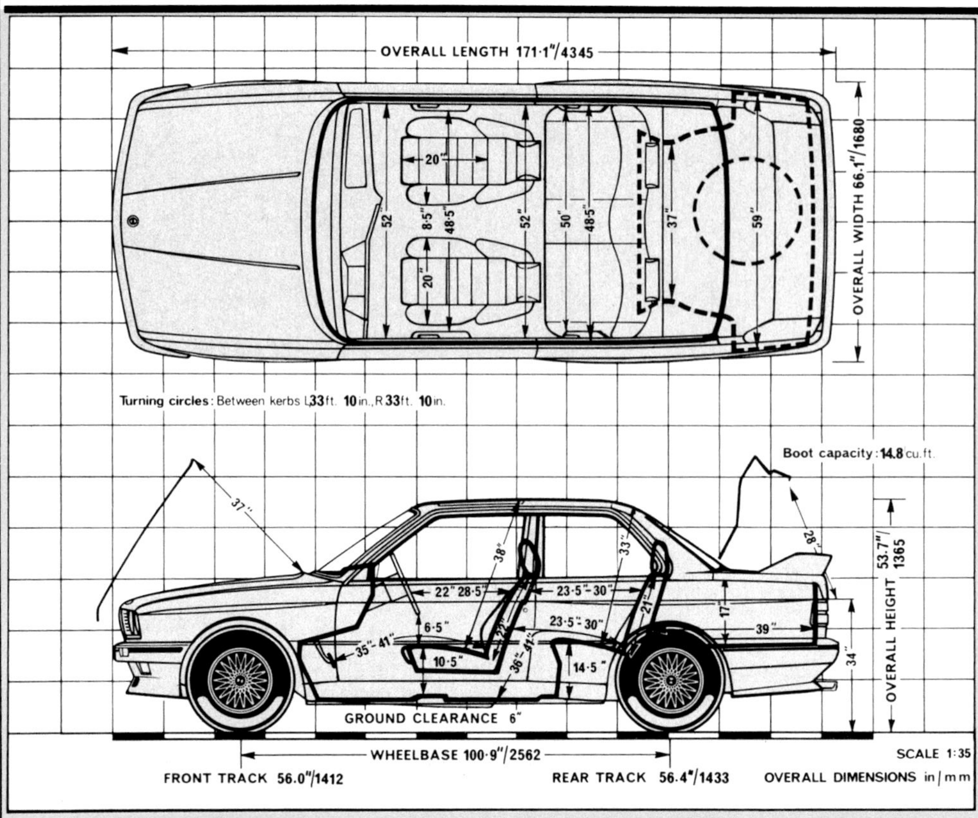

MODEL

BMW M3

PRODUCED BY:
Bayerische Motoren Werke AG,
Petuelring 40,
Munich, West Germany

SOLD IN THE UK BY:
BMW (GB) Ltd,
Ellesfield Avenue,
Bracknell, Berkshire RG12 4TA

SPECIFICATION

ENGINE

Longways, front, rear-wheel drive. Head/block al.alloy/cast iron. 4 cylinders in line, bored block, dry liners, 5 main bearings. Water cooled, electric fan.

Bore 93.4mm (3.6in), **stroke** 84.0mm (3.3in), **capacity** 2302cc (140.4 cu in).

Valve gear 2ohc, 4 valves per cylinder, chain camshaft drive. **Compression ratio** 10.5 to 1. Electronic ignition, Bosch ML-Motronic injection.

Max power 200bhp (PS-DIN) (147kW ISO) at 6750rpm. **Max torque** 177lb ft at 4750rpm.

TRANSMISSION

5-speed manual, diaphragm spring clutch, 9.0in dia.

Gear	Ratio	mph/1000rpm
Top	1.00	21.29
4th	1.26	16.90
3rd	1.77	12.03
2nd	2.40	8.87
1st	3.72	5.72

Final drive: hypoid bevel, ratio 3.25.

SUSPENSION

Front, independent, MacPherson strut, coil springs, telescopic dampers, anti-roll bar.

Rear, independent, semi-trailing arms, coil springs, telescopic dampers, anti-roll bar.

STEERING

Rack and pinion, hydraulic power assistance. Steering wheel diameter 15in, 3.6 turns lock to lock.

BRAKES

Dual circuits, split front/rear. **Front** 11.0in (280mm) dia discs ventilated. **Rear** 11.1in (282mm) dia discs. ABS, vacuum servo. Handbrake, centre lever acting on seperate rear drums.

WHEELS

Al. alloy, 7in rims. Low profile radial ply tyres (Pirelli P600 on test car), size 205/55VR15, pressures F31 R34 psi (normal driving).

EQUIPMENT

Battery 12V, 66Ah. Alternator 90A. Headlamps 55W. Reversing lamp standard. 30 electric fuses. 2-speed plus intermittent screen wipers. Electric screen washer. Air blending interior heater; air conditioning extra. Leather seats, brushed nylon headlining. Carpet floor covering. Screw pillar jack; 2 jacking points each side. Laminated windscreen.

PERFORMANCE

MAXIMUM SPEEDS

Gear	mph	km/h	rpm
Top (Mean)	139	224	6550
(Best)	140	225	6600
4th	118	190	7000
3rd	84	135	7000
2nd	62	100	7000
1st	40	64	7000

ACCELERATION FROM REST

True mph	Time (sec)	Speedo mph
30	2.8	32
40	3.9	42
50	5.5	52
60	7.1	61
70	9.5	71
80	11.9	81
90	15.2	91
100	19.0	101
110	23.7	111
120	29.8	121
130	—	131

Standing ¼-mile: 15.7sec, 92mph
Standing km: 28.3sec, 118mph

IN EACH GEAR

mph	Top	4th	3rd	2nd
10-30	—	8.7	5.6	3.5
20-40	10.0	7.8	4.7	3.2
30-50	9.8	6.8	4.3	3.0
40-60	9.5	6.7	4.1	3.1
50-70	9.4	6.4	4.1	—
60-80	9.0	6.3	4.5	—
70-90	9.6	6.5	—	—
80-100	10.7	7.5	—	—
90-110	12.2	9.7	—	—
100-120	15.6	12.7	—	—

CONSUMPTION

FUEL

Overall mpg: 20.3 (13.9 litres/100km)
4.5mpl

Autocar constant speed fuel consumption measuring equipment incompatible with fuel injection

Autocar formula: Hard 18.3mpg
Driving Average 22.3mpg
and conditions Gentle 26.4mpg

Grade of fuel: Premium, 4-star (97 RM)
Fuel tank: 15.4 Imp galls (70 litres)
Mileage recorder: accurate
Oil: (SAE 15W/40) negligible

BRAKING

Fade (from 92mph in neutral)
Pedal load for 0.5g stops in lb

	start/end		start/end
1	22-15	6	27-35
2	22-15	7	30-38
3	22-15	8	30-40
4	25-20	9	30-38
5	25-30	10	30-40

Response (from 30mph in neutral)

Load	g	Distance
10lb	0.20	150ft
20lb	0.40	75ft
30lb	0.55	54ft
40lb	0.75	40ft
50lb	0.80	37ft
60lb	0.80	37ft
Handbrake	0.35	86ft

Max gradient: 1 in 3
CLUTCH Pedal 32lb; Travel 5in

WEIGHT

Kerb 24.6cwt/2762lb/1252kg (Distribution F/R, 51.4/48.6)
Test 28.1cwt/3152lb/1429kg
Max payload 884lb/400kg

COSTS

Prices

Basic	£18,260.88
Special Car Tax	£1521.73
VAT	£2967.39
Total (in GB)	**£22,750.00**
Licence	£100.00
Delivery charge (London)	£258.75
Number plates	£20.00
Total on the Road	**£23,128.75**
(excluding insurance)	
Insurance group	O/A
Total as tested	**£23,128.75**

SERVICE & PARTS

Change	Interval 5000	10,000	20,000
Engine oil	Yes	Yes	Yes
Oil filter	Yes	Yes	Yes
Gearbox oil	No	No	Yes
Spark plugs	No	Yes	Yes
Air cleaner	No	Yes	Yes
Total cost	N/A	N/A	N/A

PARTS COST (inc VAT)

Brake pads (2 wheels) front	£47.78
Brake pads (2 wheels) rear	£87.44
Exhaust complete	£330.11
Tyre—each (typical)	£341.55
Windscreen	£203.73
Headlamp unit	£34.24
Front wing	£162.33
Rear bumper	£567.64

WARRANTY

12 months/UL, 6-year anti-corrosion

EQUIPMENT

Ammeter/voltmeter	N/A
Automatic	N/A
Cruise control	N/A
Economy gauge	N/A
Limited slip differential	●
Self-levelling suspension	N/A
Trip computer	●
Headrests front	●
Heated seats	N/A
Height adjustment	N/A
Lumbar adjustment	N/A
Rear seat belts	●
Seat back recline	●
Seat cushion tilt	N/A
Seat tilt	• ●
Split rear seats	N/A
Door mirror remote control	●
Electric windows	●
Heated rear window	●
Interior adjustable headlamps	●
Sunroof (electric)	●
Tinted glass	●
Headlamp wash/wipe	●
Tailgate wash/wipe	N/A
Central locking	●
Child proof locks	N/A
Cigar lighter	●
Clock	●
Fog lamps	●
Internal boot release	N/A
Locking fuel cap	●
Luggage cover	N/A
Metallic paint	ONC
Radio/cassette	●
Aerial	●
Speakers	●

● Standard ONC Optional at no extra cost N/A Not applicable

TEST CONDITIONS

Wind: 5mph
Temperature: 8deg C (46deg F)
Barometer: 29.4in Hg (997mbar)
Humidity: 100per cent
Surface: wet asphalt and concrete
Test distance: 747miles

Figures taken at 1975 miles by our own staff at the General Motors proving ground at Millbrook.

AUDI 200 TURBO £23,856

The 200 is essentially the Audi 100CD with a turbocharger. A healthy 182bhp is produced from the 2144cc unit as a result. In manual form (no longer available), the Audi manages an above-average top speed and generally good performance combined with reasonable economy. Power delivery to the front wheels is not a problem

Tested (Manual)	17 Dec 1983
ENGINE	2144cc
Max Power	182bhp at 5700rpm
Torque	269lb ft at 3600rpm
Gearing	23.5mph/1000rpm
WARRANTY	12/UL, 6 anti-rust
Insurance Group	OA
Automatic	●
5-Speed	N/A
Radio/cassette	●
Sunroof	●
WEIGHT	2844lb

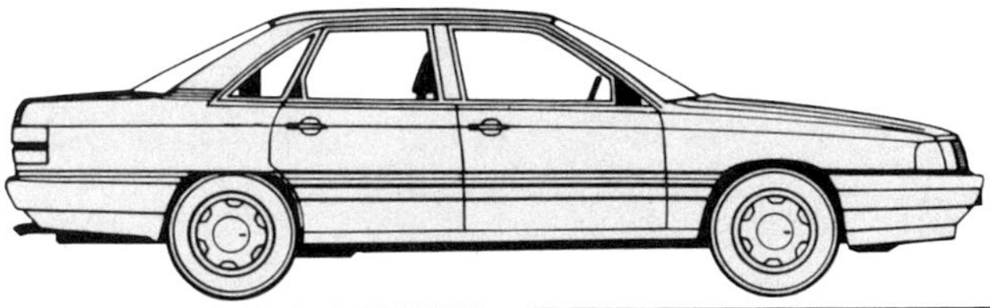

TOP SPEED	142mph	MPG	21.5
0-60mph	8.4secs	Range	378 miles

FORD SIERRA RS COSWORTH £17,100

The Sierra RS Cosworth offers brilliant performance for the price. Particular strong points are ride quality, lack of road noise from low-profile tyres, tractability and lack of fussiness from the 2-litre turbocharged engine. The car also retains all the advantages of the standard Sierra as it will transport five people and their luggage with ease

Tested	13 Aug 1986
ENGINE	1993cc
Max Power	204bhp at 6000rpm
Torque	205lb ft at 4500rpm
Gearing	22.98mph/1000rpm
WARRANTY	12/UL, 6 anti-rust
Insurance Group	O/A
Automatic	N/A
5-Speed	●
Radio/cassette	●
Sunroof	●
WEIGHT	2688lb

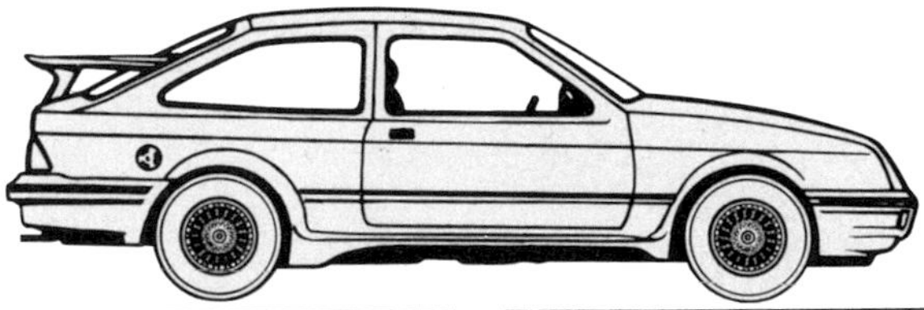

TOP SPEED	145mph	MPG	21.4
0-60mph	6.2secs	Range	310 miles

MASERATI BITURBO COUPE £24,795

Now a five-year-old design, Biturbo has only just been introduced to the UK. Strong points are its opulent and roomy interior, excellent top-end performance and well-balanced handling. Against are lack of low-end torque and turbo lag, while there are question marks over long-term reliability and build quality. Elegant and stylish 'newcomer'

Tested	N/A
ENGINE	2491cc
Max Power	192bhp at 5500rpm
Torque	220lb ft at 3000rpm
Gearing	25.0mph/1000rpm
WARRANTY	12/UL, 6 anti-rust
Insurance Group	OA
Automatic	N/A
5-Speed	●
Radio/cassette	DO
Sunroof	DO
WEIGHT	2394lb

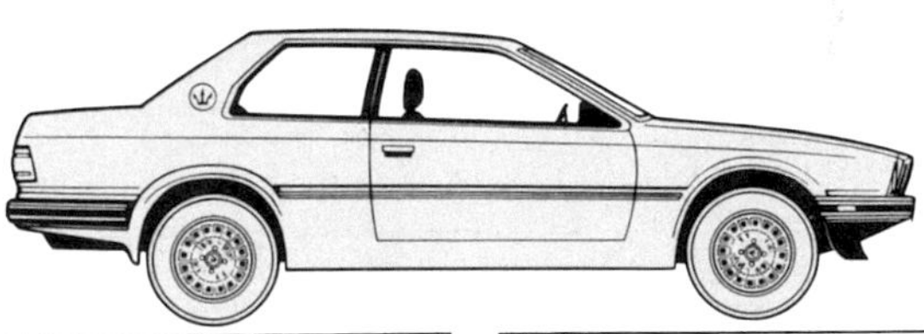

*TOP SPEED	130mph	**MPG	20.2
*0-62mph	6.6secs	Range	350 miles

MERCEDES-BENZ 190E 2.3-16 £24,670

This is exactly how you might expect Mercedes-Benz to build a sports car: thoroughly competent, well engineered and dynamically excellent. Having said that, however, it is hardly exciting in the way it performs, but the major drawback appears to be with the price-tag of just under £25,000. But what most of the opposition lacks is that Cosworth magic

Tested	7 Aug 1985
ENGINE	2299cc
Max Power	185bhp at 6200rpm
Torque	173lb ft at 4500rpm
Gearing	22.5mph/1000rpm
WARRANTY	12/UL
Insurance Group	8
Automatic	£484
5-Speed	●
Radio/cassette	DO
Sunroof	£660
WEIGHT	2954lb

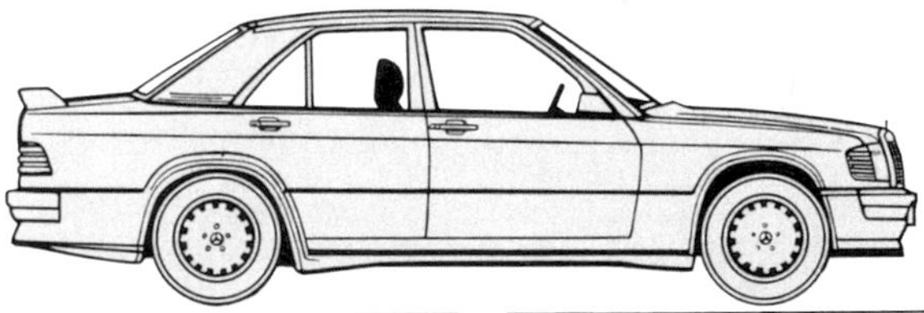

TOP SPEED	143mph	MPG	23.5
0-60mph	8.0secs	Range	360 miles

PORSCHE 944 S £25,303

Fine engineering and excellent refinement have always been Porsche hallmarks. The addition of a 16-valve cylinder head to the 944S has provided more power — of particular use for overtaking manoeuvres. Driving position is good, although rear seat accommodation is limited. It is an expensive package, but one that will hold its value well

Tested	31 Dec 1986
ENGINE	2479cc
Max Power	190bhp at 6000rpm
Torque	170lb ft at 4300rpm
Gearing	22.39mph/1000rpm
WARRANTY	24/UL, 10 anti-rust
Insurance group	OA
Automatic	N/A
5-Speed	●
Radio/cassette	●
Sunroof	£962
WEIGHT	2821lb

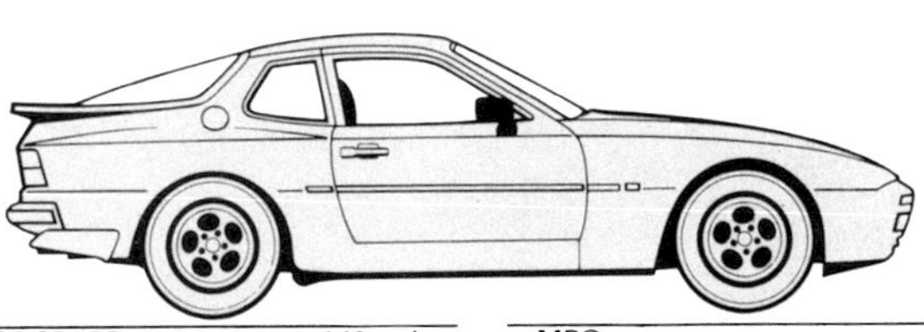

TOP SPEED	140mph	MPG	23.5
0-60mph	6.7secs	Range	415 miles

RENAULT GTA V6 TURBO £24,960

A distinctive-looking sports coupé produced at the French giant's Dieppe factory. Constructed from rust-proof GRP secured to a steel backbone chassis and powered by a rear-mounted version of Renault's 2.5-litre turbocharged V6, the Alpine provides excellent performance with a practical and surprisingly roomy interior. Luggage space is pitifully small

Tested	23 Jul 1986
ENGINE	2458cc
Max Power	200bhp at 5750rpm
Torque	214lb ft at 2500rpm
Gearing	26.4mph/1000rpm
WARRANTY	12/UL, 5 anti-rust
Insurance Group	OA
Automatic	N/A
5-Speed	●
Radio/cassette	●
Sunroof	N/A
WEIGHT	2618lb

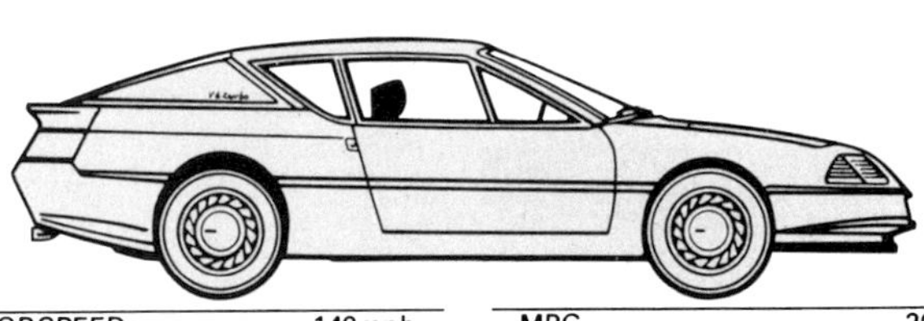

TOP SPEED	149mph	MPG	20.5
0-60mph	6.3secs	Range	325 miles

● Standard ○ Optional at extra cost ONC Optional at no extra cost N/A Not applicable DO Dealer Option * Manufacturer's figures ** European Legislative Average

The subtly *extended wheel arches, air dam and side skirts indicate that this is no ordinary 3-Series BMW*

◀ instrument layout is similar to most other 3-Series cars.

That includes column stalks either side of the wheel. The right-hand item handles wash/wipe if pulled, single flick wipe if pushed down, plus intermittent and two-speed wiper settings if lifted up. The left stalk takes care of indicators and dip/main beam settings with the actual lights switch sited in the dash at the extreme left.

The driving position feels just right; the wheel position is sensible and there is enough seat adjustment to cater for most sizes. The pedals are well placed for heel-and-toe changes and when the clutch is dormant there is a large footrest to the left of the pedal. Headroom is adequate for drivers up to 6ft in height but not for those taller than this. You can tilt the seat slightly to gain more clearance but at the expense of spoiling the driving position.

Ergonomically speaking there is not much wrong with the M3's layout — all the major controls are within easy reach, the door pulls are conveniently angled so a user does not have to strain to close the door, and the interior handles are flush fitting with no nasty sharp edges to rub against.

CONVENIENCE

Arguably this is the only area where the M3 falls down, with its boot space restricted by the more raked rear window, which also leads to a smaller load aperture with the bootlid raised. Like other 3-Series BMW models the M3 does not have much in the way of rear passenger space. Headroom is at a premium and with the front seats well back on their runners there is virtually no legroom despite the fact that the front seat backrests are cut out to help.

The rear seats are individually shaped and the M3 is clearly intended as no more than a four seater at most.

In other respects convenience levels match those of the standard 3-Series models and includes adequate cubby space with reasonably sized door pockets, glove box and the odd moulded tray in the centre console. The heating and ventilation controls include turn wheels for the four-speed fan and temperature adjustment, with three additional sliders for direction. On the most powerful setting the fan delivers a very impressive blast for quick demisting or rapid changes in temperature. On the first two settings it also works unobtrusively enough not to detract from the overall refinement levels. The standard equipment electric windows take just four seconds to lower and five seconds to raise via the push buttons mounted conveniently in the centre console. The roof mounted controls for the powered sunroof are a little more awkward to find and require a driver to look up from the road to operate. The small controls for the powered door mirrors are more conveniently placed atop the drivers door pull. Mirrors, washer nozzles and the driver's door lock are all heated to prevent icing up in wintry conditions.

Under the bootlid there is adequate space for two medium sized suitcases, but available space is hindered by the inclusion of boxes either side, one for the battery, the other for the jack. The spare wheel is hidden under the carpeted load compartment floor.

The forward hinging bonnet lifts to reveal the very impressive sight of the powerful 2.3 litre four and routine servicing looks straightforward enough, although the air box needs to be removed to get at the oil filter. Spark plug removal is far easier and the oil dipstick and fluid levels in the various reservoirs are easily checked.

SAFETY

Besides aiding the aerodynamic qualities and reducing the drag coefficient to cd 0.33, the wraparound body add-ons are also designed with safety in mind. The three piece front bumper is a composite structure comprising an energy-absorbing foam impact block and a skin of glass-fibre reinforced polyurethane foam. The rear bumper, integrated into the undervalance, is made in the same way and of similar materials. Thanks to this design just one single bumper is required to fulfil all legal standards and regulations worldwide, including the very strict US standards.

The light alloy wheels feature hidden studs behind the removable wheel centre and thereby adding a degree of security against theft.

VERDICT

Stepping into the BMW M3 is a bit like pulling on a well fitting glove, one of those rare occurrences when a driver instantly feels at home behind the wheel. The driving position is right and when you begin to use the power and experience the handling you begin to feel part of the car.

The M3 is perhaps the most successful homologation inspired road/racer offered by a manufacturer to date. The car is as docile in town traffic as any driver could wish and easy to manoeuvre due to its compact proportions. Then when you hit the open road and pour on the power the chassis handles all the demands a driver makes upon it, whatever the road surface. In this respect BMW has arrived at an excellent compromise in suspension settings bearing mind the car's *raison d'etre.*

The fact of the matter is that the M3 makes a very sensible road car; it looks the part with its decidedly sporty styling, is not over the top but very purposeful.

In road trim the M3 may not have the legs of the Sierra Cosworth but what it lacks in performance it more than compensates for with its easier road manners and better directional stability at speed. The Mercedes 190 2.3-16 can match the BMW in this respect but its engine of similar specification is less responsive, thanks to the larger and heavier body shell. Nor is the Mercedes as nimble as the BMW. ■

RACE TRACK REFUGEES

BMW's M3 and Ford's RS500 Sierra Cosworth have had mighty battles on the circuits this year. **Laurie Caddell** takes to the road and resists the lure of the track.

1987 was going to be a very special year in saloon-car racing. With Bernie Ecclestone looking after publicising it and making sure that there were rounds in all corners of the world, the major manufacturers would flood back to the sport in droves and provide spectacular action to which everyone could relate. It didn't quite happen like that, though, a last-minute £60,000 entry fee per car ensuring that only the best-heeled equipes could afford to compete, when it had been assumed by the powers that be that nobody could afford not to.

Whatever the political traumas, it hasn't stopped the racing from being exciting even with at times less than full grids. The sight of works' Alfas and works' Maseratis has ensured spectator interest that could otherwise have been somewhat lacking.

It was long before last year ended that Ford realised they were 'up against it'. Their rally season had been less than brilliant with two overweight cars to develop for use depending on conditions, while on the race tracks their almost assured success looked a little less likely with the announcement of the BMW M3. Working from the ground up, with just a modified 3 Series body as a base, BMW built a car which was a racer first and a road car second. Ford didn't have that luxury: their Sierra Cosworth has had to be more of a compromise. So it was back last year that Ford were already working on an 'evolution' RS, a model which they hoped would make up lost ground on the BMW which although competing in a class below the Sierra's would be going for — and probably taking — outright wins.

Sure enough, the original Cosworths have simply not been quick enough and, in spite of some sterling efforts by drivers of the calibre of Klauses Niedzwiedz and Ludwig and the brilliant Steve Soper, the screaming hordes of Beemers have been up there with them — and quite a few times in front. That multitude of BMWs has not been without its star drivers, either, with ex-bike World Champion Johnny Cecotto and saloon superstar Gianfranco Brancatelli always to the fore.

With the danger of a trouncing in the offing, Ford soon had the evolution on its way under the title RS500. This was homologated on 1 August and on race début, at Brno, in Czechoslovakia, the Eggenberger/Texaco works versions ran home first and second, a full lap ahead of the Bavarian opposition: mission accomplished. The upshot of all this is that, because of their on-track war, we civilians, forever confined to public roads, have some impressive combat machinery to buy. Motor sport's governing body dictates that there be 5000 examples produced of any car wishing to compete in the WTC, but only 500 need

The grid at Silverstone was as appropriate a background as could be found for the two cars which recently raced there in the TT

be made of 'evolution' variants: hence the RS500.

There may be just fractions of a second between the two protagonists on the race track, but for thee and me on the road, the two cars are like chalk and cheese. Forget tha the M3 is only available with the steering wheel on the wrong side, but one is a sybarite special with a good turn of speed, while the other is all speed with just a few sops thrown in to make it adequate for road use. Which is which we will soon find out.

Take a quick glance at photographs of the two and you will always pick the Ford as being the bigger. Three-door versions of five-door cars always look large and somewhat out of proportion, and the Sierra is no exception. Even side by side, you *assume* that the Ford dwarfs the BMW. In fact, there is just a fraction over 4 inches difference, the Ford being the longer, but hardly by enough to matter in even the closest of finishes at a WTC race! There is less than 2in difference in width and less than half an inch separating the two heights. Yes, the Ford is bigger, but only fractionally. It must be heavier, though: 2734lb plays 2645lb. The Ford is heavier, but 89lb isn't going to add many tenths to a banzai lap.

To turbo or not is the question under the bonnet, but, blowers aside, again there is plenty of similarity between the two as one would expect with Ford and BMW who have each had countless successes in Grand Prix racing.

The M3 has a four-cylinder engine, BMW engineers having worked out that the smaller frictional losses and smaller torsional vibration of a four would help the engine run to necessary racing speeds of 10,000rpm against a theoretical limit of 9000rpm for the otherwise sweet six. The motor itself is an interesting blend of cast-iron 2002 block (itself derived from the 1500 of the early 1960s and also used on the Turbo F1 motors) and the M1/5/6 alloy four-valve-head, albeit made for two fewer cylinders. With a 93.4mm bore and 84mm stroke, the 2302cc engine runs a 10.5:1 compression ratio and is fed fuel by a Bosch ML-Motronic injection and management system. The two pairs of valves for each cylinder are separated by a fashionable (and efficient) 38 degrees, and the upshot of it all is 200bhp at 6750rpm, with 177lb ft of torque at 4750rpm.

The Ford engine's pedigree is the other way up. Its iron block traces back to origins in the humble and unloved Pinto engine, but in this case it is suitably strengthened. Sitting on top is an alloy head which uses basically the same layout as in every race-winning Cosworth engine since the FVA (and, of course, including the 155GP-winning DFV, whose victory tally may even increase next year). Its valve pairs are separated by 45 degree and it feeds through Weber/Marelli injection using a compression ratio of 8.0:1; its capacity is 1993cc, courtesy of a 90.82mm bore and 76.95mm stroke. To force the mixture into the engine there is a T31/T04 turbocharger (much bigger than the T3 of last year) and this runs with a much larger intercooler and uprated oil supply. Once again, engine management keeps the various settings in order. In road-going form, the Sierra has 224bhp at 6000rpm and a fraction under 206lb ft at 4500rpm.

In race trim, about 325bhp can be extracted from the BMW, while 400bhp is easily forthcoming from the Ford.

In terms of road performance, the Ford reaches 151 mph, while the BMW is a little way back at 144mph, and in the acceleration stakes the Ford gets to the benchmark 60mph in 5.9 secs against the BMW's 6.9 secs.

Those are the cold-light-of-day figures. On the road there is a noticeable difference which could be said of most 'aspirated' engines up against similarly performing turbos. The BMW needs to rev to get there, while Ford urge is noticeable all the way. In simplistic terms you always have to press the BMW hard to get the power, while you have to try hard in the Ford not to get the power! What turbo lag there is with the Ford is matched by a ponderous gearchange with the BMW, so that really evens the score.

The BMW is really a Q-car with its only slightly bulbous arches and subtle wings — it takes a trained eye to separate it from the crowd at a distance. The RS500 stands out like nothing else and its lower spoiler catches kerbs like nothing else . . .

On motorways and fast A-roads the extra mid-range punch of the Ford leaves the BMW well back, but then so the Ford would do with most other cars on the road. On the twists and turns of the byways, the Ford has the edge, again, its much stiffer suspension set-up and 205/50-15 Dunlop D40s helping the chassis to build up to appreciably more grip than does the BMW on its 205/55-15 Pirelli P600s. The RS's steering is quite weighty, even though it is power assisted, and it's very direct, with 2.63 turns from lock to lock, so that it guides the car with precision.

The Cosworth's handling is brilliant and it takes only a few hundred miles of acclimatisation to enable a newcomer to the driving seat to charge hard into the bends,

the car slowing at the last possible minute (courtesy of brilliant brakes) before turning its nose in crisply with the tail either following directly in line or a little askew, depending on throttle position. If ever a car made life easy for its driver when pressing on, the RS500 is it.

The BMW feels altogether more of a road car than a racer, its supple suspension making light of most tarmac irregularities.

It will be well ahead on bumpy or heavily cambered roads, its suspension riding over the contours, while the Ford will be following them and taking no small amount of effort on the part of the driver to get it away from them. Where the BMW glides, the Ford jumps.

The Ford costs £19,950 and the BMW some £23,350 and that really shows up in the standard of finish. There is little, apart from bucket-style seats and a neat leather wheel, to distinguish the RS from other repmobile Sierras, and that is disappointing: it looks like an £800 car inside. The BMW by contrast is gorgeous, with beautiful switchgear and clean and attractive instruments. A case in point is the extra rubbing carpets in the footwells: they don't just sit there and they are not press-studded down; instead they have metal-ringed locating holes to slip over pins which twist and lock and then fold down in recesses. That is attention to detail.

If it's just attention that you want (good or bad!) then the Ford is *the* car to have. Its massive rear wing has been joined by a Sierra 4 x 4 lip below, while its nose spoiler is now deeper. By contrast, the spoilered and fat-arched M3 is altogether more restrained; although those in the know look at the car in wonder, you can slip by unnoticed which you most certainly can't in the Ford.

In its way, the RS500 version of the Sierra Cosworth is a little disappointing after the original. Its larger turbo takes longer to 'wind up' which, although it then helps ultimate power, means that there is less urge lower down. It really doesn't feel a great deal different through the seat of the pants, though. We perhaps unfairly expected last year's car with much more on top. We got little difference, but in the end we were really not disappointed. The Cosworth was stunning last year; this year it is still stunning.

The M3 is a real luxury car with scintillating performance. It is one rung down from the Ford in terms of speed, and its engine isn't as sweet as the 171bhp six of the 325i, but when you are taking it easy the creature comforts of the car transform it into a luxury *boulevardier*. And that engine makes a wonderful noise as the tacho needle leaps for the red line at a touch of the loud pedal.

You cannot take it easy in the Ford, it just

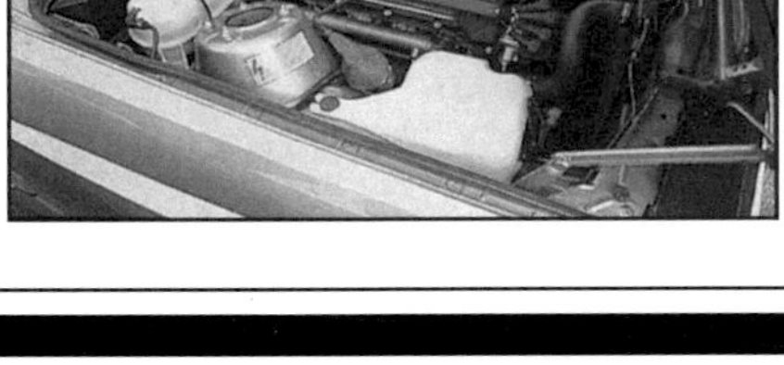

The engines of the two protagonists represent zeniths in both normally aspirated and turbocharged technology. The BMW motor is a mix of 2002 F1 block and M1/5/6 head. It is a sweet revver and smooth deliverer. The Ford has a turbo as big as you can find on a car and gives oodles of effortless power; it, too, has a four-valve head

won't let you. Its easy whistling power tries to force itself out of the engine all the time, its brakes demand that you use them hard and its chassis eggs you on to try harder. The 'Cossie' will cruise easily and will happily potter around town, but the temptation to unleash those horses is always there.

On the road then, these two 'Homologation Racers' are night and day, but it would be hard choosing. Hearts go to Ford but heads go to BMW as in the end you simply can't use the Ford to its limits all the time: the vulnerability of your licence would see to that. We photographed the two cars on the grid at Silverstone days

before the TT (for which we are indebted to circuit manager, Brian Pallet), and we finished mere minutes before some F3 cars were unleashed, their engines already barking in the background. We packed up the photographic gear and shut the boots and wandered back to the cars' cockpits. Before Publisher and Editor ducked in, one said 'fancy a race?' The other countered 'it would be interesting, wouldn't it?' Yes, it would have been, but to the relief of all concerned, common sense prevailed.

On the 'circuit' home, the Beemer would have been ahead until the B-road flattened out into a wide and fast A-road when the Cossie would have driven away. Horses for courses, they say, but these are thoroughbreds both. ■

*The biggest difference between the two is in their interiors. The Ford **(left)** has leather wheel and gearknob, bucket seats and boost gauge to separate it from 'repmobiles'. The BMW **(below)** is more luxuriously appointed*

Ford Sierra Cosworth RS500 — £19,950

SPECIFICATION

Engine	
Type	Front-mounted, water-cooled four with cast-iron block and alloy head
Capacity	1993cc
Bore/Stroke	90.82 x 76.95mm
Compression ratio	8.0:1
Valve gear	Four valves per cylinder operated by twin overhead, belt-driven camshafts
Fuel system	Weber/Marelli injection/ignition; Garrett T31/T04 turbocharger
Power	224bhp at 6000rpm
Torque	206lb ft at 4500rpm
Transmission	
Gearbox	Manual, five speed
Final drive	3.64:1
Mph/1000rpm in top	22.81
Construction	
Body/chassis	Integral
Running gear	
Front suspension	Independent, by MacPherson struts, lower track control arm and anti-roll bar
Rear suspension	Independent, by semi-trailing arms, coil springs, telescopic dampers and an anti-roll bar
Steering	Power-assisted rack and pinion
Brakes	Servo-assisted discs all round (ventilated at front) with ABS
Wheels	Alloy 7 x 15
Tyres	Dunlop D40 205/50VR-15
Dimensions	
Length	175.5in
Width	68.0in
Height	54.2in
Wheelbase	102.7in
Weight	24.4cwt

PERFORMANCE

Acceleration	0—30mph	2.2secs
	0—40mph	3.0secs
	0—50mph	4.6secs
	0—60mph	5.9secs
	0—70mph	8.1secs
	0—80mph	10.3secs
	0—90mph	12.7secs
	0—100mph	15.9secs
	0—120mph	24.1secs
Standing 1/4-mile	14.8secs (98mph)	
Maximum speed	151mph	
Fuel consumption	17-22mpg	

BMW M3 — £23,550

SPECIFICATION

Engine	
Type	Front-mounted, water-cooled four, with cast-iron block and alloy head
Capacity	2302cc
Bore/stroke	93.4 x 84.0mm
Compression ratio	10.5:1
Valve gear	Four valves per cylinder operated by twin overhead, chain-driven camshafts
Fuel system	Bosch ML-Motronic injection
Power	200bhp at 6750rpm
Torque	177lb ft at 4750rpm
Transmission	
Gearbox	Manual, five speed
Final drive	3.25:1
Mph/1000rpm in top	21.29
Construction	
Body/chassis	Integral
Running gear	
Front suspension	Independent by MacPherson struts and an anti-roll bar
Rear suspension	Independent by semi-trailing arms, coil springs, telescopic dampers and an anti-roll bar
Steering	Power-assisted rack and pinion
Brakes	Servo-assisted discs all round (ventilated at front) with ABS
Wheels	Alloy 7 x 15in
Tyres	Pirelli P600 205/55VR-15
Dimensions	
Length	171.1in
Width	66.1in
Height	53.7in
Wheelbase	100.9in
Weight	23.6cwt

PERFORMANCE

Acceleration	0—30mph	2.6secs
	0—40mph	3.5secs
	0—50mph	5.2secs
	0—60mph	6.9secs
	0—70mph	9.0secs
	0—80mph	11.7secs
	0—90mph	15.0secs
	0—100mph	18.8secs
	0—120mph	29.7secs
Standing ¼-mile	15.6secs (92mph)	
Maximum speed	144mph	
Fuel consumption	20-24mpg	

BMW M3

Don't ever think "yuppie" again.

• Let's put an end to the BMW-yuppie link. These days, all you have to do is whisper "BMW," and everyone immediately thinks "yuppie." Enough of the yups! That overpublicized group of consumers, who lust after Bimmers as they do any object perceived to confer status on its owners, could never fully appreciate the car you see on these pages. We don't mean to say that the young urban professionals won't love the new M3. After all, it's got that famous badge on the hood. And you know, it's a prestigious Eurosedan and everything. But will they realize that the M3 is the latest well-muscled, painstakingly crafted creation from BMW's esteemed Motorsport department? "Nah, but it'll sure look great in front of the condo."

The M3 deserves better. This is not a car for yuppies. This is a car for *us*. In case you haven't noticed, BMW's U.S. lineup has blossomed to include a dazzling array of leather-lined hot rods that beg to be flogged through the twisties and hammered on the superslabs. Gone are the anemic four-cylinder models that nearly ruined BMW's image. Nearly extinct are the Bimmers reserved for social climbers. The Bavarian Motor Works is back on track with a fleet of *drivers'* cars, and the M3 is potent proof of its new direction.

The M3 is the most recent of the broad-shouldered BMW Motorsport models to reach our shores. For those not yet fluent in M-speak, the M-machines are limited-edition, high-performance versions of the 3-, 5-, and 6-series sedans. For several years the M-cars were a treat reserved for European buyers, but since early this year they have been trickling into the hands of hungry American enthusiasts. The M5 and the M6 debuted stateside in February, and the M3 joined the brawny pair in June.

The M3 is available to enthusiasts because of the rules that govern FIA Group A racing. To qualify a car for Group A competition, its manufacturer must build a minimum of 5000 examples of it within twelve months. The rules also strictly limit the modifications that can be made for racing, so most of the performance hardware must be baked into the roadgoing cars. BMW Motorsport clearly knows the recipe for success in Group A road racing: after the fourth of seven European Touring Car Championship events this year, the M3 had already clinched the title.

The M3's racing heritage is immediately apparent in its steroid-injected bodywork. With its aggressive assortment of air dams, body flares, and spoilers, the M3 will quicken the pulse of any boy (or girl) racer lucky enough to catch a glimpse of one. Most of the new pieces are made of steel, though the rocker panels, the trunk lid, the front air dam, and the rear wing are molded in plastic. The rake of the rear window has been altered for improved aerodynamics, and both it and the windshield are bonded flush with the surrounding bodywork. The net result of all these aero tweaks is a drag coefficient of 0.33, down substantially from the 325i's 0.37 Cd. Perhaps more important, no one will ever mistake the burly M3 for an ordinary 3-series sedan.

The subskin make-over is equally impressive. Like its 3-series siblings, the M3's fully independent suspension has struts in front and semi-trailing arms at the rear, but the coil springs and the gas shocks have been revised and strengthened for race duty. The shorter springs drop the M3 about an inch lower than the 325i. In addition, the front anti-roll bar is attached to the struts rather than to the

control arms, and a beefier anti-roll bar is fitted to the rear.

Formula 1 fans will think they've died and gone to Monaco the first time they lift the M3's hood. Inside sits a normally aspirated, 2.3-liter version of BMW's brutal, turbocharged four-cylinder Grand Prix engine. This is the only remaining four-banger in BMW's U.S. lineup, but it's anything but a prestige-sapping weakling. Hardware enthusiasts have plenty to drool over here: four valves per cylinder, double overhead camshafts, an individual throttle for each cylinder, tuned intake and exhaust plumbing, and a new ML3 Bosch Motronic engine-management system. As further proof that this is no ordinary powerplant, its cam cover and air cleaner are emblazoned with the words "BMW M Power."

Though the "M" stands for "Motorsport," we think "Mucho Power" is more like it. The sixteen-valve four-cylinder turns out 192 hp at a lofty 6750 rpm and 170 pound-feet of torque at 4750. If you think those are remarkable figures for a 2.3-liter, you're right: the M3's ferocious four boasts a higher output per liter than any other normally aspirated piston engine available in America.

What looks impressive on paper feels equally stirring on the road. When its tail is twisted, the 2857-pound M3 dashes to 60 mph in 6.9 seconds and trips the quarter-mile lights in 15.2 seconds at 92 mph. Top speed is an autobahn-tuned 141 mph. That's enough punch to blow off the Mercedes-Benz 190E 2.3–16 and stay neck and neck with the Porsche 944S. Best of all, the M3's power delivery is wonderfully linear; it pulls willingly from its midrange all the way to its sizzling 7250-rpm redline.

Those accustomed to the silky smoothness of BMW's refined in-line sixes, how-

ever, may wince a bit when this engine starts to sing. It is, after all, a highly tuned, relatively large four-cylinder, so a little harshness is part of the bargain. BMW has softened the resonance considerably since we sampled an M3 on the autobahn a year ago, but this engine remains a howler. The noise is a fine, mechanical sound, especially when you're near the very top of the tach, but it's there whether you want it or not.

Most of the time, you won't mind a little kibitzing from the engine compartment, because the M3 is designed for driving with brio. Pushed hard, the M3 comes into its own. The five-speed transmission is tightly geared for maximum go. The chassis is more than a match for the engine, responding swiftly and surely to orders from the helm. Powering through hard corners, the tail stays firmly planted, though there is enough predictable lift-throttle oversteer available to point you back toward your line when understeer begins to be a problem. The standard 205/55VR-15 Pirelli P600 tires don't turn in as crisply as we'd like, but they do stick: the M3 squeals around the skidpad at an impressive 0.81 g.

We had a chance to put in a handful of brisk laps around Connecticut's challenging Lime Rock racetrack, and the M3 proved equal to its breeding. Few road cars can take to the track with such poise. The M3 leaps through the corners like a cat, its feisty engine spinning and spitting until you snatch another gear or the rev limiter grabs it by the tail. Excellent controls help you keep the frenzy in check: the steering is supple and superbly accurate, the shifter has just the right amount of notchiness, and the massive disc brakes—vented in front and equipped with a standard anti-lock system—are always on duty, lap after lap. Our seat-of-the-pants

admiration for the binders was confirmed by our fifth-wheel testing: the M3 clawed to a stop from 70 mph in a mere 179 feet.

The M3 may be a thinly disguised race car, but its creature-comforts list would do most luxury sedans proud. Included are power windows, mirrors, and locks; a power sunroof; air conditioning; a premium AM/FM-stereo/cassette system; a three-spoke, leather-wrapped Motorsport steering wheel; and a nine-function trip computer. Everything is laid out in typically sensible BMW fashion, and the white-on-black analog gauges are among the most legible in the industry. In view of the M3's sporting nature, an oil-temperature gauge has been substituted for the normal 3-series layout's fuel-economy display.

We have mixed feelings about the standard leather seats, however. They offer an adequate range of manual adjustment, and they're dandy for spirited maneuvers. The problem is that they aren't well designed for extended travel. Several staffers complained of a lack of lumbar support, and others suffered from pinched behinds after long drives. We'll give these thrones an overall B. Passengers banished to the rear seats should be either short or masochistic.

All in all, we're smitten by the M3. Our test car was weighed down by a $34,810 price tag—about what you'd pay for a 944S—but the Bavarian beast offers a lot in return. For that princely sum you get a stunningly distinctive design, a generous helping of luxury and quality, and the kind of cool, collected performance available only in German sports sedans.

Enthusiasts who find those attributes tantalizing should get in line immediately: BMW plans to export only 2400 M3s to the United States this year. The supply probably won't be enough to meet the demand, but it will serve to remind enthusiasts that BMW is back in the performance-car business.

Gee, what was that "y"-word again?

—Arthur St. Antoine

COUNTERPOINT

• The "batmobiles" are back! With its deep chin spoiler, fabled "bat wing," and forever-revving engine, the M3 reincarnates the spirit of the 3.0CSL racing coupes of the early seventies. This machine is meant for fast, winding secondary roads where its tight chassis can be exercised through generous use of its broad rev band and powerful brakes. Initially, it seems to understeer, but you soon learn that the trick is to brake firmly, then get on the power hard and early. Drive the M3 like that and it behaves in a wonderfully neutral manner, allowing fast, controllable four-wheel drifts that seem as if they could go on forever. As expected, the pedals are arranged perfectly for heel-and-toeing, while the sound of the sixteen-valve four in full cry pumps plenty of adrenaline into your bloodstream.

In small towns, the aerodynamic addenda turn heads while you're just cruising by at 25 mph. And on the open road, necks start snapping as you wail past at over 7000 rpm. The high, stubby, winged tail and the fender blisters give the M3 more than just a passing resemblance to the Audi Quattro Sport. And that isn't bad at all.

—Nicholas Bissoon-Dath

I've about had it with you readers. Every time we fawn all over some megadollar exotic, your collective reaction is as predictable as a California sunrise. We're blinded by the smoke, you say. We're in the manufacturer's pocket. We're crazy.

Actually, I'd probably think the same if I were in your moccasins. But here I go again. Stand back, because I'm gonna fawn. Unless you drive the BMW M3, there's no way you're going to understand the synergy at work therein.

Taken separately, the M3's engine, handling, and wild sheetmetal are stellar. Together, their effect is intoxicating. The demonic growl of the engine as it soars to the redline, the racer's-edge moves, and the rally-racer looks push this homologation special into another class entirely.

On paper, the M3 is just an overpriced small sedan with a cramped rear seat. In real life, it's the perfect toy for an upscale closet wild man. The M3 throbs with the soul of BMW's Motorsport division, and I, for one, love it. If you were standing in my moccasins, I'm sure you would, too.

—Rich Ceppos

Yuppies, keep back! The BMW M3 is keen through and through, and it cries out for only the truly keen to wield its treasury of talents. We car junkies have had it: even if you have sidestepped all the other potential addictions paraded by modern life, do not, under any circumstances, drive this car. It is *so* good that it's hopelessly addictive, and even you, NOx-breath, can't be immune. Nobody who gives a hoot about hardware can resist a tool that does everything well, and a single delirious dose of the M3's dynamics plants an emotional hook that cannot be shaken. It is finesse and muscle and fun packed into one.

The M3 looks right, too, brutish but sophisticated, and the more you drive it, the more you'll love it. In performance, it's right up there with the Porsche 944S (and has a trunk, to boot)! And in feel, stability, handling, punch, and price, it *kills* the Mercedes-Benz 190E 2.3–16. Although I dote on the kick-ass, cocoa-butter smoothness of BMW's 325is, its 27-grand tariff seems a little pricey. And yet another seven Gs seems a mere pittance to pay to OD on the M3.

—Larry Griffin

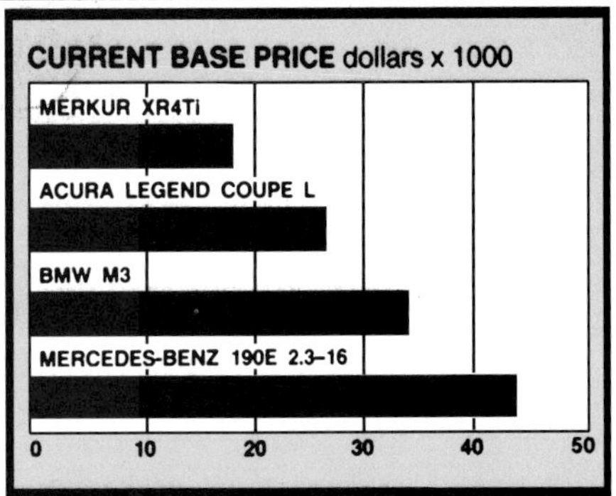

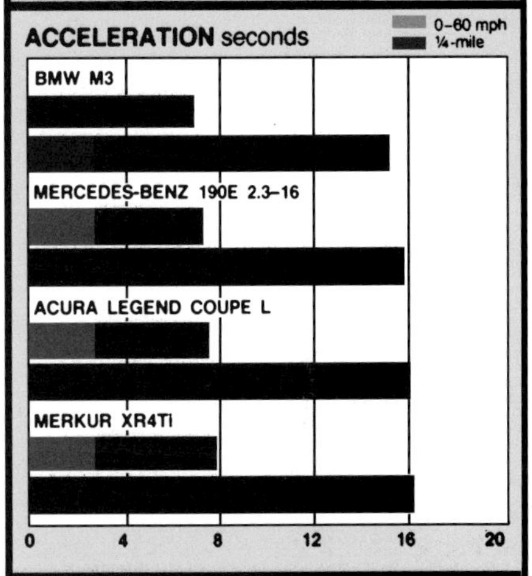

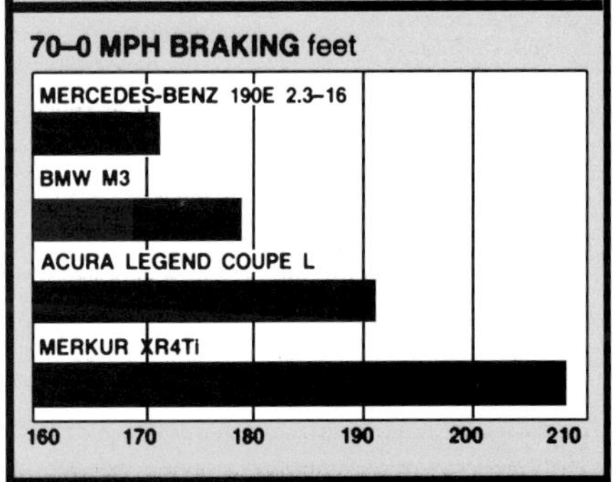

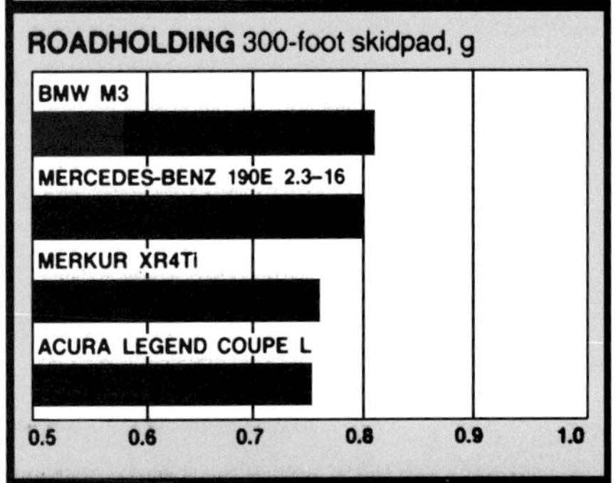

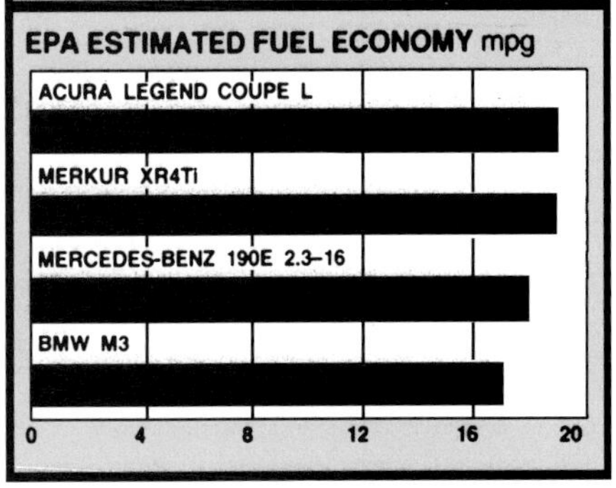

Vehicle type: front-engine, rear-wheel-drive, 4-passenger, 2-door sedan

Price as tested: $34,810

Options on test car: base BMW M3, $34,000; metallic paint, $335; freight, $475

Standard accessories: power steering, windows, locks, and sunroof, A/C, cruise control, rear defroster

Sound system: BMW AM/FM-stereo radio/cassette, 8 speakers

ENGINE

Type .... 4-in-line, iron block and aluminum head
Bore x stroke .... 3.68 x 3.31 in, 93.4 x 84.0mm
Displacement .... 140 cu in, 2302cc
Compression ratio 10.5:1
Engine-control system .... Bosch Motronic with port fuel injection
Emissions controls .... 3-way catalytic converter, feedback fuel-air-ratio control
Valve gear .... chain-driven double overhead cams, 4 valves per cylinder
Power (SAE net) .... 192 bhp @ 6750 rpm
Torque (SAE net) .... 170 lb-ft @ 4750 rpm

DRIVETRAIN

Transmission 5-speed
Final-drive ratio .... 4.10:1, limited slip

Gear	Ratio	Mph/1000 rpm	Max. test speed
I	3.83	4.4	32 mph (7250 rpm)
II	2.20	7.7	56 mph (7250 rpm)
III	1.40	12.1	87 mph (7250 rpm)
IV	1.00	16.9	122 mph (7250 rpm)
V	0.81	20.8	141 mph (6800 rpm)

DIMENSIONS AND CAPACITIES

Wheelbase .... 100.9 in
Track, F/R .... 55.6/56.4 in
Length .... 171.1 in
Width .... 66.1 in
Height .... 53.9 in
Frontal area .... 20.0 sq ft
Ground clearance .... 5.0 in
Curb weight .... 2857 lb
Weight distribution, F/R 52.9/47.1%
Fuel capacity .... 15.3 gal
Oil capacity .... 4.6 qt
Water capacity .... 11.6 qt

CHASSIS/BODY

Type ... unit construction with 1 rubber-isolated subframe
Body material ..... welded steel stampings and fiberglass-reinforced plastic

INTERIOR

SAE volume, front seat .... 45 cu ft
rear seat .... 37 cu ft
trunk space .... 13 cu ft
Front seats .... bucket
Seat adjustments .... fore and aft, seatback angle, front height, height, thigh support
General comfort .... poor fair **good** excellent
Fore-and-aft support .... poor fair **good** excellent
Lateral support .... poor fair good **excellent**

SUSPENSION

F: .... ind, strut located by a control arm, coil springs, anti-roll bar
R: .... ind, semi-trailing arm, coil springs, anti-roll bar

STEERING

Type .... rack-and-pinion, power-assisted
Turns lock-to-lock 3.7
Turning circle curb-to-curb .... 32.2 ft

BRAKES

F: .... 11.0 x 1.0-in vented disc
R: .... 11.1 x 0.5-in disc
Power assist .... vacuum with anti-lock control

WHEELS AND TIRES

Wheel size .... 7.0 x 15 in
Wheel type .... cast aluminum
Tires .... Pirelli P600, 205/55VR-15
Test inflation pressures, F/R .... 31/34 psi

CAR AND DRIVER TEST RESULTS

ACCELERATION Seconds

Zero to 30 mph 2.4
40 mph 3.7
50 mph 5.1
60 mph 6.9
70 mph 9.1
80 mph 11.8
90 mph 14.6
100 mph 19.6
110 mph 25.3
Top-gear passing time, 30–50 mph 9.4
50–70 mph 9.5
Standing ¼-mile .... 15.2 sec @ 92 mph
Top speed .... 141 mph

BRAKING

70–0 mph @ impending lockup .... 179 ft
Fade .... **none** moderate heavy

HANDLING

Roadholding, 300-ft-dia skidpad .... 0.81 g
Understeer .... minimal **moderate** excessive

COAST-DOWN MEASUREMENTS

Road horsepower @ 30 mph .... 5 hp
50 mph .... 13 hp
70 mph .... 29 hp

FUEL ECONOMY

EPA city driving .... **17 mpg**
EPA highway driving .... 29 mpg
C/D observed fuel economy .... **20 mpg**

INTERIOR SOUND LEVEL

Idle .... 59 dBA
Full-throttle acceleration .... 82 dBA
70-mph cruising .... 72 dBA
70-mph coasting .... 71 dBA

REVIEW PASSAGES

BMW's hot M3 takes off as M-B's 2.3-16 fades away.

BY KEVIN SMITH

Ann Arbor—What we have here is a story about a beginning and an ending. Think in terms of yin and yang, birth and death, the very rhythms of the cosmos. Think about the passing of a grand baton.

Or just think about exactly what's happening. An exciting new automobile is bursting on the scene, at the very moment the car that would have been its direct competitor is beating an undignified retreat.

The racy little M3 from BMW and Mercedes' 190E 2.3-16 share a basic recipe: hot sixteen-valve four-cylinders stuffed into their makers' smallest sedan bodies, along with extra-firm suspensions and fast-looking aero add-ons. Both keep one eye on European Group A Touring Car racing, the other on monied enthusiasts who are powerless to resist a personal hot rod from a German factory.

Yet these two cars come across as very different animals. We now know they differ widely in terms of success on the road (we loved the sporty Mercedes, *until* we drove it back to back with the M3), and apparently they'll differ in success on the market, too: Mercedes-Benz of North America has unceremoniously dumped the 2.3-16 from its 1988 lineup.

Perhaps we shouldn't be too surprised by these divergent fortunes. Even though Bayerische Motoren Werke and Daimler-Benz drew a bead on the same target with these high-powered missiles, they were aiming from two quite different positions. Traditionally, Mercedes cars have been stout and solid, competent to a fault, almost weighed down by their own quality and excellence. Powerful engines moved them, taut suspensions kept them in control, and firm seats propped up their occupants.

By contrast, BMWs have always had a sporting flair. Smaller, lighter, more lithe, and more maneuverable, they played the wide receivers to Mercedes' power backs, the attack subs to D-B's boomers.

Is it any wonder, then, that Munich could step up to a race-based sports sedan more deftly than Sindelfingen could pare down to one? At the very least, dealer salespeople in BMW's American showrooms could speak the sporting tongue more convincingly than their counterparts at the Mercedes stores. So today we have a genuine, 192-bhp BMW street racer sure to be in hot demand, and a Mercedes "equivalent" we can only remember (or go drive in Eu-

PHOTOGRAPHY BY TOM DREW

rope, where it remains for sale).

The M3 has a clearly focused commitment to the fast-paced life. Mechanically, it blends some serious high-speed hardware with the solid 3-series base. And it comes out better—faster, to be sure, but also more responsive, better balanced, maybe even safer—than any of its 325 siblings. At $34,000, it is the most expensive of the Three family, but, remember, the 190E 2.3-16 sold (when it sold at all) for $41,150. The M3 may be the best product BMW offers in this country, especially if we give it points for continuing the marque's tradition of appealing to the sporting spirit.

Little in this world tickles such a spirit like lots of sheer power. The 2.3-liter engine was developed by Motorsport GmbH—BMW's high-output, high-profile subsidiary, and the "M" in all those exciting cars. It spins out 192 horsepower at a lusty 6750 rpm, and is almost in the modern motorcycle class for technology and tuning. If you're a fan of specific output, and of what that tells you about state of tune, here's about as close as you'll get to 100 bhp per liter without turbocharging. The M3 develops 83.5 bhp per liter. A 3.2 Ferrari makes slightly over 81; an MR2, 70; a Corvette, under 43.

This iron-block engine uses Siamesed cylinder bores to make room for big 93.4mm holes; the short stroke of only 84.0mm helps the innards to spin past 7000 rpm without trauma. Cast pistons are designed to trim weight, and they carry the wrist pin high to permit a longer connecting rod; this reduces rod angularity in changing reciprocating motion to rotation.

Double chain-driven camshafts ride in the aluminum cylinder head and operate the light 32mm and 37mm valves directly through shim-adjusted bucket tappets. Centrally located spark plugs and squish areas around the perimeters of the shallow pent-roof combustion chambers give enough turbulence and sufficiently short flame travel so that compression ratio can be all of 10.5:1. Bosch DME (Digital Motor Electronics) controls the ignition and the fuel injection. On one side of the head is a beautiful bank of four alloy intake runners, each with an individual throttle butterfly. On the other is a tubular four-into-two exhaust header.

The torque peak of 170 pounds-

Bulged fenders are subtle, sill extensions less so, high-flying rear wing not at all.

Even the M3's interior is high-performance, with BMW's great, snug-fit sport seats.

How to get 1.37 bhp from every cubic inch: lots of cams, valves, and compression.

COMPARATIVE DATA

	BMW M3	MERCEDES 190 2.3-16
Engine type	2.3-liter, 16-valve four	2.3-liter, 16-valve four
Brake horsepower	192 @ 6750 rpm	167 @ 5800 rpm
Torque	170 @ 4750 rpm	162 @ 4750 rpm
Redline	7240 rpm	6800 rpm
Compression ratio	10.5:1	9.7:1
Gear ratios	(I) 3.83 (II) 2.20 (III) 1.40 (IV) 1.00 (V) 0.81	(I) 4.08 (II) 2.52 (III) 1.77 (IV) 1.26 (V) 1.00
Final-drive ratio	4.10:1	3.25:1
Power-to-weight ratio	14.2 lb/hp	18.0 lb/hp
Wheelbase	100.9 in	104.9 in
Length	171.1 in	174.4 in
Width	66.1 in	67.2 in
Curb weight	2735 lb	3010 lb
Weight distribution	53/47%	54/46%
Steering	power-assisted rack-and-pinion	power-assisted rack-and-pinion
Brakes, front	11.0-inch vented discs	11.2-inch vented discs
rear	11.2-inch discs	10.2-inch discs
	anti-lock system	anti-lock system
Tires	205/55VR-15 Pirelli P600	205/55VR-15 Pirelli P6

feet comes at a high 4750 rpm, further evidence of how tightly wrapped this semi-racing engine is. A five-speed gearbox with ratios that feel unusually close-spaced and short overall helps the engine run where it does its best work. In crafting the car for the U.S. market, BMW changed its shift pattern from the European sport configuration, with first outside the H, to the arrangement more familiar here, with *fifth* outside the H.

While sorting out the suspension so it could handle the new speed and power, BMW's engineers came up with a specification that brings new-found stability and dependability to the 3-series platform. True, ride height is awfully low, and spring and damper rates are quite high. But ramp clearance and ride harshness are not affected adversely enough to make us want to give up any of the M3's fine, firm control.

Front suspension geometry incorporates much more caster to give greater directional stability. Coil-spring rates are progressive in back but remain linear in front—simply because that's what worked best. Low-pressure gas-charged shocks are incorporated in the struts in front and mounted atop the semi-trailing arms in back. The shocks fight fluid aeration and its attendant heat fade, and provide degressive damping, to give way on extreme impacts and smooth out the ride.

Ambient air gives way, too, more readily for the M3's passing than for any other 3-series, and by quite a margin. Front and rear aprons with integral bumpers, gently contoured fenders, rocker panel skirts, and a raised rear deck with a wild, angular wing all slash drag coefficient from a 325's 0.37 way down to 0.33—and that's with fattish 205/55VR-15 tires.

The rear-end treatment includes a fiberglass cover for the C-pillars that changes the roofline subtly, reangles the backlight, and blends into the higher, flattened trunk lid. That wing is a sturdy slab constructed of polyurethane over a paper honeycomb core. Quality, fit, and match of the new pieces are flawless throughout; our only complaint centers on a spot where the rounded lower edge of the new deck lid wraps over the squared shape at the upper rear corner of the sheetmetal.

Frankly, we're also not sure whether the wing treatment isn't going a little far for a road car. It struck us as awfully boy-racerish, with that thing jutting up back there. On the other hand, the rest of the car is unobtrusive and conservative in the normal BMW way, and in any case, this look will shortly come to be widely recognized as simply the M3 style—giving it positive impact in the important circles, whether it's aesthetically perfect or not.

We may have felt more obvious on the street than we usually prefer, but the M3 left us with little else to complain about. Our time in the car began with a 600-mile waltz across New York State and southern Ontario, returning to Ann Arbor from the press introduction at lovely Lime Rock Park in Connecticut. Such a freeway run—particularly in that part of the continent, where the climate is hard on pavement—should show the

The factory-built, hot-rod sedan works much better as a BMW than as a Mercedes.

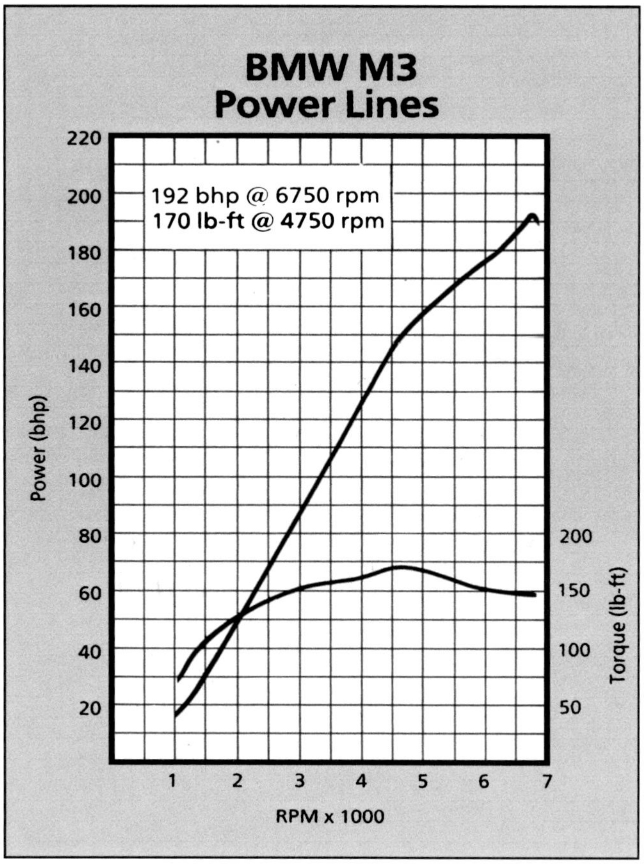

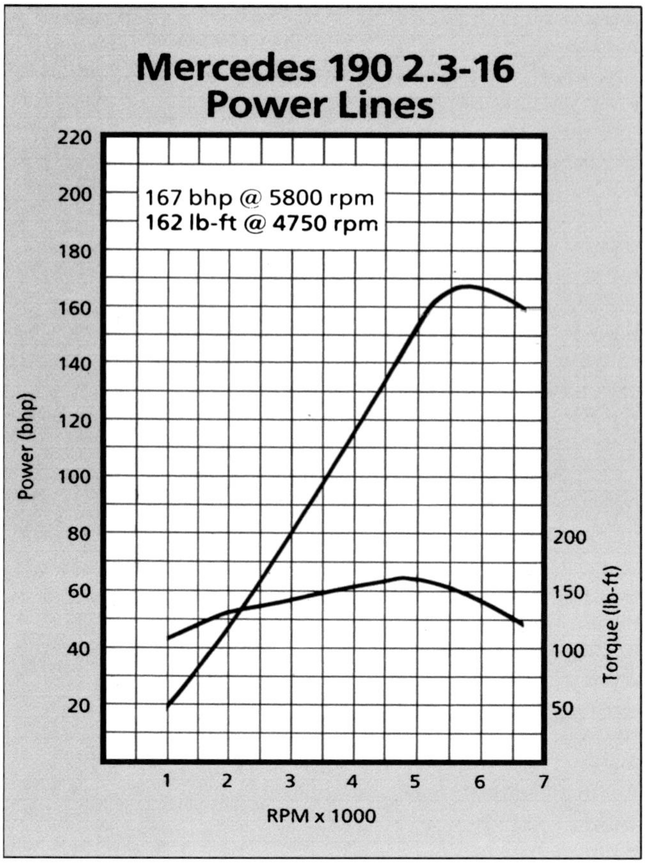

sport-tuned M3 at its worst. Well, if that's as bad as it gets, we'll take it. Yes, the car is a bit stiff-legged when hitting patches and seams at speed, but it's not too bad. Yes, its engine note is a trifle more prominent than you might prefer, but it's not too bad. Yes, engine and road vibration conspire to fuzz images in the rear-view mirror, but it's not too bad.

In short, the comfort compromises the M3 makes strike us as minor and reasonable. For a car of its type, delivering what it does in the way of performance, it doesn't really demand too much of the long-haul driver. For instance, the engine growl is obvious, but not offensive, even though it's exacerbated by the short-ish gearing (70 mph takes over 3600 rpm). Those excellent sport seats BMW uses in several of its zestier models contribute a lot, even on the Interstate. Never mind (for the moment) their aggressive side bolstering; they are perfectly shaped on the bottom as well. And the height adjustment helps place them in the car exactly the way you want them.

You'll also appreciate the M3's great seating—plus its zippy response and sharp maneuverability—around town and in the busy suburbs. You might notice the small numb spot in the steering right around center—pretty typical of most recent BMWs we've driven—but you'll also realize that the shifter and the pedals are ideally placed, and that they work so sweetly you barely pay attention to them. Instead, you drive the car.

Of course, absolutely the best place to do *that* is out on the lightly populated back roads, preferably twisty, playful ones. Here, the M3 truly hits its favored stride. Also, here, it most clearly demonstrates its superiority over Mercedes' similar but different 190E 2.3-16. The M3 is a focused, balanced, effective sports sedan; in comparison, the 190 feels a little unsure of itself, a little confused.

Both cars are comfortable, beautifully outfitted, and swift. But where the Mercedes feels soft, undertired, and resolved to plow at the nose no matter what, the BMW turns in much more crisply, gets more out of its rear tires during cornering, and is more responsive to the driver's midturn wishes. It, too, is a basic understeerer, but much less determinedly so. Its somewhat more neutral balance allows an attentive driver to obtain attitude changes (generally minor and manageable) using throttle in the bends. A quick lift lightens the tail and tightens the front; go hard back into the gas (especially over 5000 rpm), and you get a nice neutral drive out of fast turns, or a little gentle oversteer if the corner is slower and tighter.

Start working both cars hard like this, and you'll notice a couple of

PERFORMANCE*

	BMW M3	MERCEDES 190 2.3-16
0–60	7.6 seconds	8.1 seconds
Top speed	143 mph	137 mph
EPA city driving (est)	17 mpg	18 mpg

*manufacturer's data

other points the BMW scores. The Mercedes' stubby gear lever has light and lovely action, but it requires far too precise a hand—and too much attention when you're working hard—to slot into the gates correctly. The BMW's lever travels farther through a typical gearchange, but it goes where you want it without calling extra attention to itself. Also, the M3's big tachometer is much more legible, its high-bolstered seats hold more snugly, and it communicates a clearer sense of what's happening down at the tires.

Both of these sixteen-valve 2.3s are highly tuned, modest-displacement engines, both quite peaky by normal standards. They each have a little performance bubble just over 4000 rpm as they climb up onto the torque peak. The BMW's four seems to hold up a bit better off the peak, while the 190 falls off the cam into a torque pit more readily.

Looking at the torque curves for the engines confirms that impression. Although the peak values are close—within five percent, and arriving at the same engine speed—it's clear the BMW's output hangs in there better both above and below the point of maximum urge. This makes the M3 feel a little more flexible and accommodating.

As you would imagine, given the torque data and BMW's weight advantage (2735 pounds to 3010), the M3 holds the performance edge over the 190. BMW quotes a 0-to-60-mph time of 7.6 seconds versus the M-B's 8.1, and a top speed of 143, 6 mph faster than the 190. Over the broad spectrum of actual down-the-road driving conditions, however, the two cars are quite evenly matched. Credit the ideal gearing Mercedes selected for the 190, and note that the BMW's horsepower advantages are greatest above 6000 rpm. Our testing confirmed that only when both drivers work *extremely* hard does the M3 pull ahead noticeably.

Of course, in the larger race—the one in the marketplace—the BMW has pulled ahead solidly and for good. Disappointing sales and near duplication from the tamer six-cylinder 190E 2.6 finally killed the 2.3-16 in the United States. Yet there's no question that the idea of a snarky-looking factory-hot-rodded sports sedan has enduring appeal. It might not make the ideal Mercedes-Benz. But look how it works as a BMW.

1988 BMW M3

GENERAL:
Front-engine, rear-wheel-drive sedan
4-passenger, 2-door steel body
Base price/price as tested $34,000/$34,335

	POOR	FAIR	GOOD	EXCELLENT
ENGINE				
power				●
response				●
smoothness			●	
DRIVETRAIN				
shift action				●
power delivery				●
STEERING				
effort				●
response			●	
feel			●	
RIDE				
general comfort			●	
roll control				●
pitch control			●	
HANDLING				
directional stability			●	
predictability				●
maneuverability				●
BRAKES				
response			●	
modulation			●	
effectiveness				●
GENERAL				
ergonomics			●	
instrumentation				●
roominess		●		
seating comfort				●
fit and finish				●
storage space				●
OVERALL				
dollar value			●	
fun to drive				●

MAJOR EQUIPMENT:
Air conditioning standard
Sunroof standard
AM/FM/cassette standard
Leather interior standard
Cruise control standard

ENGINE:
16-valve DOHC 4-in-line, iron block, aluminum head
Bore x stroke 3.68 x 3.31 in (93.4 x 84.0mm)
Displacement 140 cu in (2302cc)
Compression ratio 10.5:1
Fuel system Bosch Motronic injection
Power SAE net 192 bhp @ 6750 rpm
Torque SAE net 170 lb-ft @ 4750 rpm
Redline 7240 rpm

DRIVETRAIN:
5-speed manual transmission
Gear ratios (I) 3.83 (II) 2.20 (III) 1.40 (IV) 1.00 (V) 0.81
Final-drive ratio 4.10:1

MEASUREMENTS:
Wheelbase 100.9 in
Track front/rear 55.6/56.4 in
Length 171.1 in
Width 66.1 in
Height 53.9 in
Curb weight 2735 lb
Weight distribution front/rear 53/47%
Fuel capacity 15.3 gal

SUSPENSION:
Independent front, with gas-pressurized damper struts, lower control arms, coil springs, anti-roll bar
Independent rear, with semi-trailing arms, coil springs, gas-pressurized shocks, anti-roll bar

STEERING:
Rack-and-pinion, power-assisted

BRAKES:
11.0 in vented discs front
11.2 in discs rear
Anti-lock system

WHEELS and TIRES:
15 x 7.0-in cast aluminum wheels
205/55VR-15 Pirelli P600 tires

PERFORMANCE (manufacturer's data):
0–60 mph in 7.6 sec
Standing ¼-mile in 15.7 sec @ 94 mph
Top speed 143 mph
EPA estimated city driving 17 mpg

MAINTENANCE:
Headlamp unit $10.62
Front quarter-panel $356.80
Brake pads front wheels $137.60
Air filter $12.08
Oil filter $3.35
Recommended oil change interval according to service indicator system

ROAD TEST

BMW M325i

It's been a long time since we last drove a BMW like the M325i. This is a finely-honed, exquisite sporting car in the best German tradition.

Recent 3-series BMWs have tended to shame owners with competitive blood in their veins. The current offerings revive the glory of the recent past, when cars like the 323i rated highly on just about everybody's most-desirable list.

Top: Big M remains secure and well-planted despite unexpected degree of body roll.
Above: Discreet spoiler and badging announce the M325i's sporting intent.
Left: Purposeful look of the 3-series battleship is emphasised by aerodynamic aids.

Munich suffered badly at the hands of catalytic converters, low compression ratios and lead-free fuel. Where some people — like Mercedes — managed to hang grimly onto their hard-won energy, BMW virtually dropped its bundle to give us cars like the 325e, and the 525e, which, with their 2.7 litre Eta engines, had all the revving ability of an old Falcon six and failed to make up in torque what they lost in power. If BMW didn't exactly lose its way at this point, it certainly lost faith with some of its customers.

Now, the company is back in the performance business. The tables are about to turn. Shortly we will have the formidable, astonishing V12-powered 750, and the new 5-series sedans which are already impressing the Europeans with their chunky looks and new-age dynamics, and are surely giving Mercedes executives some heartburn.

In the meantime, in Australia, we have the revitalized, extended 3-series range which includes the 320i convertible — tested in the last issue — and gets two new six cylinder

. . . back in the performance business

engines to replace the underpowered 1.8 litre four and the lethargic Eta six. As managing director Ron Meatchem promised us last year, the 3-series is back with real power, with the sort of performance edge BMWs have traditionally always had – the sort of equipment needed to legitimize the openly-declared challenge made by the company to Mercedes-Benz.

The M325i epitomizes the 3-series revival. Hunched on its 205/55 VR15 Pirelli P600 tyres, allowing only a sliver of daylight to sneak underneath its polypropolene aerodynamic hardware, delivering its 125 kW to the road via a close-ratio gearbox and enclosing its driver and passengers in torso-grabbing sports seats, the M325i is a synthesis of all that is good in German sporting motorcars.

It has that immensely solid, crafted feel about it that renews one's faith in the Europeans' ability to build the world's best cars, and its dynamic abilities demonstrate to us again what the word integrity really means.

"There's nothing quite like the iron-fist-in-a-velvet-glove feel conveyed by a proper high compression engine from Munich."

Without twin camshafts, without intricate induction systems and without multi-link, steered rear suspension systems, the BMW still shuts down just about anything short of $100,000 that purports to be a sporting motor vehicle. Only the M325's price – $75,750 – negatively affects one's perception of the car.

This most agile of the 3-series, although it shares its body and basic mechanicals with the two door 325i, is tuned to extract the most from the 2.5 litre engine. Perhaps the most significant changes relate to the drivetrain, where the M gets a different, close-ratio gearbox, and a limited slip differential. Overall gearing is lower than the more economy-oriented 325i to give the M a performance boost. It also tends to accentuate the deliciously harmonic sounds that emanate from all six cylinder BMWs.

BMW M325i builds on 2.5-litre six's performance with close-ratio 'box, lsd, sports suspension and aerodynamic passage.

Suspension changes – common to both 325i and M325i – to tie the car down more firmly include progressive-rate springs, gas shock absorbers and heavier-duty roll bars front and rear. M325i wheels are wider, 6.5Jx15 mesh-style alloys fitted with 205/55 tyres and the standard braking system here is all-disc ABS. The body kit – very tasteful and restrained, totally in keeping with the BMW image – comprises front and rear spoilers, rear apron and side skirts, all manufactured from fibreglass and designed to enhance both downforce and aerodynamics. The effect, on the M325i's two-door body, is unmistakeable: this is the latter-day reincarnation of the small performance BMWs that began with the 2002 in the late 1960s and were more recently represented by the sorely-missed – until now – 323i.

This is where we start talking about that sythesis between performance capabilities, design integrity, and quality.

Industrial design verges on art: quality engine castings complement neat front spoiler treatment – just part of BMW's synthesis between performance, quality and design integrity.

There's never any mistaking when you sit behind the wheel of a quality automobile: the way the doors open and close, the fit, and solid feel of all controls, and the generally understated presentation all conspire to make one conscious he's not sitting in designed-to-a-price proletarian motorcar. The seats are beautifully formed, the instrument panel is clean and completely free of gimmickry and the ergonomics are obviously the result of Germanic clear-thinking. And there's no lack of standard equipment: the car is centrally-locked, has air conditioning, AM/FM stereo and electric exterior mirrors.

Bringing the BMW's 2.5 litre six into life furthers the impression of quality. There's nothing quite like the iron-fist-in-a-velvet glove feel conveyed by a proper high-compression engine from Munich.

On the road, it's clear straight away that the gearing of the M325i is angled towards performance. 3000 rpm on the tachometer has the optimistic speedometer indicating not much more than 100 km/h and the ratio-to-ratio gaps are small indeed. Our test strip saw the car hum across the 400 metre line in 16.0 seconds, while 100 km/h came up in 8.7, pretty close to BMW's claim for the car.

The car absorbs rough roads with a nice degree of compliance, and without transmitting a lot of impact noise through to the cabin. As always, the feeling here is one of immense solidity – particularly impressive in a car like the 3-series which is really no heavyweight.

Considering the relative age of the car's design (the current shape was introduced in 1983 and has only been changed in minor ways, such as introducing new, self-regenerating bumpers, re-shaping the rear wheel arch, redesigning the tail lights and using 7-series headlight technology, for 1988), it also cleaves through the air pretty well, with a minimum of wind noise. That is partly due to the simple fact that the whole car is hung together so precisely, with no great variances in panel fit, around side window seals, or other turbulence-inducing areas.

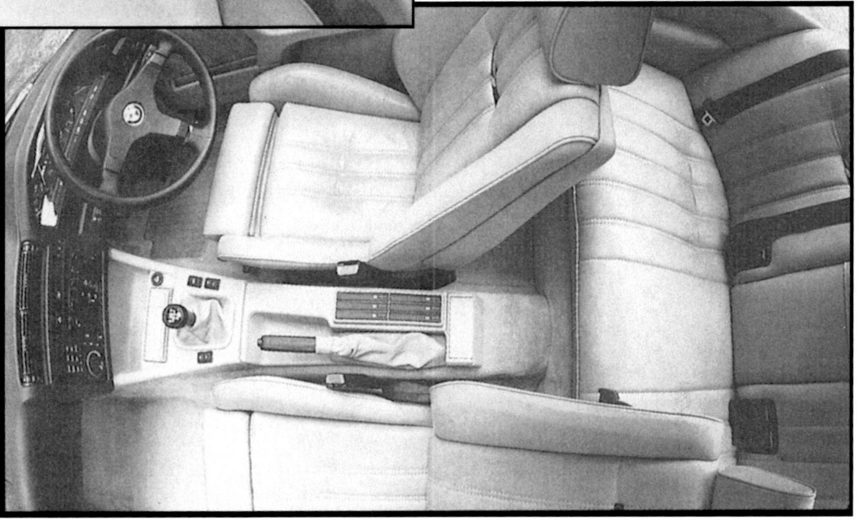

The integrity of the M comes across in the car's lack of fussiness, the way it puts its power down cleanly, and the way it turns into a fast corner.

The initial feeling, when the car is being pushed along, is that there is an unexpected degree of body roll, but once committed the amount of lean remains fairly constant, allowing a clean line to be easily maintained via the well-weighted assisted rack and pinion steering. The car is generally fairly nuetral, and responds progressively to throttle variations in mid-corner, feeling very secure and well-planted. With the ability to find precisely the right ratio to give maximum power in virtually all situations, the M325i is a very quick point-to-point car – far quicker than its straight-line figures, good though they are, suggest.

Perhaps surprisingly, there's no great sacrifice of overall ride comfort to allow the M325i its responsive, sporting character.

The aerodynamic aids on the M325i also make the car feel demonstrably better at speed on the open road, indicating that the wind-tunnel work hasn't been wasted.

The only thing that brings us back to earth with the M325i is the price. Costing considerably more working-hours than the 2002 or 323i, the BMW is a reminder that the good times for Australian motorists are now over. No matter what concessions the importers may or may not be able to wring out of the government, the fact remains that car prices – particularly imported car prices – have increased dramatically in Australia and there's no sign of this being a temporary situation. The industry is hurting, and the car buyer is hurting, and the pain is not about to go away overnight. The pain is even more intense when you realize how many aspirant prestige car buyers have been forced to lower their sights. How many people who once might have imagined themselves in a 323i have been eliminated from the list of prospective 325i buyers?

"The integrity of the M comes across in the car's lack of fussiness, the way it puts its power down cleanly, and the way it turns into a fast corner."

DATA

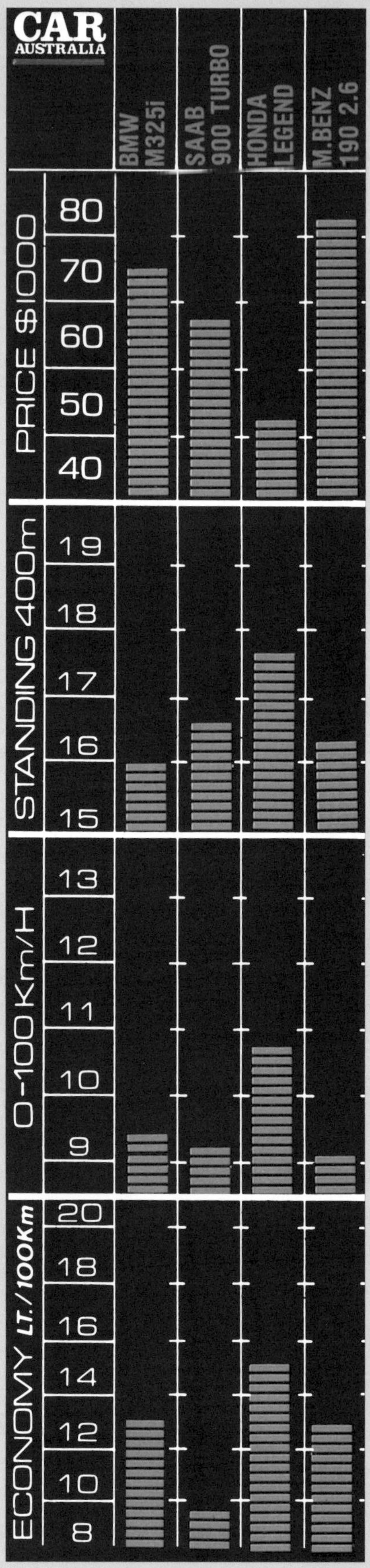

MODEL .... BMW M325i

COUNTRY OF ORIGIN . West Germany

BODY TYPE .... Sedan

SEATING CAPACITY .... Four

PRICE .... Approx $75,750

OPTIONS FITTED .... None

PRICE AS TESTED .... Approx $75,750

ENGINE:
Location .... Front
Cylinders .... Six
Capacity .... 2494 cc
Bore/stroke .... 84 x 75 mm
Block .... Alloy
Head .... Alloy
Valve actuation .... SOHC
Induction .... Electronic fuel injection
Compression ratio 8.8:1
Power .... 125 kW at 5800 rpm
Torque .... 222 Nm at 4300 rpm

TRANSMISSION:
Driving wheels .... Rear
Gearbox type .... Five speed automatic
Shift location .... Floor

Gear ratios		Calc. max. speed	At (rpm)
1st	3.35:1	49	6000
2nd	2.03:1	81	6000
3rd	1.36:1	121	6000
4th	1.00:1	164	6000
5th	0.81:1	203	6000

Final drive ratio 3.91:1

BODY/CHASSIS:
Construction .... Unitary
Material .... Steel
Kerb weight .... 1220 kg
O/A length .... 4325 mm
O/A width .... 1645 mm
O/A height .... 1380 mm
Wheelbase .... 2570 mm
Front track .... 1407 mm
Rear track .... 1415 mm
Fuel tank capacity 64ℓ

SUSPENSION:
Front .... Independent, coil over struts, stabilizer bar
Rear ..... Independent, semi trailing arms, coils, stabilizer bar

STEERING:
Type .... Power assisted rack and pinion
Turning circle .... 10.5 m

BRAKES:
Actuation .... Power assisted ABS
Front .... Ventilated discs
Rear .... Disc

WHEELS:
Material .... Alloy
Diameter/width .... 14 x 6J

TYRES:
Make/type .... Pirelli P600
Dimensions 205/55/VR14

PERFORMANCE:
WEATHER .... Warm

ROAD .... Dry

ODOMETER READING 3713

SPEEDOMETER ERROR AT:
60 km/h 56
80 km/h 76
100 km/h 93
120 km/h 113

STANDING START:
0-60 km/h 4.2
0-80 km/h 6.4
0-100 km/h 9.6
0-120 km/h 12.7
400 metres 16.0

IN GEAR ACCELERATION:

	3rd	4th	5th
60-100 km/h	6.0	10.1	13.6
80-120 km/h	7.3	10.3	16.4

BRAKING FROM 100 KM/H
Average of four tests .... 46 metres

FUEL CONSUMPTION:
Car Australia average on test
Overall combination city/highway driving .... 13.0 litres/100 km

BMW M3 racer for UK

BMW have built 500 homologation versions of their M3 racing saloon, of which 40 will find their way to the UK where they will sell for £26,960 apiece.

Power has been increased 10 per cent to 220bhp while torque has gone up to 180lb ft from 177lb ft, mainly by increasing the engine's compression ratio to 11.0:1 from 10.5:1.

These changes mean that BMW now claim a 152mph top speed and a zero to 60mph time of 6.9sec, both of which are marginally better than the standard M3's figures of 146mph and 7.0sec respectively. And half-a-second has been lopped off the 1000 metre time – now reputed to be 27.1sec.

Externally, the car has received some aerodynamic tweaks to make it more stable, as well as reducing front and rear lift. The most noticeable modifications are the front spoiler and an additional rear spoiler. That at the front is both deeper and has a forward sloping splitter to duct more cooling air into the front brakes, and there is now a lip on the boot's trailing edge.

The unladen weight of the car has been reduced – although BMW were reluctant to release the exact figures – by using thinner glass in the rear window and the rear side windows. Lighter body panels for the boot lid and the rear wing have also been used.

Pirelli 225/45 ZR16 tyres on 7.5J×16 cross spoke alloy wheels are fitted as standard. For a further £1388, potential owners can have the optional Boge three-position electronic damping system, otherwise the suspension is identical to that of the current car.

Other, more cosmetic, changes include a green-tinted screen with anti-glare strip across the top, M3 stainless steel door steps and an M Technic driver's footrest. Interior trim will be in silver cloth with leather side sections irrespective of whether the buyer chooses Macau Blue, Nogaro Silver or Misano Red bodywork. However, the most striking detail finish of the BMW racer has been reserved for under the bonnet where the cam cover and air collector box are decorated in the distinctive Motorsport colours.

The standard M3, which sells for £23,550, will continue in production. (See page 63 for Mike Smith's BMW M3 lap of Silverstone.)

EVOLUTION

The M3 Evolution is difficult to tell from an 'ordinary' M3 as the differences are subtle: the front spoiler, above, has brake cooling vents while the engine, right, gains M-sport colours as well as the extra 20bhp

BMW's M3 was born for the race track and, following racing rules, has now evolved with more power and less weight. But asks **Kevin Blick,** does it feel different?

Subtlety was out. After several false starts, there was clearly only one way to get BMW M3 Evolution number 475 off the line and down Millbrook's mile straight at its scintillating best.

And that was sheer brute force. Whip the screaming four-cylinder up to within a few hundred revs of its 7000rpm red line, then simply dump the clutch. Howling their hearts out, the massive Pirelli P700s struggled for grip on the tarmac, the car's rear end drifting almost in slow motion from side to side as it wrestled with that suddenly applied 220bhp. As grip slowly overcame slip, the engine dipped from 7000rpm to 5000rpm, then held momentarily before soaring again as the BMW speared down the track.

The awkward dog-leg shift out of first was forced through even before the wheels had stopped spinning. The revs dipped but the engine was slap bang on its torque peak and the M3's charge undiminished. Through 60mph in just 6.7 seconds, then a straight pull back on the stick to third and peak torque once more.

> This single exercise is as much about grip as it is about power. The Evolution version may have an extra 20bhp at its disposal but it's the prodigious grip that allows it to use the power with impunity. It is this grip . . . that impresses.

Another of those awkward dog-leg shifts slammed through with no time to worry about the vagaries of the Getrag gearbox's sloppy gate – but a quiet sigh of relief, nonetheless, that it had risen to the occasion well enough – and we were on to 100mph in a decimal over 18 seconds; the punch of acceleration still following forcibly through.

Brake hard and true as the end of the straight looms up, then swing round for the run back and another full-revs, clutch-dumping start. But don't get the wrong impression. The brutality of our test track treatment was not ignorant but calculated. And a tribute to the remarkable abilities of BMW's little racer.

As any tester will tell you, the technique for standing starts in a powerful, rear-drive car is usually the simplest of all to master. Half revs, drop the clutch and you'll have all the wheelspin you need for a fast getaway – too much quite often.

Not in the M3. At half revs, the big Pirellis stay glued like barnacles to the track surface. Try a thousand higher. Little better, the grip breaks, wheels spin for a yard or two, then the revs fade as the tyres claw their footholds back. Try again – peak torque revs; that usually does it. But no, the wheels spin for a few yards more, grip again and the engine fades.

And so it has to be sheer force: peak power revs, and at last we get it away with the right balance of spin and traction to keep the engine boiling until momentum has picked up.

The M3 story we've discovered in this single exercise is as much about grip as it is about power. The Evolution version may have an extra 20bhp at its disposal, but it's the prodigious grip that allows it to use the power with impunity. It is this grip, in the end, that impresses even more than the car's performance.

'Evolution' is one of those motor sport terms little understood by anyone who is not both a member of Mensa and enjoys the FIA rule book as bedtime reading.

In layman's language, having produced 5000 examples of a saloon car in order for it to be homologated as a Group A competition car, a manufacturer can then 'evolve' 500 improved versions from that original – stretching whatever the strictly defined guidelines for so doing might be as far as possible, of course.

Needless to say, this process also creates an instant, limited edition collector's piece – identified in the case of the M3 Evolution by a numbered plate riveted to the centre console.

The Sierra Cosworth, you will recall, evolved into the RS500 Cosworth via a series of nifty changes that opened up an Aladdin's Cave of rich possibilities for the race-track. A massive new turbocharger and a second rail of fuel injectors (not even connected up on the road cars) were all ready to activate a whalloping power improvement by a simple engine management chip change, while a set of additional rear suspension pick-up points (again unused on the road version) allowed track tuners ample opportunity to re-work the semi-trailing rear end into something more sophisticated. And finally, revised spoilers reduced drag and increased rear end down-force.

It was, in truth, not so much evolution as revolution. By comparison, the M3 has been through a very modest development step. The engine is substantially altered, true enough: it has new pistons, increasing compression ratio from 10.5 to 11.0:1, a lighter flywheel, revised camshafts, a new air intake system and a re-chipped Motronic management unit. But such changes are much less significant in competition terms than Ford's evolution changes for the Cosworth.

A naturally aspirated engine could not have its output radically increased as easily as Ford's turbo-unit could, and the 300bhp-odd of the Group A M3 engine is only likely to rise by 20-30bhp as a result of these mods.

The road-tune engine gains just 20bhp, too, its 220bhp being developed at the same 6750rpm as the original. Torque, likewise, changes only a little: from 177 to 181lb ft maximum at the same 4750rpm. To take advantage of the added power, the Evolution's final drive has also been stretched slightly: from 3.25 to 3.15:1.

The engine itself is, of course, the durable iron-blocked four-cylinder which has been at the core of so much of BMW's competition work since it first saw life in the BMW 1500 back in the 1960s.

In M3 guise it became a short-stroke high revving 2302cc unit, featuring a version of the twin-cam, four-valve-per-cylinder head used in the bigger, six-cylinder M-cars. Its Evolution development is identifiable at once from the vividly finished white cam cover and air collector, which sport the blue, mauve and red stripes of BMW Motorsport.

But, from a racing viewpoint, the significant alterations are those which the uninformed observer might well not spot. A delicate boot lip aerofoil beneath the existing spoiler improves downforce by between 10 and 15 per cent, and 22lb of weight have also been pared from the rear of the car by substitution of a lighter boot lid, wing and bumper supports, as well as the use of thinner glass in the rear screen and rear side windows. Wheels and tyres are also larger than the original M3's: 225/45ZR16 Pirellis on 7½J alloy wheels, though these were already available as an option in place of the standard 205/55s and 7-inch rims.

In truth, the extra power is not really discernible on the road: it takes track testing to spot the differences – for they are small, being partially hidden by that slight rise in overall gearing, which is in turn offset by the lower profile tyres.

Confused? Well, in comparison with the standard car (if a machine like the M3 could ever be termed 'standard'), the Evolution proved 0.2 seconds quicker to 60mph, a difference that had widened to just over two seconds by 100mph (18.1 against 20.5 seconds).

Top speeds are even harder to compare for we tested the original car abroad on the *autobahn*, where it reached 145.9mph. Around Millbrook's oval, the Evolution averaged 144.8mph and was clearly losing some speed through tyre scrub. How much? That's hard to say, but the original M3 has been 'maxed' round Millbrook by others at between 136 and 139mph, so BMW's 152mph claim for the Evolution looks fair enough.

But so what if the Evolution is only marginally quicker; the M3 in either guise is a magnificent performer. The four-cylinder engine is a real race-bred screamer, though with enough docility to make it a perfectly mannered road unit, too.

It will pull smoothly from below 2000rpm, though it only starts to feel at all meaningful once it is nearing 4000. From here on – it flies! The real red meat of performance, though, is reserved for the final 2500rpm from just below 5000 to the rev limiter which cuts off an engine that is still in full flight at 7300rpm.

The rather boomy exhaust note of the short-stroke four turns into a throaty howl

The new lightweight bootlid gains a spoiler below the rear 'wing', which is itself also lighter. Instruments are traditional BMW. A centre console plaque says which of the 500 the car is

and that acceleration which had started to impress a thousand revs earlier just keeps driving on.

Such an eager, high-revving power unit makes road driving not only thrilling but remarkably fuss free, too. The M3 has power and torque reserves sufficient to make gearchanging less than a priority. On a country secondary, it will punch out of corners and swallow up the short straights between in third, while on quicker roads, fourth will carry it comfortably through fast sweepers and simply devour those longer straights.

But as we said at the beginning, given the chance, the Getrag 'box's close, tight ratios can maintain the M3 at maximum momentum – when you'll discover it's a stunningly quick machine indeed. To well beyond 100mph acceleration just doesn't falter and only as it nears maximum speed does the M3 begin to slow off.

The response, too, is instantaneous. Shift up, bang the throttle hard down again and the engine's bite is immediate – quite the opposite of a turbo's slightly reluctant pick-up.

The gearbox isn't the easiest to use – especially as one is shifting with the right – or rather the wrong – hand. First is out on a dog-leg while a strongly spring-loaded gate separates second/third from fourth/fifth.

It's one of those shifts that is all too easy to fumble over when driving casually – forget the spring loading and you often wrong-slot. But, driven in anger, everything comes good. And that, of course, is what counts. All this would be to no avail, though, without the M3's terrific traction. You can slam the throttle down hard and early on the exit of a corner and those big Pirellis will just bite in and grip. There's no trace of wheelspin or tail twitching, just the instant punch of a Lynford Christie leaving his starting blocks.

It's a combination of traction and response that makes for sparkling motoring. You can drive the M3 Evolution like the racer it is: brake hard, turn in, power on, blast out.

It appears just to flow through bends – the hallmark of greatness. There's little body roll, good feel through the assisted steering and the chassis balance is impeccable. It will understeer turning in – quite noticeably so if you turn in too late and too hard – but once the power is back on it simply squirts through the corner with impunity.

And the M3 is so easy to drive, too. Grippy leather-edged sports seats hold you tightly in place and the left-hand driving position is almost inch perfect. It's one that inspires instant confidence: the pedals are properly spaced for heel-and-toe shifts and there's a massive foot-brace down alongside the clutch. All-round visibility is good, too.

If there's a fault to be found when driving the M3 (and fault-finding hardly seems fair in a car that behaves so beautifully) then it's that the steering struggles to keep up with the chassis's ability. At 3.6 turns between locks it is much higher geared than the standard 325's awful 4.5 turns, but it is still not really quick enough. Flicking the car through a complex of tight bends demands rather too much work at the wheel and you miss the Cosworth's steering quickness.

Brakes are more than up to the job, however. The car stops hard and true; there's no weaving, and not a hint of fade. And on a dry surface, you'd have to be literally screeching to a halt before the characteristic pedal thump-back of ABS made itself known.

The inevitable consequence of such crisp, racer-like road manners is that the M3's ride is hard – too hard for some, no doubt – but despite the stiffness and its associated wheel thump, even on rough country roads it remains stable and tidy, with little or no bump steer.

Our car, in fact, came with three-setting, driver-adjustable dampers – an electronic system developed by BMW in association with Boge. The three settings (altered by a turn-wheel at the base of the gearstick) roughly correspond to Sporting, Normal M3 settings and Comfort – with the last automatically up-grading itself to Normal at higher speeds.

The differences between the settings are not as great as might be expected. In fact at first you're barely aware of them. The M3's springing is stiff, and the wide, low tyres noisy even on the softest setting. But try each setting for longer and differences do emerge in the way the car copes with various types of road imperfection. In Comfort, for instance, the car is less jolty at low speed, but go faster over an undulating road and you notice a slight floatiness that isn't in tune with the hard demands made by fast motoring.

The Sport setting is harsher than the standard as well, and it can become quite unpleasantly jarring over bad surfaces. Does it improve the overall handling balance? That's hard to say: it would need a lengthy back to back test over a variety of roads to come to a firm conclusion. So perhaps at a costly £1388, it's an option that doesn't conclusively prove its worth. Not that the car is short of possible options: ours had another £2000 worth: electric sunroof (£692), headlamp cleaning (£288), computer (£337), electric front windows (£383) and heating control (£149), and anti-theft locks (£369).

As you can see, the M3 Evolution's hefty £26,960 price tag pays for that pure-bred, competition pedigree and not for a great deal in the way of added luxury.

Naturally, you do still get superb build quality with the M3 Evolution – homologation special it might be, but this is still a BMW – but for the exclusive club of 40 British buyers who'll take one home this year, the most important part of the car will probably be that aluminium plate with its limited edition serial number.

It's a collector's piece from the start, but certainly not one that should be tucked away for safe keeping. For this is the sports saloon brought to perfection: for sheer driving pleasure, you won't beat it.

BMW M3 EVOLUTION

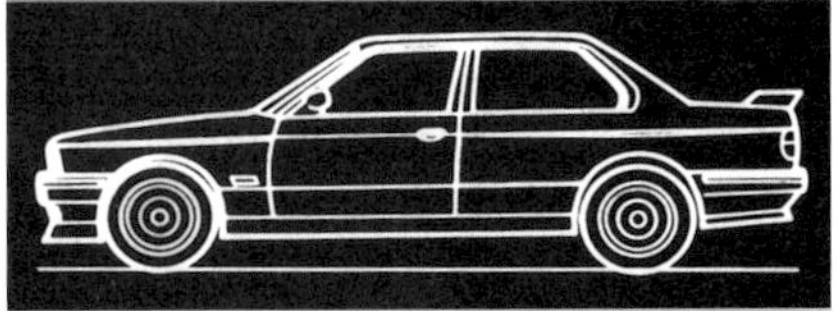

All tests with a crew of two and full tank of fuel

THROUGH THE GEARS (seconds):

0-30mph	2.5	**0-70mph**	8.6
0-40mph	3.5	**0-80mph**	10.9
0-50mph	5.1	**0-90mph**	13.3
0-60mph	6.7	**0-100mph**	18.1

STANDING 1/4 MILE:	15.2sec
TERMINAL SPEED:	93.5mph
AVG TOP SPEED BANKED CIRCUIT:	144.2mph
FASTEST 1/4 MILE BANKED CIRCUIT:	144.8mph

ACCELERATION IN 4th/5th (seconds):

30-50mph	7.4/10.5	**60-80mph**	7.4/9.7
40-60mph	6.6/10.2	**70-90mph**	7.0/10.5
50-70mph	6.7/10.0	**80-100mph**	8.3/11.5

MINIMUM SPEED COMFORTABLE PULL AWAY:
FOURTH 28mph **FIFTH** 32mph

MAX SPEED IN GEARS @ 7000rpm:

FIRST	41mph	**FOURTH**	122mph
SECOND	64mph	**FIFTH**	144.2mph@6600rpm
THIRD	87mph		

OVERALL FUEL CONSUMPTION (CORRECTED):	25.8mpg/5.7mpl
PROVING GROUND FUEL CONSUMPTION (CORRECTED):	12.9mpg/2.8mpl

GOVT FIGS: Urban 25.7mpg; @ 56mph 49.6mpg; @ 75mph 39.2mpg

TRACK CONDITION	Dry
TEMPERATURE	14°C
WINDSPEED	3mph
ATMOSPHERIC PRESSURE	1006mb

SPECIFICATION

ENGINE TYPE: In-line four-cylinder

DISPLACEMENT:	2302cc
BORE:	93.4mm
STROKE:	84.0mm
COMPRESSION RATIO:	11.0:1
MAX QUOTED POWER (DIN):	220bhp @ 6750rpm
MAX QUOTED TORQUE (DIN):	181lb ft @ 4750rpm
BHP PER LITRE:	95.7
POWER TO WEIGHT RATIO (UNLADEN WEIGHT):	183.3bhp/ton
POWER TO WEIGHT RATIO (TEST WEIGHT):	146.7bhp/ton

FUEL SYSTEM: Bosch Motronic electronic injection

CYLINDERS: Cast iron block, five main bearings

CYLINDER HEAD: Aluminium alloy, twin chain driven overhead camshafts, four valves per cylinder

GEARBOX: Getrag five-speed manual

GEAR RATIOS

TOP:	1.00	**2nd:**	2.40
4th:	1.26	**1st:**	3.72
3rd:	1.77	**Reverse:**	4.23

FINAL DRIVE RATIO: 3.15

CLUTCH Diaphragm spring

FRONT SUSPENSION: Independent, MacPherson struts, coil springs, adjustable dampers, anti-roll bar

REAR SUSPENSION: Independent, semi trailing arms, coil springs, driver adjustable dampers, anti-roll bar

BRAKES: Servo-assisted discs, fronts ventilated, ABS

WHEELS AND TYRES: Alloy 7.5Jx16, Pirelli P700 225/45ZR16

UNLADEN WEIGHT:	2625lb
TEST WEIGHT WITH CREW AND EQUIPMENT:	3304lb
WHEELBASE:	100.9in
TURNING CIRCLE:	34.0ft
FUEL TANK CAPACITY:	15.4galls/70 litres
BASIC PRICE (INC TAX):	£26,960
PRICE AS TESTED:	£30,566
OPTIONAL EXTRAS FITTED TO TEST CAR AND PRICES:	See text.

Quickest BMW ragtop for UK

The left-hand-drive M3 Convertible comes to the UK next year and with 200bhp on tap it's the most potent BMW convertible ever. Martin Vincent drives it

THE FASTEST AND MOST powerful BMW convertible ever comes to the UK early next year. The new car is a soft-top version of the race-developed M3 built by BMW's Motorsport division and will be built in left-hand drive form only. Of the 130 or so to be assembled in 1989, 40 have been earmarked for the UK to special order only. According to BMW GB, the price will be "close to £40,000."

The basis for the M3 Convertible is a 325i convertible bodyshell fitted with the M3 spoiler, rear apron, sideskirts and the distinctive flared wheelarches. This last item permits the use of M3 suspension and 16ins wheels with 7.5ins wide rims. To allow for the extra weight of the convertible body — it's about 350lb heavier than the M3 coupe — stiffer springs with different damper settings and mounting bushes replaces the standard M3 items.

The M3's 2.3-litre 16-valve four-cylinder engine with Motronic fuel injection transmits power to the fat 225/46VR16 rear tyres via a close ratio gearbox and limited slip differential. At 6750rpm, 200bhp is on tap, while the maximum torque of 177 lb ft peaks at 4750rpm. That's enough for a claimed top speed in excess of 140mph and 0-60mph time of around 7secs. Massive 11ins anti-lock brakes, ventilated at the front, keep the performance in check.

The exact specification for UK-bound cars is not yet finalised but is likely to be high. A preliminary list of standard fittings includes alloy wheels, sports seats, power steering, central locking, heated mirrors and driver's door lock, electric windows, tinted glass, M-Technic steering wheel and green tinted glass. Cloth seats will be standard with leather as a cost option.

One major development that will be standard is push-button hood operation. The 325i convertible currently is operated manually but the M3's three-layer fabric hood is opend and closed by an electro-hydraulic system via a dashboard-mounted switch. Once the hood is in place, all the driver has to do is to engage two levers on the windscreen rail. The hood automatically tensions itself and a rear window demister blower keeps the rear screen clear. The system works extremely well but a removable hardtop is also available.

The standard M3 is a delight for the enthusiastic driver — but the convertible adds a further dimension, although there are reservations. With the hood up the wind roar would become wearing on a long trip. But with the roof down it is surprisingly civilised with little buffeting for those in the front. An effective heater provides copious amounts of warm air.

It's not so good in the back where passengers are more exposed to the elements and there's the traditional lack of legroom.

Performance and road behaviour are little changed fron the standard M3. At tickover a slight lumpiness betrays the race-developed four-cylinder engine and the competition heritage also shows on the move. Below 4000rpm it feels disappointingly ordinary but once beyond that magic figure the twin cam comes alive. By 5500rpm there's an exhilarating thrust that continues unabated to the rev limiter just beyond 7000rpm. It's a willing revver and the power characteristics encourage use of the gears.

So it's a shame that the dog-leg first gear in the five-speed 'box feels clunky and old-fashioned. It improves with familiarity but there is no comparison with the sweet gearchange of the standard 3-Series.

Despite the lack of a rigid roof the Convertible shows no signs of a lack of stiffness in its road behaviour. Throttle response isn't quite as immediate as the coupe — probably because of the extra weight — but it's still crisp and responsive. Apart from wind blowing through the hair, the only other giveaway is some shaking over bumps from the dashboard area.

A brief drive in the drop-top M3 showed that it is still a thoroughbred performer. It has direct and precise steering and levels of grip and agility that are on a higher plane to most other high performance road cars. Body roll is virtually non-existent and grip is phenomenal. And it offers far better cornering balance and a more neutral attitude than we have come to expect.

The brakes too, are hard to fault; powerful but progressive, after some hard use descending a long series of hairpin bends, they showed no sign of fade.

The seats offer plenty of support and a perfect pedal layout and driving position adds to driver confidence. Inside, there is the usual solidity of build but refinement is compromised to some extent by a harsh ride — inevitable with stiff springing — and higher than normal engine and exhaust noise.

The M3 Convertible is a superb performance machine. Its looks attract admiring glances everywhere and its rarity, its dynamic abilities and its high specification add up to a fine car.

ENGINE
Longways, front, rear-wheel drive. Head/block al.alloy/cast iron, 4 cylinders in line.
Bore 84mm, **stroke** 93.4mm, **capacity** 2302cc.
Valve gear 2ohc, 4 valves per cylinder.
Compression ratio 10.5 to 1.
Ignition and fuel system fully mapped electronic ignition and fuel injection.
Max power 200bhp (PS-DIN) at 6750rpm. **Max torque** 177lb ft (195 Nm) at 4750rpm.

TRANSMISSION
5-speed manual.

Gear	Ratio	mph/1000rpm
Top	1.00	21.5
4th	1.26	17.10
3rd	1.77	12.1
2nd	1.40	15.3
1st	3.72	5.8

Final drive ratio 3.25. Limited slip diff.

SUSPENSION
Front, independent, MacPherson struts, coil springs, telescopic dampers, anti-roll bar.
Rear, independent semi-trailing arms, coil springs, telescopic dampers, anti-roll bar.

STEERING
Rack and pinion, power assistance.

BRAKES
Front 11.0ins dia ventilated discs. **Rear** 11.1ins dia discs. 3-channel anti-lock standard Vacuum servo.

WHEELS
Al. alloy 7.5ins rims. Tyre size 225/45VR16.

DIMENSIONS, WEIGHT

Length	171.1ins (4345mm)
Width	66.1ins (1680mm)
Height	53.9ins (1370mm)
Wheelbase	101.0ins (2565mm)
Track F/R	55.6/56.1ins (1412/1424mm)
Weight	2998lb (1360kg)

PERFORMANCE
(CLAIMED)

Top speed	145mph
0-60mph	7.3secs

FUEL CONSUMPTION
Urban/constant 56mph/75mph
22.8/44.1/36.2mpg

THIS WEEK
ARRIVALS

THE CAT AND THE *CREAM*

A convertible is one sure way of raising the thrill level of your motoring. The two stylish soft-tops tested here may be expensive but they're guaranteed to raise a smile: BMW M3 and Jaguar XJS V12

The saloon that has kept you warm and dry throughout the winter has probably served its purpose well. The engine fired first time every time and the heater never failed to warm the tootsies on those dark and icy mornings. Now that summer is getting into full swing, though, you can't help feeling a little envious of the slightly eccentric next-door neighbour who, having battled his way through the winter, is now taking full advantage of the weather in his stylish sports convertible.

Convertibles needn't always be impractical. In fact, today's breed of open-toppers are an altogether different ball game to the sidescreened, leaky, heaterless convertibles from days gone by. In the next few pages we provide our findings on a whole range of rag-tops, starting with the cheapest – the Skoda Cabriolet. Here, however, we concentrate our efforts at the other end of the scale; two of the most desirable and most expensive convertibles on the market: Jaguar's XJS V12 and BMW's M3.

With either car, you don't end up with a lot of change out of £40,000. But what you do get is speed – both easily topped 140mph in testing – refinement, particularly in the case of the Jaguar, and two extremely stylish motor cars.

The Jaguar is the more expensive of the two but not by much. At £38,500 it's £1250 more than the BMW, which may seem unjustified especially when you consider that it lacks the rear accommodation provided by the BMW. But in fact, at this end of the market the XJS is still considered to be pretty good value for money. For your £38,500 you may only get a two-seater but what a car it is. Underneath that wonderfully long bonnet you have at your disposal one of the finest road engines in the world, pushing out almost 300bhp. And even mated to Jaguar's

More exclusive than most: rare, race-bred M3 Convertible costs £13,700 more than saloon version. Fabulous BMW Motorsport engine thrives on high revs; sporting suspension set-up gives superb handling. BMW is a full four-seater but is left-hand drive only; electric hood-fold operation is neater than Jaguar's but, unlike Cat's, rear screen is plastic

BMW M3 CONVERTIBLE

ageing three-speed automatic box (a manual gearbox isn't available) the acceleration and top speed are highly impressive. Inside, the car is fully loaded with luxury equipment including heated leather seats, air conditioning, electric windows and mirrors and a high-class stereo. The most important 'luxury' feature though is the electric hood, which takes a mere 12 seconds to open or close from start to finish.

When BMW does something, it usually does it properly. By turning the fabulous M3 saloon into a convertible it has certainly kept up the tradition but the end result is a hefty £13,700 price hike for the wind-in-the-face version. In the UK the M3 Convertible is available only in extremely limited numbers – just 130 were built in 1988 and a similar number will be constructed in 1989, though most of these have been and will be sold in Germany and will never see this country's roads. The other drawback is that the M3 is available in left-hand drive configuration only.

Mechanically the convertible is exactly the same as the saloon, with its race track-originated four-cylinder 200bhp 16-valve engine and close-ratio Getrag dog-leg-gate gearbox. Though the chassis and suspension remains essentially unchanged the convertible actually weighs 162kg more than the saloon, owing to the extensive and highly sophisticated strengthening structures employed.

Like the Jaguar, the BMW is extremely well equipped, with electric windows, mirrors, hood and central locking. The black leather seats are heated as are the wing mirrors, and there's a hi-tech alarm thrown in too. Amazingly, though, your £37,250 still doesn't buy you a stereo.

WHAT'S NEW?

BMW M3 Convertible, £37,250: Engine, gearbox and chassis virtually unchanged from saloon though much thought has gone into body stiffening. Most significant new item is wonderful electric hood mechanism, others include heated seats, trip computer, alarm system and electric rear windows. Convertible version costs an extra £13,700 over saloon.

Jaguar XJS V12 Convertible, £38,500: Fabulous V12 engine and three-speed automatic transmission are taken directly from fixed-head version. Like BMW, the chassis remains essentially the same but extra strength has been worked into it to compensate for lack of roof. Very high standard equipment list includes electrically powered hood and semi-electric seats.

PERFORMANCE	
BMW	●●●●●
JAGUAR	●●●●●

Comparing the performance of these two cars is tricky. Both are very fast cars in their own right, with top speeds of over 140mph and sub-20secs 0-100mph acceleration to match. However, they differ greatly in the way they deliver their considerable performance. The BMW's race-bred four-cylinder engine thrives on high revs, fast gearchanging and hard braking, and actually feels more at home the faster you drive it. In contrast the Jaguar, with its fabulously torquey V12 engine and lazy three-speed automatic transmission is much more suited to being sedately driven on the cruise control down a picturesque section of dual carriageway, the air conditioning warming the feet and the stereo taking care of the entertainment.

In terms of refinement the Jaguar is

XJS styling lends itself admirably to wind-in-the-hair treatment. Though both cars have high equipment level, accent in the automatic gearbox-only Jaguar is on unadulterated luxury – but for two only. With electric hood raised, Cat feels like a genuine hard-top. Glorious V12 provides wonderfully relaxed high-speed cruising

JAGUAR XJS V12 CONVERTIBLE

in a league above the BMW. Only when the pedal is floored and the tacho rises above 4000rpm are you at all conscious that there is a mighty 300bhp lump under that long sweeping bonnet. The traditional high gearing and superb mechanical refinement combine to make the big Jag a wonderfully relaxed cruiser – to the point where it's hard to believe how rapidly it can be made to go at times. Around some very tricky Welsh mountain roads the Cat proved remarkably deceptive, for the BMW had to be worked quite hard to keep up, despite its far better set up – for such conditions – suspension. It was the effortless straightline go that gave the BMW such a hard time.

Essentially the BMW M3 is a racing car that has been detuned to suit the road rather than the track. Even so, the racing car background is still very much in evidence despite the luxury appointments. Floor the throttle in either first or second and listen to the engine note rise to a screaming crescendo at the 7200rpm cut-out point, or snick the dog-leg shift back from fourth to third to pass a slower vehicle on a short piece of straight: it's what M3 driving is all about. Admittedly the engine is noisy – much louder than the Jaguar's – and the alien shift pattern of the Getrag gearbox is odd to use at first, but it's all part of the character. For the record, the BMW hits 60mph in 6.5secs (Jaguar 7.7) and has a top speed of 143mph (Jaguar 142).

HANDLING AND RIDE	
BMW	●●●●●
JAGUAR	●●●●●

Top marks for both cars but for totally different reasons. The BMW scores primarily because of its fabulous handling whereas the Jaguar gains the full five blobs for its wonderfully refined ride. But it isn't as simple as that. While the BMW has the definite edge over the Jaguar when sprinting down tight twisting country lanes owing to its sporting suspension set-up, it is by no means uncivilised. The ride is firm, of course, as you'd expect, but the BMW copes with everyday ruts and bumps surprisingly efficiently.

On home ground – a fast section of B-road, for example – the BMW is virtually uncatchable. The traction generated by the wide, ultra-low profile tyres is fantastic in the dry (and pretty impressive in the wet, too) and combines with the car's extremely flat and surefooted cornering stance and wonderfully communicative steering to make it exhilarating to drive quickly. Unlike many supposed sports cars that get increasingly sloppy the faster you drive them, the BMW actually feels happier when pushed harder.

The Jaguar on the other hand doesn't really take to being thrown around by the scruff of the neck. When treated in such a way it becomes rather untidy and quite a handful to keep under control owing to the far softer spring and damper rates and greater overall weight. On a long fast A-road, however, it's a different story – here the extremely high levels of grip, refined chassis and sound handling make for a high-speed, effortless drive.

Where the Jag excels is ride comfort. It simply glides over uneven road surfaces as if they weren't there. The only hint the driver gets that he or she is passing over anything other than a sheet of glass is gentle feedback through the steering wheel. At 2.5 turns lock to lock, the steering itself is very fast-geared in Jaguar tradition – which means that a mere flick of the wrist is usually enough to negotiate all but the very tightest of corners. It's a shame then that Jaguar has, for a sporting car, overdone the assistance to the steering – note that the BMW too has power-assisted steering but retains plenty of feel at speed.

XJS lacks M3's raw excitement but is incredibly refined. Engine is one of the best around

ACCOMMODATION

BMW	●●●●
JAGUAR	●●

The BMW is a full four-seater and has a decent-size boot; against the two-seater Jaguar, with its odd-shaped boot, the German car looks very good indeed. In saloon guise we criticised the M3 for poor rear seat space, particularly for the head but this was down to the sharply raked rear screen (different to that on the ordinary 3-Series cars). In convertible guise, though, there is an extra three inches of headroom with the roof up and very nearly as much legroom. On one occasion during our test period we had five in the car for the best part of two hours without too much discomfort. Oddments storage is acceptable; we particularly like the big doorbins and roomy glovebox, but there are no other storage slots for cassettes and so on.

The Jaguar is a strict two-seater. Against another two-seater it would score a higher blob count for, judged on its own merits, the accommodation on offer isn't bad. There's a large compartment behind the seats for storing maps, bottles of Perrier and suchlike plus a smaller transmission tunnel storage space for other odds and ends. Actual space for the two occupants is generous in all directions with the hood up or down: passenger legroom is particularly good.

Though the Jaguar's boot measurements make impressive reading compared with the BMW, the space isn't as usable because of the various intrusions from wheel arches, spare wheels and so on. For example, we were hard-pushed to fit two large suitcases in the Jaguar whereas there is space for three big cases in the BMW.

SAFETY

BMW	●●●●
JAGUAR	●●●●

The BMW's inherently safe handling, superb brakes and immensely strong chassis ensure that it gains good marks for basic safety. The fact that the brakes are also fitted with an electronic ABS anti-lock system serves to enhance this basic appeal. One inherent feature of the BMW, though, loses it points quite heavily in this section; its left-hand drive-only configuration. When alone and overtaking on a single carriageway road it can be extremely awkward to sight a clear path.

We like the high positioning of the BMW's stereo and the fact that the trip computer can be operated by a button on the end of the left-hand indicator stalk. And the neatness of the folding system means that rear vision with the roof *down* is excellent. With the hood up, however, rear vision isn't so good. Unlike the Jaguar, in which a heated glass window is fitted the BMW merely gets a plastic screen. Two items that gain the BMW definite Brownie points are the deadlock central locking system (the Jaguar makes do with conventional central locking) and the standard fit anti-theft alarm.

Like the BMW, the Jaguar also has safe handling, good brakes with ABS as standard and a strong chassis. The fact that it weighs almost two tons is reassuring too, should the unthinkable happen. As we said, we like the superior rear window arrangement with the hood up but in contrast with the BMW the vision with the roof down is poor – the hood itself doesn't fold down far enough, so reversing into tight parking spots is extremely awkward.

The removable stereo of the Jaguar we like for obvious reasons and the door panels that illuminate when the doors are opened are also a good idea to ensure safe night-time parking. What isn't so impressive is the very low position of the stereo and, far more annoying, the lack of a linked wash/sweep on the wipers – rather a surprising omission on a £38,500 car.

LIVING WITH THE CARS

JAGUAR	●●●●●
BMW	●●●●

You have only to nestle down into the Jaguar seat and take a deep breath through the nostrils to smell the class. Unlike the BMW's rather sombre all-black leather-clad interior, the Jaguar's cabin cossets its occupants in an air of luxury that can't help bring a smile to the face. In the BMW, on the other hand, the accent is on no-nonsense efficiency.

Both, however, have highly impressive levels of standard equipment. Electric windows and mirrors, central locking and electric hoods are part of the asking price in both cases. The Jaguar has a minor advantage over the BMW in that the lumbar and recline adjustments to the seats are also electric; in the BMW, all alterations have to be made manually. However, the BMW makes up ground in that its front seats are height-adjustable; the British car's lack of this facility could prove annoying to a shorter driver as the seating position is low anyway.

In the past we have come to expect very high levels of build quality from both BMW and Jaguar, and the Jaguar did not disappoint this time. Surprisingly, we weren't so impressed by the BMW. The most noticeable demerit was the rattly dash and facia, but the doors didn't shut like a £37,000 car either. Admittedly our 10,000-mile old test car has, according to BMW, had a hard time recently but we would have expected it to wear a little better.

As far as the hoods are concerned, the BMW has the edge. The neatness of the fold-away operation is quite superb, to the extent that not a single piece of hood material is visible when the roof is folded. The system in action will also attract admiring attention but against this it takes twice as long as the Jaguar to complete its cycle. Inside the cars with the hoods up, it is the Jaguar's that is the more classy. An attractive tan velvet lining and a heated glass rear window give the Cat a genuine hard-top feel. In the BMW, though, there is no rooflining and the plastic rear window is awkward to see out of in the rain – especially as it is extremely prone to misting up in anything other than perfect weather conditions.

PERFORMANCE

	BMW	JAGUAR
Max in top (mph)	**143**	**142**
Max in 4th (mph)	120	—
0-30 (sec)	2.4	3.2
0-40	3.4	4.6
0-50	4.9	6.1
0-60	**6.5**	**7.7**
0-70	8.8	10.0
0-80	10.9	12.5
0-90	14.1	15.1
0-100	17.9	19.0
Acceleration through gears 3rd/4th/5th (sec)		
30-50	4.2/6.7/9.8	2.9 (kickdown)
40-60	4.0/6.6/9.8	3.1 (kickdown)
50-70	**4.1/6.4/9.7**	**3.9 (kickdown)**
60-80	4.4/6.5/9.8	4.9 (kickdown)
Top gear rpm at 70mph	3300	2600

BMW M3 perhaps *too* exclusive but looks and handles superbly

COSTS	
BMW	●●●
JAGUAR	●●●

It's unlikely in the long run that either of these cars will prove much cheaper to run than the other. There's an argument that German engineering skill means the Jaguar will be less reliable, but against that should be weighed the high cost of servicing in the BMW plus the higher price of spare parts.

The M3 has, in common with other BMWs, a 'service indicator' in the form of a row of small lamps: they glow green until the car approaches time for a service, when a yellow lamp illuminates as a reminder; a red warns that a service is overdue. The idea is to match service intervals to the type of use a car experiences; a carefully driven medium-mileage car might need no more than one service a year, a hard-driven hack might need three annually. There could be savings for the gentle driver, but in general services would probably crop up at around 15,000-mile intervals with an oil change required in between. There are, at least, more BMW than Jaguar dealers about.

Even in the area of resale values there's not much to choose between these two. Certainly BMW models hold their value well, but there's a possibility that the rarity of the left-hand drive convertible M3 could work against rather than with it in the secondhand market, whereas a well-maintained Jaguar XJS V12 convertible will still be seen by motorists with a taste for the traditional as a very desirable car.

What does swing the scale in the BMW's direction is the much better fuel consumption from the lean, efficient 2.3-litre engine – 26.2mpg against 15.4mpg from the guzzling V12.

VERDICT	
JAGUAR	●●●●
BMW	●●●●

The BMW is an immensely rewarding car to drive and we are very reluctant not to place it top because of this. It also looks very stylish – far more so than its already attractive saloon brother – is cheaper to run than the Jaguar and the hood mechanism is superb. It's got its downfalls, though: unexpected below-par build quality (on our car) and its left-hand drive-only configuration. But perhaps the strongest reason for placing it below the Jaguar is the M3 Convertible's limited availability.

The Jaguar isn't as exciting as the BMW but its qualities lie in other areas. The wonderful refinement that Jaguar has worked into the chassis is every bit as amazing in its own right as the BMW's out and out handling capabilities, and the effortless power delivery of the V12 engine is still an inspiration.

These are both highly desirable cars with many strong points and very few weaknesses between them, but one thing separates them. You can take delivery of the Jaguar a few weeks after ordering one but with the BMW you could be in for a *very* long wait. Now if the M3 was a production BMW with consequent BMW delivery times . . .

HOW THE CARS COMPARE		
CAR	**BMW M3 Convertible**	**JAGUAR XJS V12 Convertible**
PRICE	£37,250	£38,500
RUNNING COSTS		
Fuel consumption miles per gallon		
***What Car?* test**	**26.2**	**15.4**
Government figures: City driving/steady speed 56/75mph	22.8/44.1/36.2	15.0/27.1/22.4
Fuel grade	4-star	4-star
Fuel tank (galls)	15.4	18
Range (miles)*	380	260
SAMPLE COSTS: Three years/30,000 miles		
SERVICE		
7500 miles	£40	£55
15,000 miles	£250	£230
Annual inspection (x2)	£45	—
22,500 miles	£40	£55
30,000 miles	£280	£230
SERVICE TOTAL	**£700**	**£570**
FUEL COST	£2061	£3506
INSURANCE (Group)**	**£535 (£100 excess)**	**£764 (£100 excess)**
EXTENDED WARRANTY		
2 years' extra cover	£505 (with recovery)	£570 (with recovery)
SAMPLE DEALER PARTS PRICES		
Front brake pads	£43.03	£59.80
Windscreen	£267.49	£128.00
Exhaust system	£335.12	£259.00
Rear lamp lens	£68.68	£42.50
Warranty (months/miles)	12/UL	12/UL
Anti-rust (yrs)	6	—
Paint (yrs)	—	—
***What Car?* cost/mile† (pence)**	**93.4**	**119.9**
EQUIPMENT/OPTION COST		
Automatic transmission	n/a	yes
Power steering	yes	yes
Central locking	yes	yes
Electric windows	yes	yes
Internal mirror adjustment	electric	electric
Anti-lock braking	yes	yes
Sound system	no	rad/cass
Seat height adjustment	yes	no
Adjustable steering column	no	yes
Headlamp washers	yes	yes
DIMENSIONS		
Length (in)	171	188
Width (inc mirrors)	74	77
Height (in)	54	50
Wheelbase (in)	101	102
Front headroom (in)	38-40	36
Rear headroom (in)	36	—
Front legroom (in)	34-39	35-42
Rear kneeroom (in)	23-29	—
Rear shoulder room (in)	53	—
Boot depth: max (in)	33	23.5
Boot space height (in)	16	25
Boot width (in)	51	65
Boot load height (in)	32	25
Turning circle (ft)/lock turns	36.5/3.5	34.4/4.1
Kerb weight (kg)	1360	1062
Towing weight (kg)	n/a	n/a
MECHANICAL SPECIFICATION		
Engine: cyl/cap (cc)/fuel system	4/2302/inj	12/5343/inj
Max power (bhp/rpm)	**200/6750**	**291/5500**
Max torque (lb ft/rpm)	177/4750	317/3000
Brakes (F/R)	disc/disc	disc/disc
Suspension (F/R)	ind/ind	ind/ind
Tyres	225/45ZR16	235/60VR15

*Calculated at test mpg leaving a gallon in reserve

**Insurance rate based on a mean of five quotes for man aged 35 living in Oxford with 60 per cent no-claims bonus (figures provided by Quotel Insurance Services Ltd)

† *What Car?* cost per mile figure calculated over three years and 30,000 miles. Includes fuel, depreciation, servicing, insurance and finance costs (figures from Emmerson Hill Associates)

BMW TOURING

M3 & M 635 CSi

Two Bavarians challenge the *Alpenstrasse*

BY JOHN LAMM
PHOTOS BY THE AUTHOR

THE ALPINE ROAD is legendary for its beautiful views and challenging driving opportunities. The *Deutsche Alpenstrasse* runs east from Lindau, West Germany, at the northeast edge of the Bodensee, for 295 miles to Brechtesgaden, near Germany's eastern border with Austria. And a great run it is. Friends and I took a pair of BMW M cars for the eastern one-third of the *Alpenstrasse.* The M6 or, as some call it, the M 635 CSi, is the senior member of that line and our M3 the one most often seen in the U.S. We picked up the cars in Munich and took the number 8 *Autobahn* southeast toward Salzburg. About 30 km from Munich's center we turned south, heading for Tegernsee. It was Sunday and as good an excuse as any to stop in Tegernsee and sample strudel by the lake, washed down with a cup of strong coffee. The drive east from Tegernsee to Schliersee and on to Bayrischzell is a good warm-up for the good driving that comes later. You could also have great fun by temporarily leaving the

M AM 6807

spiel voran:
ator-Technik.

8 München
Salzburg
Traunstein 17 km
Siegsdorf 11 km
Ruhpolding 3 km
305
Reit im Winkl 21 km
Deutsche Alpenstraße
Biathlon Bundesleistungszentrum

Alpenstrasse and going instead by way of Austria, via the Urspringpass, Kufstein and Walchsee. It is as much fun as it is beautiful.

Our *Alpenstrasse* route gave us a variety in climates on our late spring drive. It was 74 degrees and short-sleeve weather just off the *Autobahn*, but we had to put on our ski jackets about two valleys to the south.

Reit im Winkl is the halfway point on our abbreviated journey, a small, vest-pocket town set at the base of a mountain in the Chiemgauer group. We stayed at the Hotel Unterwirt, a typical example of the nicely done German guest houses, finished in light wood and white plaster. The rooms are very comfortably furnished and the beds covered with down comforters. The hotel's restaurant is excellent, the food plentiful and the Pils perfect.

We found there is still something very special about the BMW 6-Series coupe. I'm not the only person who feels that way, obviously, because there are many new models influenced by the coupe's shape. The Acura Legend coupe and the new Ford Thunderbird come to mind immediately.

The coupe reminds me of the best of aristocratic Europe. Say of the gentleman who arrives at dinner in mid-February. He's wearing a classic pinstripe suit that is beautifully tailored. He's well tanned after a week's skiing at St Moritz. He gracefully mastered every slope by day; held court in the finest restaurant at night.

In contrast, the BMW M3 reminds me of a hard-charging young executive. He rushes into dinner dressed in whatever Hugo Boss has just made fashionable. This man is also tanned from skiing, but he's just in from Aspen. He attacked the deep powder every day; up late each night trying another trendy restaurant.

Both cars have the same fundamentals. The interiors are basically black with easy-to-read instrument panels that tell you everything you would care to know about the car's systems. BMW does this as well as any automaker in the world. The seats in both cars are excellent, but quite different. They are firm (these are, after all, German cars); the M3's seats hold you in place in street-racer fashion, but the M6's seats are broader and more luxurious.

Fit and finish are superb, and what the BMW interiors may lack in warmth, they make up for with unerring purpose: to go quickly.

The engine basics are also the same. Twin-cam, 4-valve technology is so popular and highly touted these days yet many automakers find it old hat. The M1 engine had its 24-valve head in 1978, when it bumped up horsepower from the standard 3.5-liter's 218 bhp to 277 bhp at 6500 rpm. These days the same engine, in the emissions trim the Germans and Swiss require, has 260 bhp, although there is a non-catalyst version that produces 286 bhp. U.S. editions have 256 bhp at 6500 rpm and 212 lb-ft at 4500 rpm, so Americans no longer take a real bite when it comes to performance.

That same 4-valve thinking has been applied to the M3 4-cylinder, and its 16-valve version has 192 bhp in the U.S. (195 bhp in Germany) with a catalyst and 200 bhp without it. That's very impressive: 83 bhp per liter in American form. Torque for us is 170 lb-ft, which is only a few less than the few non-catalyst M3s that are built. And both engines look the part, with BMW M POWER shining from the cam covers, and a neat row of injection horns. You would be proud to show off the engines of this pair even if they were slow, which they are not.

Their performance befits the motorsports heritage. BMW claims a 0–60 mph time of 6.8 seconds for the M6, and 7.6 for the M3. However, *Road & Track* recorded a 0–60 mph time of 7.1 sec for a U.S. version M3 in its February 1988 road test.

Because they are at home on the *Autobahn*, both cars have impressive top speeds. For American models, BMW claims a top speed of 143 mph for the M3 and 150 mph for the M6.

The people on our *Alpenstrasse* trip chose the M 635 CSi as the best *Autobahn* cruiser. With a route that combined both the high-speed highways and smaller secondary roads, the big coupe's ride and general refinement made it the choice. There is less general busyness in the car with its longer gearing and better noise insulation.

Given the tight roads of the *Alpenstrasse*, the M3 won. There's certainly nothing clumsy about an M6, of course, but the size of the M3, along with the firmer suspension and fat tires,

These are the things which make European trips memorable: Old World markets such as those in Salzburg, fine wines at the Hotel Unterwirt and breathtaking landscapes like the Chiemsee.

made it a natural to win on the twisties. It has initial understeer, of course, but with plenty of punch and good manners to do your bidding. This same firmness, of course, gave the *Autobahn* nod to the M6.

From Reit im Winkl we continued east for Berchtesgaden. This section is perhaps the most beautiful section of the *Alpenstrasse*. Whether the Schwarzbachwacht Pass or the Weissbach Gorges, the road is challenging when the traffic is light. There are plenty of restaurants along the way, but I would suggest a picnic lunch. If you have an M3 you can use the rear spoiler as a picnic table.

From Brechtesgaden you can backtrack a bit to get to the *Autobahn* via Bad Reichenhall. But at this point it is only minutes to Salzburg. There is Hohensalzburg castle that dominates the city and Mozart's birthplace, but we opted for Tomasellis, said to have been Mozart's favorite pastry shop. We ordered the variety tray and coffee *mit Schlag*. We wandered back to the cars through the open street market shops that were selling fruit, nuts and flowers.

On the way back to Munich via the *Autobahn*, we turned off for a short excursion to Prien, on the Chiemsee, the largest lake in Bavaria. The view across the lake to the Herrninsel island with its beautiful King Ludwig II castle, set off by the Alps behind it, is very much worth the stop.

Then we motored back to Munich, heading for the BMW enclave with its distinctive tall columns that can be seen from a great distance. Being the easiest part of the trip, it is also where we finally got lost.

M3 U.S. SPECIFICATIONS

Price	$34,950
Curb weight, lb	2865
Wheelbase, in.	101.0
Track, front/rear	55.6/56.1
Length	171.1
Width	66.1
Height	53.9
Fuel capacity, U.S. gal.	14.5
ENGINE	
Type	dohc 4-valve inline-4
Bore x stroke, in./mm	3.68 x 3.31/93.4 x 84.0
Displacement, cu in./cc	140/2302
Compression ratio	10.5:1
Bhp @ rpm, SAE net	192 @ 6750
Torque @ rpm, lb-ft	170 @ 4750
Fuel injection	Bosch Motronic
DRIVETRAIN	
Transmission	5-sp manual
Gear ratios: 5th (0.81)	3.32:1
4th (1.00)	4.10:1
3rd (1.40)	5.74:1
2nd (2.20)	9.02:1
1st (3.83)	15.70:1
Final-drive ratio	4.10:1
CHASSIS & BODY	
Layout	front engine/rear drive
Brake system, front/rear	11.0-in. vented discs/11.1-in. vented discs, vacuum assist, ABS
Wheels	cast alloy, 15 x 7J
Tires	Pirelli P600, 205/55VR-16
Steering type	recirculating ball, power assist
Turns, lock-to-lock	3.9
Suspension, front/rear:	MacPherson struts, lower A-arms, coil springs, tube shocks, anti-roll bar/semi-trailing arms, coil springs, tube shocks, anti-roll bar
PERFORMANCE	
0–60 mph, sec	7.1
Standing ¼ mile, sec @ mph	15.4 @ 91.0
Top speed, mph[1]	143

[1]Factory claim

M 635 CSi U.S. SPECIFICATIONS

Price	$55,950
Curb weight, lb	3570
Wheelbase, in.	103.3
Track, front/rear	56.3/57.7
Length	193.8
Width	67.9
Height	53.3
Fuel capacity, U.S. gal.	16.6
ENGINE	
Type	dohc 4-valve inline-6
Bore x stroke, in./mm	3.68 x 3.31/93.4 x 84.0
Displacement, cu in./cc	211/3453
Compression ratio	9.8:1
Bhp @ rpm, SAE net	256 @ 6500
Torque @ rpm, lb-ft	243 @ 4500
Fuel injection	Bosch Motronic
DRIVETRAIN	
Transmission	5-sp manual
Gear ratios: 5th (0.81)	3.17:1
4th (1.00)	3.91:1
3rd (1.35)	5.28:1
2nd (2.08)	8.13:1
1st (3.51)	13.72:1
Final-drive ratio	3.91:1
CHASSIS & BODY	
Layout	front engine/rear drive
Brake system, front/rear	11.8-in. vented discs/11.2-in. discs, hydraulic assist, ABS
Wheels	forged alloy, 415 x 195TR
Tires	Michelin TRX, 240/45VR-415
Steering type	recirculating ball, power assist
Turns, lock-to-lock	3.5
Suspension, front/rear:	MacPherson struts, lower A-arms, coil springs, tube shocks, anti-roll bar/semi-trailing arms, coil springs, tube shocks, anti-roll bar
PERFORMANCE[1]	
0–60 mph, sec	6.8
Standing ¼ mile, sec @ mph	na
Top speed, mph	150

[1]Factory claims — na means information not available

By MIKE McCARTHY

Schizophrenic style

The BMW M3 Convertible is a contradiction in terms. On the one hand there are the homologation special mechanicals from the M3, implying peaky performance and lack of refinement. On the other, the 325's fold-down top and luxurious interior, suggesting the soft life. It could be either a brilliant combination or wildly schizophrenic...

The exploits of Messrs Sytner, Weaver *et al* on the tracks have proved that those M3 mechanicals can deliver the goods performance-wise. Under the bonnet there's that unique 2302cc in-line four, with four valves per cylinder and twin camshafts which, even in road trim, produces an impressive 200bhp at 6750rpm, and 177lb ft of torque at 4750rpm. It's coupled to a Getrag five-speed gearbox with racing change pattern – first is a dog-leg left.

Suspension is 3-series derived, with MacPherson struts up front and semi-trailing arms at the rear, plus discs all round, but of course BMW Motorsport's efforts in fine-tuning and geometry alterations, helped by fat Michelin MXX 225/45ZR16 tyres, ensures that the chassis can cope. The M3 Convertible is based on the original M3, not the evolution model, by the way.

The rest of the car is a combination of 325i Convertible with some M3 panelwork, such as the wheel arches, to accommodate those wide tyres. The weight loss resulting from the removal of the metal roof is more than made up by the extra stiffening of the chassis and the roof mechanism; the Convertible weighs some 350lbs more than the standard M3. It is too a true convertible, in that the top disappears when down, and there's no roll-over bar.

This hasn't had a great deal of effect on the performance. The maximum speed is 144mph (top up, of course), and the 0-60mph time is 6 seconds dead, which is exceedingly rapid by anybody's terms. The engine is a willing charger, depending on revs, revs and more revs to deliver the goods, which takes care of the performance side of the car's character; on the hedonistic side, there's not a great deal of urge below about 4000rpm, and as the 7000 red-line is approached its racing heritage comes out in some raucousness and harshness. BMW has done a pretty good job in refining it, but then if you want refinement you'd presumably go for the standard 325i drop-head with its silky smooth 6-cylinder power unit.

The race-perfected suspension means that the Convertible is every bit as brilliant in the corners as the standard M3. If you need a word to sum it up, it would be 'bite': it corners dead flat, very neutrally, and with immense confidence. Steering precision and weighting is absolutely ideal, too. As an utterly exhilarating cross-country machine, on a bright sunny day, the M3 Convertible is near perfection.

Assuming our sybaritic owner lives in a city, however, he might find life a little less pleasant at times. For a start, the Convertible is only available in left-hand drive form which, with those invisible flared arches, makes placing the car in traffic a more cautious operation than ususal; secondly there's that dog-leg first gear

The M3 Convertible is an instant collectors' item

change. Not only is it an unusual pattern but that on the test car I'd want it improved dramatically so as not to wrong slot at quite the wrong time. On top of that, at low speeds the brakes are over-servoed. All in all, the Convertible is not at its best as a pose machine in London's West End.

On the other hand, our hedonist would have no complaints about the interior or the roof. The leather seats are properly supportive, if a little compact in the back (the top has to go somewhere), and the instruments and controls pure BMW, which means excellent. Top up, you have to be cruising at the ton or more before wind thrash on the roof drowns out normal conversation. Top down and with side windows raised there is very little buffeting until you are, again, exceeding the speed limit, and even then it's not excessive. As has been said, on a clear day and with the roof down, it's everything a sun-worshipping enthusiast could want.

And if you really want to impress the neighbours, operate the roof when you know they're watching. All you do is unclip a couple of levers on the top of windscreen, then press a button. There's a whirring and a buzzing as the rear flap opens, the roof sails majestically up then down into its bay, and the flap closes – all automatically. It's guaranteed to leave them goggle-eyed.

So: is the convertible a brilliant combination, or merely schizophrenic? The price – a whopping £37,250 – suggests that BMW think the former: in practice there's a tendency towards the latter, which, it must be said, adds to the character of the car. Dull it is not. Perfect it is not either. One thing is for sure, though: the M3 Convertible is an instant collector's item. In years to come it will be seen as an investment. Is it therefore overpriced? Who knows? ■

When is an M3 not an M3? When it's an M3 Convertible... The removal of the roof and the fitment of a soft-top transforms the car (above), making it ultra-desirable to many, but overpriced to an equal number. For all the alterations, the 2.3-litre engine (right) remains a jewel.

BMW M3 Convertible

£37,250

Cylinder/capacity	4 in-line, 2302cc
Bore/stroke	94/84mm
Valve gear	Twin ohc, 4 valves/cyl
Fuel system	Bosch ML-Motronic
Power/rpm	200bhp/6750rpm
Torque/rpm	177lb ft/4750rpm
Maximum speed	144mph
0-60mph	6.0s

GROUP C

There's fire in the belly of the new M3 Evolution Sport. This, along with predictable Bavaria

CLASSY ACT AS IT IS, THE 3-SERIES BMW range hasn't exactly sent hard-driving enthusiasts dizzy with delight until now. Ideals such as silkiness, refinement, build quality and perceived image are all very well but, when projected with an image of studied Bavarian understatement, they make a package that's just a touch predictable and forgettable if what you're really after is a nugget of genuine excitement.

Hardly the breeding-ground, you might suppose, for one of the world's all-time great sporting saloons. But the M3, BMW Motorsport's most successful and intensively developed model to date, is just that: the wild card which, in recent years, has blasted some much needed fire into the soft underbelly of the 3-series range. And, if it comes as no great shock that the £34,500 Evolution Sport is the best M3 yet, I'm sure that you can work out the broader implications for yourself.

Based on the regular 215bhp Evolution, the Sport is powered by a bored-and-stroked big-valve version of BMW's delectable 16-valve 'M-Power' four which, for this application, swells to 2.3 litres and develops an impressive 238bhp at 7000rpm. Torque, on the other hand, remains more or less the same: just 7lb up 150rpm later making 177lb ft at 4600rpm.

In line with its extra muscle, the Sport has fatter, squatter (225/45 section) tyres on 16ins alloy rims, more bulbous body blisters to accommodate them, slightly lower front suspension and a deeper chin spoiler which, along with that which forms the lid of the boot, is adjustable. This is just a homologation trick, which can be of little practical benefit to the driver, since it involves much knee-scraping activity outside the car with an Allen key.

With so much power at its disposal, the Sport turns in a fiery performance that, while lagging a little behind original Sierra Sapphire Cosworth pace, nevertheless puts most 'saloons' in the shade. A top speed of 151mph and 0-60mph time of 6.3secs are firmly in junior league supercar territory, as is the 6.7secs fourth gear 50-70mph time. Try the same thing between 30 and 50mph and it takes 6.4secs — still good, but indicative of the modest low-speed torque.

It's beautifully easy to use, though. The short-throw gearchange is light, quick and precise and, if you're in the mood, the lever can be sliced through the well-defined gate with improbable haste. That said, and mild bottom-end lugging power notwithstanding, you don't *have* to. With its sabre-sharp throttle response, urgently hard, crackling engine note and smooth, fabulously free-revving power delivery, this M3 is happy enough to play racers. Yet its fairly short, close gearing and excellent

APTAIN

›finement and quality, makes it the best 3-series car yet. David Vivian is dizzy with delight

tractability means it will lope along in fourth or fifth and still pull cleanly.

More good news. With an overall fuel consumption of 22.8mpg, the Sport is more economical than its vivid performance would lead you to expect. A sympathetic right foot should reap 25mpg or more.

The fatter and squatter rubber has contributed grip but not harshness to the BMW's brilliantly-sorted chassis. The ride is firm but outstandingly good for a car that corners so hard and with such little body roll, not only in its control at speed but in its small-bump absorbtion around town.

The handling has gained bite and precision, displaying the sort of responsiveness in a straight line that was once the preserve of track cars. Turn-in involves no appreciable understeer until the driver gets really serious, whereupon the M3 offers it, in increasing measure, as a sensible alternative to leaving the tarmac tail first. Lifting off restores neutrality. As with the previous Evolution, steering weight increases slightly with speed, but continues to feed back useful information and never becomes hard work.

The Sport Evolution, if not a revelation, is certainly the best M3. In addition to the small but significant dynamic gains wrought by the bigger engine, fatter tyres and revised suspension, it looks subtly smarter on the road. It boasts a better-equipped cabin with terrifically good leather bucket seats in the front. Add to that the established 3-series virtues of practicality, build quality and attention to details and you have a package of great potency and flair.

Not all 3-series are like this, of course, but so long as you recognise the Evolution Sport's deeper air dam, at least you can see this one coming.■

BMW M3 EVOLUTION SPORT

LAYOUT
Longitudinal front engine/rear-wheel drive

ENGINE
Capacity 2467cc, 4 cylinders in line.
Bore 95mm, **stroke** 87mm.
Compression ratio 10.2 to 1.
Head/block al alloy/cast iron.
Valve gear dohc per bank, 4 valves per cylinder.
Fuel and ignition Electronic ignition, Bosch DME fuel injection.
Max power 238bhp (PS-Din) (178kW ISO) at 7000rpm. **Max torque** 177lb ft (240 Nm) at 4750rpm.

TRANSMISSION
Five-speed manual.
Ratios top 1.00, 4th 1.26, 3rd 1.77, 2nd 2.40, 1st 3.72.
Final drive ratio 3.15, limited slip differential.

SUSPENSION
Front, MacPherson struts, coil springs, anti-roll bar.
Rear, semi-trailing arms, coil springs, anti-roll bar.

STEERING
Rack and pinion, 3.6 turns lock to lock, power assisted.

BRAKES
Front ventilated discs.
Rear discs. Anti-lock standard.

WHEELS AND TYRES
Cast aluminium alloy, 7½x16ins rims, 225/45ZR16 Michelin MXX tyres.

DIMENSIONS

Length	171ins (4345mm)
Width	66ins (1680mm)
Height	54ins (1370mm)
Wheelbase	101ins (2565mm)
Weight	2764lbs (1255kg)

PERFORMANCE (claimed)

0-60mph	6.3secs
Maximum speed	151mph

FUEL CONSUMPTION (mpg)
22.8 test, 22.6 urban, 45.6 constant 56mph, 36.1 constant 75mph.

PRICE

Total (in UK)	£34,500

With a bigger, more powerful engine, fatter tyres, revised suspension, and better equipped cabin, the BMW M3 Evolution Sport is without doubt the leader of the 3-series pack

24 PASSES IN 48 HOURS

A transalpine tour de force in a BMW M3 Sport Evolution.

Oberpfaffenhofen, Germany—

In early spring or late autumn, one could do these twenty-four Alpine passes in twenty-four hours and throw in a detour to Switzerland for good measure. But at midsummer, the Alps are one big picturesque parking lot. To make things worse, 1990 saw the collapse of an autobahn bridge in the Inn Valley, which is one of the main arteries to and from northern Italy. As a result, the alternative routes were busier than usual, and even the secret paths were infested with hidden radar traps and aimless Dutch tourists.

We left Munich at six a.m., raced southwest to Garmisch, averaging a cool 127 mph, and felt like Messrs. Berger and Senna on their way to a business meeting. At the foot of the Fernpass, however, fast forward suddenly changed to slow motion. Although it was not yet even breakfast time, the mountain road was packed like the Brooklyn Bridge on a Friday evening. We jumped queue for a little while but gave up as the gaps became more and more marginal.

Other road users tend to treat the BMW M3 with due respect, but their eyes tell you that deep within they dislike the shirt-sleeved batmobile. Why did we pick the M3, mere months before the car will be replaced by a more modern and less conspicuous model? Because it is a fantastic driving machine, a fun car tailor-made for this sick-bag slalom across three countries. Its body sports flared wheel arches that can accommodate the gumballs of a track-racing car, its suspension was redesigned for better handling and roadholding, and its four-cylinder engine is a relic of a glorious past when, in 1983, an M-Power Brabham won the Formula 1 World Championship.

The base-line M3 engine delivers a healthy 215 bhp, which used to be enough to drive circles around a 170-bhp 325i. But now that the new 325i is out, with 192 bhp on tap and a top speed of 144 mph, the powertrain magicians of the Motorsport division had to reach deep into their special effects pockets to create an even stronger range topper. Badged Sport Evolution, this highly tuned M3 is equipped with a new 2.5-liter, sixteen-valve four that develops 238 bhp. Although the production was limited to a mere 500 units (all sold within a few weeks, none in America), chances are that a similar—perhaps even more powerful—version will appear in the 1991 racing season.

To escape from the frustrating route bristling with buses, caravans, campers, and other transit lemmings, we decided to make a detour to the Kühtai Valley. Instead of taking the direct route to the Ötztal, photographer Newton suggested a loop via the Silzer Sattel. A splendid idea—there was absolutely zero traffic, the panorama looked as if it had been installed by Eastman Kodak, and the perfect road was obviously designed by the Lord Himself for occasional interludes of very worldly oversteer. The M3 flew up paradise trail like a four-wheeled mountain guide who knew every step blindfolded. Performing one stem turn after the other, the black blitz indulged in drift angles that were modest only where the soft shoulder fell straight into echo forest.

The following drive to the Timmelsjoch summit turned out to be a handicap run with international participation. Once again, the Dutch excelled by steadfastly refusing to use rear-view mirrors or turn indicators. At the border crossing to Italy, the metal centipede was temporarily halted by a cycle race. It was grand casino from bottom to top: lots of single-track sections, lots of ambitious cyclists, and lots of brain-deads stopping in the middle of hairpin bends for this year's scenic portrait of papa, mama, and the *bambini* in the Fiat. A kingdom for the Italian version of the encyclopedia of foul language!

At noon, we stopped for lunch and

BY GEORG KACHER

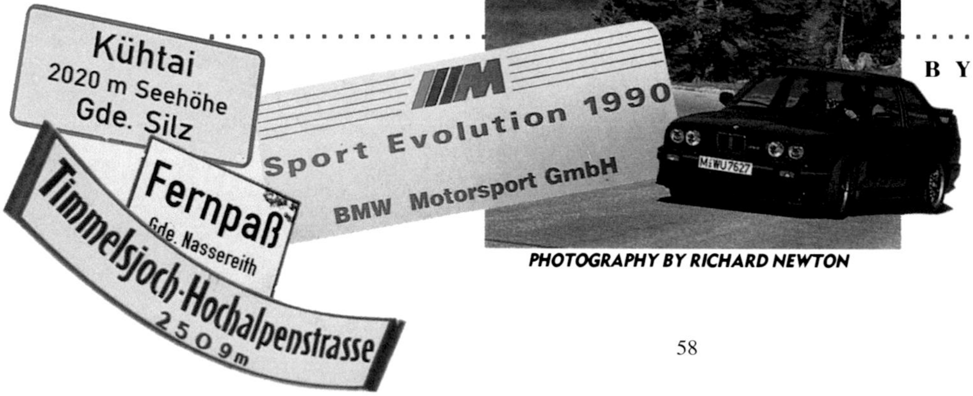

PHOTOGRAPHY BY RICHARD NEWTON

ordered a round of unleaded for the chariot and its charioteers. The car drank 14.5 gallons, which indicated an average consumption of 18 mpg. The M3 was as fit as a fiddle. The water temperature gauge had not moved, the oil level was right up on the mark, and the crackling brakes were hot but by no means fuming. The driver, on the other hand, showed the first signs of battle scars. My back was embossed with the tread pattern of the 225/45ZR-17 Michelin MXX tires, my buttocks had been remolded by the rather narrow bucket seats, and my palms were burning because the M3 Sport Evolution's steering wheel is trimmed in sandpaper suede.

But a true enthusiast knows no pain, so we headed straight for the Jaufenpass, which links San Leonardo and Sterzing (Vipiteno, in Italian). From there it's only a stone's throw down to Bozen—or Bolzano, as the Italians prefer to call it. Since the autostrada was chockablock with southbound sun worshippers, the M3 had no chance to display its 155-mph top speed. We left the tin mélange at Bolzano Nord, seeking—and eventually finding—the incredible Rosengartenstrasse. It consists of no fewer than fifty-eight tarmac garlands that rise from the Eisack Valley. The deserted spiral staircase was an ideal playground for the M3: first gear, second gear, brake, change down, turn in, change up. This is the stuff ashen-faced passengers are made of.

Next on our checklist was the Dolomites, which harbor about three dozen spectacular passes. One of the less attractive climbs is the Karerpass, which would be well suited as a natural stage for the sequel of *The Planet of the Apes*. A few miles up the road, we said *auf Wiedersehen* to south Tyrol and *buon giorno* to the truly Italian province of Belluno. Spaghetti land welcomed us with two tough arm twisters named Passo di Valles and Passo di San Pellegrino. The latter is the source of the San Pellegrino water that enjoys enormous popularity among European trendies who are not that Perrier crazy anymore.

Up here, it's bitter cold even in summer. Because of the prevailing strong winds, the chamois never leave home without crampons, and the trout in the crystal-clear mountain lakes are half-frozen even before the fishmongers arrive with the coolers. We enjoyed the change of temperature because the all-black M3 was a sauna on wheels—despite the noisy sunroof and the ventilation system that works adequately in other 3-series models. For a car costing $57,000, the Sport Evolution is rather poorly equipped. Anti-lock brakes, power steering, and central locking are standard, but a sunroof costs extra and so do electric windows, music, and the desirable air conditioning, which was only fitted to a handful of vehicles. Purists apparently prefer to sweat.

By five p.m., my hands hurt, my arms hurt, my legs hurt, and my bum hurt most of all. To relieve the pain, we bunkered an overdose of Gelati Motta ice cream followed by a bottle of San Pellegrino from the pond around the corner. After the calorie shock, we were fit for the final five passes of the day: Rolle, Cereda, Aurine, Duran, and Cibiana. Believe it or not, these hills provide more entertainment than a season ticket for the Magic Mountain. The menu prepared by the Italian road architects contains countless crests and hairpins, jumps and dives, ess-bends and dogleg bends, changing surfaces and changing radii, and bottlenecks that act like rapids when they disgorge the dammed-up traffic.

The corners add up to an intoxicating rhythm. Hard driving becomes a concert impromptu: You know how to play the instrument but never see more than two or three notes ahead. After a while, everything you do is routine; beyond that, the routine turns into trance. The movements become more and more automated, and you go faster, but without losing the quintessential smoothness.

By now, the brakes are red-hot. Whenever you touch the pedal, discs and pads instantly lock jaws. Glorified by the pervading euphoria, even the gnarled, necrotic five-speed gearbox suddenly feels as elastic as a young tree. The accurate power steering is a jack-of-all-trades that coordinates action, reaction, and Providence. And the tires, when pushed to the limit of adhesion, just keep juggling all the forces to resolve the crucial rule of three that determines grip, slip angle, and directional stability.

Hard driving becomes a concert impromptu: You know how to play the instrument but never see more than two or three notes ahead.

But the heart of the M3 is of course that raucous sixteen-valve four-cylinder engine. The displacement of the Sport Evolution variant was increased from 2302 to 2467 cc. As a result, the power output went up from 215 to 238 bhp at 7000 rpm, and the maximum torque climbed to 174 pounds-feet, available at a high 4750 rpm. Among the supporting measures are bigger inlet valves, a hotter camshaft profile, sodium-filled exhaust valves, and an improved oil cooling system for the pistons. The 2640-pound winged warrior from Munich can accelerate in 6.5 seconds from 0 to 62 mph, thus beating the new 192-bhp 325i by a comfortable 1.4 seconds.

We rejoined civilization in the Pieve Valley, which serves as a convenient *diretissimo* to go from east Tyrol to the Adriatic Sea. To unwind, the M team resorted to an unfailing recipe that included vitello tonnato, capretto al forno, and vino rosso. Although the cheapo roadside hotel was haunted by thundering trucks and a merry wedding party, we had no trouble going to sleep. After 7536 bends, the body will listen only to those noises it really wants to hear.

The alarm went off at 7:30 a.m., just in time for fresh croissants and a large bowl of white coffee. The proprietor watched us from behind the counter, and he even came running after us as we were about to enter the M3. A car fanatic like most Italian men, he would not let us go until we had explained all the details that distinguish the Sport Evolution from an off-the-peg M3. Among them, he was told, are the lowered suspension, the cross-spoke alloy wheels, the contrasting stripes on the bumpers, the bigger front wheel-arch cutouts, the additional cooling ducts to the radiator and reinforced brakes, the thinner and thus lighter glass, a more adequate 17.1-gallon fuel tank, and the body-hugging sport seats draped with silly red safety belts. But the most obvious alteration concerns the much more substantial,

The M3 had lived up to our every expectation, but we would love it even more without the fender flares and without that massive fuselage.

fully adjustable wing work, which reduces front axle lift to zero while increasing rear axle downforce. Although the stuff hates curbs and automatic carwashes, it does add to high-speed straight-line stability.

We left Pieve a little before nine a.m., heading for the Passo del Zovo, which looked from a distance like a stairway to heaven. From here it's only a few miles to the famous Passo Tre Croci and to the Col San Angelo where Reinhold Messner, that mountaineer and adventurer par excellence, learned to climb. The breathtaking panorama has since become a main tourist attraction. Once the domain of eagles, marmots, and ibexes, the Dolomites are nowadays strangled by droves of sightseeing buses and a motorized string of pearls that stretches from Cortina d'Ampezzo to Bruneck.

Monuments like the passes named Staulanza, Falzárego, Giau, Pordoi, Campolongo, Sella, and San Antonio are crumbling away as cars send their carbon dioxide messages into the increasingly polluted alpine air. Even up here, humans have taken over from nature. Above us, we had difficulty counting the hang gliders; around us, the cliffs and rock faces were dotted with climbing addicts; below us, we saw an endless trickle of hikers, mushroom pickers, and mountain bikers. Past the Grödnerjoch (Passo di Gardena), this open-air zoo ended as abruptly as it began. On the way to the Brennerpass, the trucks started to take over again, and up the Zirlerberg it was business as usual, with one slow-moving Trabant paralyzing its entire wake.

We arrived in Munich slightly ahead of schedule, feeling tired and proud as well as somewhat guilty and disillusioned. The M3 had lived up to our every expectation, but we would love it even more without the fender flares and without that massive fuselage that requires the clearance of air traffic control before you're allowed to turn the ignition key. It does not come as a surprise that BMW is already working on a less ostentatious follow-up to the M3 that should be out in early 1992. As soon as the new model hits the road, we'll be there to queue for another marathon ride. How about entering the 1993 Beaujolais Primeur wine run?

TRACK TEST

The sound of Munich

There have been faster racing saloon cars than the BMW M3 – notably the Nissan Skyline GT-R and Ford Sierra RS500 Cosworth – but there has never been a more consistently successful and durable championship winner. From its debut season as a European and World Championship winner to the 1991 version which propelled Will Hoy, Roberto Ravaglia and Tony Longhurst to the British, Italian and Australian championships, the simple but efficient M3 has garnered over 30 titles worldwide.

The naturally aspirated, 16-valve, dohc, front-engined, rear-drive design has even won a World Rally Championship qualifying event in the age of 4x4 turbo cars. Similarly the M3 brought BMW unexpected rallying titles in Belgium, France, Spain and Yugoslavia, most of these due to the activities or component knowledge of Prodrive in Brackley.

The M3 has also been a commercial success, selling over 17,000 units (they needed only 5000 to qualify for Group A in 1986).

The opportunity to drive a representative example of the German Championship M3 racing breed (they won that title in 1987 and 1989) was not to be missed, especially when Briton Steve Soper would be on hand with fellow factory racer Altfrid Heger to explain and demonstrate the niceties of their 2.5-litre steeds. When a racing school proprietor (!) crashed the six-speed, ABS-equipped, 340 bhp racer it looked as though our reporter was headed for an early Italian bath. Yet BMW Motorsport racing co-ordinator, and former Grand Prix driver, Marc Surer had us back on track within 10 minutes in an older T-car, the amiable Heger's spare M3 being readied for afternoon action, its scuffed suedette steering wheel, lack of ABS and a dash full of aged dials betraying its *muletta* status.

Soper immediately proved that it could still lap within a second of the 51.996s lap record pace . . . with a passenger aboard! That record represents an average of just 70 mph, reflecting the presence of five second-gear corners and a first gear hairpin. The overgrown kart track at Magione, one-mile long and a couple of *autostrada* hours up country from Rome, sunnily demonstrated the virtues of the M3 at speeds of up to 120 of the 180 available long circuit mph. The test car was fitted with one of 330 competition kits that BMW Motorsport has provided to over 40 countries. They will have paid the equivalent of £90,000 without a motor, or £140,000 complete with a BMW Motorsport power train.

The racing M3 is a car of enormous character, its four booming cylinders balanced to perfection by capacious brakes, simple suspension, and aerodynamic features. BMW Motorsport Racing Team Manager Karsten Engel admits: "We could make it better in some areas like the underfloor aerodynamics, but we are not allowed to do these things under German regulations, so the car will make its sixth racing season in 1992 largely unchanged." The big 3-series competition changes will come in 1993, when the company will field an M3 based on the current (E36) body shape, powered by a 2.5-litre, 24-valve version of the current 192 bhp 325i motor. Expected to give 250 bhp in road trim, it is now being readied for autumn 1992 production. A right-hand drive model will be sold in 1993.

For a preview, albeit without the extra aerodynamic appendages, watch the 1992 British Touring Car Championship, where Steve Soper will debut the new shape for his new British team, Vic Lee Motorsport. Prodrive is also scheduled to have one of the new bodies, complete with basic roll cage and body preparation from German fabrication maestro Matter.

We asked Steve to give us an insight into the differences between driving 2.5 M3s in Germany and 2.0-litre variants at home. He contrasted five key areas: weight, power, brakes, aerodynamics . . . and driving standards.

"At first," opines the now Monaco-domiciled Soper, "the British M3 actually feels quite slow. It's not just that it has 265 or so horsepower in place of 340 in Germany. You have to remember the weight. The less powerful UK car actually carries more weight. Of course it depends a bit how successful you are as a driver in Germany as to the actual weight you will carry, but the basic weights are 980 kg versus 1050 kg for the UK.

"Then there's the brakes. In Germany for 1991 we had ABS. In Britain, believe it or not, it was actually banned (it is now permitted – JW). You will also notice our German or Italian specification Evolution M3s have the front and rear adjustable spoilers. Not so in Britain. That makes an aerodynamic difference to the cornering ability I can call on, especially at the faster tracks."

During the 1990/91 winter a unique BMW Alfred Teves racing ABS braking system was conscientiously developed. Soper comments: "I tried the system back-to-back at Salzburgring and found *three* seconds in the wet, and it was better in the dry, too. It was a good thing BMW went for the system, because Mercedes had it for 1991 as well. I don't think their Bosch system is as good as ours in several important respects."

As to the opposition, Soper underlines the talent of men like ex-Grand Prix racers Jacques Laffite, Johnny Cecotto and Hans-Joachim Stuck in German fields full of rapid conductors. There were up to 15 drivers capable of winning in the German series, whereas the nascent UK equivalent naturally had a few less top runners recruited. Soper has kind words for the 'never-say-die' speed of John Cleland in the Vauxhall and Andy Rouse in his Toyota. However, since we spoke, the quality of the UK series has been augmented. Marque interest comes from BMW, Vauxhall, Toyota, Mazda, Peugeot and Nissan, at the very least . . .

Meanwhile, the Germans are looking at a leaner year than of late, with 30-car grids from only three manufacturers. The absence of Ford and Opel threatens to turn their year into another Audi rout with BMW and Mercedes squabbling over the Championship pieces.

The M3 has collected over 30 saloon car titles . . .

A conventional Getrag five-speed gearbox has synchromesh operation, but a number of pure racing six-speed alternatives are used by BMW competitors, including products from Hollinger in Australia, Getrag and Prodrive. I have experience of the Prodrive unit, and liked it very much, but I am told the Hollinger is lighter and faster to deploy.

We were seated by Recaro and restrained by

BMW M3 GROUP A (Prodrive BTCC specification)

ENGINE	
Location	longitudinally front-mounted
Cylinders	four in-line
Bore × stroke	93.4 × 72.6 mm
Capacity	1989 cc
Compression ratio	not available
Valve gear	dohc, four valves per cylinder
Power	275 bhp/8750 rpm
Torque	190 lb ft/7500 rpm
TRANSMISSION	
Type	six-speed manual, rear-wheel drive
BRAKES	
Front/Rear	ventilated discs all round
WHEELS/TYRES	
Techno 8Jx17	Pirelli
DIMENSIONS	
Race weight	1050 kg
ESTIMATED PERFORMANCE	
0-62 mph	5.7 sec
Maximum speed	170 mph

well mannered. From the start I used 9000 of the usual 9500 rpm, but during the learning curve I took advantage of its good nature and broad torque spread to pull from 5000 rpm in the lower gears. Haul it back into first for the tightest corner and the natural rev band seems to lie between 6000-9000 rpm, but this first gear section is followed by a second-gear right onto the main straight. Even the stars back off here, so most regularly exploit the sub 5000 rpm torque.

The sound levels are modest by racing standards, but exciting nonetheless. It's fun to feel the large four smooth out above 5000 revs point, yet sheer speed is not overwhelming. You might touch 115-120 mph. Until the end of the main straight, that is, when fifth is held briefly before the demands of a tight right-hander. This was the most vulnerable point of a lap for a stranger. Even the works drivers occasionally dived at the apex, still changing gears furiously. At first the choppy ride and handling was composed, then the old M3's rear wheels start to kick out of line in a manner akin to the racing RS500 with which I was more familiar.

six-point Sabelts. The dashboard looks simple at first glance, a 10,000 rpm Stack tachometer placed adjacent to a transparent pane. "That rev counter tells them all that you have done and this small readout (behind the innocuous blank pane – JW) can tell of five or six things, including water and oil temperature, oil pressure, all things like this. We keep it on the water temperature for a race, because its needs to be kept in 85 to 90 degC for the best power," explains Heger.

Walton at the controls. The onlooking Steve Soper is the only Briton currently earning a living in the GTCC.

BMW M3 GROUP A (Schnitzer GTCC specification)

ENGINE	
Location	longitudinally front-mounted
Cylinders	four in-line
Bore × stroke	95.5 × 87.0 mm
Capacity	2493 cc
Compression ratio	12 to 1
Valve gear	dohc, four valves per cylinder
Power	340 bhp/8750 rpm
Torque	214 lb ft/7500 rpm
TRANSMISSION	
Type	six-speed manual, rear-wheel drive
BRAKES	
Front/Rear	ventilated discs all round
WHEELS/TYRES	
BBS 9Jx17 (f)/9Jx18 (r)	Yokohama
DIMENSIONS	
Race weight	980 kg
ESTIMATED PERFORMANCE	
0-62 mph	4.8 sec
Maximum speed	180.1 mph

The catalytic converter is compulsory for this formula and it makes a big difference to drivers. On a hot summer day it can reach between 50 and 70 degC in the cockpit, because the converter is under the bare steel floor. Heger continued with an A-Z tour of the myriad warning lights. "The red one means you will have to stop, there is no oil pressure. The yellow ones are for the petrol tank, or the generator," he explains, although there are also lights to monitor ABS in the current frontline cars and a supplementary petrol pump. Within the white steel walls and Matter roll-cage protection lurks an old-fashioned racing car.

By the transmission tunnel, twin levers and cables lead fore and aft. "These are to operate the front and rear roll bar loads," smiles Heger. "Normally we would run with 70 per cent for the front bar, 30 per cent at the rear." Further cockpit sophistications include the usual brake bias hand wheel, an array of popout electrical fuses, a diagnostic plug for the ECU and the selector for that dashboard display of vital motor functions.

At some 136 bhp per litre, the M3 remains

As I started to use more opposite lock, the "in" board came out from the pit wall. Had I exceeded their hospitality? No, the tyres really are shot. Now I get a ferocious driving display from Soper, which produces a time despite visibly worsening grip. Ridged kerbs reverberate beneath the slewing BMW as Soper-the-Chauffeur urges more speed from flayed rubber. Rumble strips advance and retreat beneath hard worked Pirellis: tyre squeal emerges as the healthy motor and brakes are pressed to their limits. All give us an insight to what being a factory BMW driver really is all about.

Hard, but exhilarating, graft.

Soper sets a 54.77 sec best, two-up, where my best had been 57.56 sec on a solo run. The 2.79 sec gap is primarily accounted for by my plump cowardice, especially under braking at the end of the fastest straight. I am grateful to BMW Motorsport and Steve Soper for the time they allowed us to gain a unique insight into the professional saloon car driver's working environment for the '90s. I would still swap its centrally heated charms for this confounded wordprocessor . . . **JW**

M AK 8813

Worth the weight?

Behind the reborn BMW performance flagship lie at least four years' development graft and 50 prototypes. Replacing the familiar old four-cylinder warrior is a very much smoother six-cylinder M3, but the 155 mph newcomer is a very much heavier, plusher machine. It is more akin to a replacement for BMW's old six-cylinder CSi coupe. This time, British customers *will* be offered rhd from May 1993 at predicted prices in the £33-34,000 band, depending on the exchange rate and what items from the considerable options list are incorporated as part of standard UK specification.

No agreement has yet been signed to import the M3 to North America, where predicted prices look uncomfortable in a Japanese-dominated market.

Nothing but the badge and its origins in BMW Motorsport really link the new M3 to its predecessor. The 0.32 Cd body is based on that of the current 3-series coupé and much of the running gear has been developed from the 24-valve, dohc 325i.

Furthest from its 325i base is the engine. A new iron block and two-part alloy cylinder head are, statistically, very different. The 24v dohc principles are substantially modified by a variable valve timing system (VACC for English speakers, VANOS is the acronym used by Germans) that works on the inlet camshaft only. Its electro-hydraulic actuation modifies camshaft action between 80 and 120 crankshaft degrees and allows exceptional torque to accompany the generation of 286 bhp at 7000 rpm.

BMW credits its latest M50-coded three-litre (it's actually 2990 cc, 86 × 85.8 mm) with a world record in bhp per litre (95.6) at this capacity, though Honda might like to query that. The Civic VTEC manages 98.8 . . . BMW has, however, overcome Porsche's previous benchmark for torque in the normally-aspirated, three-litre class. The M3 pumps out 236 lb/ft at 3600 rpm. The most remarkable facet to that torque capability is that the peak figure is sustained all the way to 5800 rpm. Furthermore, the engine remains remarkably suave at either end of its 7280 rpm range, be it 700 or 7000.

The unit is mated to a 525i ZF five-speed, a sextet of ratios being ruled out by Germany's target price ceiling. The bulky motor is installed with at least two of its in-line cylinders forward of the axle line, and one can see why BMW and the organisers of the German Touring Car Championship came into such bitter dispute over the engine location. The company claims that 50-50 weight distribution is retained on the road, but it does not look like that in the flesh; before withdrawing from further GTCC involvement, BMW Motorsport wanted to run a lowered and relocated (moved back by 15 cm) version of the motor.

For road customers the 325i chassis has been substantially overhauled, but the principles of MacPherson strut front and Z1-derived multiple-link back axle remain, albeit with typical detail reinforcements These centre on a 1.22 in reduction in ride height after the adoption of replacement gas-filled damping, shorter and stiffer coil springs, thicker front anti-roll bar, stiffened suspension mounting joints and a ZF limited slip differential operating a 25 per cent torque preloading. The steering features a variable ratio that is not offered elsewhere in the 3-series range. The back trailing arms are physically strengthened and 850i Coupé wheel bearings are adopted, all to resist the ravages of cornering forces up that have been measured at up to 1.2G.

The biggest handling advantages come from more obvious modifications: 17 in wheel diameters are adopted with 7.5 in rims (8.5 in is a forged alloy option) and 235/40 ZR covers from the Michelin MXX3 range are prominent. Behind such large diameter wheels lurk equally impressive vented discs, effectively monitored by Teves ABS.

BMW makes much of the new M3's stopping abilities. It claims that it takes just 8.8s to go from rest to 62 mph and back again; six of those seconds are spent gathering velocity, and just 2.8 scrubbing it off.

The body has none of the old car's extended wheelarch character; even a rear spoiler is only allowed as an option. The most notable M3 panel is an extended front spoiler with under-bumper grille, but detail modifications also abound, such as prominent side sills and an extended, stylised rear apron, which wraps around stubby twin exhausts. BMW Motorsport sales personnel did feel that more M3 identity was needed, and the 'racing' mirrors, badges on each door and the kickplates reflect that lack of confidence. Originally they were going to put an M3 badge within the sacred kidney grille, but corporate defenders of the faith vetoed that intrusion, leaving the bootlid as the only place to put such a motif.

The interior is not inspired, but it does carry an individual Motorsport trim alongside the ponderous air bag steering wheel (intricately hand-stitched in bright threads around the inside circumference of the rim) and an oil temperature gauge continues to replace the econometer of the usual 3-series. Red needles record 7300 as the limit on the 8000 rpm scale and 270 km/h (168 mph) as the maximum indicated speed, but, as with all current high-performance BMWs, an electronic device interferes at 155 mph.

The engine has all the hallmarks of BMW breeding, whirring along at low rpm, where there is plentiful torque available, and gradually taking on the note that encourages lazy colleagues to recall the "turbine smoothness" of a BMW straight six.

Whether humming along melodically at 87 mph (less than 4000 rpm in top), or sprinting between second gear curves at 7000 rpm, the seductive engine is reason enough to buy. BMW engineering legend Paul Rosche told journalists: "I know of no better engine." We would endorse that for the combination of civilisation and accessible power.

Other M3 abilities that set new benchmarks are those enormous brakes and a beautifully absorbent ride, especially when you consider the 40 per cent aspect ratio tyres.

What we were not so impressed by was the communication between car and driver over roads with differing degrees of adhesion. On dry surfaces there is enormous grip, and the Michelins awaken the steering from its apparently well damped torpor to tell you that initial understeer has been traded for old fashioned power oversteer. When, as for our trip, surfaces go from dry to damp to wet and back to dry, the M3 is far from convincing. The driver – despite adjustable shoulder and headrest sections to the unique seats – is not made to feel at one with the car. The steering fails to relay either the drop in bite being achieved by the front wheels, or the disquieting speed with which the rears will now want to overtake their forward comrades. It was not the kind of hair-raising experience, or general unease, that 911s and Skodas used to generate in their original formats, but the new M3 is hard to balance in its new, heavyweight guise.

I am not advocating a traction control device, which Motorsport eschewed but is now working on again for this model, but the kind of alert feedback that characterised its 527 lb lighter four-cylinder progenitor. The new M3 can't match the old when it comes to seeking pleasure on a twisty road. It was a similar story when the 3.8-litre M5 supplanted the original.

The truth may be that journalists and purists enjoy these original Motorsport devices, but the buying public always want further equipment. Such bulk soon ruins handling pleasure, as well as putting a dent in acceleration curves and making affordable fuel consumption a challenge. In the latter respect, BMW points to a likely overall average of 31 mpg; we recorded a best of 18.7 and the most probable UK averages will be close to the urban quote 21.7. It runs on 98 RON super unleaded.

I would put the new M3 on my personal wanted list, but I wonder how many others amongst the 17,000-plus buyers of the first M3 will be amongst the 24,000 anticipated customers (over the next five or six years) for the new one? I suspect many more old 6-series clients are going to be interested, in which case the machine could have been most accurately described as a 3.0 CSi.

That would prevent purchasers gaining the false impression that the new M3 is as raunchy a driving machine as the original. **J W**

BMW M3

Supercar performance and awesome point-to-point ability have replaced feel in the new M3

PAUL DEBOIS

ANY CAR ENTHUSIAST with an ounce of soul should be itching to read this test. Why? Because it's the first proper assessment of the car that replaces what was, frankly, the best sporting saloon ever built. The old M3 was fast and involving like no other car with four seats and a reasonable-sized boot. For many on this magazine it was the one car, money no object, that we would have chosen to own for ourselves.

That's some mantle to pick up. But the writing on the wall looks good. It says that the new £32,450 right-hand-drive M3 has 286bhp worth of M-powered straight-six engine under its heavily bespoilered snout. It also hints that this could be the fastest BMW yet, except perhaps for the M1 of the late '70s, although point to point even that icon no longer looks safe from the new baby Bimmer's bullet.

Speed isn't everything, of course. The old M3 was quick but not demolishingly so, as this one promises to be. What it was was red-blooded driving appeal personified. It begged you to punt it hard and fast and cracked open the champagne automatically every time you got it right. The question is, will the new car — less aggressive visually but even more potent — do the same? Our initial encounter — no more than a few hours over the treacherous mountain roads of Majorca — hinted that the M3 might have sold its soul in favour of wider market appeal; that it had gone soft. The only way to find out for sure is to read on.

Performance

To call the new M3 quick would be a gross understatement. Devastating is more appropriate. To the extent that it blows the rest of its class clean into next week. In short, it dishes out bona fide supercar pace at half, even a third of the normal price.

At the core of the M3's haymaker punch is BMW's now legendary M Power straight six, which has been fettled to give a capacity of 2990cc. With the aid of variable valve timing, four valves per cylinder, twin overhead camshafts and sophisticated Bosch multi-point fuel injection, it thumps out 286bhp at 7000rpm and 236lb ft of torque at 3600rpm. But — and this is the secret to the M3's astonishing consistency — even at idle speed this engine develops more torque than the old car's did at its peak.

Thus it isn't necessarily the 0-60mph time of 5.4secs or the 0-100mph time of 13.1secs that ram the point home hardest, astounding figures though they both undoubtedly are. Nor is it the erroneous 162mph maximum speed (BMW is officially supposed to limit this car to 155mph). Rather, it's the in-gear times — specifically the ones recorded in fourth and top. In fourth gear the M3 puts paid to every 20mph increment between 10 and 120mph in 7.0secs or less. You'd need a Ferrari 512TR to get inside those times. And in top gear you have to be travelling at more than 140mph before the BMW enters double figures for any given 20mph increment. That's outstanding flexibility by any standards.

In the sprints, you only need to look at one figure — the 30-70mph time — to get the picture once and for all. The M3 tears up this benchmark strip in 4.7secs. A Porsche 968 is more than a second slower, a Caterham 7 HPC only a single tenth swifter. Even its theoretically quicker granddaddy, the M5, is nearly half a second adrift.

What's more, the M3's ▶

Price as tested £34,915
Top speed 162mph **0-60mph** 5.4secs **MPG** 26.2

For Fantastic engine, blistering performance, classy but understated looks, chassis security, economy
Against Not as involving as original M3, brakes lack feel, seats not as supportive as they look

performance is so easily accessible that it feels even quicker on the road than it is on the track. The five-speed gearbox — which now has a conventional gate rather than a dogleg to first gear — has no tricks up its sleeve and needs no more skill to master than that of a regular 318i. Neither do the clutch or the accelerator, both of which are beautifully weighted and encourage good, smooth driving.

And that's where the M3 delivers its final and most deadly hit. So smooth and so linear is the manner in which it accelerates, seemingly oblivious as to which gear you happen to be in at the time, that frankly there is little point in even turning up to compete if you are a sub-£50,000 rival. In fact, there is only one other six-cylinder engine in the world that is worthy of mention in the same sentence, and that belongs to the Honda NSX. Praise comes no higher.

Economy

It doesn't end there, either. With performance of the M3's calibre you'd be chuffed with 20mpg economy, perhaps high teens when running hard. But no. Overall it returned a scarcely believable 26.2mpg on test, with a best of 31.5mpg over our economy route. No other 160mph car gets even close. Especially since the overall touring range is a useful 450 miles.

Handling

This is where the clarity of the M3's purpose becomes cloudy and occasionally disappears from sight altogether. The question is this: is grip and therefore point-to-point ability everything? If so, this M3 is virtually peerless among four-wheeled transport, and that includes exotica with telephone number price tags and the front-drive Lotus Elan.

So capable is the chassis of keeping its four wheels controlled and in constant contact with the road, and so agile is the car through seemingly any sequence of bends, that it is difficult to imagine any car being notably more effective during a rapid cross-country journey. Certainly not one with four seats and a decent-sized boot.

But — and this is central to the car's sole fundamental flaw as a road car — there are a number of other cars we know of that are more involving and informative and are therefore capable of stirring up a higher degree of driver appeal during that same journey, even though they'd get there long after the M3 driver had switched off and climbed out. And the Porsche 968 is without a doubt one of them.

The M3's problem is not an easy one to pinpoint, because in black and white terms there is little doubt that it has of one of the finest rear-drive chassis we have yet to come across; its body control, damper tuning, grip and predictability are all as good as faultless on the road. As is its ability to put its power down cleanly without the aid of a traction control device. But what it fails to do is tell you, the driver, that any of this is happening in anything more than token form. Feel, somehow, is sorely lacking.

And in the old car, whose ultimate limits were lower, it was possible to explore the outer envelope of the chassis' abilities at slower speeds, which meant you could exploit it, and revel in the fact that you were able to do so, safely on the road.

In this new car the limits are so high that you can no longer go searching for them sanely on the public road. What's more, those limits are harder to seek out because the steering — a variable-ratio power-assisted rack and pinion system — fails to paint anything like as clear a picture of the road as it should. In truth, it is the car's single most disappointing aspect.

Ride

The M3 may have lost some of its finite handling qualities as a result of BMW's desire to soften the car in the name of wider market appeal, but that has done nothing but good for the ride quality. Although taut, the M3's ride never becomes harsh or uncomfortable, and for much of the time it is beyond serious criticism.

You'd need to drive very quickly indeed over an unbelievably poor road to show up any holes in the car's iron body control. Yet despite the liquorice-thin profile of the 235/40 ZR17 Michelin MXX3 tyres, the town ride is almost as accomplished. Only big potholes or badly repaired roadworks ramps cause occupants any genuine discomfort; when the suspension reaches the end of its travel it lets you know with a mighty thump, although such occasions, thankfully, are rare.

Brakes

Although faultless in their ability to slow the car time and again from implausibly high speeds, and without serious fade, we expected a little more from the M3's ventilated disc, anti-lock-equipped brakes. We expected more feel. Perhaps our car was a rogue, perhaps not; either way the middle pedal, although highly effective, was strangely dead, under light or heavy application. This is particularly disappointing given the fabulous feel of the previous M3's brakes.

At the wheel

If the new M3 lacks the purposeful quasi-racer atmosphere of its predecessor's cabin, it more than makes up for this with a cockpit of pure class and distinction. To sit behind this car's airbag-equipped,

One of the great sixes

THE M3'S NEW THREE-LITRE straight six is astonishing in a number of respects, but none more so than for the seamless tidal wave of torque it produces at virtually any revs and in any gear.

The secret is its Variable Camshaft Control (VACC), which electronically advances or retards the opening angle of the intake camshaft to give either maximum breathing at full throttle or maximum fuel efficiency under lighter loads.

VACC also ensures a very even spread of torque throughout the rev range. As a result, this new engine develops more twist action at idle speed (and at any other engine revs) than the old M3 did even at its peak. And because the engine is always working close to or at maximum efficiency all the time, fuel economy is extraordinarily good, given the car's 160mph performance.

Smoothness is the other key feature that distinguishes this engine and is attributable to a new dual-mass flywheel; this reduces vibration and virtually eradicates transmission noise.

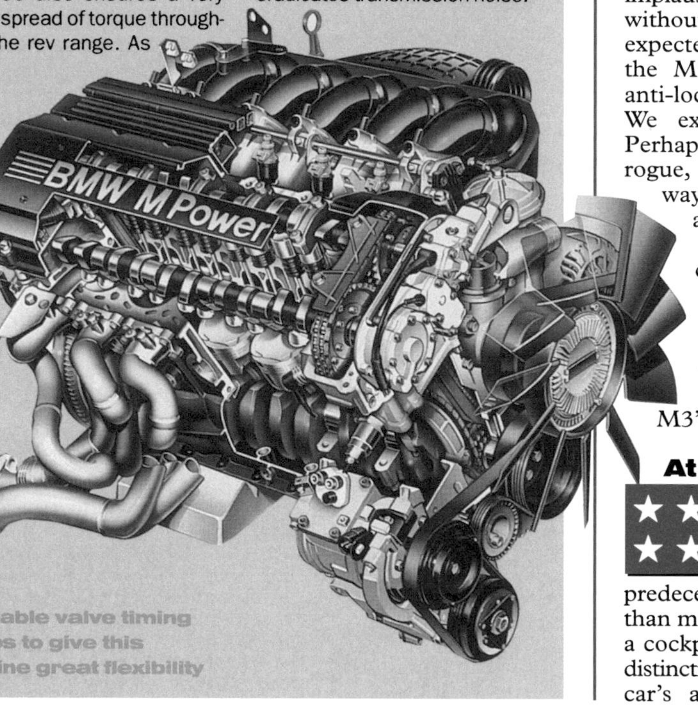

Variable valve timing helps to give this engine great flexibility

This cabin is one of the best in the business — ergonomics are first class and quality is high. Only flaw is the seats, which are very comfortable but look more supportive than they actually are

M3 is one of the few 160mph cars that can seat four adults in reasonable comfort and has space for their luggage, too. Admittedly rear seat space isn't vast, but by supercar standards it's generous, as is boot space. Two-door coupe shell is a possible limitation, but forthcoming M3 saloon will fix that

Three-litre 24-valve straight six is a magnificent unit — refined, flexible and very powerful (286bhp, no less). It gives blistering performance — in-gear times are especially impressive. Fuel economy is superb, too

Airbag-equipped sports steering wheel costs £560 extra but is a must

Fronts seats have a wide range of adjustment — base tilts at front and rear, and extends to fine-tune under-thigh support

The Autocar Road Test

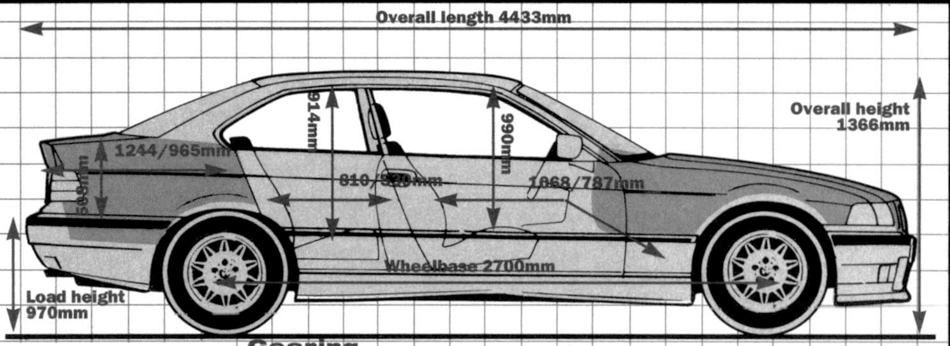

Width 1710mm
Front/rear tracks 1407/1421mm
Turning circle 10.7m
Interior width front/rear 1380/1380mm
Max/min boot width 1290/970mm
VDA boot volume 0.40cu m
Cd 0.32

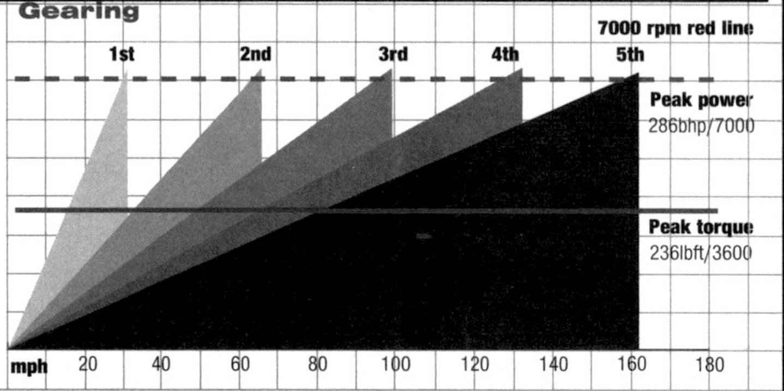

What it costs

Prices

List price	£32,450
Total as tested	£34,915

Equipment

(prices in **bold type** denote option fitted to test car)

Metallic paint	£405
RDS radio/cassette/CD player	DO
Number of speakers	6
Adjustable steering column	★
One-shot electric driver's window	★
Central locking on any door	★
Electric front seats	£975
Height/tilt adjustable driver's seat	★
Anti-theft system	**£465**
Cruise control	£375
Full leather trim	£1040
Outside temperature indicator	★
Traction control	–
Trip computer	★
Heated seats, front	£275
Automatic climate control	**£1440**
Alloy wheels	★
Courtesy delay light	★
Anti-lock brakes	★
Sports wheel with driver's airbag	**£560**

★ standard – not available
DO dealer option

Insurance group 20

Depreciation 50

Value after three years/30,000 miles as a percentage of new price. Source: Fleet News Guide to Future Residual Values

Warranty

12 months unlimited mileage, 6 years anti-corrosion, 12 months recovery

Servicing

Major 14,000 miles, service time 4.6hrs, £80 parts **Interim** 7000 miles, 0.8hrs, £12 parts

Parts costs

Set spark plugs	£55.60
Brake pads front	£50
Brake pads rear	£30
Exhaust (exc cat)	£314.15
Door mirror glass	£35
Tyre (each, typical)	£261
Windscreen	£135
Headlamp unit (twin)	£175
Front wing	£100
Rear bumper	£317.86

* Achieved over a pre-set test route designed to replicate an average range of driving conditions. **The figures** were taken at the Lotus proving ground, Millbrook, with the odometer reading 3100 miles. Autocar & Motor test results are protected by world copyright and may not be reproduced without the editor's written permission

Specification

Engine

Layout	6 cyls in line, 2990cc
Max power	286bhp/7000rpm
Max torque	236lb ft/3600rpm
Specific output	96bhp/litre
Power to weight	196bhp/tonne
Installation	longitudinal, front, rear-wheel drive
Made of	alloy head, iron block
Bore/stroke	86/86mm
Comp ratio	10.8:1
Valves	4 per cyl, dohc
Ignition and fuel	Bosch DME engine management, sequential multi-point fuel injection

Gearbox

Type 5-speed manual
Ratios/mph per 1000rpm
1st 4.20/5.4 **2nd** 2.49/9.0
3rd 1.66/13.6 **4th** 1.24/18.1
5th 1.00/22.5 **Final drive** 3.15

Suspension

Front struts, coil springs, anti-roll bar
Rear multi-link, coil springs, anti-roll bar

Steering

Type variable ratio rack and pinion, power assisted **Lock to lock** 3.3 turns

Brakes

Front 315mm ventilated discs
Rear 313mm ventilated discs
Anti-lock standard

Wheels and tyres

Size 7.5x17ins **Made of** cast alloy
Tyres Michelin MXX3, 235/40 ZR17
Spare full size

Made by

BMW AG, Munich, Germany

Sold by

BMW (GB) Ltd, Ellesfield Avenue, Bracknell, Berks RG12 8TA.
Tel: 0344 426565

Performance

Maximum speeds

Top gear 162mph/7200rpm
4th 132/7300 **3rd** 99/7300
2nd 66/7300 **1st** 31/7300

Acceleration from rest

True mph	Secs	Speedo mph
30	2.2	32
40	3.1	42
50	4.1	52
60	5.4	63
70	6.9	73
80	8.8	83
90	10.8	93
100	13.1	103
110	16.4	113
120	20.0	123
130	25.2	134
140	30.8	145

Standing qtr mile 13.9secs/102mph
Standing km 25.3secs/131mph
30-70mph through gears 4.7secs

Acceleration in each gear

mph	top	4th	3rd	2nd
10-30	9.5	7.0	4.5	2.9
20-40	8.1	6.0	4.0	2.6
30-50	7.3	5.5	3.8	2.3
40-60	8.1	5.5	3.6	2.4
50-70	7.1	5.0	3.5	–
60-80	6.0	5.0	3.5	–
70-90	6.8	5.3	3.8	–
80-100	6.9	5.4	–	–
90-110	7.9	5.7	–	–
100-120	8.3	6.4	–	–
110-130	8.5	7.9	–	–
120-140	11.4	–	–	–

Fuel consumption

Overall mpg on test	26.2
Best/worst on test	31.5/12.0
Touring*	31.5
Range	450 miles

Govt tests (mpg):
urban 21.7 **56mph** 43.5 **75mph** 35.8
Tank capacity 65 litres (14.3 galls)

Brakes

Distance travelled under max braking
Track surface dry
Anti-lock standard

30mph	9.3m
50mph	25.2m
70mph	49.4m
st qtr mile (102mph)	103m

Fade tests
Consecutive brake applications at 0.5g retardation from st qtr terminal speed

(figures on the right represent pedal pressures)

Weight

Kerb (incl half tank)	1520kg
Distribution f/r	50/50%
Max payload	470kg
Max towing weight	n/a

1 Optional radio/cassette **2** Rear demister switch **3** Heater/ventilation/air conditioning controls **4** Trip computer **5** Indicators stalk **6** Fuel gauge **7** Speedometer **8** Optional airbag-equipped sports steering wheel **9** Revcounter **10** Water temperature gauge **11** Wipers stalk **12** Lights switch

Handling, grip and body control are all first class — it just lacks the involvement that made the old M3 so much fun

◀ leather-rimmed sports wheel (an essential £560 option) is to be privy to one of the best driving environments in the business. Indeed, so thoughtfully have each of the controls and handsome instruments been designed and located that it is hard to imagine where any improvements could be made.

The only possible exception is the front seats, which appear more effective than they actually are with their serious-looking suede-tipped side wings. They boast a wide range of adjustment: the cushion tilts at the back as well as the front and can be extended to provide maximum thigh location, while the shoulder supports move up and down with the head restraint, but they don't offer sufficient lateral support for those of average girth during spirited driving — a likely pursuit in this car. On the other hand, no one found them anything other than comfortable during long stints.

Accommodation and comfort

★★★★

You need only one hand to count the number of cars that combine the M3's performance with its ability to swallow four adults and their luggage whole. BMW already makes one of them (the M5), and the Lotus Carlton is another. That leaves two fingers dangling.

Audi would argue that the Coupe S2 is a contender, but in truth this car has neither the rear seat space nor the luggage capacity of the BMW. Nor, for that matter, does it have the pace.

The M3's only compromise when it comes to space, apart from its lack of genuinely spacious rear seats (they are merely acceptable in average family car terms), is the fact that it is available only with the two-door coupe bodyshell. However, a four-door version and a convertible are already well clear of the drawing board and will, according to our sources, reach the UK by the end of next year.

Even though air conditioning is a £1440 option rather than standard (our test car had this fitted), getting comfortable in an M3 is not difficult. The standard ventilation system is first-class, while the seats, notably those in the rear, are ideally sculpted to ensure that occupants emerge ache-free even after long periods on the road.

Noise

★★★★★

Refinement is the new M3's middle name. Don't get us wrong: the song beneath the bonnet is still there; if anything the six sounds even better than the old four-pot screamer. But whereas the old M3 suffered from intrusive tyre roar and suspension rumble over anything other than roads as smooth as a billiard table, the new car damps away road, ▶

Agile M3's point-to-point ability is almost unparalleled

Ride quality and refinement are far better than that of old M3. Quasi-racer image seems to have gone forever

Striking 17ins alloys distinguish M3 from pretenders

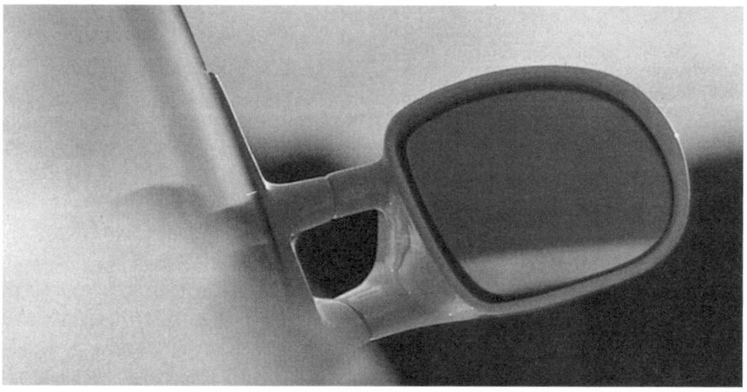

Aerodynamics play a big part in M3's terrific speed

◀ wind and tyre noise with almost limo-like aplomb.

Build quality and safety

BMWs seem to have varied in quality of late, especially the 3-series, but the M3 puts any such gremlins to rest. Our car was beautifully finished inside and out and boasted some of the most consistent panel gaps we've yet seen. The finish of the special bright yellow paint was beyond criticism, too.

The primary security imparted by the M3's chassis and its towering anti-lock brakes should not be underestimated. But should you get into trouble, there are a number of safety nets to keep life and limb intact, such as twin impact beams in each door, optional airbag (which might become standard for the 1994 model year) and bigger rear crumple zones than in the previous car.

Value and equipment

Purely because it will top 160mph and reach 60mph in less than 5.5secs, it's hard to regard the M3 as anything other than good value at £32,450. But add in its exclusivity, fuel economy, low depreciation rate and reasonable equipment tally — you get one-shot electric windows, central locking and a trip computer but no stereo (getting one fitted is a matter between you and the dealer) — and a high rating is guaranteed.

Verdict

BMW had two goals to achieve with the new M3. The first was to make it appeal to a wider commercial market, and it has certainly done that. The car is more user friendly now, not merely because it is available for the first time in right-hand-drive form but because it is quieter, roomier and a sight more economical than was previously the case.

The second was to do all of this without diluting the original car's fabulously raw thoroughbred driver appeal, but here we feel it has been only partially successful. And the trouble, we suspect, is that it was impossible to do both.

The truth is that, in its darkest confessional moment, BMW knows this just as much as we do. It is, after all, the company that produced the original M3. However, somewhere along the line a decision was taken to make the new M3 not a real M3 but instead a car more in the mould of the old M635 CSi; an easygoing tool that will appeal to more of the people for more of the time but not one that will pull so passionately on the heart strings of the serious enthusiast.

Does that mean the M3 has gone soft, then? No. Any car with an engine this good that is linked to a chassis this well developed deserves praise of the highest order, especially since it unlocks the door to such giant-killing cross-country ability. Even so, we can't help but shed a tear for the demise of the genuine M3. It was a unique car that will, it seems, remain that way forever.

BMW M3 ★★★★ £32,450

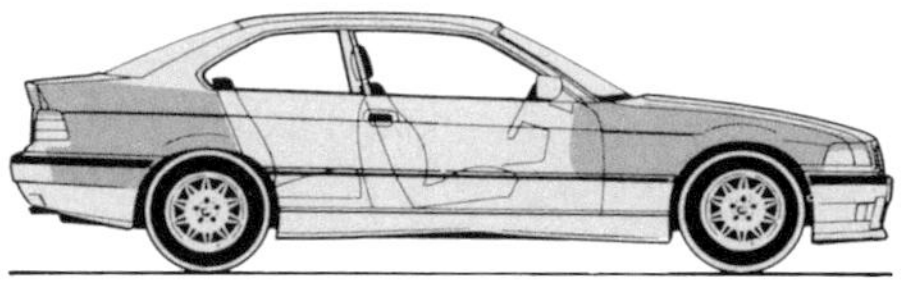

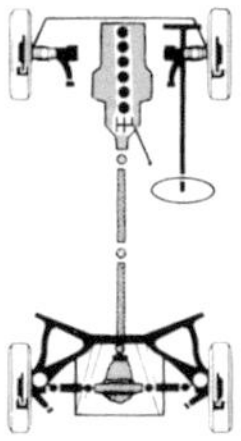

Length 4433mm **Width** 1710mm **Front track** 1407mm **Wheelbase** 2700mm **Height** 1366mm **Rear track** 1421mm **Weight distribution front/rear** 50/50

The old M3 was a tough act to follow, but for the most part the new car does a good, if not quite inspired job. Outrageously fast from point to point yet understated to the extent that you'd need a trained eye to tell it from a regular 325i coupe, the new right-hand-drive M3 is more 330 CSi than genuine M-car. That will be good enough for most people, but for us it's not quite the real thing.

Capacity	2990cc
Power	286bhp/7000rpm
Torque	236lb ft/3600rpm
Max speed	162mph
0-60mph	5.4secs
30-70mph through gears	4.7secs
Standing quarter mile	13.9secs
30-50mph in fourth	5.5secs
50-70mph in top	7.1secs
Mpg overall/touring	26.2/31.5
Mph/1000rpm in top	22.5
Kerb weight	1520kg
Date tested	4.8.93

Audi Coupe S2 ★★★ £30,495

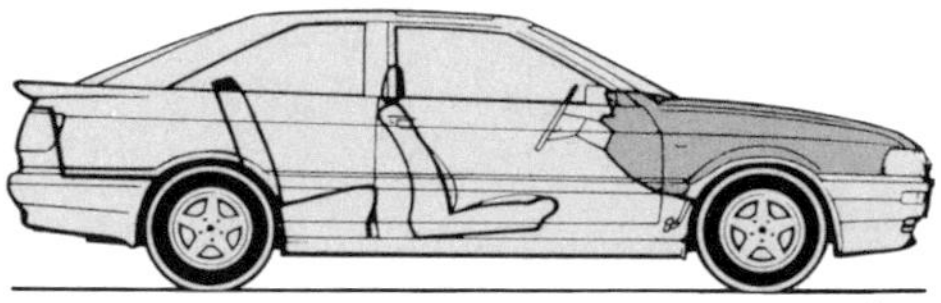

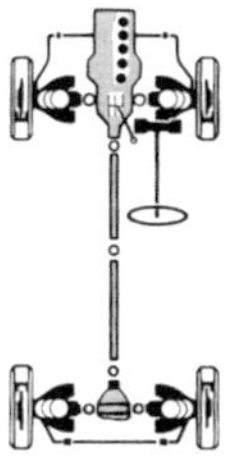

Length 4394mm **Width** 1727mm **Front track** 1448mm **Wheelbase** 2540mm **Height** 1372mm **Rear track** 1448mm **Weight distribution front/rear** 61/39

Following in the footsteps of the Quattro was never going to be an easy task and the S2, even with 230bhp, revised suspension and a new six-speed gearbox, only partially succeeds. It is quieter and more comfortable than the original but, despite secure handling and storming performance, somehow fails to inspire like its illustrious forebear. Sounds like a familiar story.

Capacity	2226cc
Power	230bhp/5900rpm
Torque	257lb ft/1950rpm
Max speed	148mph*
0-60mph	5.9secs*
30-70mph through gears	6.6secs*
Standing quarter mile	14.3secs*
30-50mph in fourth	5.6secs*
50-70mph in top	7.4secs*
Mpg overall/touring	18.2/25.6*
Mph/1000rpm in top	24.7*
Kerb weight	1475kg*
Date tested	29.4.91

* figures for 220bhp five-speed S2

Jaguar XJS 4.0 ★★★★ £33,600

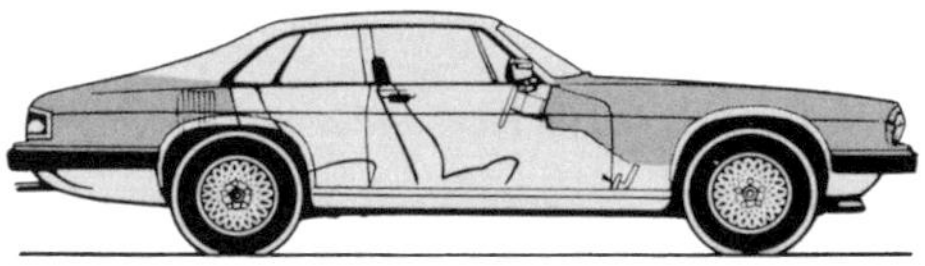

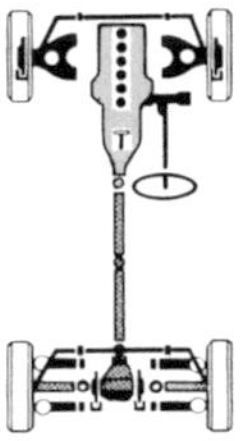

Length 4764mm **Width** 1793mm **Front track** 1489mm **Wheelbase** 2591mm **Height** 1247mm **Rear track** 1504mm **Weight distribution front/rear** 53/47

The XJS, despite recent updates to the styling, still drives a whole lot better than it looks. Straight-line performance isn't sensational, although there's no shortage of mid-range shove with the four-litre lump under that long bonnet. And you can still appreciate the smoothness, refinement and handling, along with the improved ambience within the still cramped cabin.

Capacity	3980cc
Power	223bhp/4750rpm
Torque	278lb ft/3650rpm
Max speed	136mph
0-60mph	8.7secs
30-70mph through gears	7.7secs
Standing quarter mile	16.7secs
30-50mph in kickdown	3.2secs
50-70mph in kickdown	4.5secs
Mpg overall/touring	18.8/24.6
Mph/1000rpm in top	29.1
Kerb weight	1612kg
Date tested	4.9.91

Nissan 300ZX ★★★★ £33,230

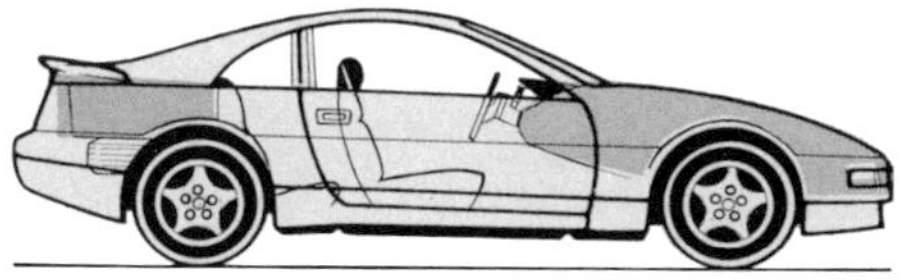

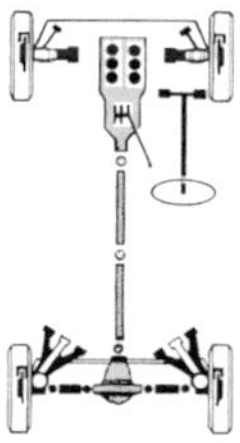

Length 4521mm **Width** 1803mm **Front track** 1499mm **Wheelbase** 2565mm **Height** 1245mm **Rear track** 1549mm **Weight distribution front/rear** 54/46

The first Japanese supercar truly to earn the title 'supercar', the 300ZX comes with stunningly butch styling and knockout power. Even with high-tech hardware such as computer-controlled four-wheel steer, it still feels like a back-to-basics street racer capable of lurid slides and slingshot acceleration. Cramped, noisy and thirsty but still fine value for money.

Capacity	2960cc
Power	280bhp/6400rpm
Torque	274lb ft/3650rpm
Max speed	155mph
0-60mph	5.6secs
30-70mph through gears	5.3secs
Standing quarter mile	14.4secs
30-50mph in fourth	5.6secs
50-70mph in top	7.8secs
Mpg overall/touring	17.0/23.0
Mph/1000rpm in top	25.7
Kerb weight	1580kg
Date tested	16.5.90

Porsche 968 ★★★★★ £36,722

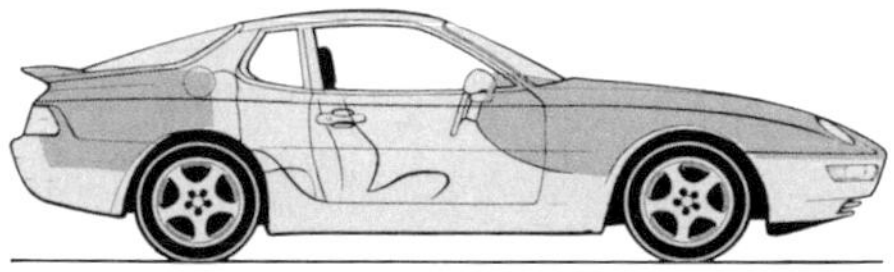

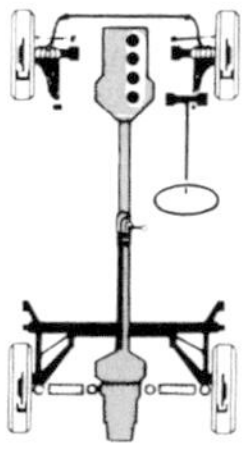

Length 4320mm **Width** 1735mm **Front track** 1472mm **Wheelbase** 2400mm **Height** 1275mm **Rear track** 1450mm **Weight distribution front/rear** 48/52

OUR CHOICE

Although it's really a thoroughly revised 944, the 968 is still an entirely convincing entry-level car for Porsche. Outstanding handling, brilliantly communicative steering and a three-litre four-cylinder engine that delivers punch exactly where it is needed are its main assets. A superb six-speed gearbox and surprisingly good fuel economy take care of the rest.

Capacity	2990cc
Power	240bhp/6200rpm
Torque	225lb ft/4100rpm
Max speed	153mph
0-60mph	6.1secs
30-70mph through gears	5.9secs
Standing quarter mile	14.7secs
30-50mph in fourth	5.7secs
50-70mph in top	8.9secs
Mpg overall/touring	23.5/24.3
Mph/1000rpm in top	24.6
Kerb weight	1420kg
Date tested	27.5.92

Renault A610 ★★★★ £29,950

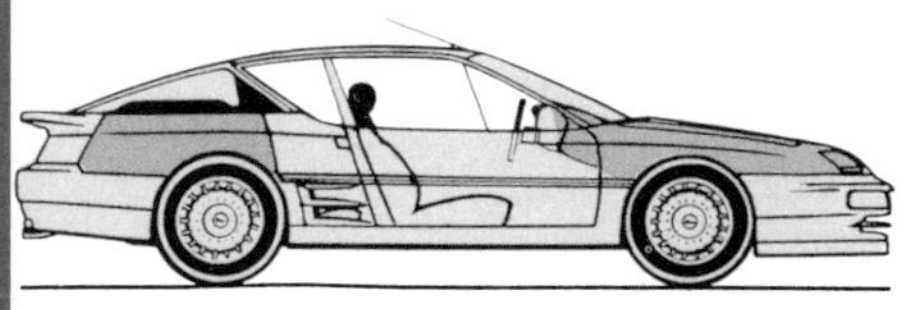

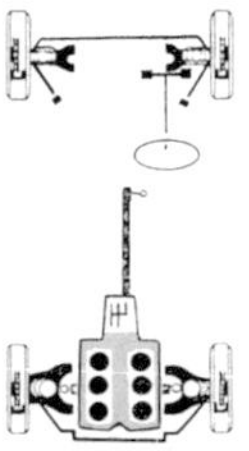

Length 4415mm **Width** 1762mm **Front track** 1504mm **Wheelbase** 2340mm **Height** 1188mm **Rear track** 1470mm **Weight distribution front/rear** 43/57

Renault has turned its GTA into a supercar and called it the A610. With meaty mid-range performance, distinctive looks and handling that proves once and for all that having an engine in the back can be fun *and* safe, it seems to be lacking little. Those looking for the inspirational steering responses of the GTA might be disappointed, but it's an interesting way to spend £30,000.

Capacity	2975cc
Power	250bhp/5750rpm
Torque	258lb ft/2900rpm
Max speed	159mph
0-60mph	5.8secs
30-70mph through gears	6.1secs
Standing quarter mile	14.7secs
30-50mph in fourth	5.8secs
50-70mph in top	6.8secs
Mpg overall/touring	20.6/24.4
Mph/1000rpm in top	27.3
Kerb weight	1380kg
Date tested	29.4.92

WORDS & PHOTOGRAPHY **IAN BROWN**

Flared wheel arches and big tyres make the new BMW M3 GTR look like a beast waiting to pounce. And with a 300bhp 3-litre V6 lurking under the bonnet that is exactly what it is...

Beauty of the beast

BMW's stunning new M3 GTR is a GT racer which is now available for use on the road. Brutally powerful and awesome in appearance, it is a real beast

One of the biggest attractions of the German Touring Car Championship is the way in which the manufacturers involved have taken their basic road-going models and given them outlandish wings, spoilers and wheelarches in order to be able to develop their racing versions. This has given rise to the crazy-looking Mercedes 190E 2.5 Evolution, a car closer in appearance to the Batmobile than the standard 190E – a staple tool of German taxi drivers.

This year, it is the turn of the new ADAC German GT Cup to spawn a radical road-going model: the BMW M3 GTR. This racer for the road is truly wild to look at, reminiscent of the BMW M1 which raced in the fabulous Procar series in 1979 and 1980.

I was given the opportunity to drive one of these beasts. And believe you me, that's the best way to describe the M3 GTR.

BMW press officer Friedbert Holz was my companion as we made our way out of the paddock at the Nurburgring, heading for the twisting undulations of the local public roads for our test run.

'We've built two of these cars for the road so far,' explained Herr Holz. 'This is one. The other is at our base in Munich. Today is the first time that it has been out on the public highway.'

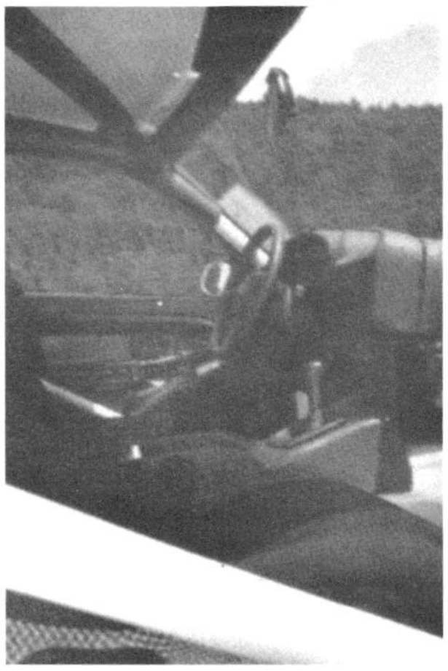

Above: M3 dashboard adds a touch of familiarity to the race car interior. Below: Boot space is reduced by the dry sump, but will still take a medium sized suitcase

The road-going M3 GTR looks and sounds just like the racing version, with flared wheelarches covering the 245/40 ZR18 tyres on 9x18in rims at the front and 285/35 ZR18 tyres on 10.5x18in rims on the rear, giving the M3 GTR a thoroughly aggressive stance.

The interior sports a full roll cage which makes it a two-seater only... The dashboard is like that on the standard M3, giving the car an unexpected air of familiarity.

The M3 GTR runs with a dry sump, which infringes on the boot space, although you can still fit a medium sized suitcase in there.

Weighing in at 1300kg and sporting a silky 3-litre V6 engine which boasts just short of 300bhp, plus a massive 320lb/ft of torque at 3600rpm, the stopping power had to be good. And it doesn't disappoint. The ABS brakes are truly impressive. Indeed, so much so that the phrase used by Herr Holz as he hauled the car down from a great velocity into the first corner we came to is not printable.

It was then that everything started to get a great deal faster. Herr Holz proceeded to dazzle me with the pure overtaking power of the car. The delight of seeing me being pushed back into my seat seemed to encourage him even more. What with the mighty brakes, I couldn't really blame him.

After this stunning example of the M3 GTR's abilities, I took over at the wheel and found immediately that the M3 GTR was a pure delight to drive. For starters, the clutch wasn't as heavy as I had expected. So in no time at all I started to feel at ease with the car.

Indeed, the ABS was one of the most impressive features of this superb road racer. The brakes imbue you with so much confidence that you seldom even consider the outrageous velocities from which you are trying to slow. You simply press the pedal and the brakes do the rest.

The gearbox was wonderfully smooth, as you would expect from a BMW, but you did tend to look for a sixth gear at around 120mph.

The handling is neutral, but nervous, something that is always in the back of your mind. There is a twitchiness that feeds back through the steering wheel in a manner not unlike that in early Porsche 911s – just to let you know that you have a sizeable power-to-weight ratio. Be committed, though, and the M3 GTR rewards, many times over.

To have a car that turns heads in Germany – the land of factory specials and wild customer conversions – it really has to be something special. Yet the M3 GTR turns heads like few others.

Costing roughly £100,000, you'd have to ask yourself whether you would pay that kind of money for a car that can only be serviced by BMW Motorsport in Munich? Well, yes, I certainly would... if I had that kind of money. ■

BMW M3

BMW introduces its "sports car for the Nineties," designed to be easy on the driver but merciless on the winding road

BY PETER EGAN
PHOTOS BY GUY SPANGENBERG

A SPORTS CAR for the Nineties? Purists may wince. How can a car that carries four people comfortably and has an excellent sound system, air conditioning and electrically operated windows be a sports car? What about the old "contains nothing that doesn't make the car go faster" ethic? Aren't sports cars supposed to be just a little harsh and difficult?

No, sayeth the engineers at BMW, they are not. With proper refinement, even a reasonably plush 4-place sports coupe can carry two (or four) people over a winding road about as fast as a car should go, with proper respect to the natives and stationary roadside objects. If a car is competent beyond all expectation, why should you suffer?

A good question. And one this car answers surprisingly well.

Previous M3s, built between 1988 and 1991, followed the old sports-car recipe a little more religiously. They were somewhat stiff and peaky, as sports coupes go, and featured arrest-me wings, dams and bodywork that left the observant police officer in no doubt as to their intentions. Suitably modified, they also won more than 150 racing and rally championships worldwide, making them the most successful competition touring cars ever built. They had an edge to them.

With the new M3, BMW has backed away from the boy-racer tradition just a bit, forging a broader sword, but a very effective one nonetheless. They have sought to build a good daily driver that is still satisfying for those who prefer to motor around wide awake, pupils occasionally dilated and a healthy dose of adrenaline surging through their veins.

Based on a 325is platform, the new M3 is extensively beefed-up, with reinforced underbody sheet metal, stronger drivetrain mounting points and spring perches, upgraded suspension, better tires and wheels, M5 brakes, variable-ratio steering that is quicker off-center and a heavy-duty ZF 5-speed manual transmission.

The 3.0-liter, 24-valve, dohc inline-6 is essentially a bored and stroked version of the 2.5-liter engine found in the 325is, hot-rodded for more power and torque. Mid-to-low-end torque is improved primarily by the larger displacement—with a 2-mm stretch in bore and a 10.8-mm lengthening of stroke. A horsepower increase at the top end comes from (among other things) a ported and polished cylinder head, more aggressive camshafts, heavy-duty valve springs and a freer-flowing exhaust system.

BMW uses the VANOS (*Variable Nockenwellen Steuerung*) cam timing system, which means Variable Camshaft Control, to get both a smooth idle and good power at high revs. This is an electrohydraulic system in which electronic sensors use oil pressure to shift cam timing. The cams operate four valves per cylinder through hydraulic lifters, which require no periodic servicing.

The result of these modifications is a substantial increase in horsepower and torque over a broad range, and a considerable improvement on the standard 325is engine: an output of 240 bhp at 6000 rpm, versus 189 at 5900, and 225 lb.-ft. of torque at 4250 rpm, compared with 184 at 4200.

Naturally, the suspension has had a going-over as well, with larger, stiffer springs, added damping on the reinforced gas-charged struts, larger anti-roll bars and reinforced control arms, front and rear. Suspension changes also lower the ride height 1.2 in.

Outward signs of high performance, as mentioned, are somewhat more subdued than they were on the M3's predecessors. The M-car is treated to a

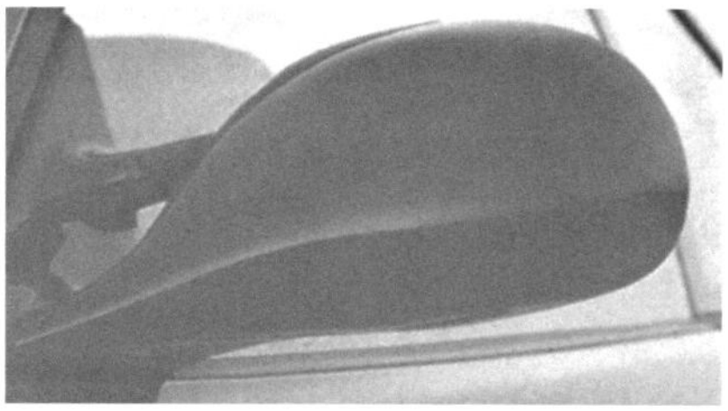

■ **The M3's 240-bhp heart, packaged in BMW's simple style.**

body-colored front air dam, a rear apron with an air diffuser to reduce body lift, and sculpted side mirrors. There are also discreet M3 badges on the door trim and sills. For those who want a little more show (as well as presumably enhanced high-speed aerodynamics), there is an optional rear spoiler. A sunroof is also available.

On this new M3, easy identification by police is achieved or negated mainly by color. The buyer may choose between flamboyant ("Hey, you with the radar gun!") Mugello Red and Dakar Yellow, or go for a stealthier effect with handsome shades of white, blue or black. There is also a Daytona Violet that this writer found both interesting and attractive, though it was not to everyone's liking at the press launch.

So. We have a nice-looking car with a good pedigree, horsepower, torque, good brakes and a developed chassis. But what about the harmony among these elements? How does it all work?

Nicely.

Out on the road, the M3 performs that rare trick of translating an impressive spec sheet into a car that is equally impressive to drive. A genuine pleasure, in fact.

First, the engine. There are few configurations nicer on the ears (or the motor mounts) than a smooth, free-revving inline-6, and the M3's 24-valver upholds this tradition in fine form. It winds up to its 7000-rpm redline with one of the most euphonious snarls this side of the Mulsanne Straight, all with a minimum of vibration and mechanical discord. Running it to redline is fulfilling but not mandatory. The engine has torque—and horsepower—everywhere.

You can duff along at 2500 rpm in 5th, from which engine speed it will pull like a truck, or downshift into any upper rpm register for snappy, instantaneous throttle response and a hard, scintillating zoom around slower traffic. The flexibility is amazing. This may be the first engine of the M-series that can be left in 4th gear and driven almost like an automatic transmission in Drive. It has a muscular bottom end, with increasing thrust all the way to redline. This is an inline-6 at its real-world best.

One of our staff found that top-end rush just a bit disappointing and said it made him nostalgic for the "peaky and nutty" performance of the old 4-cylinder M3. The six is certainly not as manic as the old four, but it is more effective under a wider variety of driving conditions.

BMW claims to have tuned this engine for the U.S. market, losing a bit of flat-out *Autobahn*-running horsepower at the top end, compared with the European version. The goal was to produce a car with the emphasis on 0–70 mph–0 performance, where most of us drive most of the time. The U.S. version has plenty of reserve speed at the top end, to be sure, but handles that U.S. speed range with either nonchalance or tightly wound alacrity, depending upon the driver's mood and right foot. With a 0–60 time of 6 seconds flat and a 14.6-sec. quarter mile at 96 mph, it's quicker and faster than the Mustang Cobra and the Pontiac Firebird Formula we tested in June 1994, and finds itself in about the same performance category as a Nissan 300ZX Turbo.

As to its 70–0 capability, BMW engineers pointed out that the M3 would have won R&T's recent 0–100 mph–0 comparison in the 100–0 mode, outbraking all the cars we ran in that test. The big 315-mm (12.4-in.) vented M5 discs and large calipers are superb on the road. They haul the car down with stable, drama-free ease and excellent feedback through the pedal. The

Teves ABS system allows almost race-car-quality threshold braking before it takes over (discreetly) and saves you from disaster. BMW, in fact, has reprogrammed the wheel-locking logic of the M3's anti-lock system to allow higher braking loads before the system kicks in.

Brakes, of course, work through four rubber contact patches, which, in this case, are not insubstantial. The M3 has wide 17 x 7 ½-in. cast-alloy wheels from BMW Motorsport, with very low profile Michelin 235/40ZR-17 MXX3 radials. Ride is firm, but remarkably unharsh, considering the tire sidewalls are about as tall as a coat of paint. The suspension has excellent compliance with minimal body roll and balanced handling with just a user-friendly touch of understeer. (Unless you badly overcook it on your first lap at Lime Rock in the rain, as I did, and slide it backward into a tire wall. Even sound engineering can't counteract the double whammy of hubris and brain fade.)

BMW introduced this car with a two-day drive from its New Jersey headquarters, through potholed city streets, over freeways, deep into the Berkshires and around the circuit at Lime Rock, Connecticut: every kind of road surface and driving. The M3 makes an excellent Interstate cruiser (even though you'd kill for a good high-speed *Autobahn*), humming along at a relaxed 3000 rpm at 70 mph, less than halfway to redline. In-town driving, too, is effortless and uncompromised by low air dams or any other sporting appurtenances, as long as you avoid the really deep potholes with those low-profile tires and expensive alloy wheels.

But where the M3 is happiest and most adept, of course, is on roads like those found in our up-and-downhill chase through the farm and horse country of the Hudson River Valley and lower New England. Always balanced, settled and connected to the road, the M3 is a predictable, easy car to drive fast. You can push it hard and play tunes on the gearbox, or choose not to. Its dual personality allows you to drive it as a comfortable, torquey sedan, or to dip into reserves of revs, power and roadholding for a scorching run up the road. There's no real downside, no price to be paid for its performance.

■ **A no-cost option on the M3 is leather, which replaces fabric splashed with Motorsport colors.**

The same may be said—generally—of its ergonomics. The M3 is easy to climb in and out of, and has firm but comfortable 12-way adjustable seats in leather or designer fabric. You can vary thigh support and slide the entire headrest/shoulder bolster section up or down. For all this adjustability, the seats seem to require a lot of fiddling to produce the exact setting you want—and don't always find. Also, the multiple adjustment levers are somewhat confusing, and it's easy to grab the wrong one.

Rear seats will accommodate a 6-ft. 1-in. passenger (just), with adequate leg room. Controls and instruments are generally straightforward and simple, though the climate-control system can take a lengthy jaw-dropped stare to master. Or, God forbid, a quick read of the owner's manual. Outward vision for the driver is excellent.

Rear seats fold forward in 50/50 configuration for more length in what is already a long, reasonably deep trunk with low liftover. Beneath the floor panel of the trunk is a full-sized spare mounted on a cast-alloy wheel to match the other four. Fit and finish throughout our test car were tasteful and flawless. The engine compartment, especially, is clean and nicely laid out; lines are neatly routed, dipstick and fluid fillers are easy to find, and that long, tilted inline-6 looks quite elegant with its curved plastic intake runners and "BMW M Power" cam cover.

Did I say there was no price to pay for the refinement and performance?

There is a price, of course. It will cost you $35,800 (suggested retail) to get one out of the dealer's showroom. A fair piece of change, but (I'm sorry to say) it doesn't sound all that high any more, given the escalation in price of nearly any car that can compete with the M3 in performance or quality. Or, indeed, compared with the astronomical prices of BMW's own upper-level 8-Series cars and their ilk.

As its competition, BMW sees such cars as the Toyota Supra, Ford's SVT cars, the Nissan 300ZX and the Mazda RX-7. Curiously, the M3 may be set to create its own broad swath of demographic appeal, cutting across the sports-car, sports-coupe and sedan markets with a well-rounded performance car that steals equal amounts of thunder from nearly all these more closely defined niches. The M3 is a formidable piece of work that will give a lot of buyers something new and pleasantly troubling to contemplate.

1995 BMW M3

PRICE

List price **$35,800**
Price as tested **$38,430**

Price as tested includes std equip. (dual airbags, ABS, air cond, limited-slip diff, leather int, AM/FM stereo/cassette; power windows, mirrors, central locking), pwr sunroof ($1120), cruise control & foglights ($455), luxury tax ($585), dest charge ($470).

0–60 mph .... 6.0 sec
0–¼ mi .... 14.6 sec
Top speed .... est 137 mph*
0–100 mph–0 .... 20.4 sec
Skidpad 0.87g
Slalom .... 62.8 mph
Brake rating .... excellent

IMPORTER

BMW of North America, Inc.
300 Chestnut Ridge Rd.
Woodcliff Lake, New Jersey 07675

TEST CONDITIONS

Temperature .... 85° F
Wind .... calm
Humidity 70%

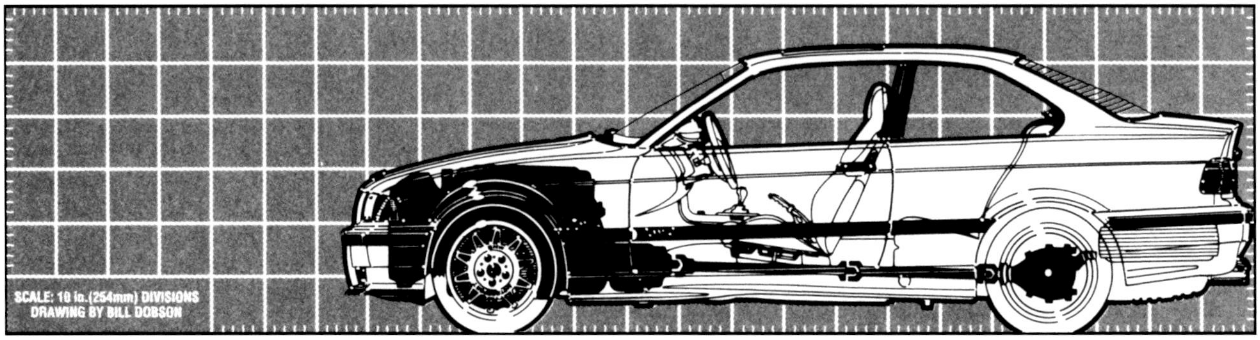

ENGINE

Type .... iron block, aluminum head, **inline-6**
Valvetrain .... dohc 4 valve/cyl
Displacement .... 182 cu in./2990 cc
Bore x stroke .... 3.39 x 3.38 in./86.0 x 85.8 mm
Compression ratio 10.5:1
Horsepower (SAE) .... **240 bhp @ 6000 rpm**
Bhp/liter 80.3
Torque .... **225 lb-ft @ 4250 rpm**
Maximum engine speed: 6800 rpm in 1st and 2nd, 6500 rpm in 3rd and 4th
Fuel injection: dual Bosch HFM-Motronic
Fuel .... prem unleaded, 91 pump oct

CHASSIS & BODY

Layout .... **front engine/rear drive**
Body/frame .... unit steel
Brakes
Front .... **12.4-in. vented discs**
Rear .... **12.3-in. vented discs**
Assist type .... vacuum; ABS
Total swept area .... 491 sq in.
Swept area/ton .... 295 sq in.
Wheels .... cast alloy, **17 x 7½J**
Tires .... Michelin Pilot SX MXX3; **235/40ZR-17**
Steering .... **rack & pinion,** power assist
Overall ratio 15.4:1–19.8:1
Turns, lock to lock 3.0
Turning circle .... 38.0 ft
Suspension
Front .... **MacPherson struts, double-pivot lower arms,** coil springs, tube shocks, anti-roll bar
Rear .... **multilink,** coil springs, tube shocks, anti-roll bar

DRIVETRAIN

Transmission .... **5-sp manual**

Gear	Ratio	Overall ratio	(Rpm) Mph
1st	4.20:1	13.23:1	(6800) 36
2nd	2.49:1	7.84:1	(6800) 60
3rd	1.66:1	5.23:1	(6500) 86
4th	1.24:1	3.91:1	(6500) 115
5th	1.00:1	3.15:1	est (6230) 137*

Final drive ratio 3.15:1
Engine rpm @ 60 mph in 5th 2725
*Electronically limited.

GENERAL DATA

Curb weight .... **est 3180 lb**
Test weight .... est 3335 lb
Weight dist (with driver), f/r, % 50/50
Wheelbase .... 106.3 in.
Track, f/r .... 56.0 in./56.9 in.
Length .... **174.5 in.**
Width .... **67.3 in.**
Height .... **52.6 in.**
Ground clearance .... 3.5 in.
Trunk space .... 14.5 + 6.0 cu ft

MAINTENANCE

Oil/filter change ... 7500 mi/7500 mi
Tuneup .... 30,000 mi/use-dependent
Basic warranty ..... 48 mo/50,000 mi

ACCOMMODATIONS

Seating capacity **4**
Head room, f/r ..... 38.0 in./34.0 in.
Seat width, f/r ... 2 x 19.0 in./52.5 in.
Front-seat leg room .... 43.5 in.
Rear-seat knee room .... 23.5 in.
Seatback adjustment .... 75 deg
Seat travel .... 7.5 in.

INTERIOR NOISE

Idle in neutral .... 44 dBA
Maximum in 1st gear .... 75 dBA
Constant 50 mph .... 63 dBA
70 mph .... 67 dBA

INSTRUMENTATION

160-mph speedometer, 8000-rpm tach, coolant temp, fuel level

Test Notes...

■ Through the slalom, the M3 reacts to quick left and right twists of the steering wheel with a flat stance, high grip and great precision. Still, it was hard to find a satisfying groove.

■ With 51 more bhp than the 325i, and the same snickety shifter, the M3 accelerates to 60 mph 1.4 seconds quicker. The straight-6 is extremely responsive, with great torque, but could use more peakiness.

■ With tall 17-in. wheels and short, stiff 40-series tire sidewalls, the M3 nevertheless rides reasonably well. Inside, the seats are highly adjustable, but it's difficult to find a comfortable position.

ACCELERATION

Time to speed	Seconds
0–30 mph	2.2
0–40 mph	3.4
0–50 mph	4.7
0–60 mph	6.0
0–70 mph	8.3
0–80 mph	10.3
0–90 mph	13.0
0–100 mph	16.0

Time to distance
0–100 ft 3.1
0–500 ft 8.0
0–1320 ft (¼ mi): 14.6 @ 96.0 mph
0–100 mph–0 .... 20.4 sec

FUEL ECONOMY

Normal driving .... 24.6 mpg
EPA city/highway .... 19/27 mpg
Cruise range .... 398 miles
Fuel capacity .... 17.2 gal.

BRAKING

Minimum stopping distance
From 60 mph .... 120 ft
From 80 mph .... 217 ft
Control .... excellent
Pedal effort for 0.5g stop ...... 14 lb
Fade, effort after six 0.5g stops from 60 mph .... 16 lb
Brake feel .... excellent
Overall brake rating .... excellent

HANDLING

Lateral accel (200-ft skidpad) ... 0.87g
Balance .... mild understeer
Speed thru 700-ft slalom ... 62.8 mph
Balance .... mild understeer
Lateral seat support .... excellent

Subjective ratings consist of excellent, very good, good, average, poor; na means information is not available.

BMW M318iS

PRICE	
£19,500 in Germany	
ENGINE	
16-valve 1.8-litre four, 140bhp	
PERFORMANCE	
133mph, 9.9sec 0-60	
DUE IN BRITAIN	
Import not planned	

BMW is selling this car to make its spoilers race-legal. But under the drastic plastic, the thing's a sham, says GEORG KACHER

THIS IS THE VERY OPPOSITE of a Q-car. Show rather than go. It's a homologation special created to improve the competitiveness of the 3-series saloon in European touring car racing, but very little of real substance matches its dramatic steroidal bodywork.

The add-ons comprise an M3-style front bumper, an additional blacked out air-intake, auxiliary driving lamps and a rubber lip designed to smooth the airflow. At the rear there is an ugly but effective double-decker tail spoiler which reduces aerodynamic lift, making the car more stable at racetrack speeds. Other drag-cutting body mods include a redesigned rear bumper-cum-air-deflector and a set of boldly sculpted sill extensions, while 'Motorsport International' badges on the rubbing strips and garish five-spoke alloys round off the boy-racer theme.

Stowed in the boot of each M318iS there is a plastic bag stuffed with rubber profiles, spacers, screws, nuts and bolts whose purpose is to convert the car's body to full race spec.

So adorned, the M318iS can hardly be described as pretty, and the story is much the same inside: a three-spoked sports steering wheel with airbag and flamboyantly trimmed bucket seats with adjustable thigh bolsters echo the elaborate wingwork. The price? Germans will be asked to fork out the equivalent of £19,500 – roughly halfway between the 150bhp 320i and the 192bhp 325i. In Britain, it won't be sold at all, because flash Germans have spoken for almost the entire run in advance.

While the familiar 320i and 325i offer the refinement as well as the extra power and torque of a six-cylinder engine, the M318iS makes do with a less cultured four. Available for the first time in a 3-series saloon (it's fitted to the mainstream 318iS coupé) this 16-valve 1.8-litre develops 140bhp at 6000rpm and 127lb ft at 4500rpm. It will readily spin to its 6250rpm red line and its throttle response is razor-sharp, but you never forget that it is not a six. Furthermore, the torque supply is ragged, and noise levels above 4000rpm decidedly unpleasant. It uses about 10 percent less fuel than the 2.0-litre six, however.

Mated to a slick five-speed gearbox, it propels the M318iS from rest to 60mph in 9.9sec, and on to 133mph. It is thus only slightly slower than the 320i saloon, and every bit as quick as the 318iS coupé – although the wider tyres feel as if they're hampering things above 100mph. The same seat-of-the-pants sensor also tells you that the fat rubber – in conjunction with M Technic suspension, tauter springs and dampers, and firmer bushings – allows quantifiably higher cornering speeds than the more sober 3-series models can muster: the M318iS feels unstickable.

Wonderful fluency and utterly failsafe on-the-limit behaviour are the keys to the M318iS's appeal. The qualities of the chassis are ably complemented by four powerful disc brakes, by the light and informative steering, by an ultra-fast clutch and by a close-ratio five-speed gearbox. Despite these qualities, however, the M318iS is too much racer and not enough all-rounder. The bodywork tweaks – though eye-catching – are worthless at legal road speeds, the stiffer suspension and wider tyres impair ride quality and cause tramlining under braking, and the rather steep price tag prevents this car from being a poor man's M3.

So Britons needn't fret that it isn't coming here. Better to go for an ordinary 320i with the optional M Technic sports suspension. It's cheaper to buy, more practical and more sensible. Most important, it's just as good to drive, and won't attract the cops and robbers.

PHOTOGRAPHS BY RICHARD NEWTON

Garish looks shroud normal innards: the M318iS is all dressed up with nowhere to go. Boot contains more DIY boy-racer bits, with instructions for fitment

The M3 Convertible retains its elegance of line even with the top-up

The possiblity of wind-in-the-hair motoring at 150mph for four people

PHOTOS: LAURIE CADDELL

M3 OPENS UP

The stunning M3's appeal has been widened now that it's available as a Convertible. This is its first ever road test

As understatements go, the current M3 must come quite high on the list. Sure, it looks different from its more run-of-the-the-mill brothers, with its standard-fit body kit, but you need to be paying attention to spot the huge, 17-inch alloys and the rubber-band 40-section Michelins. The same goes for the streamlined door mirrors and other subtle additions to the 3-Series plot.

The old and much-loved M3, from the ground up, somehow quietly made its massively effective sporting purpose clear. Yet the current model is comfortably the faster, knocking nearly two seconds off the 0–60mph time and adding more than 20mph to the top speed.

What BMW did with the 'new' M3 was to widen its appeal. For the moment, it is still two doors or nothing, but it no longer has that hint of race-track refugee about it which might deter the less committed enthusiasts among us.

Now, the Munich company has broadened that appeal still further by chopping the top off to make an M3 Convertible available for the first time. And the drop-head really does look the part. Based on the two-door Coupe, body, it has all the style, performance and practicality of its tin-top equivalents but adds that fresh-air factor that for many of us marks out a real sports car.

No special strengthening has been necessary for the M3 conversion. The latest 3-Series was designed from the start with a convertible variant in mind, so the extra stiffening that this entails could be added as a part of the package rather than an afterthought and, as the panel on page 46 reveals, there is plenty of rigidity to spare when it comes to upping the power level.

So what else marks the M3 Convertible out? From the outside, there is that handsome aerodynamic package comprising a front air dam and matching rear section, linked by sculpted side skirts. Air finds its eager way into the engine bay not just through the famous kidney grille, but via a distinctive lattice in the air dam, which also houses twin fog lamps.

Then there are the wheels, wider at rear (8.5in) than front (7.5in), but beautifully crafted in aluminium alloy in each case and shod with 235/40-ZR17 Michelin 'Pilot' tyres. Although the outside tyre diameter may be much the same as usual, the big wheels somehow contrive to give those smooth body contours a lower appearance.

Subtle 'M' badging appears on the flanks, the rear and the door sills and the smoothly curved electric door mirrors are located by twin aerodynamic struts.

Climbing into the leather driving seat (the full leather trim on the test car costs an extra £2460), you find extra clues to this convertible's motor sport heritage. Red and blue stitching on the sculpted steering wheel rim matches that on the gear knob and a subtle M3 logo on the instrument panel serves as a constant reminder to an attentive driver.

The white-on-black instrument

M POWER

The heart of the M-Power straight-six is its cast-iron block, with almost 'square' bore and stroke dimensions of 86mm and 85.8mm, respectively. The forged-steel counterweighted crankshaft has seven main bearings and is safe to a speed of 7280rpm, being linked to the lightweight oil-cooled pistons by forged connecting rods.

3-litres, 286bhp and stylish with it

A special oil-damped two-mass flywheel helps to remove such vibration as there would otherwise be in such an engine.

The aluminium alloy cylinder head houses two chain-driven camshafts, which between them act directly on 24 valves. Careful shaping of the combustion chambers, as well as the inlet and exhaust tracts, has produced the utmost operating efficiency, which is further enhanced by the VAriable Camshaft Control (VACC).

Using information based on throttle position and engine speed, hydraulic pistons steplessly vary the timing of the inlet camshaft by as much as 21 degrees, for enhanced low-speed torque, improved fuel consumption and reduced cold-start emissions.

Bosch engine management and sequential multi-port fuel injection give precise ignition and mixture control, while knock sensors keep an eye on the grade of petrol in use (it should be 98-octane unleaded) to prevent pinking.

With a 10.8:1 compression ratio, all this adds up to a power output of 286bhp at 7000rpm and torque of 236lb ft at 3600rpm – impressive figures indeed.

Driving at speed with the top and windows down is bluster free, for the front passengers at least

Subtle M3 badging on exquisite alloy wheels

display is neat, clear and very useful, the Convertible adding an oil-temperature gauge to the usual M3 package of water, fuel, speed and rpm dials. The wheel itself is a masterpiece of packaging, incorporating an airbag in a hub little bigger than normal.

Those sports seats are unique to the M3 Convertible. They are comfortable, and with multi-way adjustment combined with an adjustable steering column you can soon find a driving position that really suits you. Turn the key and you will quickly find out why BMW is renowned for its straight-six engines.

The old M3 was cherished for its all-round performance, but BMW had opted to base that superb sporting power plant on a four-cylinder block, which produced race-winning power in a free-revving format. Now, an extra pair of cylinders has brought smooth refinement to the party, with an impressively flat torque curve running from somewhere just above tickover up into the heady realms above 6000rpm.

Variable valve timing undoubtedly contributes greatly to this flexibility, as it does to economy, which averages out at an enviable 28mpg, with the hood up. They say that there is no substitute for cubic inches and the current M3 has quite a few of those, with a capacity of 2990cc.

Even with a catalytic converter, this elegantly engineered twin-cam six, turns out the horses, 286bhp, to be precise, and does so in a deceptively relaxed style. Six-speed gearboxes are becoming popular for top-performing machinery, and you might expect the M3 to have one, but we quickly found out why BMW thought otherwise.

With the superb feel and sound of this power unit at speed, there is every temptation to keep the tacho needle wound well round its dial, but there really is no need. That torque curve does not lie. Floor the loud pedal at indecently low revs, even in top, and the M3 will simply power forcefully away with absolutely no fuss. And there is none of the sudden surge that you get from other less well bred engines when they finally get 'on cam'.

So that sixth slot would be redundant, simply making more work for the driver. The five that are there, however, work fine, letting you know when you have the lever properly in place, without ever feeling notchy or obstructive.

The fuss-free temperament continues throughout the transmission. Now that the old Sierra has departed this earth, the 3-Series remains the sole bearer of the small, rear-drive saloon standard. And thank goodness that BMW has remained committed.

In the Convertible, power reaches the road through a limited-slip differential, set to cope with those few moments when the mighty rubber rings would have to give best to the engine's prodigious torque. People brought up on front drive often believe that to put the power to the other end is a recipe for cornering disaster, but with the Bee-Em, at least, this could not be less true.

Retaining the standard 3-Series suspension arrangement of front struts and a multi-link independent rear layout, the M3 is upgraded to match its sporting purpose. The spring and damper rates are increased, the longitudinal rear control arms are reinforced, the rubber mountings are extra stiff and special heavy-duty rear wheel bearings come from the BMW flagship 850i. The car sits lower than usual and

Performance

0-30mph	2.2secs
0-40mph	3.4secs
0-50mph	4.4secs
0-60mph	5.7secs
0-70mph	7.3secs
0-80mph	9.3secs
0-90mph	11.5secs
0-100mph	13.9secs
Standing-start quarter mile	14.5secs/102mph
Fuel consumption Government figures	56mph: 43.5mpg 75mph: 35.8mpg Urban: 21.7mpg
Overall on test	28mpg

Air-bag steering wheel and traditionally BMW neat and tidy dashboard

A deep nose spoiler radically alters the appearance of the 3 Series. It is less radical than its predecessor

anti-dive/anti-squat geometry is built in, which goes some way towards explaining the Convertible's great stability.

Handling balance is superb and the throttle can be used to adjust the drop-head's cornering attitude to a fine degree. If there is a tendency, it is towards understeer, but this car will not suddenly turn round and bite in an attack of terminal oversteer if you overstep the mark. Even a panic lift of the right foot will just have the back easing out, waiting for you to catch it with a gentle twitch of the wheel.

On the road, this translates into a phenomenally safe and sure device. Couple this with that wonderful power supply and a set of supremely powerful anti-lock brakes and you have one of the quickest means of cross-country transport that you could buy.

Not only is it quick, but you won't get shaken to pieces on the way. The ride quality is well sorted, particularly so given how little help can be coming from those ribbon-thin tyres. It is only when you brake hard on an indifferent surface, that they really make their presence felt, in the form of a distinct rumbling.

If there is a reservation about the ability of this chassis, it rests on the steering. BMW engineers have

CONVERSION COURSE

The shell of the latest 3-Series Convertible is around 30 per cent stiffer than that of the older car, something that has been achieved thanks to building the Convertible into the development programme from the start.

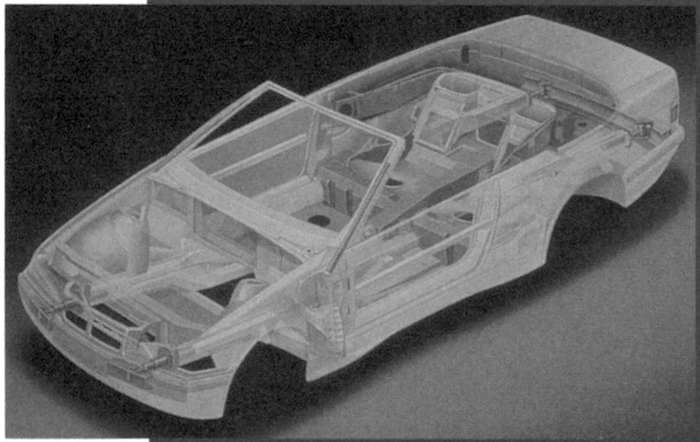

A ghost view of the Convertible's bodyshell showing how much metalwork lies beneath its skin

The areas in which stiffening has taken place to compensate for removal of the roof are numerous, but each makes its own contribution to the rigid whole. In choosing not to have a permanent roll-over bar, the engineers increased the challenge, but have compensated by adding reinforcement between the engine mountings, additional longitudinal support arms at the rear and wider door sills (although for ease of access the height of these has not been increased.

A cross-member sits beneath the rear seat, close to a further support arm running parallel to the propeller shaft. Even the wheel arches have been re-designed and the multi-piece rear bulkhead is all new, to accommodate the roll-over protection bars and the special rear seat belts.

The A-pillars are stronger than usual, the windscreen frame is stiffened and the glass bonded into place. The inner side panels, too, have additional reinforcement.

None of this is obvious to the casual observer, but other changes are. New rear side panels integrate with a longer-than-usual boot lid and, of course, the tonneau lid is unique to the Convertible.

Special damper weights, mounted on rubber cushions are known to absorb torsional vibrations, but BMW engineers, eager to avoid any extra weight penalty (the Convertible is 80kg heavier than the Coupe) have found a neat solution. They have mounted the battery on a special hydraulic base within the boot, where it provides the damping effect required.

The M3 Convertible contains all the standard reinforcement, such as a reinforced passenger cell and side-impact protection beams.

provided a sophisticated variable-ratio power-assisted rack-and-pinion set-up, which does its job well in giving about the right steering weight and gearing. Yet there is that slightly remote feel, which characterises plenty of other power systems and take just a dash of the fun out of the fare.

Convertibles are meant for driving with the top down – and we were lucky enough to have British weather that made this an attractive proposition. A power roof is standard, but our early car came with a manual version. Even that takes no more than a twist of the single catch and the small effort of opening and closing the rear tonneau to see the fabric stowed safely away. BMW have even thought about vandalism, in that the rear window is easy to replace and the cover itself comes readily away from the frame.

The electric side windows wind away to leave a proper open car, and we found it quite realistic to drive like this at speed without suffocating. If you are wondering why there is no roll-over bar, wonder no more: BMW has built in twin self-actuating roll-over supports. Located just behind the B-posts, these aluminium poles are sprung and locked in place as soon as one of various sensors establishes that the car might turn turtle. Capable of withstanding 3.5 tons, they give the peace of mind needed in an open car without permanently spoiling its appearance.

Like other BMW convertibles – and the 8-Series with its frameless side glasses – this one has windows that wind themselves down slightly as the door is opened, to prevent damage to glass or seals. A neat trick this, which is reflected in the cosy nature of the cabin when the top is in place.

It is only when the speed gets above the legal limit that you are really aware that there is only cloth above your head, and even then we found that we could still live with it. As for noise in *al fresco* mode, all you hear, apart from the rush of the wind, is that delightful six-cylinder howl from the twin exhausts.

Top up or down, the M3 Convertible is impressively rigid. At sensible speeds there is none of the steering wheel rattle, better known as scuttle shake, that accompanies less well planned conversions. It is only when you are really pressing on round corners that ask a great deal of tyres and chassis that you become aware of a slight movement. Even then, the car still does its duty.

Like its hard-top stablemates, the M3 Convertible is not over-generous with its rear legroom. Still, we found no complaints with the seats, and the sheer pleasure of fresh-air motoring makes any slight cramping worth putting up with, especially with the M3 able almost to pass through some kind of time-warp from A to B. ●

The strength of the body is evident when pressing on, and only severe bumps and high tyre loadings separate the Coupe from Convertible where the latter flexes minimally

IN SHORT

There is nothing to compare with the M3 Convertible. Other performance four-seaters don't open up and other four-seat drop-tops would be left for dead on the run up to the first bend.

For the real M3 aficionado, this car might not have the thoroughbred appeal of its predecessor. Yet this one offers cross-country abilities to take the breath away – and it comes with a soft top.

Who could fail to be stirred by that magnificent 3-litre straight-six, or wonder at the sheer grip, coupled with delicate poise, of that splendid rear-drive chassis? And just think, you can impress three of your friends with your new toy, all at the same time.

At £37,500, this is no weekend runabout, but its competence and its practicality put it up there in the rarefied atmosphere that goes with that price tag. Its build quality shines through: it feels solid throughout, it doesn't rattle, the panels all fit together perfectly and one glance under that gleaming bonnet will set any enthusiast's heart leaping.

For a car in this league, the extras list is unusually extensive, for instance leaving it to each owner to choose their own radio. But whatever the final figure on the invoice, that car in a couple of years will still be worth far more than its lesser rivals, whose values will have tumbled into oblivion.

Just don't compare it with its predecessor: they are completely different animals.

J.G. RUSSELL

Long-Term BMW M3

Fast, fluid, full of flair—but it could use the kryptonite wheel option.

BY MARTIN PADGETT JR.

It grabbed a spot on the Ten Best list. It won a recent comparison test with a near-perfect score. Most editors, given the chance, would adopt Jim Carrey as their personal savior in return for a stint behind the wheel. Need any more hints as to how we feel about the BMW M3?

Perhaps reliving the details of our long-term relationship with one might provide the final puzzle piece. In just 12 weeks, we'd used up half our allotted term, 17,500 miles, on the M3's odo. It ran a marathon from New York to Montana, shuttled weekenders to Toronto, and reeled off some 6000 miles circling the Canadian Maritime Provinces as if it were an integral part of the NORAD defense system.

By then our early impressions of the M3 were set in stone. The car has marvelous torque, tossable handling, and astounding brakes. It also has direct and faithful steering, despite the wide-load Michelin MXX3 40-series tires. The top gear is so flexible that when you hit "resume" on the cruise control, the M3 pulls strongly enough to tip your head back.

Some minor chinks in the near-flawless armor did reveal themselves, however. The M3's low-profile tires tend to jink on concrete pavement, and the engine clatters at idle on cold starts before the hydraulic tappets pump up. Still, the biggest problem was getting a reservation on our sign-out board, since most staffers attacked its slot like homesteaders headed for Oklahoma.

After we hit "engage" for the test track, the underbody shields promptly blew off at 120 mph. Yikes! We ordered replacements, but they would take a while to come.

BMW installs a self-determining service indicator in all its cars, and our yellow LEDs lit up and called for the first visit to the dealer at 9500 miles. Wary Larry Griffin hunted for a BMW shop on the fly

MARTIN PADGETT

Check out the mod accouterments: 6800-rpm redline, 240-hp in-line six, sport seats from God's own hot rod.

Rants and Raves

The seat side bolsters are so aggressive that they hang me from my admittedly wide hips. I feel arthritic after a couple hundred miles.
—Winfield

Great style—it brought out the kids from local hangouts in Toronto and caused a 54-year-old woman at the farmer's market to gaze with envy.
—Adam

This is a great car if you're late. At 100 mph, it's just hitting its stride.
—Schroeder

I was pleasantly surprised by the M3's ride quality. Call it the 'Potty Minder'—it only becomes uncomfortable with a really full bladder.
—Markus

The tires meander singlemindedly over pavement irregularities. I want one in silver, anyhow.
—Griffin

As energetic as this powerplant is, I can't say that I miss the slightly hotter Euro version, especially since it would have boosted the price by at least $10,000.
—Csere

This car changes your driving attitude. It makes you wait until the redline approaches to shift. It makes you concentrate. It forces you to enjoy yourself. Definitely not for control freaks. —Berg

and found Rice Motors and Marine of Billings, Montana. Within two hours, Rice had changed the oil and filter and adjusted the headlamps. The service cost $57.68. The mechanics forgot, however, to replace the rear-axle fluid, as recommended in the owner handbook. Also, at our request, they changed the transmission fluid, a $12 snake-oil cure for the fifth-gear whining we noticed.

The M3 returned not 100 miles later from an unlucky encounter with a pothole in Yellowstone National Park. "The impact was so horrible," Griffin wrote, "the emergency lights and flashers came on. Love those 40-series tires." And thus began our sole grievance with the M3: with its satiny but unfortunately malleable alloy wheels.

The M3 hobbled back to town, where a tire dealer put the car on the rack for a good eyeballing. Amazingly, the tires checked out fine. But the inboard edges of the right wheels were dented. A quick call to Rice saved the day. They had an M3 on the lot and graciously sold us and mounted a right-side pair of wheels for $1063.10. In the repair cost tally, by the way, we don't count damage caused by our accidents or other freak occurrences.

The M3 scooted onward and upward, at least by the odometer's reckoning. At 13,328 miles, the new front shroud arrived in Ann Arbor and was installed. Our owner warranty was voided in this case, BMW declared, since the four attaching bolts were still in place. Trash on the track or driver error could have caused the mishap, BMW claimed. Tester Markus protested this accusation and noted no detritus, but nonetheless we were out $178.85. (Since we would later repeat the exercise, we discounted BMW's explanation and included the charge in our repair costs.)

Our Bavarian-built fireball continued to blur the passing lane, bending two more expensive wheels in the process. Then tragedy struck. "I was on my way to work this morning, driving alongside a Pontiac Bonneville," Winfield wrote. "In mid-pass, there was a huge cracking sound, and the next thing I knew the dome light and flashers were on and the right-side mirror was hanging by its cable." The Bonny had kicked up a rock and pitched it neatly at the BMW's mirror.

Before a new mirror could be located, the computer called for another service, at 18,376 miles. This otherwise routine oil-and-filter swap carried with it a laundry list of inspections, from checking the brake lines and the brake pads to—holy Philip Morris, Batman—checking the lamp in the ashtray. The service technicians also adjusted the interior driver-side door handle, which had tightened up considerably. *Cha-ching,* $289.39.

The M3 begged for hard driving, and we administered it. BMW recommends against rotation, so we needed a new set of rear treads at 23,668 miles. We mounted a fresh pair of Michelin MXX3s, but didn't include the cost in the specs because the front tires had a projected life of 49,500 miles, for an average of 36,500.

Once again, the engine computer ordered a maintenance stop, this time at 27,821 miles. We were informed that both the left fog-lamp lens and the right fog lamp itself were cracked and needed to be

DICK KELLEY

MARTIN PADGETT

MARTIN PADGETT

Left: visiting Newt and friends. Right: Annapolis, the Paris of Maryland. Below: north of Helena, Montana, the Paris of, uh, never mind.

replaced. More seriously, the coolant-warning level tipped us off to a deteriorating water pump. The pump was covered by warranty, the oil-and-filter service cost $27.48, and the new outside mirror and fog lamps ran $604.36—again, an accident cost you won't see in the spec column. That's the price you pay for power mirrors and low-slung lighting.

A set of Bridgestone Winter Radial WT-05 tires kept our M3 on a true heading during the onset of winter. Squirmier and less grippy in the dry than the OE rubber, the heavy-duty shoes gave much-needed stability in crosswinds and on patchy ice.

Two incidents marred the M3's last days with us. You guessed it—we bent another wheel, for a total of five star-crossed rims. "And this car makes an *awful* noise when it hits," Schroeder moaned. This time, we didn't buy a new wheel—we instead sent it off to the Wheel Collision Center (see sidebar). We also lost another set of underbody shrouds in final testing, costing $161.97 to replace.

Bad luck with the alloys, mirror, and underbody shields notwithstanding, the M3 soldiered quickly and rather painlessly through 35,000 miles of decidedly enthusiastic driving. We did notice minor trim problems—a plastic seatbelt housing broke off, the dash sprouted a gap between its edge and the central fresh-air vent, and a slight whistle cropped up around the middle of the frameless driver-side window. But acceleration times and grip remained about the same, while braking improved a bit, to 160 feet.

JEFFREY G. RUSSELL

We've rarely been as mesmerized with a car as we have been with the M3. Its siren song—240 horsepower, graceful lines, and fluid handling—is sweet indeed. Never mind the cost of wheels and tires, where's the damn key? •

Vehicle type: front-engine, rear-wheel-drive, 5-passenger, 2-door sedan

Price as tested: $38,375 (base price: $36,642)

Engine type: DOHC 24-valve 6-in-line, iron block and aluminum head, Bosch engine-control system with port fuel injection

Displacement		182 cu in, 2990cc
Power (SAE net)		240 bhp @ 6000 rpm
Torque (SAE net)		225 lb-ft @ 4250 rpm
Transmission		5-speed
Wheelbase		106.3 in
Length		174.9 in
Curb weight		3232 lb
Performance:	**new**	**35,000 miles**
Zero to 60 mph	5.5 sec	5.5 sec
Zero to 100 mph	14.7 sec	14.5 sec
Zero to 130 mph	28.7 sec	29.4 sec
Street start, 5–60	6.2 sec	6.0 sec
Standing ¼-mile	14.2 sec @ 98 mph	14.2 sec @ 99 mph
Braking, 70–0 mph	162 ft	160 ft
Roadholding, 300-ft-dia skidpad	0.81 g	0.81 g
Top speed	137 mph	137 mph
EPA fuel economy, city driving		19 mpg
C/D observed fuel economy		24 mpg
Unscheduled oil additions		2 qt
Service and repair stops:		
Scheduled		3
Unscheduled		2
Operating costs (for 35,000 miles):		
Service		$375
Normal wear		$0
Repair		$353
Gasoline (@ $1.13 per gallon)		$1679
Life expectancies (extrapolated from 35,000-mile test):		
Tires		36,500 miles
Front brake pads		65,500 miles
Rear brake pads		72,500 miles

Don't Throw Away That Wounded Wheel

JEFFREY G. RUSSELL

At $441 each, the aluminum alloy wheels on our long-term BMW M3 cost more than the first cars of a couple of graybeard staffers around here. Worse, when combined with the thin sidewall of a 40-series tire, a Michigan pothole can prove fatal to these zooty wheels. We know—in seven months, potholes bent five of our M3's rims.

In the past, we'd be stuck for the price of new wheels. Now comes the Wheel Collision Center of Bath, Pennsylvania, a three-year-old company that says it can repair bent, cracked, gouged, or broken aluminum wheels. Since his patents are pending, company president Daryl Robbins wouldn't pass out the recipe for his process. But basically, Robbins said controlled heat is used to soften the wheel, and special machines then reshape it. The last step is to completely refinish the wheel.

We sent one of our wounded wheels, crunched at the outer top edge of the rim, to the Wheel Collision Center. The repaired wheel we received back looked as good as new. In addition, extensive testing at Lehigh University demonstrated that the strength and shape of a wheel repaired by Robbins's company equaled the original's.

Repair costs vary, though $100 to $150 per wheel appears to be in the ballpark. Ours set us back $138.25. The telephone number is 800–292–RIMS.

—*Larry Webster*

FIRST DRIVE

PHOTO BY GUY SPANGENBERG

"WE SHOULDN'T HAVE any problem getting arrested in that," photographer Guy Spangenberg said as I drove BMW's new M3 Lightweight into his driveway. An understandable reaction, considering the car's appearance: Its ground-licking front air dam, dynamic rear wing, flashy 17-in. alloy wheels and alpine white paint scheme with red/blue/purple checkers at the front and rear corners of the car turn heads on public roads like a swimsuit model in a penitentiary. But according to BMW officials, the M3 Lightweight's *raison d'être* is to race.

"Basically, the Lightweight was made in response to those who wanted to race the M3. Now, instead of tearing everything out (of the car), one can buy a car that's already partly prepared to run in an SCCA or IMSA event," Rob Mitchell, public relations manager of BMW of North America, said.

As the name implies, the M3 Lightweight is an M3 without the fat. BMW slashed roughly 200 lb. off the curb weight by deleting the air conditioning, stereo, sunroof, noise-reduction mats, tool kit, trunk lining, spare tire and even the jack. BMW also replaced the M3's doors with lighter aluminum ones. The result is a 50-state street-legal rocket that's a breath away from being show-

BMW M3 Lightweight

An M3 for those serious about competition

BY SAM MITANI

room-stock ready.

The output of the smooth-revving dohc inline-6 remains unchanged, producing 240 bhp at 6000 rpm and 225 lb.-ft. of torque at 4250, but the absence of sound deadening makes the growl of this wonderfully flexible 3.0-liter louder than ever.

Throw the shifter into 1st, stomp on the throttle and the Lightweight leaps into motion like a pouncing wildcat. The M3's 5-speed manual gearbox is one of the best in the business; its well-defined gates and short throws allow for quick flick-of-the-wrist shifts. And the clutch/brake/throttle pedals are aligned for simple heel-and-toeing—just roll your right foot over the brake pedal to blip the throttle.

Where the standard M3 accelerated impressively, the Lightweight is a half-step quicker, thanks to the car's reduced weight and a revised 3.23:1 final drive (from the standard M3's 3.15:1). It ran from zero to 60 mph in just 5.8 seconds, two tenths faster than the standard M3 (see our Road Test, August 1994).

Complementing this improvement in straight-line performance is the Lightweight's better handling. Engineers at BMW's M-Brand division lowered the M3 by a quarter inch and incorporated stiffer springs to the car's already taut suspension—MacPherson struts up front and a multilink setup at rear. They also added a strut brace to increase torsional rigidity at the car's front end. The result? More stability through corners and better overall balance—only a slight touch of understeer is detectable when the car is pushed to its limits. Turn-in response is crisp, thanks in part to the razorlike precision of its rack-and-pinion steering. And body roll is reduced.

Impressive as its roadholding ability is, the Lightweight's suspension is still significantly undersprung for competitive racing. Why didn't BMW incorporate a stiffer setup? "Because," explains Bernie Gobmeier, M-Brand manager, "we wanted a car that was still usable on the street. Serious racers can customize their own Lightweights if they want to. We offer an aftermarket package that includes height-adjustable racing suspension, adjustable camber plates and cross-drilled brake rotors."

That explains the Lightweight's efficiency as a tourer. Ride quality is smooth, and the manually adjustable cloth-upholstered front seats are comfortable. After a multi-hour drive searching for photo locations, Spangenberg and I didn't feel the least bit tired.

However, we did notice a few problems when driving in traffic. The Lightweight's enormous rear wing blocks about 75 percent of the rear view. But perhaps most distressing of all was that every passing police officer seemed to greet us with a radar gun.

All things considered, the M3 Lightweight is for performance-car enthusiasts of every order...including image-hungry ones. The bad news is that not everyone can own one. BMW is importing only 85 Lightweights and selling them for $47,900, about $12,000 more than a standard M3. Is it worth it? It all depends on how serious you are about competition—whether it's on a racetrack, on a winding road or at your 10-year class reunion.

THE BUSINESS!

BMW's new M3 saloon is brilliant. It's as simple as that, says **John Simister**

'Accelerate hard out of a damp corner and the tail will slide a little, a lot – or any amount in between. It's your decision'

ALL RIGHT, I WAS EDGY, I admit it. Torn, even. Casting doubt on the BMW 328i's dynamic invincibility (*CAR*, March) was always going to cut across the zeitgeist of the potent pleasure machine, and it was a sobering slice to make. But all is once again right with the world, perceptions are reassembled, reputations are reinstated. BMW hasn't lost it, and neither have I. For I have just finished driving the best BMW I have ever driven, and I wanted never to stop.

As it's an M3, you might not think this much of a revelation. But it's not quite that simple. As a two-door coupé, its original incarnation, the M3 does not quite gel. Great engine, stunning sound effects, magnificent pace, considerable grip, all these are in any current-series M3's repertoire. But they are not quite enough in themselves to provide the pure and perfect drive.

Blame the shortfall on the lack of steering precision that comes from trying to blend firm suspension and cosmetically right-on 40-profile tyres with a comfortable ride, a combination that calls for a lot of suspension compliance. So you never quite know where you are in a fast bend, especially when the need for knowledge is at its most pressing. The original, four-cylinder, raucous-racer M3 did not suffer this problem, and possessed a chassis of faithfulness, fluidity and endless entertainment. BMW has never shown the slightest public unease over this retrogression, citing the new M3 as a quite different and more grown-up driving experience (which it is), but it seemed deeply unsatisfactory to me.

Now you might not think that remixing the M3 cocktail in a four-door shaker would make much difference to the driving. But it does, because the cocktail's components have altered, albeit by no more than a taste. Softer springs and dampers have wrought a profound personality change. Petulant and secretive as a coupé, the M3 is athletic and open-hearted as a saloon. And those two extra doors are the perfect metaphor for its newfound accessibility.

Sceptical? So was I, at the start of our road to whatever passes for Damascus at the far end of the M6. Aim north, and moorwards. See if I could, at last, learn to love today's M3. The signs had proved promising over a weekend's pottering, the rear doors frequently flung open and pulled shut as this most potent of family cars ferried my offspring and her friends on short domestic hops that absolutely did not call for 286bhp. A snatch-free throttle action, something lacking in the first six-cylinder M3s, would be far more desirable in this habitat, and once the engine is warm the desire is satisfied.

And be the throttle blipped on the approach to a fast bend or outside the Brownies' hall or anywhere else, those enormous exhausts sound fantastic. They ooze potent purpose, as do wheels that nuzzle the very edges of their arches without quite bursting beyond the boundaries of rotary decorum. These five-spokers are different from those of coupé and convertible M3s, and have rims an inch wider at the back than at the front (although all four tyres are the same size). A deep front spoiler and skeletal door mirrors, the same as those of the Coupé apart from the absence of an aerodynamic splitter on the spoiler's lower edge, add further signals of intent. Otherwise, this 3-series saloon looks much like any other.

I'm thankful for this, and the sober dark blue paint, as we head up a damp, drizzly M1 (the road that gave its name to the first of BMW's M-cars). At 70mph the BMW is just bumbling, burbling along, ready to pour on an extra 20mph at the merest twitch of my right ankle.

Of course, six-cylinder M3s have been ever thus. This most wonderful of engines is related to the regular series of BMW six-pots, but has its own, freer-breathing variation on the 24-valve head theme and a larger (2990cc) cylinder capacity. A separate throttle valve for each cylinder gives a throttle response of electrifying crispness, while BMW's usual variable-valve-timing system makes for a torque plateau rather than a torque peak. Around 236lb ft is available all the way from 3600rpm to 5800rpm.

You can feel the valve timing varying as you accelerate through the rev range, because the intensity of the forward thrust alters in intensity with a definite stoking-up at the start of that plateau. There's enough muscle in this mid range to keep you flying without ever having to discover the fireworks further up the speed scale, but if you do venture into the stratosphere you'll find it hard to leave.

Let me give you a preview. At full stretch, the M3's motor delivers 286bhp at 7000rpm, accompanied by a granular, harmonic wail quite different from the silky blare of BMW's more sedate sixes, and rather more primal. Imagine a cross between the howl of a Porsche 911 and the

M3 saloon's cabin is unusually kitsch for a BMW. Leather seats are OK, but splashes of wood are incongruous in so purposeful a machine – albeit a very civilised one

BMW M3 SALOON

SPECIFICATIONS

Price	£33,100
Engine	2990cc 24-valve straight-six
Bore/stroke	86.0/85.8mm
Compression	10.8 to one
Power	286bhp at 7000rpm
Torque	236lb ft at 3600rpm
Specific power output	96bhp per litre
Power-to-weight ratio	186bhp per tonne
Transmission	Five-speed manual
Front suspension	MacPherson struts, coils, anti-roll bar
Rear suspension	Central Z-arm, semi-trailing links, coils, anti-roll bar
Brakes	Ventilated discs, ABS
Tyres	235/40 R17
Length/width/wheelbase	4433/1710/2700mm
Weight	1535kg
PERFORMANCE	
Max speed	156mph
Acceleration (sec)	
0-30	2.4
0-40	3.4
0-50	4.4
0-60	5.6
0-70	7.4
0-80	9.3
0-90	11.2
0-100	13.9
0-110	16.9
0-120	20.1
In third/fourth/fifth (sec)	
30-50	3.9/5.8/7.5
40-60	3.5/5.7/7.0
50-70	3.5/4.9/7.2
60-80	3.8/4.9/6.8
70-90	4.5/5.4/6.7
80-100	–/5.5/7.2
Fuel consumption	
Test	24.3mpg

Can you spot Bremner in the back (left)? Not likely: he's cowering, low down, as Simister goes into banzai mode ... again

Never again...

Gorgeous to drive, nauseous to sit in the back of

I'M THE BLOKE WHO WAS SUPPOSED TO ENJOY THIS. THAT'S WHAT I SAID before the ride. I like being driven fast if the driver isn't completely psycho, I like to hear an engine stretched, to savour the *g*-forces, to feel as if I'm strapped aboard a roller-coaster. And I enjoy trying to imagine what the car is doing, without actually sitting in the hot seat myself.

But when it came down to it, I didn't like it at all. The biggest problem is that you can't see out, because of the vision-blotting head restraints. You can look out of the side windows, of course, but twisting your neck while it's tensed up to withstand cornering loads is a good way to rick it. So you end up staring ahead. The result is rather like a blind roller-coaster ride – especially since your torso tends to flop about like a shrub in a gale, despite the bolstered backrest and a seatbelt.

It might have four doors, but the M3 is too fast and too grippy to be anything other than a sports car for one, if it's sport you want. Take a bunch of friends for a ride, and their protestations will soon overwhelm the straight-six's song. In a straight line, the M3 is comfy and very quick. But, like all its ilk, it's no fun for four.
Richard Bremner

blowy hum of a Mk3 Ford Zodiac (if you can). There are three main voices from the engine bay's choir stall, each an octave apart from the next, but it's the baritone exhaust note that dominates the soundscape.

Not that there's much opportunity for a 7000rpm symphony on the grey motorway. M1 gives way to M6, passing sad Fort Dunlop on Birmingham's outskirts, inhabited by pigeons now instead of tyre makers, and Sandbach services (one of the nastiest I have ever experienced) not much later. We stop at Forton services instead, and bolt down a Burger King. Stomachs sated, we resume our travel northward, and finally leave the functional, utilitarian motorway at the Kirkby Stephen exit in search of roads whose purpose might run to providing pleasure.

It's a wide, open road to begin with, and assaulted by fitful gusts of wind. The last 3-series I drove, the 328i coupé, proved unsteady in such conditions but this saloon-bodied M3 feels a lot more secure. It augurs well for the tighter terrain ahead, beginning at Brough with the B6276 across Lune Moor. Rock, crags and bleakness abound, and the ducking, diving road is all but empty.

Earlier in the day, the prospect of such a drive as now beckons seemed simultaneously to delight and to daunt. I remembered the launch of the M3 Coupé on tight, slippery Majorcan roads, where the dull steering and a tendency for sudden, unannounced slides put a dampener on the thrill potential. All that power was little more than a liability. But this M3 is different.

Very different. It takes a snaking section of

downhill dampness, culminating in a right-hand bend whose tightness I misjudge, to confirm my trust in the family-friendly M3. Those softer springs and dampers are the key, matching better the squidginess of the suspension bushings and the breakaway characteristics of those wide, wide Michelins (Pilot SX in marketing-speak, MXX3 in technical parlance). Put more simply, you can now tell what the car is about to do.

Actually, the communication is more two-way than that. Although still not especially sharp, the steering is smooth, well weighted and absolutely consistent. That's one benefit of the softer suspension, which soaks up cornering forces more readily without loading up the suspension arms' bushes so rapidly and corrupting the feedback. The other is that on real roads, as opposed to smooth racetracks, the tyres find it easier to hug the road surface because the wheels' movements aren't reined in as tightly.

Accelerate hard out of a damp corner and the tail will slide a little, a lot – or any amount in between. You decide. Try a more gentle and fluid approach, and you will marvel at the sheer grip on offer. Wide tyres (235/40 ZR17), especially those with no mopping-up sipes in their tread pattern, tend to be bad news in the wet, but not these. There's clearly something special about these Michelins' blend of rubber. As for dry-road grip, to all intents and purposes it is total.

And that downhill right-hander? I braked too late, as I turned into the bend, yet the M3 was unfazed. I was expecting at least a *little* wag of the tail, but no. Nor will the nose push wide as you accelerate through a fast bend; unless disturbed by steering inputs or power-induced tail

drifts, the M3 is perfectly neutral, perfectly balanced. If rear-wheel drive and an equal front-rear weight distribution make up the sacred cow of balance, poise and dynamic purity, then this M3 delivers the thickest of double cream.

It's all so *usable*, like an original M3 but more grown-up. We're on an unclassified road out of Middleton-in-Teesdale up towards Stanhope, through the remnants of snow and slush, and the M3 and I have bonded totally. Up and down through the gears, the speed range of each ratio overlapping hugely with those of its neighbours, each shift slick and neat, no other car in sight, every bump and hollow, every twist and turn tracked true: how is it possible to be so at ease while simultaneously so entertained?

And how splendid to drive on such roads in a car which never wants for thrust. The M3 is shatteringly rapid; seldom do mere figures make such compulsive reading, especially when concluded by a fuel figure as relatively frugal as 24.3mpg. Efficiency indeed.

The daylight is dimming as we draw up outside the Lord Crewe Arms at Blanchland, an ancient stone inn (once part of a monastery) in an ancient stone village. Oak doors and log fires abound, wood of a more useful sort than the glossy veneer that covers, in a masterful mismatch of media, the door pulls, the gearknob and parts of the dashboard of the M3. Like the standard-equipment leather trim, it is supposed to strike a chord with the more mature buyer who is likely to favour the M3 saloon over the flashier coupé, but for all its tactile smoothness it jars in a car of the M3's businesslike mien.

That's the carping completed, and it's a small fish indeed. Warmed by one of the Lord Crewe Arms' several blazing fires (though this particular one was gas-fuelled), we sat in awe and admiration of this best M3's self-effacing brilliance. Then, banishing the Burger King from our minds, we tucked into quail, pheasant and sticky toffee pudding and imagined ourselves able to spend £33,100 on an M3.

Saloon or coupé, the price is identical and, for most of us, way out of reach. But if I can dream, my dream will have four doors and the masterful chassis that comes with them. I'm sure my family would approve.

BMW M3 EVOLUTION

Some overdue beastliness

Well it's about time. After flogging the grossly under-powered and sluggish M3 for the past two years, BMW has made amends with the Evolution.

Instead of the original weedy three-litre, six-cylinder, 286bhp engine, there's a new 3.2-litre unit with a much more respectable 321bhp.

There's also a six-speed gearbox, bigger wheels and tyres, more direct steering and new spring and damper rates. Brakes are compound floating discs, as seen on the M5.

External changes are limited to a new wheel design on the coupe and white glass indicator lenses and black air intake on the front spoiler.

But enough of that, time to get back to the engine. Not only have BMW engineers found a further 35bhp and an extra 22lb ft of torque, they've managed to do it while improving fuel economy.

An engine management system which has been developed by BMW's racing technicians keeps track of a double VANOS variable valve control system which works on both inlet and exhaust valves. And while peak power is at 7,400rpm, you'll find all 258lb ft of torque down at 3,250rpm.

While boasting about their achievements with the new engine, they also like to mention that it uses less fuel than the smaller, weaker one it replaces. They quote a Euromix figure of 32.5mpg compared with the 31mpg of the older model. The trip computer on the car I drove reckoned it was closer to 22mpg, however.

Top speed stays artificially limited to 155mph but the 0-62mph acceleration is slashed to 5.5 seconds. Our figures on the previous car showed 0-60mph in six seconds dead.

The way the new car delivers its power is apparent the moment you step on the accelerator. Pick a high gear and you'll feel a gentle surge from around 1,400rpm, becoming a real boost from 2,600rpm which gets progressively madder and badder until you reach the power peak which coincides with the red line at 7,400rpm. The new sixth gear may be an overdrive, but it's still got bags of go, as long as you're above idle. The gearbox has a slightly clonky action, but it's positive and not too heavy. The revised steering is also light but retains feel and its reactions have been honed.

There's now no play around the straight-ahead position, giving you more confidence at high speed. At an indicated 260kph (160mph) on an unrestricted autobahn (see 'U' in the A-Z), the M3 felt completely unfussed. Even having to scrub off the best part of 100mph when a lorry pulled out was no cause for concern. The big compound disc brakes just hauled the car down, without even triggering the standard-fit ABS.

On twistier stuff the taut suspension kept body roll at bay and the huge Michelin Pilot tyres (225/45x17 at the front and 245/40x17 at the rear) glued the M3 to the road.

Only by using all the horsepower to light up the rear tyres could I get the M3 to go slightly sideways. Of course, it was bone dry and I probably wouldn't be quite so brave in the rain.

On the other hand, since BMW has been brave enough to make a fiercer, faster M3 when world opinion is dead against such horrors, maybe I'll give it a go. The weather should be just right when we get the new M3 in Feb □

Story: Nik Berg
Photography: Max Kirchbauer

The new M3 is much more of a brute than its chest-wigged forebear but better economy is also part of the package

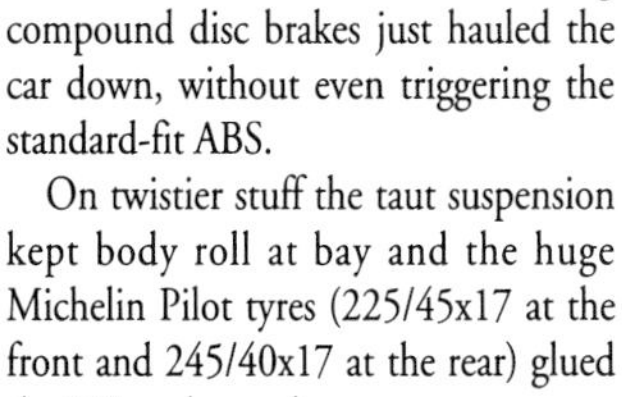

FACT FILE

Model	coupe, saloon and convertible
Engine	3,201cc six-cylinder, 24v, 321bhp
Transmission	six-speed manual, rear drive
On sale in the UK	February '96
Price	£37,000 approx
Rivals	Toyota Supra, Maserati Ghibli

BMW M3 Automatic

Removing the stick from the hot dog.

BY LARRY GRIFFIN

BMW's rockety M3, the most able sedanlet around—although it's also a born ticket receptacle—mocks overzealous speed enforcement as ably as any car we know. Now, for *pilotes* who may prefer less everyday involvement in gearshifting without giving up control, BMW whips out the M3 Automatic. It sports five forward speeds, three selectable shift modes, and way more than the usual BMW knack for inducing cop-curdling hijinks. ("Mr. Letterman, your car is impounded.")

BMW's second-generation M3 dispatches to the rear wheels a caterwauling 240 horsepower from its twin-cam, 24-valve, in-line six. At 3.0 liters, it's a bored, stroked, and breathed-on upgrade of the 325i's 2.5-liter 189-hp engine. The M3's exuberant powerplant, despite redlining at a lofty 6800 rpm, is also torquey down low, thanks to variable valve timing. That makes it ideal for the automatic. When the throttle is closed after kickdown acceleration, we sometimes note a reluctance of the automatic to upshift. That's just BMW's way of holding the revs high, ready to hurl you past even more charter members of the Anti-Destination League. Yet the M3 with the automatic does give up a little:

	M3 5-speed manual	M3 5-speed automatic
0 to 30	1.9 sec	2.6 sec
0 to 60	5.5 sec	6.7 sec
0 to 100	14.7 sec	17.1 sec
0 to 130	28.7 sec	34.5 sec
1/4-mile	14.2 sec @ 98 mph	15.3 sec @ 95 mph

(All M3s are speed-governed to 137 mph.)

The automatic's three shift modes are labeled E, S, and M. The mode-select button nests beside the shifter. The E mode is for Economy, the electronically controlled transmission's default setting, but could stand for "Everyday driving." For us, the M3 averaged fine fuel economy—24 mpg, the same as the stick-shift M3. You could say that S and M (for Sports and Manual) are the whips-and-chains modes. The M mode is best for picking a gear for pulling away on slick surfaces and then artfully sustaining your momentum, or for holding a steady pace in hills or traffic.

But the M3's automatic feels best in S-for-Sports mode. It delays shift points for quicker throttle response and has a quicker, more direct effect on the car's handling. We wish S could be the default mode, but that would undo the good EPA fuel economy. When you do switch to S, even a touch of throttle can provoke a downshift, and the M3 feels ready to fly.

The BMW Motorsport chassis magicians engineered new bushings, anti-roll bars, springs, and shocks for the M3, which remain unchanged for the automatic. Ditto the huge 5-series brakes, 17-inch wheels, and 235/40 ZR-rated Michelin MXX3s. The M3 and its deft steering really do take to cornering as if trued by magic. When the tires slither past their 0.86-g cornering limit, you can easily correct. The ABS brakes yanked us from 70 mph to a standstill in 165 feet—a few feet more than the manual M3 but, hey, the automatic carries an extra 72 pounds.

Our M3's snug cabin wore eye-popping two-tone leather and trim. The hides stretch too slickly over the firm padding of the seats, providing too little lateral support. We'd opt for BMW's handsome cloth upholstery with Motorsport logos (available at no extra cost). Oh, and under heavy braking, one cupholder hurled an unopened soda can into the front passenger's footwell, where it burst and hosed down the dash, door, and carpet.

This latest M3, outfitted as Bavaria's young-executive express, wears an air dam with a classy slatted intake rather than the original's racy mesh. Angular five-spoke alloy wheels stuff the snug wheel arches. In Ohio, two carwash kids, wiping away droplets as they studied the beefcake BMW, slowly circled the M3 and declared it the best-looking car they'd ever seen.

They didn't know an even wilder M3 is available in Europe. It's bundled in this basic bodyware but makes 317 horsepower. Meant to be the fastest production BMW, it should prolong the M3's reign as the world's greatest touring car. But with this one in our hands *now,* we took off for 2000 miles in four days, including 24 hours off for romance. Never applauding the automatic more, we found it especially easy to slip into Park—an, ah, activity ever worthy of a capital P on the shiftgate of life. ●

Vehicle type: front-engine, rear-wheel-drive, 5-passenger, 2-door sedan
Price as tested: $45,770 (base price: $38,520)
Engine type: DOHC 24-valve 6-in-line, iron block and aluminum head, Bosch engine-control system with port fuel injection

Displacement	182 cu in, 2990cc
Power (SAE net)	240 bhp @ 6000 rpm
Torque (SAE net)	225 lb-ft @ 4200 rpm
Transmission	5-speed automatic with lockup torque converter
Wheelbase	106.3 in
Length	174.9 in
Curb weight	3304 lb
Zero to 60 mph	6.7 sec
Zero to 100 mph	17.1 sec
Zero to 130 mph	34.5 sec
Street start, 5 to 60 mph	7.0 sec
Standing 1/4-mile	15.3 sec @ 95 mph
Top speed (governor limited)	137 mph
Braking, 70–0 mph	165 ft
Roadholding, 300-ft-dia skidpad	0.86 g
EPA fuel economy, city driving	19 mpg
C/D observed fuel economy	24 mpg

THIS IS A DUEL OF PHILOSOPHIES: BRAWNY SPORTINESS AGAINST SUBDUED MUSCLE, TRACK RACER MEETS HIGHWAY GLIDER, LOUD ROCK 'N' ROLL VERSUS POWERFUL CHAMBER MUSIC, 321BHP AGAINST 193

No contest?

QUITE THE CONTRARY, SAYS **GEORG KACHER**

BEFORE THE ARRIVAL OF THE HEAVILY revised, hyper-tech 1996 model M3, the 328i was a perfectly viable alternative. For BMW, almost embarrassingly so. After all, the 328i does without the loud livery of the Motorsport car, its engine is a whole cream-carton creamier, it rides much more serenely than its shirt-sleeved stablemate yet is only 8mph slower overall, it can be had with the practical Touring body, and, most important, it costs around 10 grand less. I personally preferred it to last year's M3, in Coupé guise at least, which suffered from slow steering, imperfect directional stability and handling that was flawless only as long as the road was dry and satin-smooth.

N675 PCF
N476 NDP

PHOTOGRAPHS BY TIM WREN

ENTER THE NEW M3 – even more potent, still more sure-footed, and more economical, too. On paper, at least, this 1996 version has the potential to rewrite the rules, never mind show the 328i who's boss. A 350-mile trans-Bavarian blast should settle it.

While the red 328i struggles to make a point in the mirrors of the car in front, the fly-yellow M3 has the instant overtaking power of a police car. Fortunately, the styling changes are subtle: a black air intake mesh in the front spoiler instead of body colour, white lenses for the indicators, and restyled wheels to set them apart from the rims fitted to the four-door M3 saloon and convertible.

A closer inspection will reveal wider tyres, too: the front wheels are shod with 225/45ZR17 rubber (Michelin MXX3 on our test car), while the rears wear 245/40ZR17s. One alteration you can't see concerns the doors, now made of aluminium and 12kg lighter apiece. Still in need of improvement are the tiny low-drag mirrors and the flimsy wipers – useless above 125mph.

Moving inside, we find new cloth upholstery whose redesign gives you a very good reason for specifying leather. Owing to popular demand, the new M3 comes with a six-speed transmission. Although the torque curve of the 3.2-litre engine is shaped like a giant coal dump (it peaks at 258lb ft), which suggests that five gears would be plenty, marketing called for an extra, overdrive gear to reduce high-speed fuel consumption as well as noise. It does just that – even though the engineers chose a ratio which enables you to reach the maximum speed both in fifth and in sixth. The bottom three ratios have been made slightly shorter, while fourth becomes fractionally longer.

Of course, the blame for sixth gear's apparent redundancy lies partly with corporate politicians who decided that even an M3 mustn't go faster than the arbitrarily agreed 155mph. Without the politically correct restrictor, we're talking about a genuine 170-175mph M3.

You can't tell in this view, but the M3's doors are now of aluminium and the coupé gets restyled wheels to set it apart from the four-door and cabrio. Yet more changes underneath and in the engine bay

The gearbox itself is quite quick and sufficiently light, but the double-H shift pattern is not terribly accurate. Engaging second can be a chore, and when you want to slip into first it is rather too easy to enter the cul-de-sac towards reverse, in an embarrassingly noisy fashion.

A similar problem afflicts the 328i's off-the-peg five-speeder, which also feels a bit sloppy under pressure. But while the M3 driver occasionally has one gear too many to choose from, the ratios of the lesser model are perfectly spaced. The 2.8-litre six to which it's joined doesn't play in the same league as the bigger-bore M3 unit, but the power deficit is not really a problem on the motorway. As long as you're happy to push the smooth-running 328i to its 6900rpm cut-out speed, you won't find it too hard to keep up with the M3.

THE MAIN DIFFERENCE between last year's M3 and the 1996 model is the new engine. A slightly bigger bore (86.4mm against 86.0) and a considerably longer stroke (91.0mm against 85.8) result in a displacement of 3201cc, up from 2990cc. Power goes up accordingly, from 286bhp at 7000rpm to 321bhp at a heady 7400rpm. At the same time, maximum torque climbs from 236lb ft at 3600rpm to 258lb ft at a more relaxed 3250rpm.

But there's more to the new motor than a mere capacity hike. Details changed during the three-year development process include an improved two-mass flywheel, a modified vibration damper, lightweight pistons, low-friction graphite-coated con-rods, a higher compression ratio of 11.3 to one, larger-diameter inlet valves and a second oil pump to cope with the greater *g*-forces. Other innovations include a revised exhaust manifold with six equal-length primary pipes, two quick-start metal catalysts and a new engine-management system, dubbed MSS50, which governs fuel feed, emissions control and direct ignition.

MSS50 is also in charge of the Vanos camshaft adjustment device, which now alters the

Presence of leather option in the test car means you are spared the spectacle of the redisigned standard cloth upholstery – awful, according to Kacher

Not much change here, but gearknob now boasts of a sixth ratio. It's more a matter of marketing than of mechanical efficiency

Pitch and roll are more pronounced on the 328i, but it remains fluent and offers more opportunity for tail-out tomfoolery

A mere 193bhp from the 328i's more mundane version of the straight six. More vocally subdued, too, though on a hard charge it out-drank the M3's engine

Most interior benefits of the M3 are yours on the 328i; indeed on any 3-series. Restrained, well laid-out, high quality

timing of the inlet cam as well as the exhaust cam. Employing four hydraulic valves and one big black box, Vanos is a true *wunderkind* invention which helps to boost low-to-mid-range torque, reduce fuel consumption, dampen engine noise and de-smog the exhaust gases.

Tipping the scales at a marginally leaner 1440kg, the latest M3 coupé can accelerate from a standstill to 60mph in 5.4 seconds – that's 0.7sec quicker than last year's M3, and a useful 1.4sec faster than the 328i. But mid-range pulling power is where the M3 is really at: in fourth gear, it sprints from 50 to 75mph in 5.7sec, while the 328i needs 7.6sec.

Despite this pace, official figures suggest remarkable fuel economy: the claimed 32.3mpg average is five percent better

M3 now tends towards understeer rather than oversteer, as this is the way the buyers like it, apparently. Four-wheel drift the best you can realistically hope for

than last year's model could manage. At 33.2mpg, the 328i is yet more abstemious. Unfortunately, both figures become highly theoretical if you put your foot down. The tanks of both cars were almost two-thirds empty after a hard-charging 145 miles, and when we refilled them, the M3 checked out at a sobering 17.0mpg. The 328i achieved an even worse 16.8mpg, so perhaps the M3's sixth gear does have a use.

STEPPING FROM THE 328i into the M3 is like shedding sandals for ski boots. While the red car feels loose, compliant, relaxed, its brilliant yellow sibling is taut and highly strung.

Controlled by a battery of six individual throttle butterflies, its 3.2-litre mega-motor is an all-or-nothing powerplant which reacts with gusto to every tickle of the loud pedal. Depressing the accelerator instantly frees a thousand revs, and if you're not careful with the (beefed-up) clutch, those outsize Michelins will leave fat, black and long marks on the tarmac.

Those 321 horses not only kick hard, they also produce a full spectrum of noises. The idling soundtrack is a low-key triad of hum, gurgle and boom, but as the needle of the rev counter flicks skyward, the burble turns into a rumble, the rumble into a roar and the roar into an amplified thunder.

Since the M3's intake apparatus is activated via a mechanical linkage and not by wire, this quickest BMW cannot be had with any kind of traction-control device. Luckily it doesn't need one, either, at least not in the dry when the even weight distribution and monsieur Michelin's black liquorice provide more grip than most stomachs can take. An automatic gearbox is also absent from the options list (no torque converter is man enough), but we may eventually see a sequential transmission.

A suspension re-think goes well beyond a simple uprate of springs, dampers and anti-roll bars; there are new front transverse links, reinforced ball-joints, off-centre strut tops to increase castor, stronger axle supports and stiffer spring seats. The result is a complete change of geometry and kinematics.

'The yellow devil will flick, duck and zoom through bends, lifting a wheel but never losing composure'

Upstart 328i is the more relaxed and forgiving machine, but gap between it and the M3 has been made respectable again following latter's reincarnation

Increasing the castor has improved the directional stability and reduced oversteer. But this is not achieved at the expense of steering response, because the steering rack now has a quicker ratio for a speedier turn-in, and the unsatisfactory Servotronic power assistance has been booted out in favour of a less numb, more natural-feeling arrangement. Changes to the rear suspension are less wide-ranging, but the longitudinal control arms are reinforced, the wheel bearings and driveshafts are taken from the 850Ci, and the limited-slip diff (with a locking action of 25 percent) is now M5.

WE'RE HARING THROUGH the hills and the revised suspension is turning out to be almost too much of a good thing. How can this be? It's because the handling balance has shifted from natural oversteer to natural understeer, which is what the customers are said to want.

The recalibrated anti-roll bars, the fatter rear tyres, the modified kinematics and the stiffer springs make for a slightly nose-heavy set-up which makes the new car feel less agile (BMW would say less nervous) at the limit. But you don't notice this until you grasp a knife between your teeth and go for it. Where the old car would dance along the brink before finally lapsing into a frame-filling slide, its replacement prefers to point the nose away from the apex, trying to avoid drama at all costs. In the wet and through tight second-gear bends, it must still be possible to steer the M3 via its hind legs, but as soon as the radius is wide enough for third gear, a four-wheel drift is the most you can expect.

It's this understeering bias that chips away at the new steering's alertness. Although the initial reaction is kart quick, tight corners call for rather more lock than you might expect from a rear-wheel-drive car. Getting the best from the new M3 does not call for the aggressive approach its personality might seem to demand, and which its predecessor thrived upon. Power oversteer has given way to new levels of roadholding and grip, and the excitement factor has altered accordingly. As long as you don't back off at the wrong time, the yellow devil will flick, duck and zoom through, occasionally lifting a wheel but never losing its composure.

Just as the engine needs a second oil pump, so the driver could do with an auxiliary heart pump to move the blood to those parts of the body drained by centrifugal force. It is almost impossible to upset the car's balance on smooth roads, but the M3 might need an extra foot or so of road if you hit a crest, dip or slippery patch mid-bend, and the driver will need a well lubricated sixth sense to inject that vital dash of opposite lock. Body roll is minimal, of course, and since the car neither dives under heavy braking nor squats under strong acceleration, the whole experience becomes a bit unreal, detached from real-world dangers. It's almost as effortless as slot racing.

If you're looking for old-fashioned, unbridled tail-out fun, the 328i is the better bet.

too. By the time the new M3 hits British roads early next year, it is likely to cost 'under £37,000' – about three grand more than the current M3 coupé. Mind you, the 328i coupé will probably also cost more by then. We're talking of a price gap of between £10,000 (the current difference between the M3 and 328i coupé) and £12,000.

Is it worth the extra? The 328i might be the better everyday plaything, but it doesn't match the M3's awesome competence and sophistication. It's a great touring car, scoring high for ride comfort and entertainment alike, and it represents good value for money. But instead of tarting it up with M-Style wheels, Motorsport seats and an M-Technic suspension, hoping to capture a taste of M3 magic, you could equally consider specifying automatic transmission, automatic air-conditioning and the best sound system going.

You could never countenance such a cop-out with the M3, even if it was possible. For that would be to misread the M3 entirely. It has the kind of ground-effect roadholding hitherto the province of Scalextric Magnatraction, and a truly magnificent engine. At around £37,000, this BMW must be the performance car deal of the decade. Anything that comes close, while offering similar comforts, is at least 10 grand more. If you can stretch your wallet, go for the M3.

But let's close the rapture with this thought. Crushingly competent as the M3 has become, it's a shame that its newfound maturity has squeezed out the glorious handling balance that made the original, 1986 M3 so great. That's the sort of thing that happens if you try to broaden a car's appeal. The good news is that this M3 is a good deal less compromised than the outgoing one. It's also the fastest-accelerating production BMW ever.

'The M3's motor reacts with gusto to every tickle of the loud pedal – pressing it instantly frees a thousand revs'

Step from the M3 into its underling, and you're likely to be all over the place. But after the first powerslide the aha-effect sinks in, and the red car becomes a congenial travel-mate, always at ease thanks to its much more compliant suspension. This BMW leans more and kneels deeper than the M3, and yet there is a reassuring fluency to it. Nothing happens abruptly, nothing threatens the car's composure. The steering, braking, gearshifting and clutch efforts are similarly more casual, if less precise.

If the M3 is the more mature, more physical, better-mannered car, then the 328i is the more communicative, friendlier, more forgiving one. The reassuring steering and the light clutch make for stress-free progress, but our test car's brakes were not so good: after a few high-speed decelerations they juddered and droned dreadfully. The M3, by contrast, brakes almost as well as a Porsche 911, and it will do so time after time thanks to high-tech, two-piece compound discs which dissipate heat by isolating the outer part of the disc from the inner hub.

THE LATEST M3 HAS FIXED BMW's internecine embarrassment problem, of that there is no doubt. The personality gap between the M-car and the 328i is back to the breadth it should be, which means there's now a point to the M3. You couldn't call the latest M3 flawless, but if speed is all to you, you'll be able to maintain momentum in places where other machines would have long since given up.

The price gap has broadened,

M3's engine capacity up by 211cc; power and torque take a leap, too. Makes for BMW's best ever prod-car acceleration figures

SPECIFICATIONS

	BMW M3 COUPE	BMW 328I COUPE
Price	£37,000 (approx)	£23,600
Engine	3201cc 24-valve dohc six	2793cc 24-valve dohc six
Bore/stroke	86.4/91mm	84/84mm
Compression	11.3 to one	10.2 to one
Power	321bhp at 7400rpm	193bhp at 5300rpm
Torque	258lb ft at 3250rpm	207lb ft at 3950rpm
Specific output	100bhp per litre	69bhp per litre
Power-to-weight ratio	223bhp per tonne	146bhp per tonne
Transmission	Six-speed manual, rwd	Five-speed manual, rwd
Front suspension	MacPherson struts, coils, lower wishbones, anti-roll bar	MacPherson struts, coils, lower wishbones, anti-roll bar
Rear suspension	Double control arms, coils, toe control arm, anti-roll bar	Double control arms, coils toe control arm, anti-roll bar
Brakes	Discs; ventilated front and rear, ABS standard	Discs; ventilated front and rear, ABS standard
Tyres	225/45 ZR17 front 245/40 ZR 17 rear	205/60 VR15
Length/width/wheelbase	4433/1710/2710 (mm)	4433/1710/2700 (mm)
Weight	1440kg	1320kg
PERFORMANCE		
Maximum speed	155mph (limited)	147mph
0-60mph	5.4sec	6.8sec
Average fuel consumption	32.3mpg	33.2mpg

Ford Mustang Cobra vs. BMW M3

We ask the question, Has Ford driven the Mustang Cobra to the European high ground?

BY MARK GILLIES

Los Angeles—

G*ran turismo.* Say the words, and you'll summon up visions of motoring at its most romantic. You'll imagine French-blue Delahaye 135s and Bugatti Type 57s sweeping along poplar-lined *Routes Nationales,* dusky light reflecting off long, graceful hoods and sleek curves.

You'll picture spiffy little Alfa Romeo coupes tearing up helter-skelter Alpine passes, raucous twin-cam engines straining away at the expensive end of the tachometer dial, tires squealing, brakes fuming. Or you'll envisage debonair Aston Martins devouring whole countries between breakfast and dinner, trunks laden with Louis Vuitton luggage.

One doesn't, somehow, think of GTs as American cars. A GT is European, almost by definition. In the days before Europe was crisscrossed by autobahns, autoroutes, and autostradas, you needed a car that could tackle long, straight roads and twisting mountain passes with equal aplomb, if you wanted to go quickly across the continent.

Yet some of the greatest GTs had prosaic roots, being turned from the mundane into the magnificent by intelligent development. Look at the Alfa Giulietta Sprint (sired by an Alfa sedan), the Lancia Aurelia B20GT (developed from a family car), and the sleek BMW 3.0 CS/CSi/CSL (another GT spawned from a sedan).

Both the BMW M3 and the Ford Mustang Cobra have been developed from existing hot metal by enthusiastic, knowledgeable engineers who love cars: the Cobra from the current Mustang GT by the Ford Special Vehicle Team, and the M3 from the 3-series coupe by BMW's M division.

We know just how great the M3 is: It won our 1995 Automobile of the Year accolade and is a 1996 All-Star. The Cobra has made firm friends here, too, winning an All-Star berth this year and being one of the standouts of our Four Seasons fleet. In the past, you'd never have mentioned Ford Mustang in the same breath as BMW M3, but we like to think that the Cobra really measures up. And at the same time, it poses the question, Has the Mustang been transformed from a pony car into a genuine *gran turismo*?

For the purposes of this test, the Harbor Freeway through Los Angeles serves as our Autoroute du Soleil, and the Angeles Crest Highway and some of L.A.'s serpentine canyon roads double as our Futa and Raticosa passes. Good substitutes they make, too, roads that will show up the slightest deficiency in either of these automobiles.

As we roll north, beyond the choking traffic and smog of Los Angeles, it's obvious that both cars fulfill the mile-eating segment of the GT repertoire. The M3 may have slightly more rear-seat room, but both vehicles' back seats are for occasional use and nothing more. The trunks are reasonably accommodating, and both cars ride the rutted pavement of the Los Angeles freeway system with a suppleness that laughs at their sporting suspension setups.

If the highway patrol isn't looking, both will amble all day at 100 mph, cruising fast and easily. The Mustang's longer gearing makes for more relaxed mile-eating, as well as a 15-mph-higher top speed—although that's academic unless you're a Montana resident who considers 152 mph "careful" and "prudent."

Turn onto challenging pavement, and you're going to have big fun in both cars. The Mustang's engine is a marvel, a quad-cam 305-bhp V-8 that combines the hard-edged snarl of a high-tech race unit with the kind of flowing midrange we've always associated with Detroit V-8s. But where in the past the power might have died away as the tach needle spun around

PHOTOGRAPHY BY GREG JAREM

the dial, the Cobra's engine keeps the power coming to the point where you fear for its innards. Or your own. Given its head, the Cobra accelerates harder than the M3, whose twin-cam 3.0-liter, 240-bhp straight-six also sounds wondrous as it chases the redline with the relish of a dog pursuing a juicy bone.

When the roads start twisting, you'll find that the Cobra's fat BFGoodrich Comp T/As have plenty of grip, and the car changes direction as fluently as an expert linguist switches languages. Over canyon roads, the Cobra goes really hard and balances the tricky handling/ride equation expertly: soft enough to be comfortable, but firm enough to keep body roll at bay.

The BMW M3 has excellent steering, brakes, grip, and handling. Six-cylinder 3.0-liter engine develops willing 240 bhp, has good midrange, and sounds superb. Car looks classy, elegant.

Overt hooligans will find you can break traction from the rear tires around tight hairpins, but it's more rewarding to settle into a rhythm and go with the flow, dialing out mild understeer with power to sweep through bends in a neutral, stable attitude. Occasionally, you'll notice the live rear axle's legacy over midcorner bumps, but the Cobra is a miracle of damper engineering over what many construe as an outdated design. Your only real disappointment is the steering: It's accurate, but too light on initial entry into corners and not talkative enough through them.

Over these selfsame roads, the BMW reinforces its status as one of the world's great sporting cars. The steering whispers sweet nothings into the palms of your hands while the chassis dismisses bumps and bends. Almost immediately, you can drive really fast in this car, yet it is never upset by the under-tire terrain or by ham-fisted driving such as applying the brakes in midcorner. It turns and points into corners with the alacrity of an alcoholic downing a drink and makes you feel like

Over roads where the Cobra is really exciting, the M3 can come across as a little boring, a little too accomplished. Push it further, to the edge of the envelope, and it lives for the moment like few other cars.

Michael Schumacher even if you know the limits of your driving talents.

Over roads where the Cobra is really exciting, the M3 can come across as a little boring, a little too accomplished. At 90 percent, it's so polished that you don't realize just how fast you're driving. Push it further, to the edge of the envelope, and it lives for the moment like few other cars in the world, its true greatness lying in territory few drivers will ever explore.

Even at a halt, the M3 impresses. The cabin décor may be as gloomy as a winter's day in Detroit, but its layout is heavenly for keen drivers. The seat affectionately cradles your shoulders and thighs and forces your rear end into a cozy relationship with the cushion. (Any racing driver or fighter pilot will tell you it's your butt that does the talking when the machine into which it is strapped starts defying the laws of physics.)

The M3 wraps around you, cocoons you, involves you. Its driver-centricity is summed up by the center console's being angled toward the left seat and by the immaculate juxtaposition of the throttle and brake for heel-and-toe downshifts. BMW people know about driving and driving pleasure: You can tell by the easy way your right foot can cover both pedals at once, rather than groping for the throttle while decelerating.

The Mustang's interior may be made from less classy materials—Levi's to the BMW's Versace—but this car is a great deal cheaper, and the overall effect is brighter and more cheery. For $26,645,

The Ford Mustang Cobra uses sensational quad-cam 4.6-liter V-8, developing 305 bhp. Changes by SVT add muscle to already appealing shape. Car rides well and changes direction fluently.

FORD MUSTANG COBRA
Front-engine, rear-wheel-drive coupe
4-passenger, 2-door steel body
Base price $24,810/price as tested $26,645

POWERTRAIN:
32-valve DOHC V-8, 281 cu in (4605 cc)
Power SAE net 305 bhp @ 5800 rpm
Torque SAE net 300 lb-ft @ 4800 rpm
5-speed manual transmission

CHASSIS:
Independent front, live-axle rear suspension
Power-assisted rack and pinion steering
Vented front and rear disc brakes
Anti-lock system
245/45ZR-17 BFGoodrich Comp T/A tires

MEASUREMENTS:
Wheelbase 101.3 in
Length x width x height 181.5 x 71.8 x 53.4 in
Curb weight 3446 lb

PERFORMANCE (manufacturer's data):
0–60 mph in 5.9 sec
Standing 1/4-mile in 14.0 sec @ 101.6 mph
Top speed 152 mph
EPA city driving 18 mpg

the Cobra comes with all the bells and whistles you could ever desire, including a brilliant sound system, leather trim, and electric seat adjustments. The more ascetic BMW costs more—much more—but does without a CD player and has fiddly manual seat movements. You can enjoy the Cobra's slightly contrived interior architecture, but the car's GT aspirations are compromised by clumsy detailing. The gearshift lever is tall and requires manly maneuvering around its gate, whereas the BMW's stubby lever has svelte movements.

The Mustang's seats are comfortable over long journeys, but lack the cozy intimacy of the BMW's by being too squidgy and set high relative to the steering wheel. And, finally, it requires podiatric contortion to heel-and-toe in the Mustang. Minor gripes they may be, but these things spoil ultimate driving pleasure and would have cost only a few dollars to fix.

Over the Angeles Crest Highway—and several other unsuspecting California byways—the Cobra felt bigger, more brutal, and less deft. Yet it has more character than the BMW, in the same way that you warm to the outspoken American rather than the reserved and cautious European aristocrat.

We also suspect that potential buyers will prefer the Cobra's butch shape to the M3's understated looks. A deep air dam, more scoops than the *National Enquirer,* and neat wheels add muscularity to what is already a great-looking car. The Cobra looks more expensive than it is, and you can be sure that the valet parker will be keen to rip the keys from your hand.

The M3 is also a looker, in a complete-

BMW M3
Front-engine, rear-wheel-drive coupe
5-passenger, 2-door steel body
Base price $37,950/price as tested $40,195

POWERTRAIN:
24-valve DOHC 6-in-line, 182 cu in (2990 cc)
Power SAE net 240 bhp @ 6000 rpm
Torque SAE net 225 lb-ft @ 4250 rpm
5-speed manual transmission

CHASSIS:
Independent front and rear suspension
Variable-power-assisted rack-and-pinion steering
Vented front and rear disc brakes
Anti-lock system
235/40ZR-17 Michelin Pilot SX MXX3 tires

MEASUREMENTS:
Wheelbase 106.3 in
Length x width x height 174.5 x 67.3 x 52.6 in
Curb weight 3180 lb

PERFORMANCE (manufacturer's data):
0–60 mph in 6.1 sec
Standing 1/4-mile in 14.5 sec
Top speed (electronically limited) 137 mph
EPA city driving 19 mpg

ly different way. Whereas the 328is is a little effete, the M3's subtle body addenda, brawny seventeen-inch wheels, and rubber-band tires endow the BMW coupe's graceful shape with the suggestion of force—like Sean Connery dressed in a tuxedo, playing James Bond. The Bavarian car appears classy and expensive, as witnessed by the $13,550 premium over the Cobra.

Take away the German competition and consider the Cobra in isolation—as I did over the following weekend—and you draw the conclusion that the SVT people have elevated the Mustang into a legitimate GT, a car you can really believe in as a long-distance mile eater rather than a short-haul tire smoker. By shoehorning in a truly outstanding engine, by working on the ride comfort, and by pushing their own management, SVT has come close to matching the Europeans in one area that remains their specialty.

The Cobra is a car that America can feel proud of and that car enthusiasts are going to adore. Yet we'd like to see Ford and SVT go the whole hog and elevate the Cobra onto an even higher plane. (We're like that.) The Cobra still suffers from naïveté in the detail areas that make the M3 so effortless at covering ground at such high speed: things like control and pedal feel, seating position, and steering feedback. It would take time, which costs money, to rectify them and turn the Mustang into a car that can run with the M3 all the way. And it would probably mean a Mustang with a $40,000 price. But we'd like to think that, even if the market for it is small, Ford needs a car like this.

FORD SVT VERSUS BMW M

Creating the culture of speed.

Ford first went shopping for its own in-house specialty-car operation back in 1962, but the $10 million deal unraveled at the last second when the owner of the tiny outfit in Maranello balked at the final contract. That's why the Mustang doesn't wear a Ferrari badge today. Afterward, Ford moved on to its own efforts. First, Shelby American produced the Cobra and Mustang GT-series cars from 1962 to 1970. Then Ford Special Vehicle Operations (SVO) went into business in 1980. Although it couldn't get its mid-engined GN34 supercar into production, the turbocharged Mustang SVO was produced from 1984 to 1986.

In sales terms, neither venture rewrote the books, so the lesson here is that it's necessary to sell high-performance cars as well as build them. When Ford gave the Special Vehicle Team (SVT) a charter to produce limited-production high-performance cars in 1991, a marketing program was the key to success. SVT has designated 705 Ford dealers in the United States and thirteen in Canada as authorized outlets for its products, and that assures the commercial success of the 10,000 Mustang Cobras (8000 coupes, 2000 convertibles) that will be built this model year. In fact, Ford SVT is the kind of company that might have been created had the deal with Ferrari gone down: a self-contained entity with engineers, dealers, and even a dedicated marketing agency.

Ford hopes its SVT operation will generate a culture of high performance that will rival BMW's remarkable M division. BMW's company grew out of a motorsport department founded in 1972, but its first attempt at a specialty car, the Lamborghini-engineered mid-engined M1 introduced in 1978, proved to be a commercial failure. A small number of special projects kept the Motorsport division in the car business, however, and BMW finally formalized the company's responsibilities in 1993 as BMW M. About 500 employees at BMW M are now involved with production cars, special-order cars, driver training, motorsport, and cooperative technical ventures with outside companies. BMW M put 14,000 cars on the road in 1995 and modified some 30,000 more.

—Michael Jordan

In the blood

PHOTOGRAPHY: STEVE MORRIS

With famous a driver as an uncle, racing is in James Cunningham-Reid's blood and he finds the M3GT the perfect outlet. Mark Chillingworth met him

What would the nephew of a great 1950s' racer drive? A performance coupé with almost unrivalled performance and handling, naturally. And what colour would such a car be? British Racing Green.

James Cunningham-Reid is a true car enthusiast, owner of a rare M3 GT and nephew of Noel Cunningham-Reid, celebrated Aston Martin and Jaguar sports car racer of the '50s. The car bug bites even deeper than this, though. James has followed in his uncle's racing footsteps and the family talent seems to have been passed down to him.

His passion for motorsport started early. He was fortunate enough to attend Stowe School, near Silverstone, and every spare moment was spent at the Northamptonshire circuit. 'I was spoilt really,' he says. As a boy, though, BMWs seemed unobtainable. He says: 'I thought they were beyond my reach.'

Cunningham-Reid Senior had given up racing by the time James was born, but the sport still flows in the veins. In 1995 James contested six GT races in an E30 M3 to get the signatures for his race licence, ready for a full onslaught in 1996.

James tackled the BMW Car Club Championship this year and won his class – not bad for his first year. He is not alien to the tough environment of the track, though. Before racing, he had driven an E36 M3 at club track days. This was no ordinary M3 either, James built himself the ultimate street racer, fitting uprated AP Racing brakes (those used by single-seater F3000 cars) and a Safety Devices roll-cage, the first fitted to an M3 by the Cambridgeshire company.

He says: 'I did just about everything on that car, a Schnitzer exhaust and no sunroof for rigidity'. This car, his everyday hack, was taken to the limit around most British and European racing circuits for two years.

In his first race of 1996 he finished second overall. 'I was terrified in that first race, but I soon realised that I could challenge for a reasonable result,' he says with

Right: James wondered why such a rare car should be on sale so soon, but the M3 GT has proved a real gem

typical modesty. The class B championship went down to the wire at the last meeting, where James picked up class honours, but not the prestigious title of BMW Car Club Champion.

'There has been a lot of contact in this year's series, I think people are surprised at how close and competitive the racing is,' comments James 'But it is a real gentleman's class and great fun. I think someone has been looking down on me and given me a really good result.'

His racing car has been prepared by Alex Elliot of Munich Legends this season and James speaks very highly of the team, saying: 'The car was very consistent, you felt an element of the race was already dealt with. We all worked well as a team,'

James got his first BMW aged 24, a 325i Sport. 'Ever since then there has been no looking back and I have now had five,' he says. 'People buy a car to reflect on themselves and the M3 GT does that for me. I feel a car must be a real driving pleasure, that is a very big criteria. The old 'yuppie' image of BMW has gone now, they are cars that represent fun, reliability, performance, and style.'

His latest BMW is a bit special though. James gave up BMWs as his road transport in favour of a Jeep Cherokee to ferry his race E30 M3 to meetings. The Cherokee failed to live up to expectations so, having sorted out his transport problems, he wanted another BMW road car. He started looking for a used M3 Evolution, a new one would mean waiting. James had read about the GTs, but could not justify spending the extra cash. So he rang a number of dealers and told them what he was looking for, how much he was prepared to spend and mentioned that he might be interested in a GT.

Six months ago, Frank Sytner's BMW dealership in Nottinghamshire called and said they had something they felt James should look at. 'I got on a train and went straight up there. As soon as I saw the car on the forecourt I bought it,' he says.

Now buying a car just because of the colour may seem a little unwise, but he did negotiate that the car would be inspected by top BMW gurus Munich Legends within a couple of weeks of purchase. 'I was a little concerned that such a rare and new car was on sale so soon,' he said, 'But it turned out to be a gem.'

Sitting in James' Clapham office, surrounded by memorabilia of the racing adventures he and his uncle have sought, it becomes obvious how deep the motoring bug has bitten. As well as five 3-series BMWs, he also owns an Aston Martin DB4 and an MG Metro 6R4. 'My uncle had a huge association with Aston Martin so it is rather nice to own such a beautiful car,' he reveals.

He talks with informed ease and enthusiasm which you find carries you off with his infection. The M3 GT was a 'buy from the heart' and is probably all the more important for being so. 'The car carries the colour so well, to have a car in British Racing Green is great and especially one as special as this,' he explains. 'I have never seen another M3 GT in the flesh apart from mine'

However, this is no blind obsession. 'The 325i had one of the best six-cylinder engines in production, I think,' says James. 'BMW has an incredible history in every aspect, as mass producers its mentality of wanting to get everything right and above the ordinary is admirable. Porsche has gone one step beyond that,' he continues on a more practical note, 'but the BMW service in this country is fantastic, you are made to feel quite special.'

James is one of the lucky few who can truly answer the argument of whether the E30 or the E36 M3 is the better. 'I have driven both cars on the track, and I would like to stress I am referring to track driving,' he summarises, 'But the E30 is definitely the better car. When an E30 does let go, it is far more involving and tells you more than an E36 will.

'That said, I will hang onto the M3 GT for as long as I can,' he concludes. Then again, he may well have to as BMWs are the only cars he ever feels comfortable in. Why? James is 6 feet 8in tall, so there is quite a bit of James Cunningham-Reid for a car to accommodate. ■

Above: plenty of head and leg room for 6ft 8in driver
Below: factory decal confirms M3 GT finished in BRG

Below: James in his racing M3 which he says is better than an E36

Six-speed sequential gearbox an option on M3 from March, for £1735. Gearbox is a little slow to react to shifts, but mostly it's smooth and enjoyable

Sequential M3: sorry for delay

BMW M3 Evolution SMG
PRICE £40,155
ON SALE March

Picture this. You are in a BMW M3 on a twisting mountain road. Stamp on the throttle and the road behind vanishes in a puff of tyre smoke.

Tug the gear lever towards you and you're into second. Do the same again and you're into third, followed by fourth, fifth and sixth. Then it's hard on the brakes for the hairpin. Four successive forward jabs bring you back down to second for a perfectly smooth exit. No clutch, no heel and toeing. Just a flick of the wrist and eyes focused on the road ahead.

Enticing, isn't it? And soon to be a reality, because – after what seems like an interminable wait – BMW's new Sequential M Gearbox (SMG) will soon be offered as an option on the M3 coupe and convertible (the saloon has been discontinued).

Pull to change up, push to go down

STAN PAPIOR

Dash display shows gear selection

The UK could have had this car a year ago. It's been on sale in Europe since last March, but BMW GB wasn't happy with the way the gearbox's automatic mode coped with UK traffic conditions and insisted on a few changes. When you're the second largest market after Germany for M cars, you can afford to be fussy.

The hardware of the SMG is similar to that in the Ferrari F355 F1. Hydraulic valves and actuators take care of the clutch and gear selection, while the gearbox itself is straight from the manual M3. Trouble is, unlike the Ferrari there is a noticeable delay between tugging the lever (paddles were dismissed as too confusing) and the gearchange occurring. BMW claims the change itself is as quick as the F355's, but it appears that the electronics take longer to set things in motion. As a result, you have to second guess exactly when it's going to happen. Time it right and it's as smooth and enjoyable as any manual. Get it wrong and the gear bangs through with an uncomfortable jerk.

You really have to learn to get the best from the SMG, whether it's in manual mode or one of the three automatic settings, and in our experience this takes some time.

Engine and ratios identical to M3

Whether M3 buyers will be prepared to shell out £1735 in the hope of growing to like SMG is questionable. But if the UK follows the European trend, more than half eventually will.

Hugo Andreae

FACTFILE

0-62mph 5.5sec
Top speed 155mph
Combined mpg 25.7

HOW BIG?

Length 4433mm **Width** 1418mm
Height 1393mm **Wheelbase** 2700mm
Weight 1535kg

ENGINE

Type 6 cyls in line, 3201cc
Installation Front, longitudinal, rear-wheel drive
Max power 321bhp at 7400rpm
Max torque 258lb ft at 3250rpm
Gearbox 6-speed sequential

CHASSIS

Suspension MacPherson struts, coil springs, anti-roll bar (f); Z-axle, coil springs, anti-roll bar (r)
Steering Rack and pinion, power assisted, 3.2 turns lock to lock
All manufacturer's figures

VERDICT

Not as fast or intuitive as Ferrari F355 F1 paddle gearchange, but sequential gearbox still shows enormous potential. However, book a long test drive before buying one.

BMW's M3 Evo Convertible puts a hurricane in your hairpiece and a bloody gr

Blown away

Words Brett Fraser
Photography Colin McMaster

It's down there in the footwell, if you look for it hard enough. The extra punch, that is – the stuff that separates the brand new 321bhp BMW M3 Evolution from the outgoing 286bhp M3. You just have to keep forcing down hard with your right foot to overcome a point of resistance in the pedal travel, beyond which you'll find an extra paddock full of raging horsepower.

Until you learn to keep on pressing with every gearchange in the six-speed 'box, you could convince yourself the Evo isn't all that special – quick, certainly, but not super-spectacular. But hell, a bit of right leg stretching ain't much of a price to pay for acceleration which makes passengers grunt loudly with appreciation and gives you a sky-high, day-long buzz of satisfaction and pleasure. Oh yeah, and because this is the convertible version, you'll need to nail your hairpiece in place, because it's not just a breeze that blows through the cabin, it's a hurricane. Warn Michael Fish now!

Owners of superseded M3s are going to be mighty pissed off when they test-drive an Evo, because good though the old car was, the new one's a huge improvement in the way it goes, handles, and stops. If the M3 had been like this from the start, there wouldn't have been a single grumble from the press, and no-one would have bemoaned the passing of the previous series, four-cylinder M3. Still, the 'real' M3 is here now, so let's just be thankful, shall we?

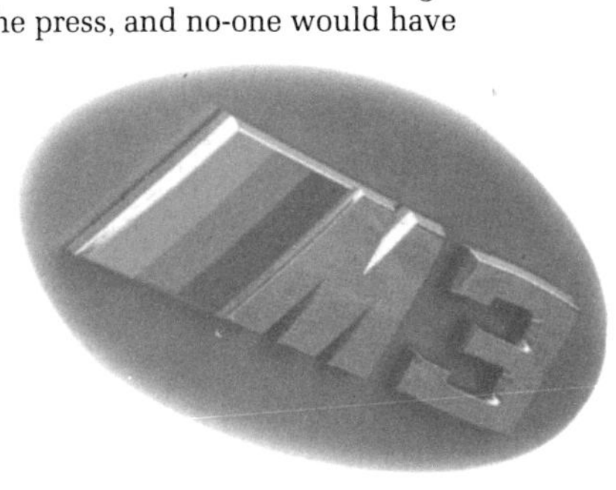

Although it looks much the same as before, the Evo is a substantially different beast. God's greatest straight-six 24-valve engine has been given a thorough working-over to make it even more heavenly. Capacity jumps from 3.0-litre to 3.1-litre, helping raise power and boost torque by 10 per cent to 258lb ft, developed at 3250rpm. Upping the capacity is only a small part of what's been done to the engine; more important are the introduction of BMW's very own engine management system, engineered specially for the Evo, and the adaptation of the company's VANOS variable inlet cam timing system to work on the exhaust cams, too.

BMW's very proud of the fact that as well as tickling the enthusiast's fancy, the Evo's engine also satisfies a load of sissy 'green' requirements. But as that means fewer trips to the petrol station, we can all be glad to be green – well, as green as you can be in a car that'll do 100mph anywhere other than a multi-storey car park.

With the extra go comes extra stop, in the form of 'floating' discs, common on competition cars; picture the disc as a ring, attached to the wheel hub by a set of pins, or mini-stilts, so that it stands clear of the hub. The advantage of this arrangement is that heat is spread more evenly across the disc and dissipates much quicker. It's an expensive way of doing things, but it means discs last up to five times longer, and you get more life out of the pads, too. Combined with a new Teves MkIV anti-lock system, the Evo will smack to a standstill from 62mph (100km/h) in 2.8secs, with enough force to knock the wind out of you.

The major criticism of the old car – lack of feel through the variable assistance power steering at high speed – has been answered by fitting constant ratio power steering, combined with new geometry for the front suspension struts to give more feel around the straight-ahead. All the suspension's been fiddled with (new springs, retuned dampers), and the tyres are now different sizes front and rear: 225/45s at the front, 245/40s out back.

Maybe it's because you know what's been done to the car, or maybe it's because with the hood down you can hear so much more, but when you fire up the Evo for the first time it does seem different. Blip the throttle and the engine rocks the car as if it's trying to break out and run off on its own. You can hear the extra dose of animal in the Evo, crackling from the tailpipes, threatening bystanders while thrilling occupants. With all this promised potency reverbing through your body, it's as well you remember the pedal-to-the-metal advice, so you don't end up disappointed.

On second thoughts, what are the chances of having 321bhp underfoot and not booting it as hard as you can? So go on, do it. Wham-*bam*, the Evo squats at the rear and your head whips back from the *g*-force. The tacho needle seems to take an age to work its way round to the 7500rpm rev cut-off point, but at the same time you're snatching second almost immediately – spooky. No time to ponder this apparent contradiction of the laws of physics because you've whacked past 60mph in 5.5secs and are closing in on 70mph and you need to grab third. Now!

All the Evo's gearchanges are quick and metallicky, as if it's on the verge of metamorphosing into a genuine track car. This feeling of a racer for the road is enhanced by the engine note, which is competition-crisp, tinged with (but not tainted by) a mechanical hardness. Once you discover the Evo's happy to be held at high revs, and that there's a stack of power to play with at the top end, then you'll play at keeping the thing humming on the high side of 5000rpm. You'll have to hang

Under new management: 3.1-litre 24-valve straight-six now gives 321bhp

Fraser extends his right leg, the M3 surges forward, and a stiffening breeze begins to tease playfully with what's left of his hair (you're fired – ed)

The Evo has landed. Convertible even looks horny with the hood up

onto your hat and your hairdo though, because above 90mph it's getting a bit wild inside the car, and 90 is just the start of the action to come.

Which isn't to say there's nothing going on lower down the speed range. The straight-six pulls cleanly from idle, although there are a couple of noticeable hiccups in the delivery (at 1300rpm and 2200rpm) as the VANOS gizmo does its stuff.

But now you're hooling down towards a corner and braking later than you'd have dared in the old car because you know the uprated brakes can cope. Even light pressure on the pedal wipes off 20mph, and a decent push hauls you up a long way short of the bend. Amazing. You end up experimenting with just how late you can leave it before stamping on the anchors, and unless you're extremely brave (or monumentally stupid), you're unlikely to out-fox the stoppers.

Into the corner you go now and the steering is awash with all the feel and feedback a landlubber could wish for; turns to port and starboard can now be accomplished with apex-crushing accuracy every time.

Which is just as well, because you're going to spend a lot of time exploring new lines through favourite corners in a bid to get the rear end to swing out. And I promise you, it ain't going to be easy, even in the wet. The Evo grips the road like toffees stick to your fillings, and there's a certain amount of risk involved in making either of them let go. In the dry you can try all sorts of outrageous abuse and the Evo'll scoot round unfussed and at extremely high speed. Dump an excessive amount of power into the equation at the exit to a tight bend and you'll get a concilliatory wag from the back end, but it tucks in again so quickly you'd swear it was just playing with you.

Wet roads make a bit of difference, but not as much as you'd expect given the grunt factor. Again, the tail slides out gently, then sidles gently and briskly back on track. These slides are so controlled you can convince yourself that you're a hero, when in fact it's the car doing most of the work.

Remember, too, that this is the convertible and sun-toppers generally don't handle as well as their tin-top cousins. The fact that in the Evo you hardly notice whether or not it's got a roof, is proof of what an involving drive it is.

It's a stonking car, the M3 Evo, every bit as rapid point-to-point as a Porsche 911 and, at £41,800 for the convertible and £36,550 for the coupé and saloon, more than 20 grand cheaper. It's easy to see why the previous M3 was a best seller in its class; the Evo deserves even greater success. Using the performance per £ ratio, the revised M3 is the most outstanding performance car bargain on the market today; if you're considering cars in this price bracket, you can just reduce your shortlist. To one.

This comparison is between—inarguably—the two most desirable compact four-door sedans ever built. The limited-production BMW M3 four-door and Mercedes-Benz C36 are each so fantastic, so fundamentally tremendous, that this test could degenerate into a love-fest of praise. They're quick, handle brilliantly, brake instantly, and are built with the structural integrity of a beryllium molecule. We could almost put the critical blinders on, engage WordPerfect's excellent built-in thesaurus, and let the superlatives fly. Still, though this test will draw out the subtleties and distinctions, it will lapse into a few gooey gushes. Forgive us, we're human.

Neither the M3 nor the C36 looks particularly intimidating. Sure, they have deep front spoilers, oversize wheels, our test M3 is painted vivid yellow, the C36 has carbon fiber on its B-pillars, and they hunker seductively to the ground, but these are familiar shapes. If one isn't conscious of the performance details, they blend into the gang of "lesser" 3s and Cs in the associate parking stalls at any Minneapolis law firm. However, their low-key decoration belies the substance of the changes within. Both the M3 and C36 emerge from a German tuning tradition that demands elegantly engineered components to complement extra power with handling and braking. That tradition has little to do with ornamentation.

The M3 sedan comes from BMW's own Motorsport Division, which has developed special high-performance road and race machines from the exotic M1 mid-engine sports car of the early '80s to the luscious M5, M6, and 850CSi models of more recent memory. Until the sedan's late arrival in the United States, the M3 extension of BMW's 3 Series had been available here only as a coupe. The European M3 sedan, however, has been available for a while, and we still don't get the M3 convertible. Except for the extra set of doors, the M3 sedan is mechanically identical to the M3 coupe, right down to its suspension calibration. And that's a good thing.

What "mechanically identical" means is that, under the same sheetmetal that skins the 138-horsepower, four-cylinder 318i sedan lies a 240-horsepower DOHC 24-valve inline-six. Boring the iron-block 328i's six cylinders an additional 2.4 millimeters and lengthening the crankshaft's stroke 5.6 millimeters results in a 359-cubic-centimeter bump in the M3 engine's displacement

BATTLE OF THE TWO QUICKEST COMPACT FOUR-DOORS ON EARTH

BMW M3 VS. MERCEDES-BENZ C36

PHOTOGRAPHY BY RANDY LORENTZEN

by John Pearley Huffman

up to 3.2 liters. Combined with a slight compression increase from 10.2:1 to 10.5:1 and the appropriate fuel injection, intake, exhaust, and engine management systems, the result is 50 more horsepower than in the 328i.

ROAD TEST

That horsepower rating is deceptive, though, because the engine's greatest advantage actually lies in torque production. The M3's peak horsepower rating occurs at a relatively high 6000 rpm, 700 rpm higher than the 328i's peak, but the maximum 236 pound-feet of torque are available at only 3800 rpm. That's 150 rpm lower than the 328i's 206-pound-foot torque zenith. Basically, whatever gear the M3 is in, or wherever in the rev band the engine is turning, there's always a glut of grunt available.

Behind that torrent of twist, BMW mounts either of two ZF five-speed transmissions: a sublime-shifting manual or a superb automatic. Our test car had the manual, giving it a somewhat unfair edge in acceleration over the automatic-only C36.

The M3's suspension geometry is familiar to anyone who's peeked under any BMW 3 Series coupe or sedan, but it's optimized by the M Division with specific springs, shocks, and anti-roll bars. Also, unlike other 3 Series, the M car gets a variable-rate power assist on its rack-and-pinion steering system, which has a slower ratio at parking-lot speeds and a much quicker ratio when the car is romping. Braking is the responsibility of giant 12.4-inch front and 12.3-inch rear vented discs with ABS.

Sharing shoe size, the M3 and C36 both wear 225/45ZR17 front and 245/40ZR17 rear tires on 17x7.5-inch front and 17x8.5-inch rear wheels. The M3's tires are Michelin Pilot SXs, while the C36 sports Bridgestone Expedias.

To create the C36, Mercedes conspired with famed tuner AMG, a firm that recently has evolved into Benz's practical equivalent to BMW's M Division. Based on the C-Class sedan introduced in '95, the C36 represents the first time Mercedes has sold a vehicle explicitly modified by an outside firm as its own. It won't be the last, however; soon the E50 version of the E-Class sedan will appear on these shores. If you want a C36, hurry; only 200 will be imported this year, and the company swears there will be no '98 version.

The C36's engine has only 1.1 millimeter extra bore diameter

Derived from the 2.8-liter BMW six, the 3.2-liter/240-horsepower M3 engine retains the legendary smoothness and friendly torque curve and then amplifies it, big-time.

After six years in production, the basic elements of the BMW 3 Series interior are familiar. The M badging, great front buckets, tri-color seat stripes, and steering wheel all transfer over to the sedan from the coupe unchanged.

than the 2.8-liter DOHC 24-valve C280 six it's based on, but the crank's stroke is a daunting 18.9 millimeters longer. Along with that increase, AMG bumps the compression up half a point to 10.5:1, calibrates the electronics to work with more-aggressive camshafts, and throws on a freer-flowing exhaust. That results in 3.6 liters, a full 454 cubic centimeters more displacement than the M3 engine offers. That advantage works out to 276 horsepower at 5750 rpm—82 more than a C280 and 36 more than the M3. It's also eight more horsepower than was claimed for the C36 upon its introduction two years ago.

The only transmission offered with the C36 is a five-speed automatic, which, using the traditional Mercedes gated shifter, is very effective when shifted manually.

Fortification of the C-Class chassis was accomplished with careful raiding of the AMG and Mercedes parts bins. For example, the AMG "Monoblock" wheel design is also used on the SL500 (albeit in an 18-inch diameter), and the mammoth 12.6-inch front and 10.9-inch rear vented disc brakes were scavenged from the 905-pound-heavier SL600 V-12 roadster. The basic C-Class suspension design remains unaltered, though equipped with much stiffer springs and shocks and specific-diameter anti-roll bars. The C36's recirculating-ball steering's 13.3:1 ratio is much quicker than the C280 Sport's 15.4:1 gearing.

Slide into the M3, and the car seems to wrap around you. The dash and cowl feel high, while the aggressively contoured bolsters of the M-spec seats almost embrace you. Climb into the C36, and you feel as if you're in a much larger car. Although the C36 is just 0.8 inch wider, 2.9 inches longer overall, and the wheelbase is actually 0.4 inch shorter than the M3's, you feel as if it were closer in size to a BMW 5 Series. The C36's dash sits lower, the glass area seems greater, and the driver sits atop, rather than in, the splendidly comfortable seat. It's a question of mood: The M3 feels aggressive and ready to pounce, the C36 confident and in command for a long bout. It's the difference between being outfitted for guerrilla warfare or an open-field tank battle.

Attractive as both interiors are—with their supple leathers, upholstery detail, and subtle logos reminding occupants of the specialness of the vehicles they're in—all is not perfect. In the M3, there's no adjustment available for the steering wheel, and the shallow center-console cupholder looks like an afterthought more appropriate for a conversion van. On the C36, the door armrests and center console are formed from a rigid plastic lacking the tactile sophistication that should be taken for granted on any car this expensive.

The C36 may feel bigger, but the interior dimensions provided by each manufacturer indicate that the difference in accommodations is minimal. BMW claims 41.1 inches of front and 34.0 inches of rear legroom in the M3, while Mercedes asserts there are 41.5 and 32.8 inches, respectively, in the C36. When it comes to really packing people in—and that's the essence of a four-door's talents—the contest is a draw.

To get the maximum performance from either car, it's first necessary to turn off the traction control. Fortunately, that's possible. Unfortunately, there's no way to program either system not to reengage every time the car is started. When on, both systems are unobtrusive and reassuring during day-to-day motoring, yet prove to be absolute fun-robbers in aggressive driving.

When the traction control is turned off, each car displays a big orange triangle warning light on the dash indicating that, while the manufacturer appreciates you're an adult responsible enough to afford the car, you must be nuts to do what you have in mind. If the C36's warning light were any more obnoxious, it would auto-dial the suicide prevention hot-line on the cell phone. What makes this all so bizarre is how perfectly mannered both cars are without traction control—among the least likely vehicles to betray a driver.

It takes a bit of delicacy to obtain the fastest dragstrip launch from either car (a bit more with the manual transmission in the M3), but both are massively rapid. The 3175-pound M3 takes just 5.5 seconds to reach 60 mph, while the 3550-pound C36 does the trick in 5.9. BMW claims the automatic-equipped M3 sedan takes 0.8 second longer to 60 than

From the C280's 2.8-liter six, AMG's 3.6-liter/276-horsepower C36 engine is the highest specific-output powerplant Mercedes has ever offered.

In its third year, the Mercedes C-Class' interior exudes a stoic confidence. For people wider of girth, the C36's power seats are a godsend, while the generous glass area gives the passenger module a more airy feel than that of the M3.

its manual brother, which would leave it slightly behind the C36. Pull up to a new Z28 in either car, and it'll be the drivers' relative skill that determines the winner of a stoplight drag. The BMW shows its power best coming off a corner when its heady torque insanely rockets the car from any apex. By contrast, the C36 shines brightest when the driver pounds the accelerator while cruising at about 70 mph; once the transmission kicks down, the car's acceleration to 120 is breathtaking. Top speed won't separate the two, as both are electronically limited to 155 mph.

In ultimate handling, the M3 has the clear advantage. The BMW's 69.4-mph eruption through *MT*'s 600-foot slalom has been surpassed only by the Ferrari F355, Porsche 911 Turbo, and Dodge Viper GTS among all current production cars. That's impressive company, and what's more amazing is that the M3's steering response may be the best of the bunch. Matching that dynamic performance are awesome brakes (60-0 mph in 113 feet). Around a tight road course, the M3 could well be the quickest production four-door ever.

Still, the C36 is no handling slouch; its 66.5-mph slalom speed betters some normally aspirated 911s we've tested, and its suspension isn't quite so harsh in normal driving. While the BMW beats the Mercedes' 114-foot 60-0-mph stopping distance by a foot, the C36's 28-foot 0-30 anchorage is that foot better than the M3. As good as the C36's steering is, however, it can't match the M3 for precision feel.

The C36's more compliant suspension combines with more efficacious gearing to make the car a superior cruiser. At about 70 mph, the M3's 1.00:1 fifth and 3.23:1 final-drive ratio have the engine turning well over 3000 rpm, and the drone is noticeable. The C36's 0.83:1 fifth-gear overdrive and 3.07:1 rearend make for a more relaxed 2550 rpm at the same 60 mph.

The M3's barely compromised prowess has its allure, and so do the C36's longer, more compliant legs. But ultimately the victory here must go to the M3 for one simple reason: price. Every C36 comes loaded with power seats, a moonroof, cruise control, a Bose stereo that could be used to shout propaganda into North Korea, and a $51,925 base price. By the time options like an integrated cell phone, CD changer, adjustable steering column, and destination charges were added, the test car had earned a $57,260 sticker. That's up there with the larger, incredibly attractive E420 Sport and 540i six-speed.

In contrast, the M3 sedan starts at a much lower $39,280 without a sunroof, power seats, cruise, or a lot of things. But even with options to match the C36, it's still a full Honda Civic DX cheaper. And in the realm of performance cars, that makes it one of the great bargains out there. No matter how many doors it has. **MT**

TECH DATA

GENERAL

	BMW M3 Sedan	Mercedes-Benz C36
Importer	BMW of North America, Inc, Woodcliff Lake, N.J.	Mercedes-Benz of North America, Inc., Montvale, N.J.
Body style	4-door, 5-passenger	4-door, 5-passenger
Location of final assembly	Munich, Germany	Afalterbach, Germany
EPA size class	Subcompact	Compact
Drivetrain layout	FE, RD	FE, RD
Airbag	Dual	Dual
Base price	$39,280	$51,925
Price as tested	$39,280	$57,260
Options included	None	Traction control, heated seats, $1875; CD changer, mobile phone, $1495
Ancillary charges	Destination, $570	Destination, $595

DIMENSIONS

	BMW M3 Sedan	Mercedes-Benz C36
Wheelbase, in./mm	106.3/2700	105.9/2690
Track, f/r, in./mm	56.0/56.6/1422/1438	58.9/58.2/1497/1478
Length, in./mm	174.5/4432	177.4/4506
Width, in./mm	66.9/1699	67.7/1720
Height, in./mm	53.7/1364	56.1/1425
Ground clearance, in./mm	3.5/89	5.0/127
Mfr's curb weight, lb	3175	3550
Weight distribution, f/r, %	50/50	55/45
Cargo capacity, cu ft	10.3	11.6
Fuel capacity, gal.	16.4	16.4
Weight/power ratio, lb/hp	13.2	12.9

ENGINE

	BMW M3 Sedan	Mercedes-Benz C36
Type	I-6, liquid cooled, cast iron block, cast aluminum head	I-6, liquid cooled, cast iron block, cast aluminum head
Bore x stroke, in./mm	3.40x3.53/ 86.4x89.6	3.58x3.64/ 91.0x92.4
Displacement, ci/cc	192/3152	220/3606
Compression ratio	10.5:1	10.5:1
Valve gear	DOHC, 4 valves/cylinder	DOHC, 4 valves/cylinder
Fuel/induction system	Multiport injection	Multiport injection
Horsepower, hp @ rpm, SAE net	240 @ 6000	276 @ 5750
Torque, lb @ rpm, SAE net	236 @ 3800	284 @ 4000
Horsepower/liter	76.1	76.5
Redline, rpm	6800	6600
Recommended fuel	Premium unleaded	Premium unleaded

DRIVELINE

	BMW M3 Sedan	Mercedes-Benz C36
Transmission type	5-speed manual	5-speed automatic
Gear ratios		
(1st)	4.20:1	3.59:1
(2nd)	2.49:1	2.19:1
(3rd)	1.66:1	1.41:1
(4th)	1.24:1	1.00:1
(5th)	1.00:1	0.83:1
Axle ratio	3.23:1	3.07:1
Final-drive ratio	3.23:1	2.55:1
Engine rpm, 60 mph in top gear	2800	2250

CHASSIS

	BMW M3 Sedan	Mercedes-Benz C36
Suspension		
Front	MacPherson struts, lower arms, coil springs, anti-roll bar	Upper and lower arms, coil springs, anti-roll bar
Rear	Multilink, coil springs, anti-roll bar	5-links, coil springs, anti-roll bar
Steering		
Type	Rack and pinion, power assist	Recirculating ball, power assist
Ratio	15.6:1	13.3:1
Turns, lock to lock	3.0	3.0
Turning circle, ft	38.1	37.2
Brakes		
Front, type/dia., in.	Vented disc/12.4	Vented disc/12.6
Rear, type/dia., in.	Vented disc/12.3	Vented disc/10.9
Anti-lock	Standard	Standard
Wheels and tires		
Wheel size, f/r, in.	17x7.5/17x8.5	17x7.5/17x8.5
Wheel type/material	Forged alloy	Forged aluminum
Tire size, f/r	225/45ZR17/ 245/40ZR17	225/45ZR17/ 245/40ZR17
Tire mfr. and model	Michelin Pilot SX	Bridgestone Expedia

INSTRUMENTATION

	BMW M3 Sedan	Mercedes-Benz C36
Instruments	160-mph speedo, 8000-rpm tach, fuel level, water temp, digital clock	160-mph speedo, 7000-rpm tach, fuel level, coolant temp
Warning lamps	Battery, low fuel, check engine, brake, brake fluid, airbag, seatbelts, brake pressure, ABS	Low fuel, engine oil, seatbelt, traction control, front brake-pad wear, coolant, washer fluid, ABS, engine electronics

PERFORMANCE AND TEST DATA

	BMW M3 Sedan	Mercedes-Benz C36
Acceleration, sec		
0-30 mph	2.0	2.2
0-40 mph	2.9	3.2
0-50 mph	4.1	4.5
0-60 mph	5.5	5.9
0-70 mph	7.2	7.7
0-80 mph	9.0	9.9
0-90 mph	11.5	12.3
0-100 mph	14.3	15.2
Standing quarter mile, sec @ mph	14.0 @ 99.2	14.4 @ 97.7
Braking, ft		
30-0	29	28
60-0	113	114
Handling		
Lateral acceleration, g	0.91	0.87
Speed through 600-ft slalom, mph	69.4	66.5
Speedometer error Indicated/actual	30/29 40/39 50/49 60/59	30/28 40/38 50/48 60/58
Interior noise, dB		
Idling in neutral	48	45
Steady 60 mph in top gear	71	70

FUEL ECONOMY

	BMW M3 Sedan	Mercedes-Benz C36
EPA, city/hwy., mpg	20/28	18/24
Est. range, city/hwy., miles	328/459	295/394

hard core soft top

BMW M3 CONVERTIBLE

STORY **Jonathan Hawley**
PHOTOS **Helmut Mueller**

There's only one thing I can think of which is good about the M3 Convertible. Hang on, rephrase that: there's only one thing about the convertible which could possibly make it *better* than the coupe. If you suffer from claustrophobia then being open to the elements by flipping back a fabric lid is going to help solve a few fears.

Otherwise, consider this. The M3 coupe is a sensational car. It is very, very fast, but manages to fold loads of sensibility into its potent packaging. A big back seat, reasonable boot, bodywork which is slave to nobody's fashion, and driving manners more like a Honda Civic than the Porsche 911 it comes near to matching in a straight line. Heck, it ran away with our 1996 PCOTY award.

Now slice through the C-pillar and across the windscreen header rail. There's the small problem that either end is only kept together by the floorpan and a couple of door latches, but that's okay thanks to some 100 kg of strengthening under the floor pan

The 3-Series convertible is a stiff little number as convertibles go. Far from rock solid, but scuttle shake and those intimate little groans which infest the roofless body are minimal.

But no fabric roof can match steel, so wind and road noise levels are inevitably higher. Still, the Bimmer's canvas does do it better than most.

The 3.2-litre straight six, of course, is still gloriously crisp with 236 kW available in the upper reaches of its VANOS valve gear's oscillatory limits but will drive like a lamb in stop-start city traffic.

The back seat and boot are still useful enough that you can load up your spouse, mother-in-law or little nephew Nathan, take them out to your favourite piece of road and terrify the living shit out of them.

The convertible does come with a host of extras to celebrate BMW M Division's 25th birthday: Nappa leather, forests of woodgrain and heated seats. Those things can be found on the coupe as well, but there's a catch. The benefits of convertible ownership come, surprisingly enough, at a price. Sans roof, the M3 will lighten your bank account by $147,500.

One of the coupe's main attractions is it is such a potent performer and yet looks

relatively anonymous. There's a certain satisfaction in having the ability to excel without advertising it. In the convertible's case, don't forget that while you're looking out, the world is also looking in.

speccheck

engine	*3.2-litre 24-valve six*
power/weight	*236 kW / 1590 kg*
drive	*rear-wheel*
on sale	*now*
price	*$147,500*

ROAD TEST

BMW M3 Superb engineering, **supercar performance**

Motoring writers often refer to the "grin factor" as a mark of how much they enjoyed driving a car, but to borrow a line from a BMW advertisement about their new six-speed gearbox, we'd raise that to an unqualified "Yeee ha" after two weeks with the mighty M3.

Back in 1966 the Bavarian manufacturer defined the small sports sedan genre with the 1602 and, from then to the present, has continued to improve the breed, culminating in what ranks as an exceptional high-performance automobile. It seems a tad gung-ho to speak of value-for-money in a car costing R260 000 sans options, but what else can one buy for the money that offers supercar performance and has the running gear and refinement to match?

Not that the M3 is perfect – we have our share of gripes – but we'd go so far as to say that anyone who loves fine high performance machinery without attachment to status, must come away highly impressed with this latest execution of BMW's most agile sedan.

Quite the opposite of wimpish, the top 3-Series requires continuous involvement just to drive smoothly, let alone to explore its responses. The gearbox, designed to take the motor's walloping torque, is of necessity chunky in action and the clutch action stiff by luxury-car standards. Likewise, the driveline has a fair amount of backlash, especially noticeable in first if the clutch and throttle are not synchronised correctly. Naturally, practice makes it easier, but the driver still has to pay attention if he prides himself on smooth shifts.

Another irritant is the small dimensions of the designer-style door mirrors. Their limited field of reflection can lead to a feeling of unease in cut-and-thrust traffic situations.

Standard luxury and convenience items on our test car included power steering, nappa leather upholstery, lacquered wood cappings, electric windows, electric sunroof with tilt and slide functions, temperature-controlled air-conditioning with microfilter air recirculation, electric front seat adjustment and integrated CD sound system. SRS airbags are standard for both front occupants. Optional extras include folding rear seats to increase luggage space, automatic air recirculation, an enhanced sound system, remote central locking, cruise control, car 'phone, park distance control and metallic paintwork.

On the subject of paintwork, our test car was finished in an attention-getting colour, called Santorini blue, that really suited the macho looks provided by the aerodynamic enhancements and special alloy wheels. The front air dam incorporates cooling air vents for the ventilated disc brakes, and low-level driving lamps. The downside of this was that we soon learned to treat even shallow driveway dips with caution as the ramp angle proved to be particularly small.

Our last test of an M3 was for our

Main picture: distinctive exterior features include double-spoke forged alloy wheels and special aerodynamic body kit.

Right: the M3 interior has lacquered burr walnut cappings and the seats and door panels are upholstered in nappa leather. Airbag collision protection for front occupants is standard equipment.

February 1994 issue, when we featured the three-litre coupé, which was a fully built-up import priced at R209 998. Running happily on 97-octane leaded petrol at the coast, that motor had a capacity of 3,0 litres, a compression ratio of 10,8 to 1 and variable inlet camshaft control, along with Bosch's DME engine management system, all helping to deliver a rated peak power of 210 kW at 7 000 r/min. The current unleaded fuel motor has been bored and stroked to take it up to 3,2 litres, and the compression ratio has been dropped to 10,5 to 1. Improvements include a double Vanos (BMW's variable valve-timing system for inlet and exhaust cams), solid state ignition with individual coils, and further advanced engine management. Power is up by 18 kW and torque by 30 N.m, but based on our 1994 figures, the power-to-weight ratio is improved by only 0,74 per cent because of the extra weight penalty imposed by the sedan bodyshell.

From the above, it follows that we were not pinning our hopes on any significant improvement in performance but we expected, and were not disappointed, by the same M3 magic we remembered of old. In addition, the new car has some serious running gear improvements such as the six-speed transmission, with lower intermediate ratios but a higher top (fifth gear is direct). Spring and damper settings have been completely revised and matched to different tyre dimensions on the familiar double-spoke forged light alloy wheels. Braking has been upgraded by switching to compound aluminium brake disc covers with grey cast iron friction rings for improved heat dissipation. In addition, the ABS system has been upgraded and there is a new vacuum servo.

Little can be said about the snug but ergonomically sound driving position of the current 3-Series that has not already been said frequently in the pages of CAR, but it's worth noting that the M3 sedan with its burr walnut trim and fine nappa leather upholstery has a considerably more opulent interior than the previous coupé version. Quality of workmanship is in the BMW tradition, right down to practical metal twist-clips that hold the floor mats firmly in place to prevent the irritating sliding that so often takes place due to foot movement in cars that are not so well appointed. One small criticism concerns the lack of a kick pad on the commonly vulnerable spot at the base of the door, where we noted that the leather

Right: the heart of the M3 is its 228 kW in-line six motor with Vanos variable valve timing for both inlet and exhaust camshafts, solid state-powered individual ignition coils, cylinder-specific knock control and state-of-the-art Bosch digital motor electronics.

KEY FIGURES:

Maximum speed	255 km/h
1 km sprint	26,37 secs
Fuel tank capacity	62 litres
Litres/100 km at 100	N/A
*Fuel index	N/A
Estimated fuel range	N/A
Engine revs per km	1 382
Odometer error	0,06 per cent over
National list price	R260 000

(*Consumption at 100 plus 40%)

covering was already marked on the relatively new test car.

From the moment that you fire up the latest 3,2-litre six, you know that this is a very fast car. The motor kicks into life to the tune of a deep bass exhaust that switches to a sound like tearing canvas as you blip the throttle, accompanied by a gentle rocking of the body to the right in response to the accelerating mechanical components. First is a start-off gear, pulling 8,5 km/h per 1 000 r/min, so it bumps the peak power/rev limit of 7 400 at 63 km/h ludicrously quickly, and jack-rabbit starts will trigger vigorous rescue action on the part of the limited slip differential . Second, on the other hand, at 14,36 km/h per 1 000 r/min, is still low enough to allow the motor to pull like a steam train from only 500 r/min right up to 106 km/h. Third is even more impressive, pulling strongly from around 1 000 r/min on the flat all the way up to 143 km/h, by which time the M3 is bulleting forward with seat-mashing acceleration. From there on, it's really a case of that aforementioned "Yeee ha" feeling as the scenery starts passing by ever more rapidly, and wind-roar drowns out the bass exhaust and mechanical noise of the spinning in-line six. During our performance testing we posted a zero to 100 km/h time of 6,19 seconds, a slight improvement over the 6,34 seconds taken by the previous coupé model, with a kilometre sprint of 26,37, just 0,42 seconds worse, confirming that – like its predecessor – the M3 sedan is still firmly seated in supercar territory. For the record, top speed is nominally limited to 255 km/h, but our test car took us up to a steady 250 km/h one way and made the return run at 256. Free of a rev-limiter, it would likely red-line in fifth at close to 267 km/h.

With this kind of performance capability on hand, it stands to reason that the M3 could cruise effortlessly at speeds of over 200 km/h if it were legal to do so. More importantly, the powertrain shows none of the usual signs of distress when called upon to perform to the limit. Apart from a very slight valve gear rattle at idle, the motor retained its turbine-like quality, even after some hours of really tough road testing.

The integrity of design extends to the chassis which is, if anything, even ahead

SPECIFICATIONS

POWER AND TORQUE

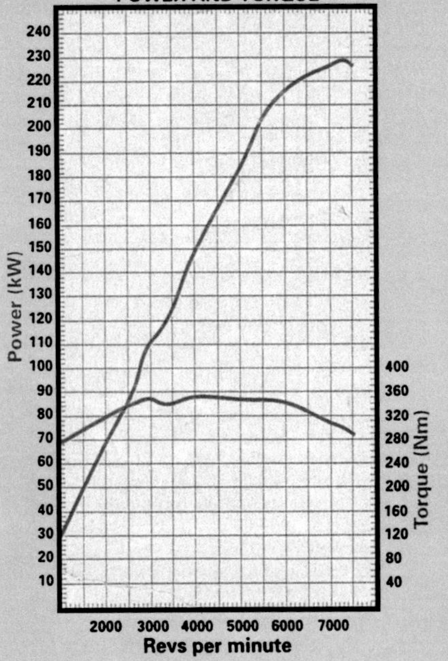

ENGINE:
- Cylinders: six in-line
- Fuel supply: Bosch DME
- Bore/stroke: 91/86,4 mm
- Cubic capacity: 3 201 cm³
- Compression ratio: 10,5 to 1
- Valve gear: d-o-h-c, double vanos
- Ignition: Bosch DME
- Main bearings: seven
- Fuel requirement: premium unleaded
- Cooling: water

ENGINE OUTPUT:
- Max power I.S.O. (kW): 228
- Power peak (r/min): 7 400
- Max usable r/min: 7 400
- Max torque (N.m): 340
- Torque peak (r/min): 3 250

TRANSMISSION:
- Forward speeds: six
- Gearshift: console
- Low gear: 4,23 to 1
- 2nd gear: 2,51 to 1
- 3rd gear: 1,87 to 1
- 4th gear: 1,23 to 1
- 5th gear: 1,00 to 1
- Top: 0,83 to 1
- Reverse gear: 3,75 to 1
- Final drive: 3,23 to 1
- Drive wheels: rear

WHEELS AND TYRES:
- Road wheels: alloy
- Rim width: 7,5J front, 8,5J rear
- Tyre make: Michelin Pilot SX
- Tyre size: 225/45 ZR17 front, 245/40 ZR17 rear
- Tyre pressures (front): 230-280 kPa
- Tyre pressures (rear): 240-330 kPa

BRAKES:
- Front: compound ventilated discs
- Rear: compound ventilated discs
- Hydraulics: ABS
- Boosting: vacuum
- Handbrake position: console

STEERING:
- Type: power-assisted rack and pinion
- Lock to lock: 3,3 turns
- Turning circle: 10,6 metres

MEASUREMENTS:
- Length overall: 4 433 mm
- Width overall: 1 698 mm
- Height overall: 1 366 mm
- Wheelbase: 2 710 mm
- Front track: 1 422 mm
- Rear track: 1 444 mm
- Ground clearance: N/A
- Licensing mass: 1 530 kg
- Mass as tested: 1 533 kg

SUSPENSION
- Front: independent
- Type: struts, coil springs, anti-roll bar
- Rear: independent
- Type: multi-link, coil springs, anti-roll bar

CAPACITIES:
- Seating: 4/5
- Fuel tank: 62 litres
- Luggage trunk: 256 dm³

WARRANTY: Motorplan 5 year or 100 000 km

TEST CAR FROM:
BMW South Africa

of the M3's pulverising performance. During really hard cornering the test car displayed prodigious levels of grip combined with faithful responses to steering inputs. Turning into our favourite test corners at high speed elicited much pleasure as the steering loaded up with micrometer-like precision to perfectly communicate the side forces induced in the process. Like its predecessor, this latest M3 is impressively neutral. High speed stability is, in a word, Teutonic, and pedestrian-speed ride is firm but compliant enough to avoid being uncomfortable. As we said, this is a macho performance car with some inevitable compromises.

Due to the complex in-line six extending far enough back in the engine bay to make the fuel lines particularly difficult to access, and considering the test results would be of academic interest to those wealthy enough to buy an M3, we decided to restrict our fuel testing to tank-to-tank measurements. These returned an overall figure of 15 litres/100 km, covering lots of enthusiastic driving and tough performance testing. This should be taken as a worst-case scenario, which is why we believe the claimed urban cycle figure of 13 litres/100 km to be reasonable.

Test summary

As we remarked in the beginning, the M3 is really good value if you stack up its performance capability and integrity of engineering against anything else with similar agility. We'd say that it is as close to the ultimate combination of performance, handling and luxury as is technically possible in a sedan of this size at present. Who could ask for more? ●

TEST RESULTS: BMW M3

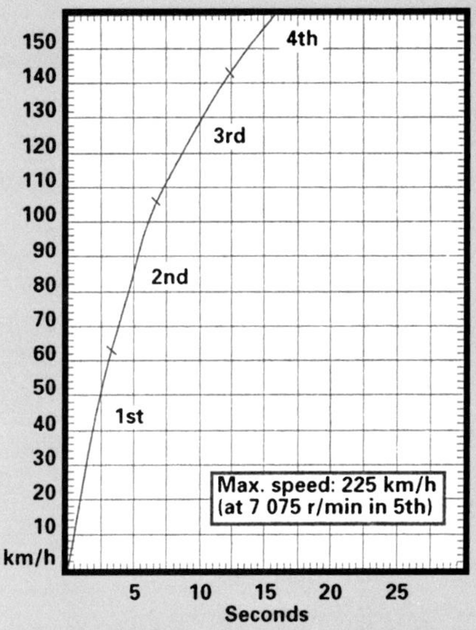

BRAKING DISTANCES

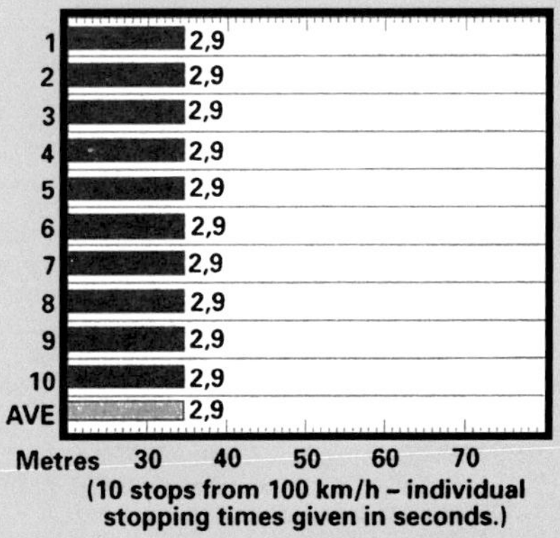

(10 stops from 100 km/h – individual stopping times given in seconds.)

GRADIENT ABILITY

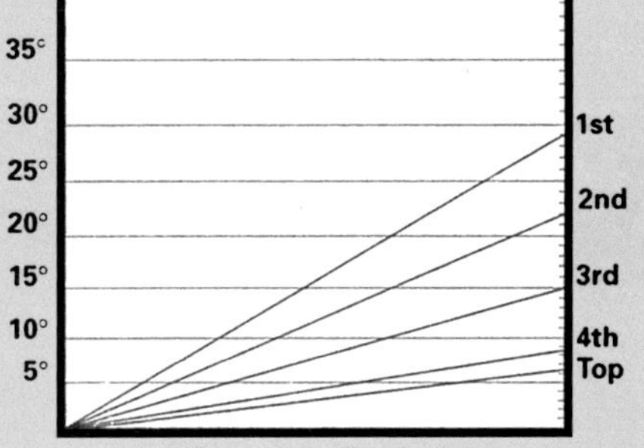

(Degrees inclination)

MAXIMUM SPEED (km/h):

True speed	255			
Speedometer reading	260			

(Average of runs both ways on a level road)

Calibration:	60	80	100	120
True speed:	58	76	95	115

ACCELERATION (seconds):

0-60	3,09
0-80	4,61
0-100	6,19
0-120	8,59
1 km sprint	26,37
Terminal speed	206,4

OVERTAKING ACCELERATION (seconds):

	3rd	4th	5th	Top
40-60	2,50	3,90	5,41	7,10
60-80	2,26	2,51	4,49	6,70
80-100	2,30	3,26	4,37	6,50
100-120	2,44	3,31	4,27	6,10
120-140	2,49	3,60	4,10	6,32

FUEL CONSUMPTION:
(claimed according to EEC/80/1268)

90	6,5
120	7,9
Urban	13,0

BRAKING TEST:
From 100 km/h

Best stop	2,9
Worst stop	2,9
Average	2,9

(Measured in seconds with stops from true speeds at 30-second intervals on a good bitumenised surface.)

GRADIENTS IN GEARS

Low gear	1 in 1,8
2nd gear	1 in 2,5
3rd gear	1 in 3,7
4th gear	1 in 5,3
5th gear	1 in 6,7
Top	1 in 9,1

(Tabulated from Tapley (x gravity) readings, car carrying test crew of two and standard test equipment.)

GEARED SPEEDS (km/h):

Low gear	63*
2nd gear	106*
3rd gear	143*
4th gear	217*
5th gear	267*
Top gear	321*

(Calculated at engine power peak* – 7 400 r/min and at max. usable r/min – r/min.)

INTERIOR NOISE LEVELS:

	Mech	Road
Idling	40	–
60		55–
8058	65	
100	62	67
120	65	71

(Measured in decibels, "A" weighting, averaging runs both ways on a level road: "mechanical" with car closed; "road" on a coarse road surface.)

ENGINE SPEED

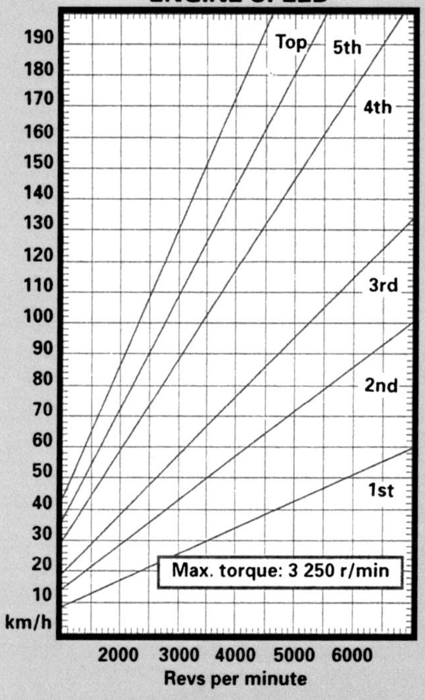

PERFORMANCE FACTORS:

Power/mass (W/kg) net	148,7
Frontal area (m²)	232
km/h per 1 000 r/min (top)	43,41

(Calculated on "mass as tested", gross frontal area, gearing and I.S.O. power output)

TEST CONDITIONS:

Altitude	at sea level
Weather	fine, light wind
Fuel used	95 octane
Test car's odometer	2 603

CAR'S ROAD TESTS

CAR is the only South African motor magazine whose performance road tests are carried out at sea level – where naturally aspirated car engines achieve their (rated) peak performance – on a flat road to internationally comparable standards.

The test car carries a crew of two, a full tank of fuel and German Peiseler electronic road test equipment. CAR's fuel consumption testing is done with a Pierburg flow meter linked to the Peiseler computer. Top speed and overtaking run times are averaged both ways on a level road.

M BRACING

DRIVE BMW M3 EVOLUTION Time to take the straight six for one final fling through the bends it revels in. By Andrew Frankel

It's easy to forget just how fast the BMW M3 is. Easy because it doesn't look that fast, easier because supercars are exotic things that are rarely sighted. Yet if you know where to look, you will find more M3s loitering on the corners of city streets than pigeons on Nelson's Column.

Second thing. The speed with which M3s are driven is inversely proportional to the power under the bonnet. Find an old-shape M3, with its 200bhp four-pot motor, and I'll wager you've also found in its owner a true enthusiast. Find this, the last Evolution model of the M3, and almost anyone could be behind the wheel. And usually is. These cars have 321bhp, but I don't think I've ever seen the performance being used to the full, other than in the artless pursuit of another few hundred yards' advantage on the M4.

Yes, I am generalising, but in the two years since I last drove an M3, its memory had fled my mind so completely that when I approached it again it was with the expectation of no more than another pleasantly swift BMW.

The few fibres of previous experience that remained suggested this was a good car, one that was better than many had given credit at the time. The problem was the car it was based on, the first M3 to use this bodyshell. This wasn't a bad car, merely a bad M-car, one which had no right to that badge despite its 286bhp engine. The steering and suspension were wrong for such a car – calling it a 330CSi would have been more accurate.

Our purpose with the Evolution was to spend a day's hard driving in Wales in the hope of being able to produce a satisfactory valediction for a car no longer in production and about to be replaced by one based on our chase car, a new BMW 328Ci.

Step from one to the other and at once you are struck by how old the M3 feels already. It's everywhere you look, from the position of the pedals to the fact that the steering wheel adjusts only for rake. There are straight lines where now there are curves, slightly busy switchgear where now brilliantly marshalled order reigns.

Twist the key, hear the engine catch and let it settle. There's nothing old sounding here, and nothing old looking about a revcounter whose circumference turns into unbroken red only beyond 7500rpm. Back at idle, it sounds cultured, but makes no promise of what is to come.

I discovered it sprinting away from the toll booths on the old Severn Bridge. A quick squirt through the first couple of gears to gain a preview of what's in store. And now the memories returned as swiftly as they had left. If this is not quite Ferrari punch, it is closer than anything your mind's eye would have you believe.

BMW has never made an uncivil straight six in its life, but this one, with its searing 100bhp per litre specific output, piles on the power with grace and remarkable even-handedness; for sure it goes harder at 5000rpm than at 3000rpm, but there are no steps from idle to red line – it is just relentless.

Yet the car feels old. The gearchange requires seemingly double the effort of the new 328. The steering is different, too. Better, in my book. As in so many new cars, the new 3-series has a vagueness engineered into

Hot BMW coupe has to live up to its own badge

Rapid progress on ordinary roads is uneventful

Big 315mm discs provide huge stopping power

Ask the BMW M3 to challenge and entertain you and it will

its character when the wheel is straight. It allows your high-speed progress on motorways not to be disturbed by tiny hand movements which then have to be corrected. However, it does make a car feel less responsive, and you only have to spend five minutes in this M3 to know it. The M3 feels more alive, positive and direct and, if still falling far short of the reactions of a racing car, does at least respond to the helm with something resembling alacrity.

Such were the thoughts that ambled across my mind as the junctions of the M4 ticked away. It's still a refined car by any standards, its sixth gear ratio being kept long for such purposes while the other five are given over to the provision of fun. It's comfortable enough, with big M-emblazoned chairs and a ride quality that would not disgrace many entirely unsporting cars.

It was, I pondered, a car I could live with every day, and as this thought occurred so did another. Perhaps that *is* the trouble with this car, perhaps that's why so many owners fail to appreciate the true nature of the commodity they possess. It looks good, has the right badge and is easy to own. These are the foothills of its talents, but if trundling around below base

Cabin is comfortable place to be, but already feels old

Steering feels much more alive than in new 3-series

STAN PAPIOR

camp is where you're happiest, why bother putting your crampons on?

For me there was one good reason, and it was the same reason that brought us to Wales in the first place. The M3 and I were going mountaineering; we were going to push ourselves a little bit harder than usual to hopefully find out a lot more than usual. I needed to be sure of the values it would hand to its successor, and that it was rid of the one thing that haunted its immediate predecessor – the fact that, for all its speed, it wasn't really a driver's car. We were going to go to roads, through corners and over crests behind which no car without the requisite talents could hide.

The weather was closing in as we left the M4, but the roads to the hills were clear. At first, the M3 was more fluent than fun. There was little doubting the rate of progress or its composure through corners. But were we having fun? No, to be honest. The awful suggestion that this was another car more confident in its own abilities than those of its driver nagged at me. Cars that think they are better than you miss the point – you don't want to be that good, you just want to enjoy yourself.

In the end, it took seriously challenging terrain to tempt the M3 into dropping its veneer of efficiency and join in the fun. The moment it happened I was sold on the car, in the same way that the discovery of a sense of humour in a very serious person is instantly endearing. The M3 had, after all, not forgotten the bloke behind the wheel.

It was an uphill, second gear, left-hand hairpin with all the visibility you could wish for. The car didn't even need to be provoked – just a little too much throttle at the apex was enough to prise the rear Michelins from their grasp on the road and kick the back just a few degrees out of line, where it would stay so long as the power remained applied and the slide was not killed too swiftly with the steering. I should be old enough to have grown out of amusing myself in such a cliched fashion, but it seems I am not. Besides, I didn't do it for a cheap thrill; I needed to know what lay beneath the surface of this car. ➧

Just a touch too much throttle and the M3 drops its civilised veneer, though it's always safe – even in the rain

LATEST EVOLUTION OF THE M3

The M3's evolution entered a new phase at the Frankfurt Motor Show last month when BMW revealed its next-generation model.

To offset the extra weight of today's safer, stiffer body, the engine capacity has risen to 3.4 litres. BMW's M division has promised to maintain the high-revving straight six's output at 100bhp per litre, which equates to 230bhp per tonne.

***Autocar*'s sources report that in secret tests the car will sprint to 60mph in under 5.0sec, but no official claims have been made. The new model goes on sale in autumn 2000 and is expected to cost £46,000.**

THANKS TO CHEYNE BMW, LONDON SW6 (0171 736 8481)

You see, nothing lies beneath the surface of the 328Ci. Do not mistake me, I think it's a superb car, but it is what you see, and its handling is entirely linear. Push a bit and it will understeer; push a bit more and it will add a commensurate amount more understeer. Hoof it, lift off, boot it again and the greatest reaction you're likely to elicit is the blinking of the traction control light. Such reactions are fine from a less than overtly sporting car, but they do not befit an M-car, and I was relieved to discover the M3's sense of fun remained intact.

The rest of the day was straightforward because now I understood. We were truly in the mountains, and all its attributes, hitherto impressive on their own, came together to create an experience you'd not have suspected on the way here. The brakes and the engine make a fabulous double act, for both possess unlikely reserves of power. As I'd ask more of the motor as we howled up to the next curve, so too would I ask more of the discs to shed the extra speed.

I never did fully make my peace with the steering. It was just a bit too slow and a shade less communicative than I'd hoped, but at least it no longer spoiled the fun like its predecessor. And there was no sign of that car's on-limit nervousness. Even when the rain set in and driving fast became more a matter of restraint than exuberance.

I returned home happier than I'd ever expected to be with the M3. There hadn't been any seminal driving experiences, nor was I left with that moment of truth when you know you have driven a truly extraordinary machine. This, however, was not on the agenda. More surprising even than how old the M3 feels, is how bloody good it is at so many things, and I wonder now as then how many owners actually know what their M3 will do if shown the right roads.

It is, however, fair criticism to say most of us do not find ourselves in the Brecon Beacons every day, and a truly involving sports car should not require such a trip before the fun starts. If this M3 does make a mistake it is that it's so effective on more ordinary roads that the driver feels almost cut out of the loop. And if such roads make up your everyday motoring, how could you discover that, elsewhere, the M3 is also beautifully balanced, adjustable and indulgent?

Even so, for me it was enough to know that the M3 Evolution truly regained for the breed the ability to challenge and amuse an appreciative driver on the right roads while cossetting and comforting the rest of the time. It may have put a different spin on it, but these are the core values of the original M3. The latest M5 suggests BMW has not forgotten this, and we must hope that the new M3, due here next year, will prove it. ●

Smooth-spinning 3.2-litre straight six produces a seamless and relentless stream of power – 321bhp at its peak

FACTFILE

BMW M3 EVO

HOW FAST?

0-60mph	5.3sec
0-100mph	12.2sec
Top speed	155mph

HOW THIRSTY?

Touring	29.3mpg
Best	29.3mpg
Worst	15.8mpg
Average	22.8mpg

HOW BIG?

Length	4433mm
Width (inc mirrors)	1920mm
Height	1366mm
Wheelbase	2700mm
Weight	1510kg

ENGINE

Layout 6 cyls in line, 3201cc
Max power 321bhp at 7400rpm
Max torque 258lb ft at 3250rpm
Specific output 100bhp per litre
Power to weight 212bhp per tonne
Installation Front, longitudinal, rear-wheel drive
Made of Alloy head, iron block
Bore/stroke 86.4/91.0mm
Valve gear 4 per cyl, dohc
Ignition and fuel MS S50 Digital Motor Electronics

GEARBOX

Type 6-speed manual
Ratios mph/1000rpm
1st 4.23/5.4 **2nd** 2.51/10.1
3rd 1.67/13.6 **4th** 1.23/18.5
5th 1.00/22.8 **6th** 0.83/27.4
Final drive 3.23

SUSPENSION

Front MacPherson struts, coil springs and dampers, anti-roll bar
Rear Multi-link, coil springs and dampers, anti-roll bar

STEERING

Type Rack and pinion, power assisted
Turns lock to lock 2.8

BRAKES

Front 315mm ventilated discs
Rear 315mm ventilated discs
Anti-lock Standard

WHEELS AND TYRES

Size 7.5Jx17in (f), 8.5Jx17in (r)
Made of Alloy
Tyres 225/45 ZR17 (f), 245/40 ZR17 (r), Michelin Pilot MXXV SX

VERDICT

Stays true to the core values of the original M3. A scorching driver's car lurks under a civilised veneer, but needs challenging roads to show its mettle.

Soul of Gold

BMW's new M3 ups the ante on its performance legacy.

BY IAN KUAH · PHOTOGRAPHY BY THE AUTHOR

BMW'S M3 STORY STARTED back in the mid-1980s when BMW laid plans to homologate a sports sedan for the European Touring Car Championship. The 3-Series was the ideal size and weight, but needed suspension modifications and a potent motor, which could be tweaked for racing. The task was given to BMW Motorsport and the first customer cars wearing the M3 badge were delivered in 1987.

A 2.3-liter four-cylinder twin-cam motor set far back in the chassis made for a 50/50 weight distribution while substantial upgrading of the E30 3-Series suspension turned a fairly evil-handling luxury compact into one of the best-handling cars ever. By the time the E30 M3 line was shut down with around 17,000 sold, engine capacity had grown to 2.5 liters, and the model had won Touring Car championships all over the world. The M3 legend was carved in stone.

No wonder then when the E36 M3 arrived in 1992, great things were expected of it, especially since the four cylinder engine had been replaced by a 3.0-liter twin-cam iron-block straight-six boasting 286 horsepower.

This engine was not destined for the US, however. Instead of the sophisticated DOHC 286-hp engine and the later 321-hp version, the US M3 received a stroked version of the 2.5-liter 3-Series inline-six with 240 hp. The expensive and complicated continuously variable VANOS system on the DOHC head was ditched in favor of a simpler VANOS system with just two points of adjustment. Even when it was enlarged to 3.2 liters, the US engine remained at 240 hp.

Planning for the E46 version started about the time the M3 went into production in 1992. In a development program that took three years to complete, the first move was to increase engine displacement slightly from 3201cc to 3246.

New, lighter pistons were mated to graphite-coated connecting rods, the inlet valves were enlarged and the compression ratio bumped up from 10.8 to 11.5:1. A second oil pump was added to make sure the vital fluids continued to reach the right parts under sustained hard cornering. While the previous VANOS variable valve system had timing on just its inlet cam, a significant improvement in torque was found by adding this feature to the exhaust cam as well. Open the hood, and you'll spot the M3's new VANOS mechanism on the front of the timing chain cover. The equal-length primary pipes on the exhaust header are another giveaway. The engine management system is also new. The latest Bosch MSS50 system looks after fuel, spark, emissions and the VANOS units simultaneously.

The complexity is worth it. Now there's 333 hp at a staggering 7900 rpm and 262 lb/ft of torque at a lower 4900 rpm. In a car weighing 3400 pounds, this is a recipe for dynamite performance. We clocked a 0-60 mph time of 4.8 seconds, and the quarter-mile came up in 13.5 seconds with a 104.5 mph terminal speed! Top speed is electronically limited to 155 mph (250km/h), but the engineers say that 170 mph is a realistic maximum if the car is given free rein.

BMW's engineers knew what its US customers wanted in a new M3—more power than the previous model and the intimate steering feel and fine handling of the original E30. A tall order if ever there was one, but within the first mile, we knew they had succeeded.

The Heart of the Matter

The heart of any car with sporting pretensions is the engine. The 18 months leading up to the launch saw a huge amount of speculation in the press as to whether the new car would use a sleeved-down V8 from the M5 or a 3.4-liter version of the old M3 motor. In the end, BMW stuck with the straight-six in 3.2- liter form.

M3 Project Manager Siegfried Friedmann explained that "3.2 liters is the sensible limit of the block, plus the fact that mathematically 3.4 liters is not an ideal capacity in terms of bore and stroke for what we needed to achieve. It is a heavily modified block and we are using strengthened and lightened components to achieve the much higher piston speeds. In

the end, we have 45cc more, so the new capacity is 3246cc."

This time, Europe and the US get the same engine, though there is a ten horsepower difference, five of them owing to the conversion to SAE horsepower from DIN and the other five attributable to US-spec catalytic converters. The European version is rated at 343 hp with 269 lb/ft of torque.

Styled at M

Chris Bangle's styling department has done a terrific job of muscling up the M3. At the sweep of a pen, it has lost the near anonymity of the E36 M3, a car that was visually far too close to its lesser 3-Series Coupe.

Wanna-bes will find the new M3 look hard to forge without some serious sheet metal work. The differences start with the aluminum hood, which sports a purposeful power bulge. Form follows function, and the engineers say this bulge is needed to clear the taller motor, while the side vents are also functional, drawing hot air away from the engine bay.

Below the bumper line, the signature M-Style front intake and spoiler configuration introduced on the M5 gives the new M3 significant visual touches up front. The new side mirrors also take their cue from the M5, as does the subtle spoiler lip on the rear deck.

The flared wheel arches cover the wide wheels and tires perfectly. Coupled with the new rear valance and four big exhaust pipes at the business end, the M3 looks taut and purposeful from any angle. Despite this visual toughening, the drag coefficient has only slipped a fraction from 0.29 to 0.32.

The styling department's work in the cabin has been equally effective. We could hardly fault the E46's interior to begin with, but the M3's additions turn it into a more serious office for the enthusiast driver. The first thing noticed are body-hugging sports seats. Recognizing that M3 drivers are not all the same size, BMW has incorporated pump-up adjustable side bolsters so you can tailor the seat to your build.

The exquisite M-Style sports steering wheel now has a thicker rim, helping to make the ergonomics perfect. The instrument faces are grey and as on the M5, the rev counter has orange and red lights on the needle's approach to redline, some of which turn off as oil temperature reaches normal. In present M-car fashion, the knob of the six-speed gearbox is illuminated.

High Limits

As good as the E46 chassis is, BMW M engineers desired even higher handling parameters for the new M3, requiring significant geometry changes. One of these was controlling geometry under hard cornering and for that, longer suspension arms were needed. "The (M3) is 40mm wider (20mm per side) than a 3-Series Coupe," explained Friedmann. "We even had prototypes 50mm wider, but they looked weird."

Feel the width, and feel the quality. The act of widening the track for stability and minimizing geometry change is but one element of the suspension modifica-

Standard US Spec M3 interior will feature "Anthracite" fabric and M multifunction steering wheel. Full Nappa leather is an option. US speedometer reads to 190 mph. The 19-inch wheels shown are for Europe only. First cars will go on sale in January, with 3000 projected sales.

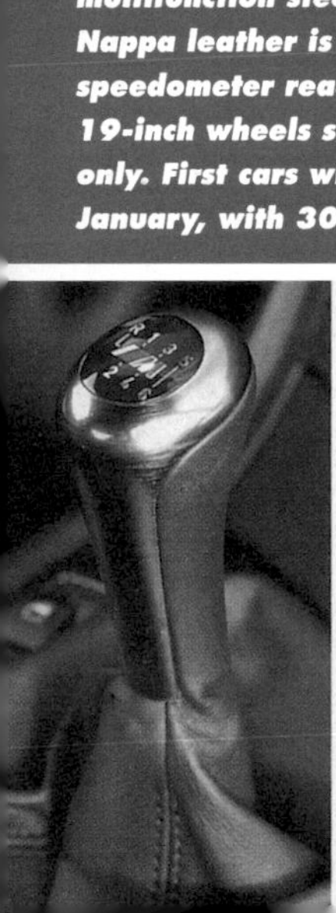

tions. The longer lower wishbones are a unique design made from forged alloy and use different mounting points and bearing system for additional stiffness. Sachs makes the upgraded dampers and the coil springs are linear rate. The top mounts are the same as on the 330Ci, but the bearings are decoupled.

A significant component is a 3mm thick alloy tray, used for additional stiffening of the whole front subframe/suspension assembly. This is bolted to the subframe and wishbones at eight points, helping to distribute cornering loads more evenly, resulting in very precise geometry control. The tray even has a NACA duct to push cooling air towards the gearbox. These boys don't miss a trick!

At the rear, the central arm axle introduced on the E36 3-Series has been further developed. The steel subframe is new and has a new mounting system utilizing a V-shaped tie bar. The upper track control arm is alloy and the rear track is also 20mm wider per side like the front.

The final drive is new, and incorporates what BMW calls the variable M differential lock. This is a torque sensing differential lock using viscous fluid technology. Apart from enhancing traction and stability in slippery conditions, it makes the M3's handling more consistent at the limit.

BMW will not offer the optional 19-inch wheels and tires in the US that Europe gets. Instead, 18s are it. BMW has homologated two brands of tires, Michelin and Continental for this car. These are a special compound developed for the M3, so you can't just replace them with tires of the same 225/45ZR18 and 255/40ZR18 sizes.

Smooth as a turbine all the way to 8000 rpm, the M3's powerful inline-6 promises many smiles per mile with 333 horsepower lurking under the drive-by-wire throttle. Phoenix Yellow is one of four metallic colors available in addition to four solid colors. Aluminum hood provides a 40% weight reduction over steel.

Like all BMWs, the new M3 has a perfect 50/50 weight distribution. While that does not always translate into a 50/50 mass distribution in a moving car, in this case, the car's fabulous balance in cornering indicates that the numbers are right. Significantly, when we checked the amount of tire scrub on each of the fat Michelins after a few hot laps on the Jerez, Spain race circuit, the loaded front left and the two rear tires were evenly feathered, a sure sign that the balance is good. The unloaded front right obviously had to work far less on a clockwise circuit.

The revised power rack and pinion steering is great. Its weight is spot on and there is far more feel than the old E36 M3. In fact, it is easily as tactile as the original E30 M3, a classic handling and steering icon of the cognoscenti. Turn into a bend on the race line, and you feel a gentle increase in loading, totally linear in relation to the chassis. Understeer is mild unless you have turned in too early. Get it right, and the car goes where you point it. You can use the throttle to influence the cornering attitude in a way that was denied to the E36 M3 because of too much initial understeer and denied to the E30 M3 through sheer lack of grunt.

The innovative rear differential does exactly what the engineers claim. Power oversteer is so progressive and predictable that playing with the tail is enjoyable if you are halfway good—the warning of impending breakaway is as loud and clear as a brick through a plate glass window and the seat of the pants tells you how much opposite lock to apply. So long as you keep the power on and don't overdo it or run out of tarmac, you will look like a hero.

What it comes down to is that the new M3 has even more inherent chassis poise than its predecessor. Significantly, it now has more than enough midrange torque and response to influence the car's attitude at any point in a curve. The handling is so good that unless you're out to take a Banzai lap time, you just have so much more fun playing with the car's attitude through the curves.

Of equal importance for fast and consistent lap times, the brakes are superb. As with the previous M3 and the old and new M5s, US versions will have one-piece vented brake discs. These are deemed more suitable for the lower average speeds in the US, and are claimed to be quieter in daily use than the drilled rotors that are standard for European models.

Ten years ago, we would not have believed that electronics could influence engine response so much. The Sport button bumps the ECU into its "fun" mode, noticeably sharpening up throttle response and adding more meat to the power steering. Normally, response is razor sharp, but with Sport mode engaged, it is truly exceptional.

Blip the throttle and the revs rise instantly like a race car. "The E36 M3 also had a single throttle per cylinder, but these were grouped in pairs, so their opening was not absolutely synchronized," Friedmann explained. "We use a single rod now and the drive-by-wire system, so all six throttle open precisely together."

One of the strengths of fuel injection and fully mapped ignition is all-round tractability. The new M3 will pull away convincingly from 1000 rpm in third gear and goes like hell once you double those revs. It is quite highly geared in top however, so asking it to pull from anything strongly from anything less than 2000 rpm in fifth or sixth is still a tall order. Another thing immediately apparent after the first shift is that the slightly sticky throttle of the old car and its annoying shunting in stop-go traffic is gone. The new car's throttle action and transmission behavior are nothing short of creamy smooth.

You will be simply astonished at how much faster the car feels than the previous M3. From the word go, even if you haven't had seat time in an E36 M3 for some months, the difference is crystal clear. For US customers who have never had the opportunity to drive the European E36 M3, it will be like stepping from a sedan into a racer.

Overtaking ability is nothing short of spectacular. Clear road, right gear, move out, nail the throttle and the vehicle being overtaken is history. In fact, often whole lines of slower traffic can be munched in the intermediate gears. Third is a really useful ratio both for passing and holding on twisty roads.

It is therefore hard to believe that an engine which does its best work close to 8000 rpm, is also heroic at commuter speeds. We guarantee a huge culture shock in this respect, no matter what you are used to driving.

Jumps tall buildings in a single bound—that about sums up the new BMW M3. It looks great, goes and handles like a thoroughbred sports car, and yet is capable of taking four adults and a reasonable amount of luggage on long trips. And it doesn't need an oil refinery to fuel it either, even if you use its performance energetically. This is a car that you'll want to say hello and good night to in the garage every day. It has soul and an engaging personality, and that for us means it is worth its weight in gold. ●

SPECIFICATIONS

2001 BMW M3

General
Vehicle type: Front-engine, RWD 2-door coupe
Structure: Steel unibody
Market as tested: US
MSRP: $46,000 (est.)

Engine
Type: Inline-6 with iron block and aluminum head
Displacement (cc): 3246
Compression ratio: 11.5:1
Power (bhp): 333 @ 7900 rpm
Torque (lbs. ft.): 262 @ 4900 rpm
Intake system: EFI
Valvetrain: DOHC, 24 valve, variable valve timing

Transmission
Type: 6-speed manual
Final drive: 3.62

Dimensions
Curb weight (lbs.): 3460
Wheelbase (in.): 107.5
Track, f/r (in.): 57.9/58.2
Length (in.): 176.8
Width (in.): 70.0
Height (in.): 54.0

Suspension, brakes, steering
Suspension, front: MacPherson struts with lower control arms, coil springs, twin-tube gas shocks, anti-roll bar
Suspension, rear: Multi-link, coil springs, twin-tube gas shocks, anti-roll bar
Steering type: Rack and pinion
Wheels, f&r: 8 x 18, 9 x 18 cast alloy
Tires, f&r: 225/45 ZR18, 255/40 ZR18
Brakes, f&r: 12.9-inch, 12.8-inch vented discs
ABS: Standard
Traction Control: Standard

Performance
0-60 mph (sec.): 4.8
Top speed (mph): 155 (electronically limited)

Contact
www.bmwusa.com

THE M-PIRE STRIKES BACK NEW BMW M3 AIMS TO CAPTURE MAGIC OF BIG BROTHER M5 BY PUMPING IRON IN A MAJOR WAY

'There are teeth to back up that "come and have a go" demeanour. With power output up to 343bhp, this promises to be the quickest M car yet'

Story by Matthew Franey. Photography by Anton Watts

IT ARRIVED WREATHED IN THE SMOKE OF SELF-destructing space shuttles, amid the fall-out of Chernobyl. It developed in the blink of an eye its own critical mass. It thrilled and enthralled all who had a chance to sample it. In a more simple time, when Nintendo was still trying to push us Donkey Kong, we were given space rocket, nuclear reactor and video game wrapped up as one. In 1986 we learnt the true meaning of M-Power. A holy trinity. M. Three.

It was, in so many ways, ahead of its time. In an era of conspicuous consumption, M3 was subtle, even understated. As city slickers popped another bottle of Krug, brushing squared-off shoulder pads in Square Mile wine bars, M3 sat unpretentiously outside. Yes, it was a BMW. Yes, it was homologated, a race-bred special. Yes, it had a spoiler. But compared with whale-tail 911 Turbos and Ferrari Testarossas? Blink and you'd miss it.

But the fuse couldn't burn brightly forever. M3 may have set off Geiger counters everywhere, but it had a half life. And a short one at that. By the early '90s, BMW was beginning phase two of the 3-series story and second generation M3 sat, rather sadly, in the shadow of what had come before. In the touchy-feely decade, M3 had developed a gut. Gone was the white hot flash of performance, to be replaced by a slow burn that appealed to a new breed of owners. Out went the razor-sharp steering, out went the race car handling. In came purchasers buying into little more than a name. That the name now began with a lowercase 'm' should have mattered more to those wielding their chequebooks.

BMW's decision to remove so much of what made the original M3 memorable is, perhaps, symptomatic of the company's direction 10 years ago. Refinement was a '90s buzzword and, alongside Conran restaurants and New York-style loft conversions, BMW carved its niche with cars that performed, but pampered too. Fine if you're wafting along on a 5-series cloud, but M3? I don't think so.

And neither, finally, did BMW. A mid-decade attempt to evolve the portly M3 was a step in the right direction, but there remained a sense that the project itself had lost its overall direction. It *was* quick, its straight-six engine *was* a masterpiece, but it was almost indistinguishable from the remainder of the 3-series fleet and, more pointedly still, people continued to go misty-eyed whenever the original, perpendicular left-hooker was mentioned.

Credit to BMW, then, for its sense of dramatic timing. Just when it seemed that the mania for all things 'M' might be on

BMW has worked hard to reduce unsprung weight and improve steering in order to sharpen up new M3's handling. But don't expect an original M3 reborn

the wane, along came the V8-powered M5, a devastatingly fast super-saloon that put the frighteners on many an unabashed sports car. And then, for the *piece de resistance*, a tantalising glimpse of M nirvana.

On a stand at the Frankfurt Motor Show, a full 18 months before the car was due to go on sale, a vision in gunmetal grey confirmed that M3 was back. No longer, it seemed, would BMW make the mistake of disguising its high-performance cars. No longer would a mere blue and red chevron hint at what lies beneath. If previous M3s had slipped into a performance hinterland, the new car screamed its presence from every square centimetre of that polished alloy paint job. (A paint job, incidentally, that set BMW back a cool 20 grand. It's unlikely to make it on to the options list.)

This was the verge of a new millennium and with it came a new breed of M car. Wheel arches flared like the shoulders of a heavyweight boxer throwing clubbing haymakers; the front spoiler snarled and grimaced as you cowered before it; bonnet louvres and bulges marked its surfaces like the welts and creases of a testosterone-charged bodybuilder. BMW 318i? Hardly.

Stand square on to the front wheels and there is a distinct, animalistic profile to the reshaped nose. BMW describes the M3 as 'bullish', but that bluff snout is more pitbull, even bull shark, than bovine. Sidle up close to those wraparound headlight clusters and you sense how an underwater cameraman feels as one of those cold, lifeless eyes glides into shot.

There should be teeth to back up that 'come and have a go' demeanour, for beneath that ridged bonnet line rests the latest in a series of straight six-cylinder engines that have become a part of the M3 legend. That BMW has been able to improve on the existing unit is a feat in itself but power does rise, from 321 to 343bhp, as the 3245cc engine displaces a morsel more normally aspirated fuel and air. Without recourse to superchargers or spinning turbos, M division's engineers have relied on good old-fashioned revs to release that increased output, with the redline now posted at 8000rpm. Torque is also up, with 269lb ft on tap at just under 5000rpm.

It's all honed from BMW's standard M3 unit – cast iron block, aluminium cylinder head, four valves per cylinder – but further work has been done on the double VANOS variable valve timing system, which operates with new rocker arms and an in-house engine management system for the electronically controlled throttle butterflies. Performance, as you might expect, improves along with the increase in power. Acceleration time to 62mph (100km/h) is down to 5.2sec, while in-gear acceleration between 50 and 75mph is an equally impressive 5.4sec. Have no doubt: under full throttle, new M3 will be a match for all but the fleetest of supercars. Come what may, this will be the quickest M car BMW has ever built.

There's technology, too, at the driven wheels, where power from the tried and trusted Getrag six-speed gearbox is channelled through a new, variable M differential. Rather than detecting torque levels at either rear wheel, the M diff acts by measuring the difference in wheel rotations and applying

Price: £43,000 (est) **Engine:** 3245cc dohc 24V in-line six **Power and torque:** 343bhp at 7900rpm, 269lb ft at 4900rpm **Transmission:** Six-speed manual, rear-wheel drive **Suspension (f):** MacPherson struts, coil springs, anti-roll bar **Suspension (r):** Z-beam, coil springs, anti-roll bar **Performance:** 155mph (limited), 5.2sec 0-62mph

appropriate power to each side through an electronically controlled clutch depending on traction levels. Allied to the third generation of BMW's Dynamic Stability Control system and ABS and traction control, the M3 will, at less conservative speeds, potentially be the most poised of its kind yet.

Look between that trick differential and the wheels for further clues as to exactly where that poise and sure-footedness come from. Suspension geometry has been revised at each corner, with even wider tracks being governed by new aluminium track control arms, as well as an additional thrust arm at the front. While MacPherson struts are retained in the nose, and BMW's unique Z-beam remains at the rear, much work has been done to stiffen and strengthen the subframes on which they are mounted, in order that the suspension can cope with the extra torque and power.

BMW claims it has worked hard to minimise unsprung weight at each corner of the car, ensuring the sort of direct response that was missing from its predecessor. Newly geared steering should be sharper, more exact, and it's safe to say you can expect decent feedback, too, for there will be plenty of contact patch with which to chat freely with the asphalt. The rear wheels are shod with colossal 255/45 ZR18 tyres (there's 10mm less width at the nose), while the newly designed M Styling double-spoke alloys are ultra-lightweight. The company has equally high expectations of the brakes (floating steel discs, 325mm in diameter), predicting stopping potential equivalent to that of the car's big brother M5.

Like the top M car, new M3 also boasts an interior that is as luxurious as the first M3s were spartan. Over the past 15 years, BMW has veered dramatically away from the stripped-out homologation racers that allowed the firm to field its Group A touring cars in the mid '80s. Today's M3 is as upmarket as any top BMW. Stylish sports seats offer not only all the 'bucket' required from a car where lateral *g*s appear at the top of the spec list, but also, for the first time, the option to widen the backrests depending on the broadness, or slope, of your shoulders.

Four aluminium-rimmed dials are housed within the instrument binnacle, with an M sports steering wheel housing remote buttons for the in-car entertainment system and cruise control. Trim levels will range from a combination of fabric and leather, climbing through alcantara and leather, levelling out at as much leather as you could possibly desire.

Not that you buy an M3 for the width of its seats or the patina of its cowhide. At least, not *this* M3. This is a car that will be bought on external looks alone. Looks that carry the promise of such latent potential, looks that should mean the M3 name no longer stumbles forward under the pretence of something that it clearly should not have been. When you're dealing with bloodline and heritage, then every so often that family tree needs chopping back to its roots to discover what made the tree so strong in the first place. This new M3 may be no more a racing thoroughbred than the second generation cars which have thankfully been put out to stud. What it is, is a vision of something far more courageous: an M3 that satisfies allcomers and, in doing so, revives a name that lay dormant for too long.

BMW M3 Convertible

The fabulous M3 loses its roof – but is that all it loses in the transformation to convertible?

Hood up, the M3 is a snug place to be, even in a downpour. Optional 19in alloys don't help ride, highlighting the convertible's lack of stiffness

The arrival of an M3 at Evo Towers usually results in a polite tussle for the keys. The merits of each claimant are weighed up, and then a full blown argument erupts. Then Harry walks in, mutters some far-fetched excuse and nicks the keys.

So when I heard that another M3 was arriving I reckoned that the chances of getting a quick blast were remote. That was until I saw it pull up. First of all it was a convertible – never a winner in the office. The colour didn't help. Laguna Seca Blue isn't too offensive on the subtly aggressive coupe but on the convertible, in combo with optional glitzy alloys (huge 19 inch diameter), the convertible looked every-inch the pimp-mobile. Peter declared that he wouldn't be seen dead in it. John was on holiday, Dickie grimaced at the thought of the biggest alloys on the wobbliest model and Harry didn't mutter a word. I donned my best gold chains and prepared to be subjected to some unwanted attention.

Happily you can't see the questionable aesthetics once ensconced in the rather more tasteful, black leather trimmed interior. From the driver's seat it's business as usual, which means perfect ergonomics, superb quality and a general feeling of well-being, and that continues when you fire-up BMW's latest straight-six masterpiece. We've talked a lot about this superb engine but it's great to jump back into an M3 and revel in the smoothness, power and noise that the 3.2-litre six generates. It may be 'only a 3-series' to some, but the M3 comes with one of the truly great supercar engines.

Hood down on a smooth, sweeping A-road, you could almost be forgiven for choosing the convertible over the coupe. The chassis feels admirably shimmy-free, the engine sounds even more spectacular than I remember and acceleration isn't perceptibly dulled. According to BMW's figures, it should be good for 0-60 in around 5.3secs (we recorded 5.1secs for a the coupe) while top speed is limited to 155mph.

However, put it on your favourite stretch of B-road – the twisty, bumpy sort littered with off-camber corners and tightening bends – and gaping holes begin to appear. Wicked mid-corner bumps that the coupe would shrug off elicit shudders and groans of protest. Sharp ridges send an almighty jolt through the body and screen surround, encouraging a slightly gentler pace. BMW is not a company to cut corners, but despite a heavily reinforced windscreen frame and strengthened floorplan, the convertible cannot hope to match the structural integrity of the coupe. The steering highlights this, kicking back severely when the going gets really tough.

Those 19in wheels don't help. The ride is by no means destroyed but certainly suffers. Both urban and fast open roads reveal a noticeably more fussy ride which soon becomes a bore. The convertible is less of a weapon and more of a cruiser.

Don't think that the M3 has gone completely soft. Most of the time it remains a very fast and effective tool. But it's that last 15 or 20 per cent of ability that defines the Motorsport BMW. That the convertible becomes less convincing on the sort of road where the coupe excels, and from which we all derive so much fun, is a real shame. Predictable, but a shame none the less.

If you're rubbing your hands together in glee, waiting for the first time you come across an M3 convertible driven by someone more interested in posing than power-sliding, hoping to humble him in a more affordable pocket-rocket, don't get too carried away. Even in inexperienced hands the M3 is blisteringly quick, soft-top or not. The traction control system is well-judged – allowing just a little tail-slip before cutting in rather than spoiling the fun before it has even begun. Turning it off results in as much tail-out tomfoolery as anyone could possibly want, but either way you'll be making rapid and fluent progress. And enjoying yourself.

The gear change can feel a little vague and rubbery at town speeds but smooths out when used briskly. Steering feel is disconcertingly light initially but still manages to convey the vital messages about the road surface and the onset of understeer or oversteer. Normally it's the latter, metered out in progressive, satisfying style by the smarty-pants M-diff. Heroic car control skills aren't required to make the M3 dance. Forgiving yet involving, the M3 chassis is about as good as it gets.

But here's the rub. When choosing an M3, surely chassis dynamics are right up there with performance on the list of reasons to buy. If I was helping fund all that development work on the 'Ring, I'd like to think that I had the ultimate expression of BMW's know-how. With the convertible that isn't the case. Each evolution comes with claims of greater structural rigidity – compared with the previous convertible the new car is said to be a huge improvement, with torsional rigidity up by 20 per cent. Trouble is, the coupe is making strides just as fast, and highlights the inherent drawbacks of chopping the roof off.

Despite a snug hood which manages to keep wind noise to a minimum and does a good impersonation of a hard-top most of the time, when that dream road snakes out into the distance, distractions like scuttle shake and compromised steering become a nagging reminder that the coupe is still the M3 to have.

Jethro Bovingdon

SPECIFICATION

Engine	In-line 6-cyl, 3246cc, 24v
Max power	338bhp @ 7900rpm
Max torque	269lb ft @ 5000rpm
Top speed	155mph (limited)
0-62mph	5.5secs (claimed)
Price	£41,400
On sale	Now

evo RATING ★★★★

+ That engine

– That colour, those wheels. And the wobbly ride

Photography: Andy Morgan

ROAD TEST NUMBER 4480

BMW M3

MODEL TESTED M3 coupé
LIST PRICE £38,500 **TOP SPEED** 160mph
30-70MPH 4.1sec **0-60MPH** 4.8sec
60-0MPH 2.6sec **MPG** 21.7
FOR Stunning performance, handling, looks, brakes, price
AGAINST High seating position, firm low-speed ride

REINTERPRETING AN icon is never easy, and BMW knows this better than most. While the first M3, launched in 1986, created a legend, the follow-up in 1993 was criticised for being too big and heavy to match the precision and agility of the four-cylinder original. This did not, however, dissuade 7421 people in the UK from buying one.

The criticism hurt BMW, which vowed to create a new M3 with both pace and involvement – a much purer machine. And here it is; the new M3 that goes on sale in the UK in April. With the current M5 a firm favourite at *Autocar*, expectations of its smaller brother are sky high.

At £38,500, the Porsche Boxster S is the BMW's natural rival, but the M3's performance puts it head to head with the much more expensive Porsche 911 and Audi RS4.

DESIGN AND ENGINEERING

If the outgoing model looked a little soft compared to the first M3, then this latest version hits back hard with bulging wheel-arches, a massive chin spoiler and gorgeous 18in alloy wheels.

These aren't just for visual effect. The larger wheel-arches accommodate the extended front and rear tracks, now both increased by 40mm, and the front of the bodyshell has been substantially stiffened. The 18in alloys wear 225/45 (front) and 255/40 (rear) Michelin Pilot Sports. But it's what sits beneath the aluminium bonnet and behind the gaping front air intake that excites the most.

The 3.2-litre straight-six engine is a masterpiece by BMW's M division. It retains the iron block from the previous M3, but BMW claims the new engine shares only five components with the old engine.

A 0.6mm increase in bore has raised capacity by 44cc to 3245cc. Each cylinder has its own composite intake duct and butterfly throttle control, while the engine is controlled by a vastly uprated MSS54 engine management control system. The result: 343bhp developed at 7900rpm and 269lb ft of torque at 4900rpm.

Like the M5, the M3 has a Sport option that sharpens the engine's electronic throttle response. That power is handled by a reinforced version of the six-speed Getrag 'box from the old M3 – albeit with a different final drive – channelling power to the rear wheels via BMW's new variable M differential. Developed jointly with British engineering specialist GKN, the diff varies rear-wheel lock between zero and 100 percent.

Naturally, the brakes and suspension have been uprated to match the hikes in power and performance. Behind those big wheels lurk 325mm ventilated front and 326mm rear discs, electronically backed up by anti-lock. BMW's Dynamic Stability Control, Cornering Brake Control and Traction Control systems are also fitted as standard.

The brake calipers are made of aluminium to reduce unsprung weight. The M3's suspension has also been revised. The front MacPherson strut and rear Z-arm multi-link layout has been reinforced to cope with higher cornering loads. Firmer bushes, dampers ➧

HISTORY

The original M3 from 1986 was a left-hand drive homologation special, producing 195bhp from its 2.3-litre four-cylinder engine. Only 5000 were built. It was followed by an Evo version with an extra 35bhp, revised suspension and adjustable rear spoilers. This was superseded in 1993 by the bigger, more luxurious E36. Its 3.0 straight-six had 286bhp but the agility and nimbleness of the original were lost. An E36 Evo – the most popular M3 – gained an extra gear and 200cc, bumping power up to 321bhp.

X908 SUT

and springs have also been introduced to enhance body control, and overall stability is improved by the widened axle tracks and a 15mm reduction in ride height.

Despite its extensive use of aluminium, the M3 weighs 1577kg – 106kg more than the model it replaces. Still, with a power-to-weight ratio of 218bhp per tonne, the M3 is hardly going to be slow.

Muscular body hides superb chassis
★★★★

PERFORMANCE AND BRAKES

The M3's ability to both gain and shed speed is striking. It takes a delicate touch to get the M3 cleanly off the line with the traction control deactivated and the Sport button on. But launched successfully, it scorches to 60mph in 4.8sec, touches 100mph in 11.5sec and covers the quarter mile in 13.4sec. That's a storming set of figures, good enough to shame the old M3, which reached 60mph in 5.3sec and 100mph in 12.2sec.

In short, the M3 is quick enough to sit on the tail of a Porsche 996 Carrera, and even the powerhouse Audi RS4 would feel the hot breath of the M3 on its collar. It's only one tenth of a second quicker to 60mph and three tenths quicker to 100mph.

These cold figures do little to impart the BMW's hot-rod manner, however. Below 2000rpm the engine seems slightly unwilling to pull tall gears, but once past that threshold the engine hurtles to its 8000rpm limiter with one explosive shove. It's almost brutal in its delivery, the slightest movement of the drive-by-wire throttle resulting in an instant response from the motor. Thankfully, the driveline snatch that plagued the old car has been eradicated. The drivetrain now feels solid.

The grunty rumble from the quad exhausts at idle gives way to a serrated wail as the straight-six climbs to its red line. It's enough to make you wish you had an on-board tape recorder.

Accelerate hard in the first three gears and it's best to keep your left hand fixed on the gearlever, ready to snap the slick shift up a gear, so quickly does the engine hit the red zone. Dig deep into the M3's power and it will whip from 30-70mph in 4.1sec, just shy of the 911's 3.8sec time but ahead of the RS4's 4.2sec.

In-gear thrust is equally electrifying, if not as quick as the lighter 911 or the turbo-charged Audi. But let's put these figures into perspective. The M3 is trading blows with cars much further up the price ladder. Cast it among similarly priced rivals like the Boxster S and Lotus Exige, and the BMW eats them whole.

If the M3's ability to gain speed astonishes then its brakes are little short of heroic. They can be beautifully modulated right up to where the anti-lock system kicks in. Really stand on them and they haul the M3 down from 60mph to a standstill in just 2.6sec. Neither the 911 nor RS4 can do better.

Scorching 0-60mph time of 4.8sec backed by brilliant handling and brakes

Terrific performance matched by superb brakes
★★★★★

HANDLING AND RIDE

Despite its massive performance, the M3's on-road behaviour strikes an almost perfect balance between supple tourer and hard-edged racer for the road.

The chassis and suspension play strong supporting roles to that astounding engine. The suspension informs you of each rut and ripple, every change in camber and road surface. But there's a subtlety to this flow of information. Think of the visceral nature of the original M3 combined with the refinement of the current 3-series and you get the picture.

This balance means the M3 can be pushed very quickly and confidently down virtually any road. Motorway expansion joints and abrupt ridges are both felt and heard within the cabin but progress is never as jarring or as brittle as you would anticipate considering the size of the wheels and tyres.

The M3's chassis was tested extensively on the Nürburgring circuit in Germany, and it

PERFORMANCE AND SPECIFICATIONS

ENGINE

Layout 6 cyls in line, 3245cc
Max power 343bhp at 7900rpm
Max torque 269bhp at 4900rpm
Power to weight 218bhp per tonne
Torque to weight 171lb ft per tonne
Specific output 106bhp per litre
Installation Front, longitudinal, rear-wheel drive
Construction Alloy head, iron block
Bore/stroke 87.0/91.0mm
Valve gear 4 valves per cylinder, dohc
Compression ratio 11.5:1
Ignition and fuel Bosch ignition, MSS54 engine management, sequential multi-point fuel injection

GEARBOX

Type 6-speed manual by Getrag
Ratios/mph per 1000rpm
1st 4.23/5.1 **2nd** 2.53/8.5 **3rd** 1.67/12.8
4th 1.23/17.4 **5th** 1.00/21.4 **6th** 0.83/25.8
Final drive 3.62

MAXIMUM SPEEDS

6th 160mph/6200rpm **5th** 157mph/7350
4th 139/8000 **3rd** 102/8000
2nd 68/8000 **1st** 41/8000

ACCELERATION FROM REST

SURFACE DRY

True mph	sec	speedo mph
30	2.0	32
40	2.9	42
50	3.8	53
60	4.8	64
70	6.1	75
80	7.7	85
90	9.4	96
100	11.5	107

Standing qtr mile 13.4sec/107mph
Standing km 23.7sec/139mph
30-70mph through gears 4.1sec

ACCELERATION IN GEARS

mph	6th	5th	4th	3rd	2nd
20-40	9.7	6.5	4.5	3.3	2.1
30-50	10.1	6.6	4.5	3.0	1.9
40-60	7.6	5.4	4.1	2.9	2.0
50-70	7.7	5.4	4.3	2.9	-
60-80	7.6	5.4	4.3	2.9	-
70-90	7.8	5.5	4.3	3.0	-
80-100	8.3	5.7	4.5	3.7	-

STEERING

Type Rack and pinion, power assisted
Turns lock to lock 3.2

CONTROLS IN DETAIL

1 Chunky leather-clad steering wheel looks and feels fantastic **2** Six-speed gearbox has illuminated-top gearlever **3** Revcounter ringed with engine temperature lights, shared with the M5 **4** Electrically adjustable seats offer superb support but are set high **5** Stylish brushed aluminium trim adds to cabin's air of sophistication

SUSPENSION

Front MacPherson struts, lower wishbones, coil springs, anti-roll bar
Rear Multi-link, coil springs, anti-roll bar

WHEELS & TYRES

Wheels 8Jx18in (f), 9Jx18in (r)
Made of Alloy
Tyres 225/45 ZR18 (f), 255/40 ZR18 (r) Michelin Pilot Sport
Spare Foam repair kit

BRAKES

Front 325mm ventilated discs
Rear 326mm ventilated discs
Anti-lock Standard

BRAKES

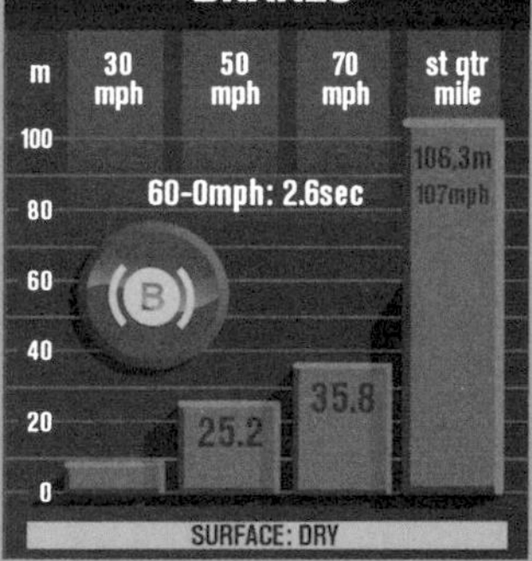

GEARING

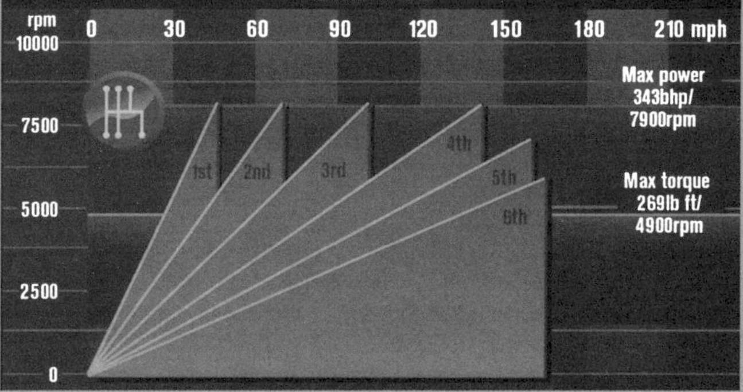

FUEL CONSUMPTION

TEST RESULTS

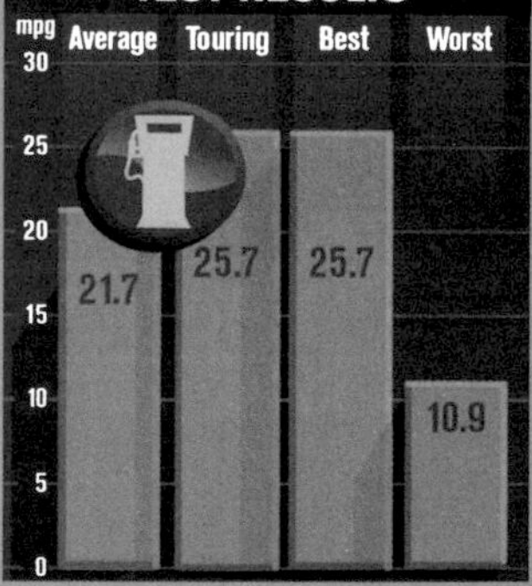

GOVERNMENT CLAIMS

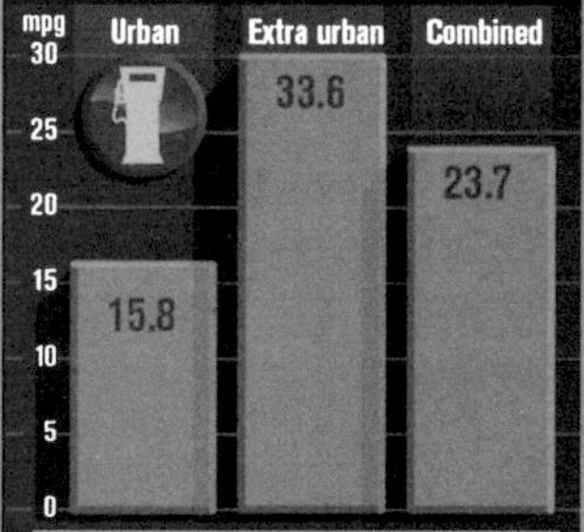

Tank capacity: 63 litres (13.9 gallons)
Touring range: 360 miles

NOISE

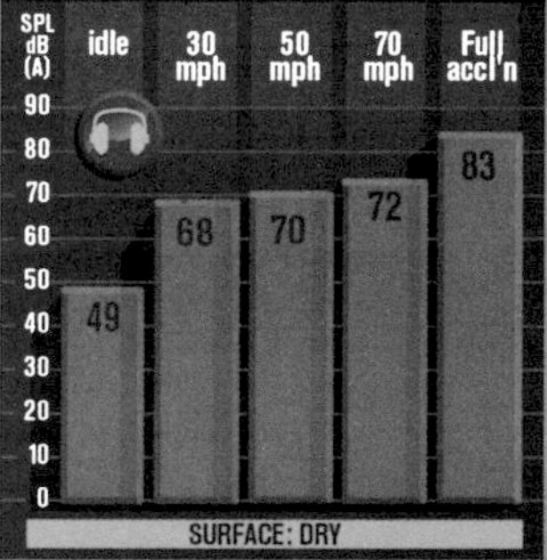

LAYOUT

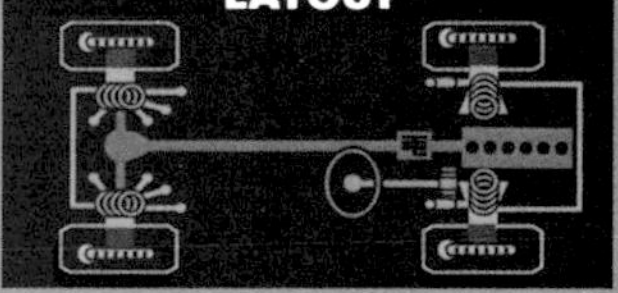

Body 2dr coupe **Cd** 0.29 **Front/rear tracks** 1508/1478mm **Turning circle** 10.3m **Min/max front legroom** 910/1110mm **Min/max rear legroom** 1170/970mm **Min/max front headroom** 860/970mm **Interior width front/rear** 1480/1420mm **Min/max boot width** 760/1340mm **Min/max boot length** 1000/1660mm **VDA boot volume** 410 litres/dm³ **Kerb weight** 1577kg **Weight distribution front/rear** 49/51 percent **Width (inc mirrors)** 1947mm

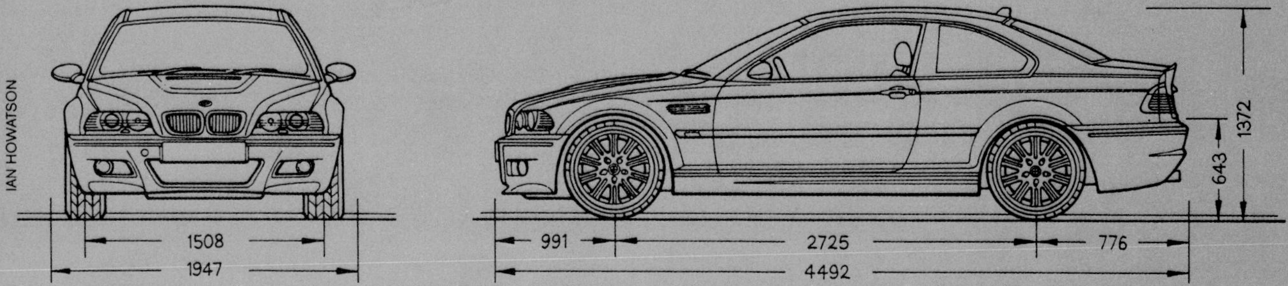

Straight-six engine, increased to 3245cc, now develops a stunning 343bhp; leather trim is standard on the steering wheel and supportive sports seats

Plenty of room for rear passengers; M division logo adorns side air vent; familiar fin aerial sits on rear window; gas discharge headlights very powerful

shows. Its race-inspired handling is evident the first time the M3 takes a bend. The lowered ride height, stiffer suspension and widened front and rear tracks allow it to spear flatly through corners. There's little roll even in the most aggressively taken corners, and body control at all speeds is exceptional.

The combination of the chassis' beautifully neutral balance and the generous footprint translates into a phenomenal level of grip. The steering, while still not in the same feel-all category as the Porsche 911, still supplies your hands with a constant flow of details. It feels heavier than the 330 Ci due to reworked valving, while kickback is also well damped when the front wheels encounter mid-corner ruts.

The M3 is remarkably accurate on turn-in, with the quicker rack that M division engineers insisted on fitting allowing you to slice through curves with greater precision. But it's the super-smart variable differential that really allows the chassis to exploit the engine. It provides astounding levels of traction – up to a point.

While the front end's natural inclination is to run wide eventually, that understeer can be dialled out with a quick prod of the throttle. If you flick off the Dynamic Stability Control, getting the tail out becomes a doddle.

Entertaining and rewarding in equal measure
★★★★

COMFORT, SAFETY AND EQUIPMENT

The restrained and subtle layout of the M3's cabin is the perfect counterbalance to the pumped-up exterior. Its atmosphere is perfectly suited to the M3's no-nonsense character.

The leather-covered seats, electrically adjustable in every direction, are fabulous – both supportive and comfortable. Yet the electrical engines inside them mean that even the lowest setting is higher than you would chose in a bespoke sports car like a Porsche 911.

It's not too much of a problem because all other driver contact points are perfectly positioned. The fully adjustable three-spoke steering wheel has to be one of BMW's most tactile units, the thick leather-bound rim hand-finished in Motorsport's distinctive blue, mauve and red.

Behind the wheel are two pairs of chrome-ringed dials, but it's the revcounter that holds your attention. Like the M5's, it wears a crescent of lights that wink on start-up and then turn off as the engine warms up.

The M3 also borrows its illuminated gearlever top from the M5. The positioning of these three elements – pedals, gearlever and steering wheel – make for a driver-oriented cabin. Not that passengers feel excluded. The interior may be intimate but there's plenty of room for occupants both front and rear.

The boot is also capable of swallowing four people's luggage for a weekend away, making the M3 effective as both sports car and high-velocity tourer. It may be a hothead at heart but as befits its flagship status, the M3 is still an opulent car to sit in. The list of standard equipment is extensive and includes an excellent sound system, leather trim, cruise and climate control and classy brushed aluminium detailing.

Nor is the driver shortchanged when it comes to safety features. The full complement of driver and passenger airbags is backed up by the sophisticated electronic traction and switchable Dynamic Stability Control.

Stylish, comfortable, safe and well equipped
★★★★★

MARKET AND FINANCE

The £38,500 M3 provides a level of ability few – if any – cars at this price can match. It may cost £9000 more than BMW's 330 Ci coupé but when you consider its lavish level of kit and staggering engine, the M3 looks like a bit of a bargain. High demand and guaranteed exclusivity should further boost its residuals. The UK's limited allocation of 800 M3s for this year is already all sold. Like all new BMWs, the M3 comes with a full 36-month/ 60,000-mile warranty.

A performance bargain
★★★★

Boot is far bigger than a conventional sports car's; knob is from the M5

Chrome-ringed dials reinforce sporty feel; styling is subtle yet purposeful

ECONOMY

For a car capable of humbling all but a handful of supercars, the M3 returns some impressive fuel figures. Driven enthusiastically, it returned 21.7mpg, rising to 25.7mpg over our touring route. That gives it an impressive touring range of 356 miles form the 63-litre fuel tank – better than the 911 and RS4 can manage.

But that said, drive it flat out and you're unlikely to improve on our worst figure of 10.9mpg, recorded after high-speed testing.

Exceptional economy in spite of raw performance
★★★★

WHAT IT COSTS

On-the-road price	£38,500
Total as tested	£38,500
Cost per mile	111p
Contract hire per month	n/a
CO_2	286g/km
EQUIPMENT	
(**bold** = options fitted to test car)	
Air conditioning	●
Traction control	●
Leather trim	●
Height/tilt-adjust steering column	●/●
Anti-lock brakes	●
Airbag driver/passenger/side	●/●/●
Satellite navigation	£1400
Alarm/immobiliser	●/●
RDS stereo/CD player	●/●
● standard - not available	
INSURANCE	
Group	20 (est)
Typical quote	£1669 (est)
WARRANTY	
36 months/60,000 miles, 6 years anti-rust	
SERVICING	
Electronically controlled, up to 18,750 miles	
PART PRICES	
Oil filter	£6.20
Air filter	£15.58
Set of spark-plugs	£176.62
Brake pads f/r	£51.50/£80.86
Tyre f/r	£231.5/£263.35
Windscreen	£119.65
Front wing	£182.07
Door mirror	£149.38
Rear bumper	£212.77

TESTER'S NOTES

We counted no fewer than 18 M division logos while scrutinising the M3 both inside and out. They are even found on the tops of the front suspension turrets.

The M3 received a rapturous welcome from a 3am motorway driver behind the wheel of an enthusiastically driven 318i. He followed our test car for as long as he could, flashing his lights and giving the car an emphatic thumbs-up as he rode alongside.

It's no wonder the BMW's gas discharge lights are so powerful. The legend on the headlamp covers warns that the gas discharge units consume 25,000 volts.

The M3's Orwellian electronic black box seemed to take a rather relaxed attitude to our test car's top speed. Despite being offically limited to 155mph, the BMW recorded 157mph in fifth and then clocked a true 160mph in top gear on the Millbrook high speed bowl.

THE AUTOCAR VERDICT

STAN PAPIOR

BMW has taken the spirit of the original M3 and improved it in every way

THE M3 IS a return to form that rekindles the excitement of the original M3.

The company's pride may have been dented by previous accusations that the last M3 never quite captured the purity of the original, but this time round the M division has a stronger hand.

The intimacy and involvement that charmed us in 1986 is now joined by unprecedented levels of performance married to exceptional refinement. They blend to create a wonderfully complete performance car.

Seeking out chinks in the M3's armour is therefore no easy task. It is blindingly quick and gorgeously styled. It's refined, comfortable and can swallow four adults and their luggage with ease. The intense driver involvement it provides is addictive and way out of proportion with its relatively low price.

But ultimately, what makes the new M3 such a special car is its ability to appeal to the core enthusiast. For us, it's the best M car yet.

Best M3 yet – a stunning return to form
★★★★★

Third time's a Charm

by ALEXANDER PALEVSKY
photography by SCOTT DAHLQUIST

The previous two convertible versions of BMW's M3—the very limited production, Europe-only E30 and last-generation E36—seriously compromised the chassis rigidity and great handling of the coupe. The latest one doesn't; it's a legitimate M car.

With a few exceptions, we're not huge convertible fans here at *SCI*. Sure, we've been known to occasionally indulge in the warm sunshine while gazing out at picturesque surroundings from the inside of a drop-top. But convertibles add weight and take away rigidity, two major strikes against performance driving. For a group more concerned with our cornering lines than our tan lines, that's usually enough to steer us away from an open-top machine and towards its coupe counterpart. But factor in the ubiquitous melody of squeaks and rattles that few convertibles are immune to, and it's downright surprising how an otherwise fabulous car can become significantly less fabulous once its roof is removed.

A perfect example is the last iteration of the BMW M3, known as the E36. As a closed coupe, we raved about this mighty Bimmer's impeccable combination of power, handling and practicality. But with-

out a top, the M3 became something of an embarrassment to the whole M ethos. Sure it still had decent power and practicality, but the laughable amount of flexing and creaking that was perpetrated upon the chassis by the stiffened, M-tuned suspension instantly transformed the handling from class star to class clown. And frankly, a heavier, slower M3 stripped of its handling prowess is an M3 we could do without.

So it was with much trepidation that we sunk our bottoms into the latest E46 M3 convertible, a mightier, pricier and more rigid (hallelujah!) machine than its older namesake. It makes a good first impression. We've never had any qualms with how the E36 M3 looked in drop-top form, but the new one seems to work even better as a convertible. Perhaps it's because the ultra-aggressive front fascia, widened fenders and two sets of dual exhaust tips work to inject a healthy dose of testosterone into the otherwise demure shape of the E46 cabrio. Or maybe it's because the new body style, though not radically different from that of the previous 3 Series in overall design philosophy, has made the old model suddenly seem antiquated by comparison. Whatever the reason, it's clear that the myriad of M styling enhancements (said to exist as a result of the old M3 looking too much like a normal 3 Series) make this one great-looking convertible.

There's no question that the new M3 has tons of posing value, but don't mistake it as merely a car for the boulavardier. For under its bulged hood lies the S54 engine, surely the finest motor yet to emerge from the BMW M facility. Like the old M3 powerplant, the S54 remains a 24-valve inline-6 with an iron block and a capacity of 3.2 liters (actually 3,246 cc compared to the old engine's 3,152 cc). Those characteristics aside, there's not much in common between the old 3.2 and the new one. For starters, all E46 M3s sold in North America use essentially the same S54 engine sold elsewhere, so that means we finally get the individual throttle plates and continuously variable Double VANOS valve timing system that was denied our market on the previous model. Those features, along with countless upgrades to the head, intake, exhaust, engine management and just about everything in between, give the E46 M3 an additional 93 horsepower (now 333 at 7,900 rpm) and 26 lb/ft of torque (now 262 lb/ft at 4,900 rpm) over the old car.

Yet the figures only convey a vague notion of the new powerplant's magic. For starters, there's the sound. The engine itself emits a rich, even purr, like a good straight-6 should. But the noise that exits through the quad tailpipes is more high-pitched and mechanical, not unlike that of a finely tuned motorcycle engine. Drop the top, and the two are instantly melded together into a glorious duet that makes you want to head for the redline over and over.

But it's the power delivery that really gives the S54 its sublime character. Though not quite as punchy right off the line as the old 3.2, the new engine loves to rev, so the first few thousand rpm flash by in an instant. Before long, there are 4,000 rpm on the tach and things are starting to get interesting. By now, the more aggressive cam lobes have probably been called into active service, unleashing a healthy dose of mid-range grunt. The M3 would certainly be considered a very quick car if the power dropped off after this, but there are still several thousand rpm left to go! With peak power achieved just short of the 8,000-rpm redline, keeping your foot planted until the rev limiter kicks in results in the kind of ferocious acceleration that, until recently, was the exclusive domain of ultra-exotic supercars.

This is especially impressive considering that the M3 convertible has put on a few extra pounds, precisely 366 of them compared to the current M3 coupe or 290 more than the old M3 convertible. That brings the grand total up to 3,781, a hefty chunk of mass by any standard and nearly as much as a 540i sedan. Yet the M3 convertible rarely feels like it lacks grunt. In fact, the performance barely feels blunted under most conditions. If anything, initial acceleration is a tad less brisk (confirmed by BMW's claimed 0-to-60-mph time of 5.4 seconds, versus 4.8 seconds for the coupe), but it's easy to overcome the extra mass by simply dialing in a few extra revs. As you can imagine, this is hardly a chore.

So thumbs up in the styling and performance departments, but what about the small matter of chassis stiffness? Well, it's better than the last M3 convertible. A lot better. In fact, the M-tuned suspension (forged aluminum control arms, modified rear subframe, underbody stiffening, M-spec springs, shocks, anti-roll bars) gives the convertible nearly as much poise as the coupe. No longer does the steering column shake violently over railroad tracks. No longer does the inside rear-view mirror vibrate at freeway speeds. No longer does the handling deteriorate if the tires are on anything but freshly paved asphalt.

There are moments where the added weight and reduced rigidity do take their toll, such as in tight, poorly paved corners where the chassis must absorb high cornering forces and the road's imperfections simultaneously, but the majority of the M3 coupe's highly tactile feedback remains uncorrupted. With such a stable platform to work with, it's not at all scary to extract the most from the M3 convertible's wonderfully throttle-sensitive chassis, light yet razor-sharp steering and unfadable brakes. That said, we probably wouldn't feel entirely comfortable wringing the convertible out at 10/10ths on a racetrack, but then again, that's what the coupe is for.

Alas, there is one final area where the M3 convertible cannot fully escape the burden of open-top cars: squeaks. With just over 1,500 miles on the odometer, our test car already possessed a cacophony of chirps and rattles whenever its soft top

Right: The interior of the M3 Convertible is essentially the same as the Coupe, meaning it is both ergonomically and tastefully laid out; for 2002, the black gloss trim will be replaced with a titanium finish. Below: The M3 Convertible corners nearly as crisply as its fixed-top sibling. Opposite top: Unlike the Porsche 911 Carrera Cabriolet, the M3 Convertible offers an extremely high level of performance *and* room for four passengers. Opposite: The silky-smooth S54 inline-6 produces 333 horsepower and a wonderful exhaust note.

was closed. With several thousand more miles on the clock, we're sure there will be even more. It's hard to imagine that any top that has to cover front and rear seats via a complex power-operated mechanism can be completely devoid of unwanted noises, but we weren't expecting them to appear so quickly. Various fixes (lubrication, new seals, etc.) may quiet the noises temporarily, but any M3 convertible owner should realize that the interior is never going to offer the cocoon-like solitude of a closed coupe.

Of course, there is one way to get rid of the squeaks: put the top down. This is easy enough to do, requiring only that you apply the brakes and depress a button on the center console for as long as it takes to lower all four windows by a few inches and retract the canvas roof under its hard tonneau cover. Once down, the M3 convertible is quite a nice place to be, especially if equipped with two inexpensive options: heated seats ($500) and the Harmon/Kardon sound system ($675). The former are a must on any convertible, if only to make night-time alfresco driving more tolerable. In the M3 (and all E46 3 Series), the seat heating can be adjusted in three degrees of intensity, though only the top setting is really adequate. We wouldn't normally consider the Harmon/Kardon audio system (40 percent more power, upgraded speakers) a must-have, since the standard system is already quite good. But with the added road, wind and engine noise that the convertible brings to the equation, it's nice to be able to crank up the tunes without unwanted distortion.

SPECIFICATIONS

BMW M3 Convertible

ENGINE	3246-cc 24-valve DOHC inline-9
POWER (hp)	333 @ 7400 rpm
TORQUE (lb/ft)	262 @ 4900 rpm
TRANSMISSION	6-speed manual
BRAKES	12.9/12.8-inch vented discs
WHEELBASE (in.)	107.5
LENGTH (in.)	176.8
WEIGHT (lbs.)	3781
0-60 MPH (sec.)	5.4
TOP SPEED (mph)	155
AS TESTED PRICE	$55,745

Added exposure to the elements aside, the M3 convertible's cabin is more or less like the coupe's. Same thick three-spoke steering wheel, same M instrument cluster with illegible white-on-gray numerals, same black "high-gloss" trim on the dash and doors. (For 2002, the M3 has more appealing titanium trim as standard equipment.) The main exceptions are the leather-clad seats which, because of the integrated seat belt arrangement required by the convertible body, are more similar to the regular 3 Series sport seats than those fitted to the closed M3. Though perfectly comfortable after many hours behind the wheel and decently supportive in the corners, they're not quite as good as the coupe's seats, and are a far cry from the hip-hugging Recaros of the original E30 M3 and other BMWs of the late 1980s.

But we'll gladly give up some seat support when the rest of the car is this good. BMW has made a great effort to correct the old M3 convertible's biggest faults and has succeeded in almost every way. Though it still doesn't quite achieve the handling brilliance of the coupe and remains plagued by squeaks and rattles, this is a far, far better machine than the previous M3 convertible and undoubtedly the best open-top BMW yet. If it were our 50 grand, we'd probably still opt for the coupe, if only because we'd want to wring it out on the track from time to time. But don't think that the convertible wouldn't be tempting. After all, this is the only BMW that can improve your cornering line and your tan line at the same time. ●

AUTOCAR ROAD TEST

BMW M3 CSL

Number 4612 Meet BMW's lighter, harder, faster M3. Worth the full £58,455? You bet

Trick semi-slick tyres and 130kg less to haul around equals 1.6*g* of cornering grip

JULIAN MACKIE

BMW M3 CSL
List price £58,455
Top speed 161mph
30-70mph 4.2sec
0-60mph 4.8sec
70-0mph 41.2m **MPG** 21.1
For **Astonishing engine, handling, looks, focus, noise, performance**
Against **Gearbox, high price, ride**

HOW YOU approach the new M3 CSL will probably depend on whether you accept the simple concept of a £58,455 BMW 3-series. If you feel the image simply can't support the £60k tag, then you'll never consider it a genuine Porsche 911 rival.

But our brief outing with the fastest production BMW indicates that in doing so, any petrol-blooded enthusiast would be ignoring one of the most exciting cars currently on sale. But before we start delving into the considerable list of alterations an M3 requires to earn BMW's most coveted badge (for CSL read Coupé Sports Lightweight, by the way), it's crucial to acknowledge that in the showroom, on the road and from behind its Alcantara-trimmed wheel, this car does feel like a £60,000 experience. And that is arguably the biggest test of all.

Not that doing something this radical from an M3 was ever going to be easy. Stripping weight from production cars means losing luxury features and fittings and shelving hefty safety equipment – neither of which amuses the marketing department. All credit to BMW M for sticking to its guns, then, and producing a car of unique focus.

Dealers will tell you that BMW chose to cap this car's 360bhp at 7900rpm (the standard car has 343bhp) because the cumulative effect of removing 130kg from the kerb weight (carbon roof, no electric seats or side airbags, extensive use of composites for other components) and the modest power gain produced the necessary performance. There's some truth in that, but the reality is that the Motorsport straight-six is at the very limit of its abilities now; hence the reason that the next car will use V8 power.

It is, by any conventional, unconventional, race or road-car yardsticks a quite astonishing powertrain: one whose raw performance data doesn't properly convey how much more it offers over the standard car. Working in conjunction with a modified SMG paddle-shift gearbox, it will happily knock out the 4.8sec 0-60mph and 10.9sec 0-100mph runs we recorded all day; but at a time when every other Mercedes seems capable of cracking 10sec to the ton, such numbers are merely impressive. Maximum speed depends on your having a current international racing licence. BMW has decreed those who don't will retain the 155mph limiter, whereas those who do can explore up to a claimed 172mph. In operation, the combination of thinner exhaust walls, enormous air intake, optimized exhaust valves and revised camshafts perfectly amplifies the engine's finest characteristics: instant throttle response and straight-six music. The noise is something else – as loud as it is delectable – trumpeted up through the single intake nostril and snarled out of the bespoke carbon airbox inside the engine bay.

Unsurprisingly, given the track credentials, this gearbox works best in the fastest shift mode (a staggering 0.08sec), but despite righting many of the wrongs committed in the standard SMG M3, we still found the software incapable of replicating the perfect blipped downshifts the concept CSL managed last year.

If the engine modifications and outputs seem relatively tame, then what BMW has

"ALL CREDIT TO BMW M FOR STICKING TO ITS GUNS AND PRODUCING A CAR OF UNIQUE FOCUS"

Straight-six produces 360bhp and one of the greatest engine notes ever; SMG 'box improved but not yet ideal; steering still a bit numb

done to the chassis, or more precisely the rubber the chassis sits on, is plain radical. The CSL now joins the Ferrari 360 Challenge Stradale as one of only two cars sold with Michelin Pilot Sport Cups (semi-slick, minimal tread-depth, soft-compound rubber) tyres. Michelin Pilot Sport tyres come as standard, but for the full CSL experience, the fancy rubber is a must.

BMW claims 1.6*g* of lateral acceleration is possible in this car (a 911 Turbo is slithering away at 1.1*g*), and when warm and working on a decent surface that is entirely believable. On a dry road it is nearly impossible to reach a point of under- or oversteer, but factor in some precipitation and that situation changes; although not as dramatically as some people or the disclaimer every owner will need to sign would have you believe. The Cups do, in fact, offer better damp- and wet-road adhesion than a conventional tyre, they just don't have the tread depth to shift standing water, so the aquaplaning tolerance is that much lower.

No other production car's overall performance is so tightly governed by its footwear. With added grip comes added road noise: the CSL is only just tolerable on the motorway. Super-stiff sidewalls take the edge off an already hard ride, but the damping control is so good that you spend more time marvelling at the economy of motion than you do moaning about some added head-bobbing.

But then, road cars just don't come much more exciting than this. A sharper steering rack, revised suspension geometry, trick springs and dampers, and a wider front track make it a far more direct device. However, the standard car's Achilles heel – that numb steering rack – has only been marginally improved. There's now more weight, but for simple, interactive feedback, this is the one area a 911 trounces the CSL.

That isn't the case in many other departments though. Subtle interior tweaks (carbon inner door panels, fixed buckets and the coolest pair of rear chairs in existence) complement the raised bootlid, new front splitter and special alloys perfectly. Yes, the silhouette remains basic 3-series Coupé, but the detail is so obvious and the stance so much more purposeful that even the uninitiated will spot this car as something very special.

As such, the base-origin stigma will be of less hindrance to buyers than the CSL's uncompromising nature. But the basic M3 covers the everyday needs of most people and this car always needed to offer the definitive, unexpurgated driving experience – which it does, quite brilliantly.

Performance and specifications

Engine

Layout 6 cyls in line, 3246cc
Max power 360bhp at 7900rpm
Max torque 273lb ft at 4900rpm
Power to weight 260bhp/tonne
Specific output 111bhp/litre
Installation Front, longitudinal, rear-wheel drive
Construction Alloy head, iron block
Bore/stroke 87.0/91.0mm
Valve gear 4 per cyl, dohc
Compression ratio 11.5:1
Ignition and fuel MSS 54HP engine management

Gearbox

Type 6-speed SMG
Ratios/mph per 1000rpm
1st 4.23/5.1 **2nd** 2.53/8.5
3rd 1.67/12.8 **4th** 1.23/17.4
5th 1.00/21.4 **6th** 0.83/25.8
Final drive 3.62

Maximum speeds

6th 161/6250 **5th** 161/7500
4th 139/8000 **3rd** 102/8000
2nd 68/8000 **1st** 41/8000

Acceleration from rest

Surface dry

True mph	sec	speedo
30	2.0	31
40	2.6	42
50	3.8	52
60	4.8	62
70	6.0	73
80	7.6	84
90	9.2	94
100	10.9	104
110	13.2	115
120	15.7	125
130	18.7	136
140	23.1	146
150	28.9	157

Standing quarter-mile 13.2sec/110mph
Standing km 23.1sec/140mph
30-70mph 4.0sec

Acceleration in gears

mph	6th	5th	4th	3rd	2nd
20-40	-	8.9	6.7	3.4	2.0
30-50	9.2	5.7	4.5	3.1	1.9
40-60	7.3	5.4	4.2	2.8	1.9
50-70	7.3	5.3	3.9	2.7	-
60-80	7.3	5.2	3.8	2.8	-
70-90	7.3	5.1	3.8	2.9	-
80-100	7.4	5.1	4.0	3.2	-

Steering

Type Rack and pinion, power assisted
Lock to lock 3.0 turns

Suspension

Front Struts, coil springs, anti-roll bar
Rear Multi-link, coil springs, anti-roll bar

Wheels & tyres

Wheels 8.5Jx19in (f), 9.5Jx19in (r)
Made of Alloy
Tyres 235/35 ZR19 (f), 265/30 ZR19 (r), Michelin Pilot Sport Cup

Brakes

Front 345mm ventilated discs
Rear 328mm ventilated discs
Anti-lock Standard, with CBC, DSC and M differential lock

Braking

From 30/50/70mph 7.8/21.3/41.2 metres
60-0mph 2.3sec

Noise

At idle 30/50/70mph/max revs in third gear 51/70/73/76/85dB

Fuel consumption

Govt figures: urban/extra urban/combined 15.9/33.6/23.7mpg
***Autocar* figures: test/touring/average** 11.4/27.9/21.1mpg
Tank capacity 63 litres
Range 328 miles

Layout

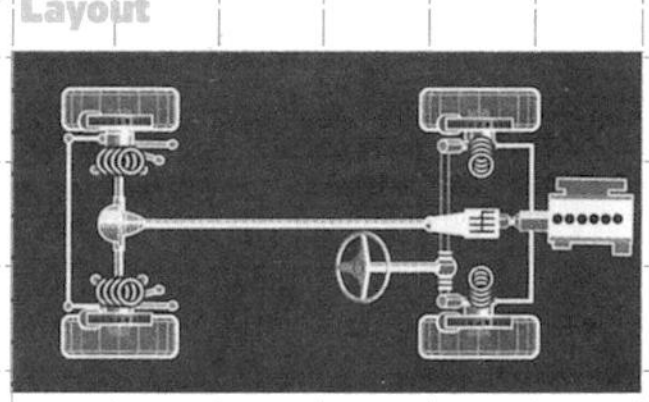

On-the-road price	£58,455
Total as tested	£59,130
CO_2	287g/km
Cost per mile	na
Contract hire per month	na

Equipment

(**bold** = options fitted to test car)

Metallic paint	●
19in M light alloy wheels with Michelin Pilot Sport Cup tyres	£0
Xenon headlamps with wash	**£770**
Automatic air conditioning	£0
Rear parking sensors	£340
Radio/cassette	£0
Single CD	£100
Airbag driver/passenger/side	●/●/ -
Alarm/immobiliser	●/●

● standard – not available
£0 no cost option

Insurance group 20e
Typical quote na

Warranty

3years or 60,000 miles

Servicing

As per indicator

Body 2-door coupé **Cd** 0.33 **Front/rear tracks** 1518mm/1525mm **Turning circle** 11.0m **Min/max front legroom** 910/1110mm **Min/max rear legroom** 970/1170mm **Min/max front headroom** 860/970mm **Max rear headroom** 840mm **Interior width front/rear** 1480/1420mm **Max boot width** 1340mm **Boot length** 1660mm **VDA boot volume** 410 litres **Kerb weight** 1385kg **Width (inc mirrors)** 1950mm

PETER LIDDIARD

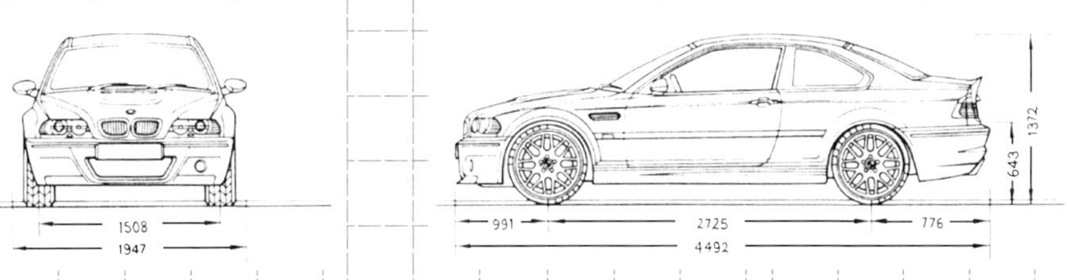

The performance figures were taken with the odometer reading 2340 miles. **AUTOCAR** test results are protected by world copyright and may not be reproduced without the editor's written permission

The M3's finest hour
9/10

BMW M3 SMG

Our favourite BMW now has a sequential gearbox that shifts even quicker than a Ferrari 360 F1's

When the original SMG (sequential manual gearbox) was fitted to the M3 some five years ago, it wasn't considered particularly important in terms of sales, while the target buyer was someone who preferred convenience to outright performance. A lot has changed since then, and the second version of SMG is not only hugely different from the first; BMW now sees it commanding a major chunk of M3 sales in the same way the F1 option has on the Ferrari 360 Modena.

The BMW M department boffins and bigwigs have obviously been paying a great deal of attention to the Ferrari system and have produced a system that not only shifts cogs faster, but allows the driver greater choice of speed and type of change.

The system, a £2400 option, offers no fewer than eleven different settings, five in automatic mode and five in sequential, controlled by either the paddles on the back of the chunky steering wheel or by the lever in the centre console. There is one further, special mode, which we'll come to later. The controls actuate the standard M3 six-speed gearbox electro-hydraulically and as the extra equipment required for this is mainly sophisticated software, it adds only 8kg to the overall weight. A small LED display indicates the mode and gear selected and, despite the wealth of options available, it is clear and easy to use.

Even in the softest sequential setting, S1, upshifts happen swiftly, although the system allows itself enough time to smooth the change even if you keep the throttle on hard. Press the small buttons just behind the lever to select S5 and the shift characteristics change completely. They now come hard and very fast. Keep your foot in and the transmission takes a thump as the cog engages and the clutch releases almost simultaneously, although a very brief lift eases this.

The Formula 1 feel is further enhanced by the yellow and red shift-lights encrusted around the outside of the tachometer, illuminating in the opposite direction to the needle between 7000 and 8000rpm. Downshifts are equally fast and impressive, with a full double-declutch and a throttle blip perfectly matched to the engine speed that encourages you to exploit it to the full by changing down as early as possible.

Push the gear lever to the right to move into the automatic mode and the changes are very similar. A1 is a winter setting where the M3 will move away in second, but the rest are almost a mirror image of the sequential options. This means that it isn't as relaxed as a true automatic when smooching around town and often gets caught hunting around between one of the six gears, even in A2, though you do adapt to it once you understand the way it works.

Sequential shifts activated by paddles (above) or gearstick (right). Above left: shift lights

The final, party-piece setting is designed for the racetrack and can only be accessed with sequential selected and the DSC traction control system turned off. Each gearchange takes an astonishingly short 80 milliseconds to complete. The mechanically sympathetically minded will wince on every shift but the rest will marvel at the incredible speed at which everything happens. There are other tricks too, including hill-start assistance and a launch control system. Hold the gear shift selector forward, flatten the throttle and the engine will spin-up to 3500 revs; release the lever and a full-blooded, tyre-squealing take-off ensues.

Is it better than the manual? That depends entirely on how much personal satisfaction you gain from making a perfect change yourself. Only the talented few can work the gears as fast as the SMG and even fewer get it right every time. Even if you can, remember

that with this system you always have two hands on wheel. And this, don't forget, is an option added to the car that last month we described as being the best driver's BMW yet.

Roger Green

SPECIFICATION

Engine	6-cyl, in-line, 3246cc, 24v
Max power	338bhp @ 7900rpm
Max torque	269lb ft @ 5000rpm
0-60mph	5.2secs (claimed)
Top speed	155mph (limited)
Price	£40,900
On sale	Now

evo RATING ★★★★1/2

+ The best semi-automatic yet

− Not as smooth as a regular auto in town

'There are other tricks too, including a launch control system. Hold the gear selector forward, flatten the throttle and the engine spins up to 3500 revs; release the lever and a full-blooded tyre-squealing take-off ensues'

Brothers in Arms—

BMW M3 & M3 GTR

Separated at birth, but sharing the same family values

BY KIM WOLFKILL • PHOTOS BY GUY SPANGENBERG

FOR BMW FANS EVERYWHERE, the past year has been an exciting, if not memorable one. Last spring, the introduction of the new E46-based M3 put an end to the Euro-spec-vs.-U.S.-spec engine argument, long a sore point with U.S. owners. Starting with the 2001 model, all M3s come equipped with the same smooth 333-bhp 3.2-liter inline-6. Complemented by an equally entertaining chassis, this more powerful M3 has the sort of performance to go toe-to-toe with perennial

sports-car favorites like the Porsche 911 Carrera and Chevrolet Corvette.

Last racing season, BMW also enjoyed enormous success campaigning its new M3 GTR racer. Based on the E46 platform but powered by a purpose-built 4.0-liter V-8, the controversial M3 GTR completely dominated the 2001 American Le Mans Series (ALMS) season, sweeping both the driver and manufacturer titles in the GT class. However, from its inaugural victory at Sears Point (About the Sport, October 2001) to its season-ending triumph at Petit Le Mans, the GTR encountered more challenges off the track than on it.

Controversy aside, there's no denying that the GTR is the most highly evolved M3 to ever turn a wheel. From its meticulously crafted chassis to the hand-built V-8, it represents the pinnacle of M3 development.

Which brings us to Sebring International Raceway, the track where, in a cruel twist of fate, the M3 GTR did not compete in this year's 12 Hours of Sebring (see sidebar). Thanks to BMW of North America and Tom Milner, owner of the Prototype Technology Group racing team, I was given the opportunity to compare the street M3 to PTG's Petit Le Mans-winning M3 GTR. Two distinctly different cars, for sure, but both sharing common DNA, and as such, the same quest for speed.

M3 ROAD CAR

Walk up to the M3 and there's no mistaking it for a standard 3 Series coupe.

Subtle yet suggestive fender flares, 18-in. wheels, sleeker mirrors and a more purposeful nose quietly hint at the serious performance hidden within. Turn the key, stab the throttle and the M3's sporting intentions become self-evident. This car is about more than simply eclipsing its E36 predecessor; it's about totally rewriting the books.

With more horsepower and torque, and one of the industry's sexiest exhaust notes, the engine alone is worth the price of admission. With 3.2 liters of smooth-revving snarl, it belts out a solid 333 bhp and 269 lb.-ft. of torque with power at just about any rpm. Thanks to its larger displacement and such tricky technical items as six individual and electronically controlled throttle butterflies, high-pressure double VANOS valve operation and an 8000-rpm redline, the M3 enjoys a massive 108-bhp advantage over its tamer 330Ci sibling. Or when compared with the previous E36 M3, the new car tromps it by 93 horses on its way to surpassing the vaunted 100-bhp-per-liter mark.

At our test at Sebring, the first order of business is to turn on the Sport mode and flip off the Dynamic Stability Control. Selecting Sport tells the engine-management system to apply a more aggressive map to the gas-pedal travel and throttle butterfly openings, while disengaging the DSC simply makes it easier to slide the car around. In the Sport setting, throttle response feels instantly more reactive and is accompanied by a decidedly more menacing bark from the M3's exhaust. Power on upshifts is almost instantaneous as the car leaps forward with nary a pause in acceleration. Helping matters is a slick 6-speed transmission that makes short work of gear changes to optimize time spent in the meaty part of the powerband. The sweetest range comes between 5000–8000 rpm when the engine just keeps pulling harder and screaming louder.

After a few familiarization laps, it's easy to see why this latest iteration has quickly proven such a favorite among serious enthusiasts. It possesses an instantly reassuring composure that makes it easy to push hard almost right away. Around Sebring's high-speed sweeping Turn 1, for instance, the M3 maintains excellent at-limit balance that allows it to be drifted predictably through the corner's exit lap after lap. At lower speeds, hints of understeer can be easily remedied by simply maintaining light braking to add front bite followed by a welcome dose of the gas pedal.

This track-happy balance comes courtesy of some thoughtful tuning of the MacPherson-strut front and multilink rear suspension along with the M Variable limited-slip differential. At speed, the M3 soaks up Sebring's infamous bumps and surface changes with little protest and puts its power down effortlessly. When a change in attitude is required in most any part of a turn, a little throttle dancing produces the desired result. And despite its rather hefty 3415-lb. curb weight, the M3 still manages to stay relatively light on its feet and handle quick transitions with a surprisingly deft touch. For pure track use the suspension tuning could be firmer, but given the demands of the street, this setup strikes a good compromise between comfort and performance.

The steering, on the other hand, could stand some firming up and a bit less power assist. It lacks some of the trademark feel of previous M3s, instead coming across as overboosted and a little on the light side. This probably doesn't hurt lap times around a racetrack, but it certain affects the overall driving experience on a day-to-day basis. This has been a common complaint of E46 owners in general, so let's hope BMW has been listening.

Steering quibbles aside, it's back to business, as all things that accelerate must also slow down. In the case of the M3, this is dutifully accomplished by a quartet of beefy vented brake rotors (12.8-in. front, 12.9-in. rear) and the accompanying electronic aids (ABS, Dynamic Brake Control). Mysteriously, our test car at Sebring did not exhibit the same level of braking performance we've experienced in other M3s, which have all been excellent. In this case, the Sebring M3 suffered from brake fade to a degree that isn't necessarily reflected in the test numbers but could certainly be felt at higher track speeds.

On the street or at the track, the BMW M3 is a car that you can simply get in and drive. Whether it's the first few turns of an unfamiliar road or the warm-up laps at a new track, there are few cars as easy to feel comfortable with.

■ Balanced, predictable and a blast to toss around, the M3 feels right at home around Sebring's many turns.

A well-engineered balance of power, performance and civility makes it one of the most enjoyable sports cars around. With that in mind, what better place to start when building a championship-winning race car?

M3 GTR RACER

Purpose-built race cars are designed to do one thing and one thing only—go faster than every other car in the field. With that in mind, the engineers at BMW Motorsport set about building the fastest production-based race car the 2001 ALMS GT-class rules would allow. They utilized data not only from the E46 street-car program, but also valuable technical input from Tom Milner's Team PTG to create a car that would be superior to the 2000 version in every significant way.

As the regulations were written at the

time, this meant they could take a heavily tweaked production E46 unit-body and drop in an all-new specially developed 4.0-liter V-8. Provided BMW also built a street version within a year of the M3 GTR's introduction, it was eligible to compete in the 2001 season. They accomplished that midway through the season, thereby validating the race car, at least in the eyes of the rulebook.

The No. 6 Team PTG M3 GTR represents BMW's interpretation of those rules and the masterfully executed end product. Practically reengineered from the wheels up, the M3 GTR suffers few compromises on its way to being the world's most complete GT-class racer. It goes beyond simply bolting a more powerful V-8 into a revised chassis. The M3 GTR also handles better, brakes better, has better aerodynamics and is a more responsive car overall.

Starting with the chassis, engineers significantly stiffened the unit-body and reworked the suspension design to better accommodate the lower ride height required for racing. The standard MacPherson-strut front and rear multilink configuration remains, but all the major suspension components (shocks, struts, springs, anti-roll bars) are race-tuned and fully adjustable. The front and rear tracks have also been increased significantly to accommodate massive 11 x 18-in. wheels and Yokohama racing slicks. The combination of 15-in. front brake rotors and 6-piston Brembo calipers with 12.3-in. rears and 4-piston calipers delivers stopping power on par with many faster GTS-class cars.

Nestled low and set back in the engine bay sits BMW's now notorious 4.0-liter V-8. Pumping out a claimed 444 bhp and 354 lb.-ft. of torque, this remarkable powerplant makes no secret of its highly developed nature. BMW denies it was originally earmarked for the German DTM series, but it's still tough to hide its very high-tech roots. An oversquare bore and stroke, four valves per cylinder and a 180-degree crankshaft make for a powerful, high-revving mill with an exhaust note more akin to a Formula 1 V-10 than a traditional V-8. And thanks to its featherweight flywheel and vastly reduced reciprocating mass, this V-8 revs quicker than almost any engine in the paddock. A carbon clutch and 6-speed Hewland gearbox round out the powertrain that's easily the most advanced in GT racing.

Strapped in and fired up, the toughest task is getting the M3 GTR out of Sebring's pit lane. The engine's lightweight internals

"Rolling on the throttle **unleashes an intoxicating blast** of smooth, linear power that continues unabated in every gear."

■ **The cockpit, left, includes only the essential controls, switches and instrumentation necessary for racing. Heavily reinforced chassis and rollcage members stiffen the production unit-body while offering extensive driver protection. The trunk, below, houses the carbon-fiber fuel cell and additional bracing. The heart of the M3 GTR is BMW's purpose-built 4.0-liter V-8, right. With more horsepower and torque than the inline-6 it replaced, this controversial engine powered the GTR to driver and manufacturer championships in 2001.**

and touchy carbon clutch require a slow constant drag to launch without stalling. Release the clutch any quicker and the engine instantly dies. Out on the track, it's surprisingly easy to drive for such a potent race car. As speeds climb and cornering forces increase, its considerable talents quickly begin to make themselves known.

Immediately apparent is the overwhelming sense of precision. This car goes exactly where it's pointed with no wasted energy or unwanted commotion. It arcs through turns with laser-like accuracy and absolute consistency. Combined with uncanny balance, the GTR inspires confidence in its ample limits. Around corners, over bumps or under braking, it's generally unaffected by what's happening around it. Instead, it allows the driver to concentrate on more important matters like consistency and speed.

Rolling on the throttle unleashes an intoxicating blast of smooth, linear power that continues unabated in every gear. Excellent torque throughout the rev range guarantees strong acceleration out of turns, while individual rev limits for each gear further optimize engine performance. Straight-cut gears make gear-

changes ultra-quick and, like the rest of the car, exceedingly precise.

Rounding out the M3 GTR's bag of tricks is braking performance with few, if any, rivals. Even the almighty Porsches, famous for amazing brakes, can't compete with this M3. Apart from the sheer stopping power, what's more impressive is the uncanny control it possesses under hard braking. Jumping on the binders at 150 mph produces huge deceleration forces without the penalty of unwanted instability. Instead, it tracks true when slowing for corners, takes a solid set turning in, then

■ Team PTG driver Bill Auberlen, left, explains to Kim Wolfkill the nuances of driving the M3 GTR quickly around Sebring.

rockets out with utter confidence.

While its V-8 engine garnered most of the attention during the 2001 race season, the M3 GTR is about more than just its controversial powerplant. Surrounding this engine is one of the sport's most complete and well-developed race cars. Whether it complies with the spirit of the production-based GT class is still open to debate, but what isn't debatable is that in the world of M3s they don't get any better than this.

HOW SIMILAR ARE THEY, REALLY?

Truthfully, there aren't that many similarities between the street M3 and its M3 GTR sibling. From a technical standpoint, they do share the same unit-body, drivetrain layout, suspension configuration and overall shape, but beyond that, they're two very different cars with entirely different purposes.

However, what they do share are core BMW traits like balance, control and predictability. Even with their wildly disparate goals, both make it easy to get acquainted and up to speed. The street M3 is obviously the milder of the two, but even the GTR, at least by racing standards, is a surprisingly benign car to jump into cold. Both possess a similarly reassuring degree of balance that encourages you to have some fun. So while the M3 and M3 GTR may seem worlds apart, common traits still hold them together, leaving no doubts about their family lineage.

Why no M3 GTR in the ALMS?

Before it had ever turned a lap, the M3 GTR was the center of controversy in the ALMS GT class. A category for production-based cars with road-going counterparts, GT has been the playground of Porsche's GT3R/RS for the previous two seasons. With the arrival of the BMW GTR, however, all that changed as the V-8-powered coupe decimated the competition, winning six straight races en route to both the driver and manufacturer championships.

And while it was built in accordance with the Automobile Club de l'Ouest's (ACO) 2001 homologation requirements (at least one V-8-powered street M3 need be offered for sale within a year of the race car's debut), critics felt the GTR hurt the class and, as Porsche officials put it, violated the "spirit" of the rules.

After all the political chips had fallen, BMW found they'd won the battle but lost the war. For the 2002 season, the ACO drew up stricter eligibility requirements for GT-class cars competing in the 24 Hours of Le Mans and ALMS. Aimed squarely at the M3 GTR, the 2002 rules require GT cars to be based on a vehicle in series production with output of one car per week using an engine derived from a production model built in numbers of 1000 or more.

Any manufacturer unable to meet these criteria is still permitted to compete, but with a 20 percent reduction in their air intake restrictors and the addition of 100 kg. of ballast.

Following careful evaluation and testing over the winter, BMW management concluded that the company could neither meet the required production numbers nor compete effectively with the additional air restrictor and weight penalties. During pre-season testing at Sebring, the restricted M3 GTR was off the pace significantly, turning laps some 3 seconds slower than last year.

Consequently, the BMW Motorsport and Prototype Technology Group teams withdrew from the 2002 ALMS season just two months prior to the 12 Hours of Sebring season-opener. So no more M3 GTR and no Porsche-BMW battles this year. Both BMW and the ALMS say they're hopeful of a return in 2003, but until then, the GT class sadly returns to nearly an all-Porsche affair.—*KW*

ROAD & TEST

2001 BMW M3

BMW of North America, Inc
P.O. Box 1227, Westwood, N.J. 07675; www.bmwusa.com

BMW M3 GTR

Prototype Technology Group
441 Victory Rd., Winchester, Va. 22602; www.ptgracing.com

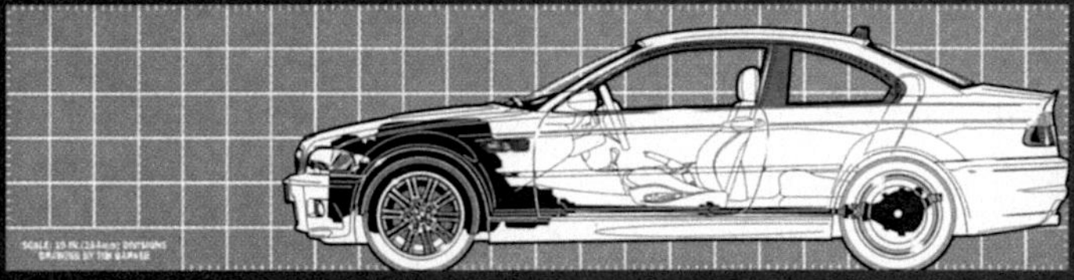

List Price: $45,400 **Price as Tested: $53,591**

List Price: $470,000 **Price as Tested: $470,000**

Price as tested incl std equip. (stability control, traction control, dynamic brake control, limited-slip diff, ABS, air cond, power windows, mirrors & door locks; cruise control, remote locking, dual front airbags & side airbags, head-protection airbags, onboard computer, anti-theft alarm), cold weather pkg (heated front seats & headlight washers, ski bag) $700, Luxury pkg (power moonroof, dual power front seats w/memory, Nappa leather, rain-sensing windshield wipers) $3100, adjustable seatback width ($500), titanium silver metallic paint ($475), xenon headlights ($500), AM/FM/CD player ($200), Harman Kardon sound system ($675), gas-guzzler tax ($1000), luxury tax ($396), dest charge ($645).

Price as tested incl BMW Motorsport rolling chassis, engine, transmission, electronic data acquisition & telemetry system.

General Data

	BMW M3	BMW M3 GTR
Curb weight	**3415 lb**	**2425 lb**
Test weight	3595 lb	2731 lb
Weight dist (with driver), f/r, %	est 53/47	50/50
Wheelbase	107.5 in.	107.5 in.
Track, f/r	59.4 in./60.0 in.	63.3 in./63.1 in.
Length	176.8 in.	181.6 in.
Width	70.1 in.	74.8 in.
Height	54.0 in.	52.0-52.4 in. adj.

Engine

	BMW M3	BMW M3 GTR
Type	dohc 4-valve/cyl **inline-6**	dohc 4-valve/cyl **V-8**
Displacement	3245 cc	3997 cc
Bore x stroke	87.0 x 91.0 mm	94.0 x 72.0 mm
Compression ratio	11.5:1	12.0:1
Horsepower (SAE)	**333 bhp @ 7900 rpm**	**444 bhp @ 7500 rpm**
Torque	**269 lb-ft @ 4900 rpm**	**354 lb-ft @ 5500 rpm**
Redline	8000 rpm	8500 rpm
Fuel injection	elect. sequential port	elect. sequential port
Rec. fuel	prem. unleaded, 91 pump oct	Elf race fuel, 100 oct

Chassis & Body

	BMW M3	BMW M3 GTR
Layout	**front engine/rear drive**	**front engine/rear drive**
Body/frame	unit steel	steel, fiberglass/unit steel
Brakes, f/r	**12.8-in. vented discs/ 12.9-in. vented discs**; vac asst, ABS	**15.0-in. vented discs/ 12.3-in. discs**; driver adjustable balance bar
Wheels	aluminum alloy; **18 x 8J f, 18 x 9J r**	forged aluminum, **18 x 11**
Tires	Michelin Pilot Sport; **225/45ZR-18 f, 245/40ZR-18 r**	Yokohama Racing; **290/650-18 f, 290/680-18 r**
Steering	**rack & pinion,** power assist	**rack & pinion,** vari power assist
Overall ratio	15.4:1	na
Turns lock to lock	3.0z	1.25
Suspension, f/r	**MacPherson struts,** double-pivot lower L-arms, coil springs, tube shocks, anti-roll bar/**multi-link,** coil springs, tube shocks, anti-roll bar	**MacPherson struts,** coil springs, adj tube shocks, adj anti-roll bar/**central link,** coil springs, adj tube shocks, adj anti-roll bar

Accommodations

	BMW M3	BMW M3 GTR
Seating capacity	**5**	**1**
Head room, f/r	38.5 in./35.0 in.	na
Seat width	35.0 in.	na
Front-seat leg room	46.5 in.	na
Rear-seat knee room	21.5 in.	na
Seat travel	9.0 in.	na
Trunk space	10.7 cu ft	na

Acceleration

	BMW M3	BMW M3 GTR
Time to speed, sec		
0-20 mph	1.7	1.5
0-40 mph	2.8	2.1
0-60 mph	4.7	3.3
0-80 mph	7.8	4.9
0-100 mph	11.6	7.1
Time to distance		
0-1320 ft (¼ mile)	13.3 @ 106.8 mph	11.3 @ 125.3 mph

Braking

	BMW M3	BMW M3 GTR
Minimum stopping distance		
From 60 mph	112 ft	94 ft
From 80 mph	200 ft	165 ft
Control	excellent	excellent
Brake feel	excellent	excellent
Overall brake rating	excellent	excellent

Handling

	BMW M3	BMW M3 GTR
Lateral accel (200-ft skidpad)	0.89g	na
Balance	mild understeer	na
Speed thru 700-ft slalom	66.6 mph	na
Balance	mild understeer	na

Fuel Economy

	BMW M3	BMW M3 GTR
Our driving	na	4.8 mpg
EPA city/highway	16/24 mpg	na
Fuel capacity	16.6 gal.	26.4 gal.

Interior Noise

	BMW M3	BMW M3 GTR
Idle in neutral	54 dBA	na
Maximum, 1st gear	86 dBA	na
70 mph	74 dBA	na

Drivetrain

	BMW M3	BMW M3 GTR
Transmission	**6-speed manual**	**6-speed manual**
Gear/Ratio/Overall/(Rpm) Mph		
1st, :1	4.23:1/15.30:1/(8000) 40	2.50:1/8.66:1/(7500) 69
2nd, :1	2.53:1/9.15:1/(8000) 66	2.07:1/7.16:1/(7500) 83
3rd, :1	1.67:1/6.04:1/(8000) 100	1.69:1/5.85:1/(7500) 102
4th, :1	1.23:1/4.44:1/(8000) 138	1.38:1/4.79:1/(7500) 125
5th, :1	1.00:1/3.62:1/est (7250) 155*	1.18:1/4.10:1/(7500) 146
6th, :1	0.83:1/3.00:1/est (6000) 155*	1.04:1/3.62:1/(7500) 165
Final drive ratio	3.62:1	3.75:1
Engine rpm @ 60 mph in top gear	2400 rpm	3604 rpm

*Electronically limited.

Subjective ratings consist of excellent, very good, good, average, poor; na means information is not available.

shift no lift

by DAVID COLMAN
photography by JOHN KIRIKOS

The Sequential Manual Gearbox-equipped BMW M3 allows you to paddle-shift like an F1 driver or kick back and let the car do the shifting.

When James Bond (in print, not on screen) did a "racing downchange" in his Blower Bentley, he took care to blip the throttle, match the revs and double de-clutch with masterful dexterity. Sadly, 007's pride in stirring the gears without shaking them has been rendered obsolete by BMW's SMG M3. Here's a car that will do a racing downchange all by itself. Not only that, it will also perform programmed smoky burnouts followed by racing upshifts. BMW has every reason to feel smug about SMG. One of every two M3s sold abroad are SMG-equipped. It's the first ever automatic gearbox I would buy in lieu of a manual.

But the Sequential Manual Gearbox isn't really an automatic transmission at all. Rather, this $2,400 option harnesses an electrohydraulic shift mechanism to operate the same synchronizers and shift forks that control the M3's standard-issue Getrag Type-D 6-speed. BMW deletes shift linkage and clutch pedal, replacing them with a hydraulic pump and three solenoid valves. A computer orchestrates the hydraulics by relying on information provided by 11 different sensors.

Of all the magic tricks the SMG performs, three stand out for the enthusiast. You can leave 150 feet of rubber in first gear by just standing on the gas and letting SMG dump the clutch for you. Then, you can speed shift upshifts without lifting off the throttle, because SMG requires no lift to shift. And when the first turn looms, you can bang downshifts like Juan Pablo Montoya.

SMG will also allow you to potter around town slower than a Meals-On-Wheels step van. Just push the stubby stick on the center console over to the right and you've left Montoyaland for the AARP Kingdom. In what BMW calls "the automated mode," upshifts and downshifts occur continually. The objective here seems to lie in keeping engine rpm under 3,000. No matter how much you fiddle with the five-position slide switch controlling BMW's Drivelogic system, automated SMG invariably chooses a higher gear than you would ever select on your own.

The M3 receives no special SMG badging on the exterior or underhood, but once inside, the short, chrome-rimmed shifter and steering wheel paddles let you know right away this is no ordinary M3.

Side View

THIS IS ONE piece of technology I'd rather leave to F1, regardless of how impressively efficient it is. Pulling on the paddles simply isn't as satisfying as executing a perfect manual shift, however archaic it might be to operate the throttle, gearbox and clutch oneself. And as has become all too common on BMWs of late, SMG is an overly complicated variation on a theme—does it really *need* 11 modes?—*Jacqueline Jouret*

IT'S ODD THAT BMW touts the benefits of having the SMG paddles on the steering wheel, as opposed to the steering column, when the steering technique it teaches at its own driving schools, shuffle steering, renders them largely useless in spirited driving. The paddles are great in stop-and-go traffic—they work better than the fussy automatic mode—but when the going gets twisty, it's time to reach for the shifter.—*Eric Gustafson*

Climbing a hill at 30 mph? Why not try fifth, suggests Drivelogic? Exiting a tight turn and entering a short straight? You'll find yourself in sixth faster than you can say EPA duty cycle. Clearly, the automated mode of SMG was selected to give the M3 passable gas mileage statistics. Even so, the rating reads 16 city and 24 highway, burdening this Bimmer with a $1,000 Gas Guzzler tax.

If brain-dead trolling is your bag, then Driveillogic is happy to accommodate you. But if you want to experience F1-style shifting, then move the Jekyll-Hyde lever back to the right, or tap a paddle on the wheel, and you're instantly transported into Sequential mode again. Here, you control every upshift and downshift, with but two exceptions. SMG will not perform a downshift that could damage the engine or gearbox. SMG will also automatically downshift to first if you come to a complete stop, obviating the need for you to manually cycle down through the gears. The rest of the time, you're on your own. Just be sure to watch those illuminated tach lights as they sweep from amber to red. The 333-hp engine peaks so quickly that keeping up with its demands can be a daunting task.

Those paddles move with the wheel, unlike the stationary column-mounted ones Ferrari chose for the 360 Modena. And if you're having trouble getting a grip, your BMW dealer can sell you a pair of optional, oversized paddles. On curvy roads it can be difficult to get a grip on those paddles as the wheel saws 3.2 turns, lock-to-lock. The problem is your hands become crossed-up as the wheel pivots. This makes it hard to keep track of which paddle is up and which down.

The big difference between your SMG M3 and Montoya's F1 car is that his wheel travels less than one turn lock-to-lock, so paddle disorientation is never an issue for Pablito. If you find you can't chew gum, rub your tummy and pull a paddle at the same time, however, there is an alternative: You can use that shifter between the seats to bang off downshifts by pushing forward, upshifts by yanking back. In curvy terrain, this is the best solution of all.

There is room for improvement in the design of the information panel on the lower right edge of the instrument cluster. At 1.75 x 1 inches, it's too small for easy viewing, especially when the fat-rimmed, paddle-festooned wheel is cocked sideways. This SMG digital screen includes information about which gear you've selected, which mode you've chosen and which echelon of Drivelogic you've picked. Oddly enough, the letter "A" appears in the slot for "displayed shift mode" when you have chosen sequential mode. Why an "S" does not appear defies logic. BMW would do well to relocate this panel to a spot directly between the speedo and tach, enlarge its size and rethink the abbreviations on the pictograph. In fact, the SMG M3 would seem to be an ideal candidate for an all-digital, F1-style instrument cluster, like the one Honda uses on its S2000.

The switch for toggling Drivelogic from one setting to another sits on the center console, just aft of the shift lever. In automatic mode, you can dial yourself one of five settings from soft and sloppy to hard and nasty. A minute bar graph on the dash panel indicates which setting you have chosen, but frankly I couldn't tell much of a difference between any of them in automatic mode.

In sequential mode, you can access a sixth bar of goodness—if you first delete Dynamic Stability Control (DSC) with a button on the console. With the tranny set in sequential mode and six bars dialed up on the Drivelogic graph, as well as the electronic throttle placed in Sport mode, the M3 is heaven to drive really fast. Completely controlled by you, SMG will snap off shifts in just 0.08 second, and make you feel like the F1 hero you really are. ●

SHORT TAKE

BMW M3 Convertible

The four-seat sports car.

BY CSABA CSERE

"This is just as bad as a Corvette, except it has a back seat," muttered my wife, Mary, and she was not employing *bad* to mean *good* in the modern urban vernacular. Mary has developed an aversion to riding in Corvettes with me because the powerful plastic sports cars always seem to stimulate my aggressive driving tendencies. She had correctly perceived that the BMW M3 convertible has precisely the same effect.

To readers of this magazine, this effect is a virtue rather than a vice because, just like the Corvette, the M3 convertible has the combination of effortless energy, secure grip, and linear controls that make any driver feel like Michael Schumacher–and want to emulate him.

Okay, so the M3 convertible can't quite match the quarter-mile time of 13.1 seconds at 111 mph of the latest Corvette convertible. In fact, the M3 convertible's 13.7-second quarter-mile at 104 mph is 0.3 second and 2 mph in arrears of the closed-roof M3 (June 2001), thanks to the convertible's shocking *398-pound* weight gain from its power top and various and sundry reinforcements.

Even so, the M3 convertible is by far the quickest droptop on the market with an adult-feasible rear seat. Turn off the traction control, drop the clutch at 4500 rpm, and you rocket to 60 mph in 5.1 seconds. A mere 7.4 seconds later, you'll hit triple digits.

Passing on a back road is simply a matter of using the beautiful shifter to select third gear and planting your right foot. Accompanied by the determined metallic rasp from the rev-happy 3.2-liter six, you will surge around even a double tractor-trailer in astonishingly little time and space. Keep your foot in it, and the M3 convertible will still be pulling strongly when you run into the electronic governor, which truncated the acceleration curve at 157 mph in our car, although the speedo needle was nearly touching the 170 mark.

At top speed, on an admittedly uneven road, the M3 cabrio did want both hands on the wheel. But in most other circumstances, it inspires immense confidence. We found ourselves hurling the M3 into corners ever faster, knowing the car was so well-planted on its big Michelin Pilot Sport tires that we would simply track through as if on a tether. Even in fast corners, midcourse corrections are always an option because there's invariably sufficient bite to tighten your line.

Although the current line of 3-series suffers from steering that is too light (soon to be corrected, BMW promises), the M3's nicely sculpted three-spoke wheel is beautifully weighted and so intuitively responsive that after driving a few blocks, you position the car with the casual accuracy that normally comes from years of ownership. Pretty soon, you're "driving it like a Corvette."

Unlike the latest version of Chevy's sports car, however, the M3 convertible accommodates more than luggage in the rear. Although its back seat is narrower than the one in the sedan, it's roomy enough for two average-size adults for short trips. The trunk will hold a pair of stacked, unfolded garment bags and some odds and ends, even with the top down. With the top up, you can fold a panel out of the way and fit another duffel bag or two.

As you would expect in a $58,000 car, this trunk is neatly trimmed, as is the nappa-leather-upholstered cockpit. All the usual power adjustments and conveniences are standard, including one-touch top operation incorporating a mechanized hard boot. Dropping the top is so painless, we often did it for five-minute trips.

This top is fully lined and impressively tight. Even during an extended 90-plus-mph cruise–people sure drive rapidly in central California–air leaks and wind roar were so low that we almost forgot we were driving a convertible.

Droptop 3-series models have never been paragons of structural rigidity, and this latest M3 still can't match a Corvette convertible in twist resistance. Although stiffer than its predecessor, which is quite an achievement given the new model's much firmer suspension, the M3 convertible will quiver and shake in pothole-infested Michigan. On California roads, however, we rarely noticed any sheetmetal jitters.

The structural quibble aside, if you want a convertible that's fast and has a real back seat, this M3 is the best there is. Just don't let the four seats fool you. It's a sports car, and it encourages you to drive it like one. •

Vehicle type: front-engine, rear-wheel-drive, 4-passenger, 2-door convertible
Price as tested: $57,989 (base price: $55,727)
Engine type: DOHC 24-valve 6-in-line, iron block and aluminum head, Siemens MSS 54 engine-control system with port fuel injection

Displacement	198 cu in, 3246cc
Power (SAE net)	333 bhp @ 7900 rpm
Torque (SAE net)	262 lb-ft @ 4900 rpm
Transmission	5-speed manual
Wheelbase	107.5 in
Length	176.8 in
Curb weight	3838 lb
Zero to 60 mph	5.1 sec
Zero to 100 mph	12.5 sec
Zero to 130 mph	22.8 sec
Street start, 5–60 mph	5.8 sec
Standing 1/4-mile	13.7 sec @ 104 mph
Top speed (governor limited)	157 mph
Braking, 70–0 mph	162 ft
Roadholding, 300-ft-dia skidpad	0.81 g
EPA fuel economy, city driving	16 mpg
C/D-observed fuel economy	19 mpg

BMW
Meader
nal BMW parts

twister

Meet BMW's biggest, baddest M3 of all: the flame-spitting M3 GTR. We grab a unique chance to sample this invincible 911 GT3-eating, rule-bending racer

Words: Richard Meaden | **Pictures:** Dominic Fraser

Fearsome M3 GTR roasted Porsche's 911 GT3 in last year's ALMS. Flames and earsplitting backfires accompany downshifts. No wonder Meaden (below left) looks a bit anxious

No one likes a cheat. However, in the nefarious world of motorsport a 'creative' approach to interpreting the rulebook is often the most effective way to gain a decisive advantage. When challenged, the best exponents of such an approach to racing merely claim they've exploited a loophole; those unfortunates on the receiving end will inevitably cry foul.

While galling for the opposition, the upshot for car nuts like us are fabulously exciting race-cars, machines conceived right on the cutting edge of the sport. Just such a machine is BMW's M3 GTR, an alleged road-based racer that took Porsche to the cleaners in last year's ALMS, or American Le Mans Series. I stress the 'alleged' bit, for despite the ALMS rulebook calling for GT-class cars to be based on a road-going car, a V8-powered BMW M3 is still yet to hit the streets. Porsche, past masters at the old loophole exploitation trick, were understandably miffed.

Cheats? Well, to be fair BMW did announce a price for the M3 GTR road car (a modest £157K) and show a picture of a GTR prototype alongside the M3 GTR racer in the autumn of last year, so you could argue the intention was there to build it. But with 2001's ALMS silverware already gathering dust in the BMW Motorsport trophy cabinet, and the M3 GTR subsequently withdrawn from racing, we're more likely to see this year's Jaguar F1 car in pole position than see an M3 GTR in our local BMW showroom. Shame.

But do I really care? To be honest right at this moment I couldn't care less. For here before me is the very M3 GTR racer that slayed Porsche, literally with my name on it. Sat on its air jacks and primed for 20 laps of the sinuous Vallelunga circuit on the outskirts of Rome, it looks spectacular and, if I'm honest, a rather bigger bite of Bavarian racing muscle than I feel able to chew on. Intimidated? You bet your life.

The best racing cars always have a menacing air about them, but the GTR is so purposeful the atmosphere in the pit garage positively crackles with aggression. Engorged wheelarches struggle to contain a gargantuan set of wheels and slick racing tyres, while the extended front and rear bumpers incorporate all manner of mesh-filled vents and intakes. A pair of shin-scorching side-exit exhaust pipes threaten to flame-grill anything within a metre radius, while perched atop two sturdy stanchions sprouting from the bootlid is a surfboard-sized wing to keep the GTR's fat behind pressed firmly into the asphalt.

Activity amongst the BMW Motorsport mechanics intensifies as my time draws near. Sensing my nerves, the GTR's regular peddler, Dirk Muller, invites me to get belted in, then gives me a guided tour of the cockpit. Biggest surprise is the conventional H-pattern gearbox. I'd been expecting a push-pull sequential transmission, but the ALMS rules require a good old-fashioned 'box, which gets my palms sweating even more as there's a chance I could wrong-slot and send the GTR's steel conrods clean through the side of its bespoke 4-litre engine bock. That's right, the GTR's motor isn't derived from BMW's familiar V8 road motor, but a completely new design penned specifically for racing. Dry-sumped and running an eye-watering 13:1 compression ratio, the GTR's V8 is conservatively rated at 450bhp and 400lb ft of torque. However, remove the asphyxiating ALMS inlet air restrictors and 650bhp is nearer the mark, which doesn't really bear thinking about in a car weighing just 1100kg.

The sun is beating down as the GTR's air jacks hiss into the chassis and its four sticky Michelin slicks unceremoniously hit the garage floor. It's been suggested I do half a dozen laps or so to get

'The GTR is so purposeful the atmosphere in the pit garage positively crackles with aggression'

Below: despite its brutal appearance, the GTR is far from a brute to drive. Brilliantly stable under braking, fantastically progressive under power and with huge stonk from tickover to redline, it is awesomely effective

comfortable with the car and circuit, return to the pits and then go back out for fifteen uninterrupted laps, which sounds like a good idea to me. Keeping my quivering right foot well away from the throttle (as instructed) I press the starter button and the V8 erupts into life. Grab the rubber golf-ball-topped gear lever and push purposefully into first, let the revs settle into a fast idle and feed the clutch in with my jelly-like left pin. Amazingly we're trundling along the pitlane and out onto the circuit.

Perhaps it's because the GTR still resembles a road M3. Perhaps it's because with power steering and that H-pattern gearbox the GTR doesn't require you to learn any fancy techniques to drive. Whatever the reason, I soon feel unusually comfortable in this $500,000 race car, and by the end of my first session not only have I got a good idea of the circuit, my nerves have gone as well.

Happy that I'm happy, the BMW crew wave me back out of the pit, but as I reach for the starter and the GTR sticks its square jaw out into the daylight once more, the huge thunder-cloud that's been circling Vallelunga turns on the sprinklers. Despite a full-face helmet, the BMW bods see the look of alarm on the Meaden visage and sensibly push me back into the garage, only to bolt on a set of wets and send me out again! Thanks chaps. Not.

Compared with the massive grip levels generated by those big slicks, the not-fully-wet-but-too-greasy-for-slicks surface feels like ice. There isn't a huge amount of feedback from the steering, and it's easy to lock a front brake without noticing. Typically thorough, BMW cottoned on to this early in the GTR's race career, which is why there are two small red lights on the dash to warn when one or both fronts are locked. It's easy to get them lit into the low-speed corners, but even in the damp it takes a surprising amount of effort to provoke a flicker into the one big braking area, when we must be slowing from 130mph or so. Later, Muller says the GTR eats the 911s under braking, such is its stability, though he also admits the Porsche's rear-biased weight distribution allows it to get the power down harder and earlier than the hairy-arsed M3.

The gearbox is fantastic, and my fears of wrong-slotting soon fade. It responds best to clutchless upshifts, aided by the faintest lift of the throttle to unload the transmission. Driven thus you can punch up through the 'box with amazing speed, each change accompanied by a sharp, percussive rifle-shot from the exhaust and, if you're lucky, a three-foot stab of flame, a party piece it performs more readily under braking The engine pulls with the relentless insistence of gravity itself, with enormous power punching you into the seatback from 3500rpm to just over 7500rpm, and bellows with the full-blooded, goosebump-inducing force of an angry Norse God. In fact it's all so dramatic I can't quite believe I'm strapped into the epicentre, directing proceedings from the driver's seat. In keeping with the unreality of it all, I have a stab at sliding the thing around, and not only get away with it, but discover that the GTR positively enjoys such juvenile behaviour. As Muller concedes, smooth is fast and kinder to the tyres, but when you need to go off-line and beast your way past a stubborn rival, the M3's benign character means it's on your side even when you overdrive it. In the less do-or-die circumstances of a hack, sorry, track test, it flatters uncertain, inky hands like no other racing car I've ever driven.

Then, in an instant the rain turns torrential, and within a lap I can barely see where I'm going, despite the big wiper slicing across the screen for all its worth. BMW bods hang over the pit wall and wave me in before I bury it in a barrier. Engine cut, I coast down the pitlane, absorbing the last precious moments in this most amazing car. It might have been the product of dubious rule-bending, but this ruthlessly effective machine is a warhorse in the finest Bavarian tradition. As a road car (without those air restrictors) it would be devastating. Perhaps Stuttgart should be thankful the GTR hasn't hit the streets… ■

'In an instant the rain turns torrential, and within a lap I can barely see where I'm going'

TURNED UP TO 11

BMW calls the stripped-out CSL the '110 percent M3', cranking the driving experience up to new heights. Where better to taste the purity than the Nürburgring? Story by Mike Duff. Photography by Tom Salt

THE LINE BETWEEN MORTAL CAR AND supercar is getting finer. This is the golden age of the unlikely performance car: ordinary-looking vehicles with deeply exceptional amounts of go. Among all the super-saloons, one car stands out as exemplar: the BMW M3. Step back to grab some perspective and the M3 is a gloriously unlikely thing. Take the coupé version of a well engineered small executive saloon that's sold by the boatload to red-braced thrusters. Make it wider, lower and meaner. And then force it to swallow a bristly six-cylinder engine that more than doubles the power of the cooking versions. A bit of tweaking, a bit of fiddling and – hey presto – you've got a vehicle capable of keeping pace with all but the most exotic supercars. It's BMW's brand values of performance and driver focus taken to the *n*th degree.

But the standard M3 wasn't enough. Too much never is; you want *way* too much instead. And BMW was determined to squeeze even more from the package: less weight, more power, even sharper reactions. Which led, via some intensive tinkering, to the car we've come to the Nürburgring in Germany to drive: the M3 CSL. Feel free to get *quite* excited, but hold the full-bore enthusiasm briefly; the cars on show here are still prototypes (albeit effectively production-ready), and the finished car won't be along for another year or so. Roughly translated, 'CSL' comes out as 'coupé, sports, light', and it's an acronym that's been knocking around the corporate boot badge drawer for a while. Ever since the original CSL of the 1970s and its race-winning 'Batmobile' variant. The M3 CSL is here to usurp the M3 as ultimate brand champion: lighter, faster and more hardcore. The standard M3 is a near-perfect focusing of product and brand; the CSL is the same, only slightly more so. Think in terms of concentrating sunlight through a magnifying glass. Or, as BMW puts it, 'M3 CSL: the 110 percent car'.

THERE ARE LOTS OF BIG QUESTIONS TO be asked of the CSL. And there's only a very limited time to conduct the interrogation; I may need to be brutal. Is this a car that's really worthy of the hype, and a likely 50 grand-plus price tag? BMW invited what seemed like every motoring journalist in Europe to come and find out, meaning that (with only six prototype CSLs on hand) we're limited to 20 minutes each in the car and not a second longer. A large part of the PR message is that the CSL has been engineered with plenty of exposure to the Nürburgring's notorious *Nordschleife*, the 13-mile-long former grand prix circuit that's now basically a toll road for nutters. Thing is, corporate cowardice (or more likely common sense) has prevailed, BMW obviously figuring that the odds of getting its precious prototypes back intact after a day on the *Nordschleife* are very slight. Hence we learn that we're only going to be allowed to play on the considerably less scary, gravel trap-equipped

Spine-tingling 3.2 straight six has more power in CSL, but BMW can't say how much more yet – possibly 350bhp. Sequential 'box to be recalibrated to allow for new tyres, reduced weight

modern grand prix circuit. Still, in predictable Eifel mountain fashion, the day is overcast and rainy for some added no-cost excitement.

Right, the CSL. This is a car that's definitely about engineering. The M division's white coat wearers must have reacted with glee when asked to take the standard M3 and, in *Spinal Tap* fashion, turn it up to 11. But this is also a car that has caused some serious beard scratching in the marketing department. Just how expandable are the company's oh-so-cherished brand values? Will people really pay Porsche 911 money for a BMW 3-series, however fast it goes? This is a pertinent question. Remember the Peugeot 306 Rallye (or its smaller 106 Rallye sister)? In a far more modest way, it was basically offering the same deal as the CSL: take a great driver's car, strip out all the luxuries, and then market it as a hardcore driving device. For a more contemporary take on the same theme, check out the forthcoming Renault Clio Sport Cup. But there's one very important difference: the stripped-out rally replicas cost considerably *less* than the cars they were based on. BMW is being very tight-lipped about the CSL's eventual price tag (and similarly cagey about all other relevant details), but one thing's for sure, it's going to cost considerably *more* than the standard M3. Quite likely somewhere on the fat side of £50,000. It's the sort of trick that only the likes of Porsche have got away with in the past. Are we having our legs pulled?

Okay, so what exactly is the CSL? The standard car's digital climate control, electrically adjustable leather seats and stereo have been binned. The prototypes didn't even have air conditioning. Technology is on display with a rash of carbonfibre-reinforced plastic (CFRP); the front bumper, sill extensions, rear diffuser and centre console are all made from the stuff. The floor beneath the boot has been replaced by a lightweight aluminium honeycomb material. And the rear screen is made from thinner-gauge glass. It's not quite as extreme as the CSL concept seen at the Frankfurt show last year; that had a carbonfibre roof and bootlid as well. The company is being extremely coy about the actual weight saving over a standard M3. 'These cars are all prototypes and the production specification will be different,' summarises the corporate line. But don't anticipate the 200kg discount claimed for the original concept, especially as the massive 19-inch alloy wheels and massively uprated brakes might well have brought some extra mass to the party.

Other changes are down to that fine old tradition of incremental tinkering. The steering has been revised with a reworked rack and new front suspension geometry to sharpen reactions. There are new spring and damper settings, moving the ride/handling balance considerably further to the right. And the enormous alloys wear bespoke, specially designed Michelin ▸

'THE SLIGHT SLACK YOU INSTINCTIVELY EXPECT IN ROAD CARS, EVEN FAST ONES, JUST ISN'T THERE'

Cabin much more purposeful with all luxuries stripped out, plus glassfibre buckets and suede-trimmed wheel. Say goodbye to understeer and slack, hello to near-telepathic reactions

◂ Pilot tyres. They're basically cut slicks, losing some wet-weather performance in return for ultimate dry grip. And BMW confirms that production cars will wear them, even in damp old Blighty. Engine modifications are limited; the air mass sensor has gone and fuelling is now based on engine speed and throttle position algorithms, in the same vein as a race car. Together with a retuned ECU, this should help to sharpen the M3's not-exactly-blunt throttle response. And the prototypes came with a very rorty free-flow exhaust system, keeping the four shotgun-like tailpipes of the standard car. All in all it's not about power; don't anticipate much of a gain on the standard M3's 343bhp. Rather, it's about control, sharpening responses and reducing reaction times.

Predictably, all CSLs will come with BMW's SMG sequential gearbox as standard, paddles behind the steering wheel and a big push/pull lever enabling you to change gear without the clutch pedal. When the system works well, it can cut gearchange times noticeably compared with a standard cog 'box. But, as ever, it was presented to us with a generous garnish of 'F1-derived technology' hogwash; it's really a completely standard synchromesh gearbox fitted with clever hydraulic actuators.

THAT'S THE THEORY. NOW FOR A BIT of practice. Approach the M3 CSL and even with your spotter's radar turned up to maximum you're hard pressed to spot the differences: bigger wheels, a slightly lower stance, an almost imperceptibly deeper front bumper. Only ultra-discreet 'CSL' badges on the front wing air vents actually tell you what the car is.

It might be conservative on the outside, but it's radical within. Getting into the CSL is a culture shock for anyone used to comfortable, well equipped 3-series variants. Where have all the buttons gone? The dashboard stares blankly at you, without stereo, climate control and all the rest. Instead, there are blanking plates, some nice carbonfibre detailing and rotary heater controls unseen by anyone except the drivers of absolute base 316is. Nothing is allowed to get between you and the driving experience, that's the message. Standard seats have been replaced by huggy glassfibre buckets, the door linings are plain except for big, chunky carbonfibre pull-handles, held in place by some very purposeful-looking exposed bolts. The rational rules of car assessment cease to work; people are going to be asked to pay considerably more for considerably less. But from the driver's seat, the CSL's interior really does look the business.

Start the engine, waggle the eternally confusing gearstick from '0' (for neutral) to '1', apply gentle power and head out onto the track. There's a fine drizzle coming down and conditions are decidedly wet. The Nürburgring grand prix circuit has recently been extended ▸

BMW M3 CSL Price: £55,000 (est) **Engine:** 3246cc dohc 24V straight six, 350bhp, 269lb ft (est) **Transmission:** Six-speed sequential manual, rear-wheel drive **Performance:** 4.7sec 0-62mph (est), 155mph (electronically limited) **Economy:** n/a **Weight:** 1420kg (est)

◂ with an extra complex of tight corners after the end of the start/finish straight. Apparently Mercedes was irritated that its corporate guests could only see cars for three seconds at a time, so it offered to pay for it all to be done. So thanks for that, Merc. Because within the first few tight, greasy corners it becomes clear, in a non-intimidating fashion, that the CSL is a seriously hardcore driving machine. The sort of slight slack you instinctively expect from road cars, even fast ones, just isn't there. No understeer of note, no delay in the throttle pedal's reactions. If you make an input, the car presumes that you mean it and reacts accordingly. It would be very easy to get it wrong.

But then, although it's considerably less easy to get the CSL right, it's one of those cars that will keep you trying. The accuracy reduces your capacity for excuses; if you find yourself on the wrong line, or braking too late, or in the wrong gear, it's your fault rather than the car's. In the prevailing wet conditions, the steering is a friendly point of dynamic contact, getting lighter to warn you of an impending front-end grip overdraft. The throttle requires serious respect, though: you need to feed the power in oh so gently to stop the back end from making a bid for freedom. Small, inadvertent power slides are corrected instinctively. Dramatic oversteer is there for the taking if that's your thing. Compared with some laps in a standard M3 that BMW laid on for comparison purposes, the CSL feels like a car transformed.

The rest of the experience is very similar. The solid brake pedal gives excellent feel and works very well. The only slight problem is that whoever laid down the road cones marking braking, turn-in and apex points (an inevitable feature of track-based launches) seems to have done so in the dry. And, of course, it's wet. Meaning that the first time I get to the tight 90-degree left Michelin corner and brake at the appropriate moment, a less-than-anticipated amount of retardation arrives and the gravel trap almost claims me. Later on I'm very nearly crunched in the same spot by another CSL doing the same thing. Which would have been embarrassing for all concerned.

Even the SMG gearchange – never my favourite system – is at home on the track, swapping ratios near-instantaneously with the 'speed' button turned up to maximum. The only real problem is its tendency to momentarily lock the rear wheels on downchanges under hard braking. The system hasn't been recalibrated to take into account the new tyres and different weight. Apparently it will be sorted by the time of the launch. It's still hard not to feel slightly disappointed that there won't be a proper manual gearbox option for those of us who like to change our own gears. Still, SMG is here to stay so we'll have to get used to it.

Rationally, there's no way that the fractional differences between the standard M3 and the CSL can be justified with the enormous increase in price. (Dynamically this might be the 110 percent M3, but in terms of cost it looks certain to be the 130 percent M3). But of course, this isn't rational. It's not about raw speed or fractional changes in the centre of gravity. It's all about experience. And even on the briefest of acquaintance on the slipperiest of race tracks, it's immediately obvious that the CSL offers a dramatically improved driving experience. That's what you'll be paying for, and that's what seems *almost* worth the extra.

GIVE A LITTLE RESPECT TO STANDARD M3

The regular M3 is an enormously capable car. All it lacks is passion...

YOU HAVE ENORMOUS respect for the standard M3 on the *Nordschleife*. But this isn't a car to engender the sort of dribbling, lustful admiration that the Porsche 911 does. The M3 is hugely competent, enormously fast and, in the not unlikely situation that you've forgotten where the track goes next and got it all horribly wrong, it's highly forgiving as well.

There's something about the lightness of the power-assisted steering (and the gearchange paddles of our SMG-fitted car) that makes you think of a PlayStation game. The CSL is meant to change that situation.

Granted, there are lots of very good reasons for the M3 to be engineered as it is. It's massively talented at crossing country quickly and accurately, it overtakes lines of traffic in a gulp and it tracks absolutely

straight on the autobahn. Well over 90 percent of the time it will be all the M3 anybody ever wants. But it's missing that vital, almost intimate connection you get with the Porsche 911. Or the CSL.

BMW M3 convertible

Sizzling M3 power and all the style of an open-top 3-Series – how good a combo is that?

STORY Michael Taylor PHOTOS Thomas Wielecki

Were it not for the involuntary shivers and deathly pallor the boys get when the M Roadster is mentioned, I'd happily state that an M3 motor is a surefire recipe for a bloody good car.

But shiver and discolour they do, so a dialed-back conclusion would be that an M3 motor is a huge head start. At the very least. After all, shy of the rarified atmosphere of 200K, it's about as good an evolution of the four-stroke, fossil-fuel-burning, fast motivation caper as you'd find anywhere in the world.

The biggest difference is that where the M3 coupe is a charging, hard-cornering jet,

A real nice way to ruffle a pricey hairdo

MT wants a matching lounge suite...

Strut brace keeps it stiff

the M3 convertible is, well, a convertible. There's a bit of a rule with such things, which goes as follows: if it was designed to have a fixed roof, and you unfix it, the whole thing's gunna get awfully soggy.

So BMW's worked hard to amend that (with the Z3 in its recent history, it's quite familiar with soggy) and, as a result, the M3 convertible is a full 195kg heavier than the coupe. Part of that extra weight is in the electronic roof system, but a fair bit of it goes towards bracing to counter the roof removal, including a strut brace under the bonnet.

Where the coupe runs to 100km/h in 5.39 seconds and does the 400-metre sprint in 13.59, the extra weight pushes the convertible to 5.93 and 14.17 seconds – both of which are pretty sharp numbers for wind-in-the-hair jobbies.

There are a few other dimensional changes, including a significant reduction in rear elbow and shoulder room, while headroom, obviously, becomes infinite once you've flicked the button and watched the beautifully lined roof fold back, in and under.

And that's when the world gets nice. All right, it's not as rigid as the coupe – it was never going to be – but it's still not bad, especially compared with the stock 330Ci version.

It loses a bit in mid-corner grip and on turn-in on those optional 19-inch boots, but, hey, when you can fire out of a corner with an M3 engine punching its pistons up and down at 24 metres per second, it's not going to hurt you much.

If anything, the engine sounds more metallic and slightly tinnier than it does in the fixed-roof M3, and not everybody agrees that's a good thing.

Obviously it's well equipped, with a telly, satellite navigation, a gun sound system, parking distance control and leather everywhere (though, thankfully, you can choose nicer colours than this particular one…)

Good? Yes. As good as the coupe? It was never going to be. Worth having? To find a faster four-seat convertible, you'll have to spend a hell of a lot more than $158,000.

BMW M3 convertible

FAST FACTS

engine	3.2-litre DOHC 24-valve straight six
power/weight	252kW/1720kg
drive	rear-wheel
on sale	now
price	$158,000

To find a faster four-seat convertible, you'll have to spend a hell of a lot more than $158,000

SO, WAS THE M3 CSL

The choice: AC Schnitzer-tuned M3 (right), M3 CSL (centre) or BMW M3 (left). The

> 'In one bold gesture BMW exposed just how many people wanted a CSL to move on quickly through the classifieds'

The purpose of this gathering is less empirical, more theoretical. In 2003, I drove three very different BMW M3s. They were the very same cars gathered for this test. Two of them are merely brilliant, whereas one is quite exceptional. This is their story.

Let's begin with the grey car. Odd to think that the dust is already settling on the BMW M3 CSL. New sales have ended in the UK just six months after the first customer car was delivered and now we are left to chew over what has become something of a saga. Of the 422 cars built for our shores, a good few remain within the franchised dealer network brandishing the old £POA (Please Offer Anything) sticker, as punters wait to see just how low prices will stumble.

BMW's handling of the CSL reintroduction/branding exercise has, at face value, not been the smooth ride we might have expected from such a market-savvy operator. The car was certainly right, but the trade is currently smarting from BMW's aggressive pricing and volume strategy. As such, this will become a crucial case study for future trends in the sports car market and lessons need to be learned. And in fairness to BMW, it needs to spend less time in the classroom than most other parties involved in the story.

I first heard about the CSL in September 2001. Then I drove the prototype in June '02 and it was sensational. An M3 with 15 per cent more of everything. Only one question wasn't answered by the marketing types: how much? Tellingly, I now remember writing out the spec panel for the magazine and working out what I thought was a reasonable estimate – that number was £45,000. I was a mere £13k shy of what the actual price would be. People were already flocking to order one and around 500 prospective customers had shown serious interest when the full-fat £58,455 tag was revealed. It was a steep number, but given the press interest, added performance and circulating rumours that fewer than 100 cars would be coming to the UK, the speculator market felt confident.

Ah, the speculators: punters up for a quick quid, brokers and dealers sniffing a potential 'overs' model. They were all at it and for once BMW decided not to limit supply. I say 'they', when I mean 'we'. Not wanting to miss out on the party, yours truly very nearly took a bath with a CSL back in September, but that's another story. Instead BMW decided to try something radical: count interested heads and make exactly that number of cars. No other manufacturer has ever done such a thing at this end of the market. In one bold gesture BMW exposed just how many people wanted a CSL to move on quickly through the classifieds. It would be fascinating to know how many buyers actually financed their CSLs with a view to conventional ownership: I'd guess at maybe 75, 100 maximum, leaving a balance of around 350 vehicles squabbling for classified ad space. Residual mayhem began immediately, with cars advertised at list for no more than a week. Prices promptly dropped to the mid-50s before Christmas, and right now the trade values a 1000-mile car at £50k. People don't like losing £10k in six months, especially when they thought it was going to be money spinner.

So they blame BMW for making too many CSLs. And in some respects, they have a point. But think about BMW's primary role in the marketplace for a

'Basic' M3 is a great car but Schnitzer matches CSL on ability. It's the best here

WORTH IT AFTER ALL?

prices? £40k, £58k or £50k. Is the CSL really £18k better, asks **Chris Harris**

FACT FILE	RED BMW M3	SILVER BMW M3 CSL	BLUE BMW M3 (TUNED)
HOW MUCH?			
Price	£39,830	£58,455	£50,000
On sale in UK	Now	No longer	Now
HOW FAST?			
0-30mph	2.0sec	2.0sec	2.0sec
0-60mph	4.8sec	4.8sec	4.8sec
0-100mph	11.5sec	10.9sec	11.0sec
0-150mph	na	na	na
Standing qtr mile	13.4sec/107mph	13.2sec/110mph	13.2sec/109mph
Standing km	23.7sec/139mph	23.1sec/140mph	23.2sec/140mph
30-70mph	4.1sec	4.2sec	4.1sec
60-0mph	2.6sec	2.3sec	2.3sec (wet)
Top speed	160mph	161mph	165mph (claimed)

second. It exists to sell as many cars as possible, so if 500 people hand over a £500 deposit, why shouldn't it tool up for the full quota? Why should it effectively subsidise an overs market it can't take advantage of? Baseline: isn't the CSL's rapidly diminishing residual stock as much a product of individual greed as BMW's lofty sales targets?

Which brings me to the blue car you see here. In trying to quantify whether or not the fantastic bona fide M3 CSL was actually worth the staggering price increase over the standard car, we all dabbled in hypothetical tuning – take one 'normal' M3, chip it and add some beefier seats and trick tyres and it would surely do roughly the same job as a CSL. It may even be as fast in the real world. But these were all fumblings in the conditional tense, until the car in question turned up at an *Autocar* track day a little while back. At last, here was the answer to the CSL quandry: someone unhappy at the CSL's cost and willing to try his hand at creating one out of a standard M3.

And what a car it is. A standard M3 SMG, but with the full benefit of AC Schnitzer's options brochure liberally applied where it matters most. I first drove it at the end of last summer and was blown away: DMS chip, larger air intake and Schnitzer exhaust for a circa 25bhp increase, adjustable Schnitzer suspension with a 30mm drop in ride height, gorgeous Schnitzer Recaros, bespoke Schnitzer front splitter, a set of uprated AP stoppers and the requisite set of Michelin Pilot Sport Cup tyres – the very same rubber that lends the CSL its other-worldly grip. Total cost £10,000. Or, in other words, still £8k less than a CSL.

And it matches almost all of the CSL's on-track benefits to a tee (although, admittedly, the SMG 'box isn't quite as sweet because it doesn't benefit from the same software). Look at the performance figures, accept that they offer identical levels of dry-weather grip (with the blue car just losing a little agility with its extra 100kg) and the CSL's case looks shaky indeed.

Of course, the CSL is by any marker a superb car, but it was one saddled with unfortunate market positioning: 30bhp shy of justifying the big price given the proposed volumes and yet £10k above what an interested party would really want to pay. By the end of 2004, the CSL will be *the* performance car bargain and prices will no doubt begin to creep skywards once more.

And what of poor old red? Cooking 343bhp, no extra performance, no special bits. The 'normal' M3 is still a conspicuous exercise in what constitutes real value. For, more than any other factor listed here, it's the unbridled talent resting in every standard E46 M3 that has caused the CSL the most problems. It remains the most sensible M3 choice of them all – if you could ever call an M3 sensible while keeping a straight face. ●

Sporty essence

Street-brawler becomes exquisite supercar

CSL is an evocative name in BMW history. Back in the '70s, when not battling Cologne Capris, BMW's CSL (which, in its extreme form, became known as the "Batmobile" because of its outrageous aerodynamic appendages) often took the fight to hot versions of Porsche's 911 on the racetracks of the world.

Subsequently, the two German rivals followed somewhat different, though still decidedly sporty, paths. BMW's growing importance as a manufacturer of luxury sporty saloons led to subtle changes in focus, and raw road-race performers took something of a back seat in the company's priorities. So much so that people have tended to forget that Munich is capable of building cars which, while having the powerunit at the opposite end of the chassis, are able to challenge the 911 in spirit as well as in handling and performance. Until the advent of the M3 CSL, that is.

Local test car had a radio/CD player, optional overseas (top). Gears can be shifted using the stubby lever (inset, above right) or wheel-mounted paddles (inset, left). Front seats are lightweight CFP-shelled buckets (above).

Only a limited number of M3 CSLs – 59 was the total originally bandied about – were imported into South Africa, and virtually all of them were pre-sold, so the model no longer appears on the company's local price lists. On top of that, despite being far and away the country's biggest circulating motoring magazine, CAR's Cape-based operation was last on the roster to receive the one and only test unit, having to wait until after the Gauteng-based publications, situated close to BMW SA's head office, had all had a go. So we make no apology for delaying this report even further, to fit in with our January performance issue...

Priced at R940 000 when it was sold here, the CSL has a 911-style price tag. That's a whopping R395 000 more than you'd pay for a current M3. Some may dismiss this difference as plain ridiculous, and use the marginal gains in performance to support their contention. But they would be overlooking the sheer attention to detail employed in distilling out the M3's sporty essence, turning a dynamic, brutally quick "everyday" coupé into an exquisite supercar.

BMW says CSL stands for Coupé, Sport and Lightweight, and our Longacre scales gave an immediate indication of the lengths to which the car's design and development teams went in their quest for mass reduction: the test unit weighed in at 1 470 kg, compared with the 1 603 kg we recorded with the standard M3. The M division used what it calls "intelligent" lightweight technology, selecting the most appropriate materials for each specific application. For example, the use of carbon-fibre-reinforced plastic (CFP) at the front and rear of the car doesn't simply help to trim overall weight: its positioning also cuts mass at the front and rear ends, helping to improve stability and handling. Components using this F1-derived material include the front airdam and rear diffuser. "Endless glass-fibre plastics", appropriated from the aerospace industry, are used for sections of the front and rear crash structures, and the rear lid is in lightweight sheet moulding compound. As on the standard M3, the bonnet lid is in aluminium. The roof is also made of CFP – with the weave of the mat visible for all to see – to lower the car's centre of gravity, and a paper-honeycomb sandwich panel is used on the luggage compartment floor. Such is the attention to detail that even the exhaust system is made up of thinner material, and the air-collector for the engine is in carbon fibre.

Of course, removing weight from a luxury car also entails some "sacrifices". So the CSL eschews side airbags and electric leather-covered sports seats. Instead, there are manually-adjustable CFP-shelled bucket seats, upholstered in Amaretta and fabric. Rear seats also have the cloth and Amaretta covering. The floor carpets are laid over a weight-optimised foam layer, and there is no navigation system. And, although our test unit came with a radio/CD player and an air-conditioner, even those items are not offered as standard equipment on cars overseas. Centre console and door-coverings are also in CFP.

The engine has been tweaked to

Challenging the 911 in spirit as well as handling and performance

In search of a supercar

Can BMW build a car to mix it with the likes of the 911 Carrera and Maserati Coupé? The answer lies in the M3 CSL, a car that features the same painstaking attention to detail, the same careful choice of materials and componentry, as these supercars. Of course, that means a massive escalation in price compared with the standard M3, but true "exotics" don't come cheap...

Rivals — *Our choice*

	BMW M3 CSL SMG	Porsche 911 Carrera	Maserati Coupé	BMW M3
price	R940 000 (off market)	R895 000	R950 000	R545 000
cyl/capac	6/3 246	H6/3 596	V8/4 244	6/3 246
power	265/7 900	235/6 800	287/7 000	252/7 900
torque	370/4 900	370/4 250	451/4 500	365/4 900
power/mass	180	157 est	170 est	157
engine revs/km	1 509	n/a	n/a	
gears/drive	6/R	6/R	6/R	6/R
0-100 km/h	5,44	5,0 est	5,4 est	5,48
max speed	255	287 est	290 est	250
fuel index	14,64	11,1 est	18,0 est	11,89
boot space	296-708	160-456	–	296-708

Porsche 911 Carrera. The benchmark by which all such cars are judged, and still the best, in our eyes. In new, 997 form, the archetypal Porsche is as sharp as ever, only more usable. The standard fitment of PSM and the new variable ratio steering have increased its real-world usability, making it a comfortable cross-country cruiser as well as the world's best "on-the-edge" sportscar.

Maserati Coupé. Latin style and red-blooded performance are two highly-regarded facets of the unboosted Maser's character. It shares its basic engine architecture with Ferrari's new F430, and should offer Maranello-like levels of usability and reliability. Sumptuous detailing and classic styling will seal the deal for lovers of the Italian art of sportscar building.

BMW M3. A real value-for-money performer in this company, the standard M3 shows just how good a car can be without resorting to the extra-trick componentry and materials of more exotic creations. Its beautifully balanced chassis serves as a solid base for the CSL's quest for the ultimate in road-holding, agility and performance.

produce 265 kW at 7 900 r/min, 13 more than the standard M3, with torque up by 5 N.m to 370 at 4 900. Modest increases, and evidence that the classic Motorsport straight six has really reached the end of its development life. Next-generation M3s, we believe, will have V8 power...

Probably the most controversial thing about the CSL is its use of SMG, BMW's sequential manual gearbox, featuring Drivelogic electronic control. Developed from the company's Formula One programme, it can be operated either with the shift lever or paddles on the steering wheel. The system automatically blips the throttle to match revs to road speed in downshifts, and offers eleven gearshift modes, including an auto function, tailored to specific driving requirements. A control on the console behind the shift lever allows the driver to adjust the speed of the changes, which can be varied from slow, slurred, reasonably comfortable shifts, to quick, sharp, almost violent cog-swops that switch ratios in just 0,08 seconds. The set-up also includes launch control, a function that automatically shifts the gears in sprints from take-off, achieving optimal acceleration and, integrated into the DSC system, an M Track Mode for racetrack driving.

The front track has been widened compared with the normal M3, and the suspension geometry modified. Dampers and springs are tailor-made, the steering has been re-aligned for cutting-edge turn-in, and the brakes have been upgraded. The CSL also comes with special Michelins, shared only with Ferrari's 360 Challenge Stradale. Designated Michelin Pilot Sport Cup, they are semi-slick creations with vestiges of minimal-depth assymmetrical tread and soft-compound rubber. In front, the size is 235/35 ZR 19, with 265/30s wrapped around the rear alloys. The wheels, too, are special alloy units designed specifically for the CSL.

Out on the test strip, we found out about one of the launch control system's hidden limitations. The set-up's electronics are designed to protect engine and drivetrain life by going into a kind of "protective" mode if they detect that components have been highly stressed. Which effectively means you have to go for a leisurely 10-kilometre cruise between jack-rabbit starts, not the way to get optimal times, which generally require back-to-back experimentation with throttle technique and the level of wheelspin...

Still, we managed to get the test car to 100 km/h from rest in 5,44 seconds, a fraction quicker than the 5,48 seconds achieved with the standard M3. However, given the car's reduced weight and slightly higher power output, we believe we could have improved on that considerably with a straightforward six-on-the-floor. The test car covered the kilometre in 24,45 seconds, and topped out at a limited 255 km/h in sixth. Apparently, BMW sells versions without the limiter (claimed top speed 277 km/h) overseas, but you have to produce an international competition licence to clinch the deal! The uprated brakes provide stopping

F1-derived 'intelligent' lightweight technology

Insets, left to right: CFP roof meets steel A-pillar; stability and traction control buttons; tweaked M3 motor produces a massive 265 kW at a heady 7 900 r/min.

Likes and dislikes

DESIGN
- ✔ Purposeful lines with subtle differences from standard M3
- ✔ Compact, wieldy sports coupé

POWERTRAIN
- ✔ Inspirational engine
- ✔ Throttle blip by SMG is neat
- ✘ Finicky SMG gearbox

COMFORT AND FEATURES
- ✔ Workmanlike stripped-out interior
- ✘ Seats not ideal for taller drivers
- ✘ Gearshift paddles should be separate from wheel

PERFORMANCE AND BRAKING
- ✔ Ferocious acceleration
- ✔ Excellent stopping ability
- ✘ Frustrating "time-out" mode for launch control

FUEL ECONOMY
- ✘ Thirsty if you drive it as intended

RIDE AND HANDLING
- ✔ Firm, controlled ride
- ✔ Huge grip from semi-slick tyres
- ✘ Tyres not the best in wet conditions

VALUE FOR MONEY
- ✔ Exquisite detailing is worth the money
- ✘ Not much better performance than an M3 for the extra R395 000

power to match, averaging a cutting-edge 2,68 seconds in our 100-to-zero emergency braking test.

But straight-line performace is not really the CSL's strongest suit. This car really comes into its own on winding, smooth roads, or even a race track. In these conditions, the Michelins provide leech-like grip, the new steering rack allows near-perfect positioning, and the SMG achieves rapid gear-shifts (with those addictive throttle-blips), to keep the responsive engine in its power-band. For exhilarating track driving with the DSC safety net in place, you can engage M Track mode using a button on the steering column.

Nit-picks? The steering, improved though it is, does not have the nuanced feedback of a 911, and those Cup tyres can only be really exploited in the dry. They're fine even on a slightly wet surface, but heavy rain dramatically reduces grip levels as aquaplaning becomes a real problem.

Test summary

Forget the price and the "humble" standard M3 origins. This car is an exercise in proving that BMW really can challenge Porsche if it puts its mind to it. This is a car one cannot really judge by normal standards. For what it was designed to be, the CSL is difficult to fault. Perhaps a slick manual gearbox would provide better straight-line performance. But then again, the paddle-shift system could hardly be bettered in the heat of battle on a twisty road. One thing is certain: the CSL is destined to become a classic. ●

BMW M3 CSL SMG ★★★★★

SPECIFICATIONS

ENGINE:	
Cylinders	six in-line
Fuel supply	multipoint sequential fuel injection
Bore/stroke	87,0/91,0 mm
Cubic capacity	3 246 cm^3
Compression ratio	11,5 to 1
Valve gear	d-o-h-c, four valves per cylinder
Ignition	electronic
Main bearings	seven
Fuel requirement	97 unleaded
ENGINE OUTPUT:	
Max power ISO (kW)	265
Power peak (r/min)	7 900
Max usable r/min	8 000
Max torque (N.m)	370
Torque peak (r/min)	4 900
TRANSMISSION:	
Forward speeds	six
Low gear	4,227 to 1
2nd gear	2,528 to 1
3rd gear	1,669 to 1
4th gear	1,226 to 1
5th gear	1,000 to 1
Top gear	0,828 to 1
Reverse gear	3,746 to 1
Final drive	3,620 to 1
Drive wheels	rear
WHEELS AND TYRES:	
Road wheels	front: 8,5Jx19 alloy; rear: 9,5Jx19 alloy
Tyre make	Michelin Pilot Sport Cup
Tyre size	front: 235/35 ZR19; rear: 265/30 ZR19
Tyre pressures (front)	240 to 280 kPa
Tyre pressures (rear)	240 to 320 kPa
BRAKES:	
Front	345 mm ventilated discs
Rear	328 mm ventilated discs
Hydraulics	ABS with CBC and DSC
STEERING:	
Type	rack and pinion
Lock to lock	3,0 turns
Turning circle	11,0 metres
SUSPENSION	
Front	single-joint sprint struts, positive steering roll radius, transverse arms, anti-dive
Rear	longitudinal control arms, double track control arms, coil springs, gas dampers, anti-squat and anti-dive
CAPACITIES:	
Seating	4/5
Fuel tank	63 litres
Boot space	200 dm^3
Utility space	708 dm^3

WARRANTY AND SERVICE INTERVALS:
3 years/100 000 km warranty
Service according to indicator. Sold with Motorplan

TEST CAR FROM:
BMW South Africa

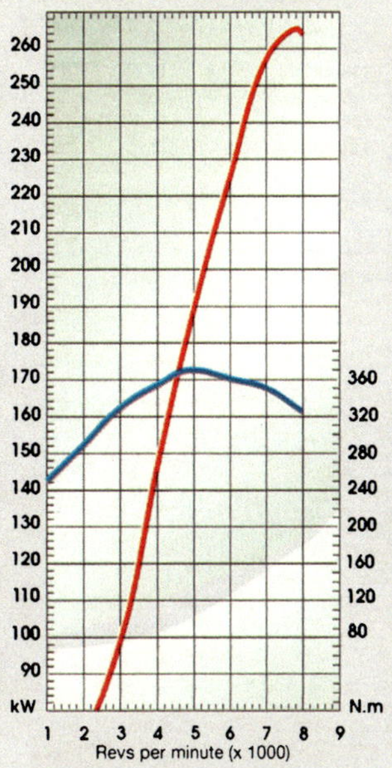

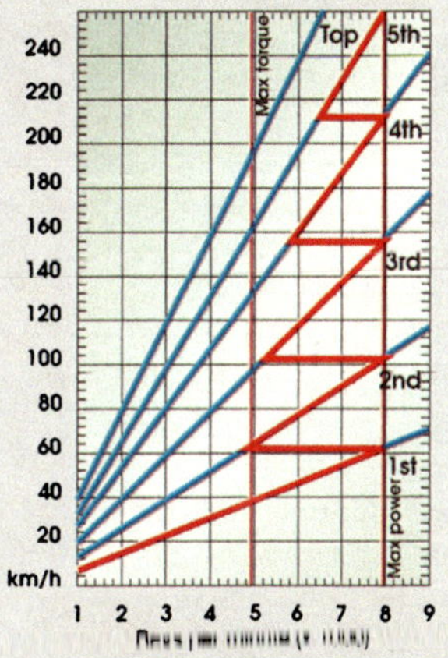

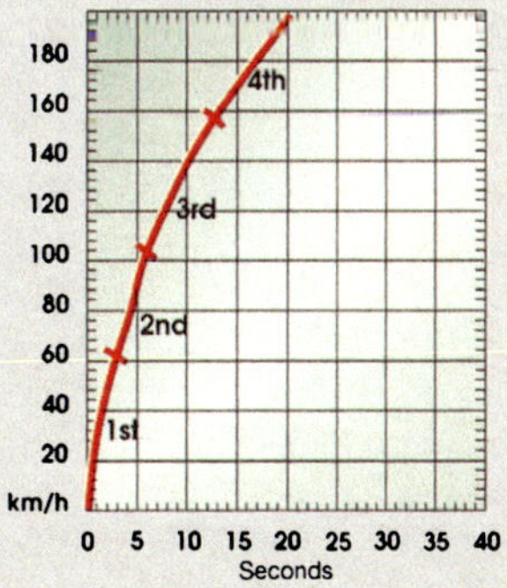

TEST RESULTS

MAXIMUM SPEED (km/h):

True speed	255 at 6 410 r/min in top gear
Speedometer reading	268

(Average of runs both ways on a level road)

Calibration:	60	80	100	120
True speed:	56	74	93	113

Odometer error	0,20 per cent under
ACCELERATION (seconds):	
0-60	2,51
0-80	4,11
0-100	5,44
0-120	7,44
1 km sprint	24,45
Terminal speed	222,2 km/h

OVERTAKING ACCELERATION (seconds):

	3rd	4th	5th	Top
40-60	2,19	3,15	–	–
60-80	1,88	2,96	3,86	5,02
80-100	1,74	2,64	3,53	5,44
100-120	1,76	2,50	3,44	4,80
120-140	1,99	2,59	3,43	5,00

FUEL CONSUMPTION (litres/100 km):

*Fuel index	14,64 litres/100 km
	6,83 km/litre
Estimated tank range	430 km

(*Calculated overall consumption)

BRAKING TEST:
From 100 km/h

Best stop	2,58
Worst stop	2,78
Average of 10 stops	2,68

(Measured in seconds with stops from true speeds at 30-second intervals on a good bitumenised surface.)

GEARED SPEEDS (km/h):

Low gear	62*	62
2nd gear	103*	104
3rd gear	156*	158
4th gear	212*	215
5th gear	260*	263
Top gear	314*	318

(Calculated at engine power peak* – 7 900 r/min and at max. usable r/min – 8 000 r/min.)

INTERIOR NOISE LEVELS (db, A-weighted):

	Mech	Road
Idling	48	–
60	63	–
80	66	78
100	69	80
120	72	82

PERFORMANCE FACTORS:

Power/mass net (W/kg)	180
Frontal area (m^2)	2,10
km/h per 1 000 r/min (top)	39,76
Mass as tested (kg)	1 470

(Calculated on "mass as tested", gross frontal area, gearing and ISO power output)

TEST CONDITIONS:

Altitude	at sea level
Weather	cool, windless
Fuel used	97 octane unleaded
Test car's odometer	5 170

TRACK PHOTOS DITO MILIAN, DETAIL PHOTOS JACKIE JOURET

BMW M3 Competition Package

Has BMW finally given its U.S.-market M3 a dash of the Europe-only M3 CSL's hard-core flavor by offering a Competition Package? We head to the track to find out.

FINDING OUT THAT BMW was not importing its M3 CSL to the U.S. was a mighty bitter pill for American Bimmer enthusiasts to swallow. With its carbon-fiber roof, racing seats, track-tuned suspension and tweaked engine, the CSL seemed like the ultimate "Ultimate Driving Machine."

Several years hence, BMW has finally thrown the U.S. market a bone with the release of the M3 Competition Package. We couldn't wait to sink our teeth into it, and booked a track day with Hooked on Driving at nearby Thunderhill Raceway Park in anticipation of its arrival.

With its unique Interlagos Blue paint and gorgeous 19-inch forged alloy wheels, the car certainly looks the part. The larger front brake rotors (13.6 inches vs. 12.9) nicely fill out the taller wheels, while cross-drilling gives all four discs a racy look. The high ride height raised our suspicions, however: The fender gaps seemed to be larger than on the last M3 we drove. Wasn't the real meat of the $4,000 Competition Package supposed to be the sport suspension?

On the inside, the package includes an Alcantara-trimmed steering wheel and parking brake lever, straight from the CSL. The wheel includes a single button which, when pressed, places the Dynamic Stability Control system into M Track mode. This particular M3 was fitted with cloth seat inserts and a standard manual transmission—just the way we like it.

The M3 was a real pleasure on the three-hour drive from San Francisco to the track. We'd forgotten just how quickly the 333-hp 3.2-liter inline-6 propels this 3,460-pound coupe, and how great it sounds in the process. The ride is surprisingly good—stiff, but no harsher than the standard car's.

Once we got off the highway and onto a twisty ribbon of tarmac, the car's handling had a chance to shine. It took us a few corners to acclimate to the Comp Pack's faster steering (2.7 turns lock-to-lock vs. 3.0), but once we did, the improved turn-in response was much appreciated. The car exhibited fine poise and high cornering speeds on this sunset run, heightening our expectations of the next morning's Thunderhill session all the more.

Our run group was the first out of the paddock. The track surface was dry, but the previous day's heavy rain had washed most of the rubber off the asphalt, making it a bit slippery in a few corners. Still, we were surprised at how quickly we ran out of grip; the tires started squealing in protest far sooner than we had anticipated. More troubling, however, was the excessive body roll we encountered. Through the faster bends this wasn't such an issue, but while negotiating one of the slower, left-right-left combinations, we found ourselves waiting for the car's body motions to catch up with our steering inputs. *You call this a competition package?* we asked ourselves as we rolled into the pits.

"Competition" is obviously a loaded word, but we didn't go into this test thinking we would be belting ourselves into a race car. However, we did interpret the word to mean track-ready, or at least *more* track-ready than a standard M3. For the most part, this is simply not the case.

As it turns out, while the suspension on the M3 Competition Package is tuned differently than last year's M3, its settings are shared with *all* 2005 M3s. Apparently,

Specifications

ENGINE	3.2-liter DOHC inline-6
POWER (hp)	333 @ 7900 rpm
TORQUE (lb/ft)	262 @ 4900 rpm
TRANSMISSION	6-speed manual
Weight (pounds)	3460
0-60 MPH (sec.)	4.8
BASE PRICE	$51,995

Top: Heavy body roll took the fun out of lapping Thunderhill. Above left: 19-inch forged alloys house 13.6-inch front brake rotors. Above: Engine is unchanged. Left: Alcantara-wrapped steering wheel includes button for M Track mode.

BMW engineers wanted to dial out some understeer—a worthwhile goal in any enthusiast's book—but instead of increasing rear roll stiffness to accomplish it, they softened the front. This works fine on the road, but out on the track you end up with too much body roll.

The other problem we immediately confronted was heat damage to the outside edges of the tires. After just that first session, the outer treads on all four brand-new Michelin Pilot Sports were "cupping," where the tread edges lift up. It was clear that the suspension was in desperate need of some negative camber to try and get the inside of each tire to lend some rubber to the effort; the car was effectively circulating Thunderhill on its tip toes. It's no wonder one of the other participants fitted camber plates to his E46 M3. He also mounted significantly wider front tires—255s vs. the standard 225s—which seems like a better way of battling understeer to us; that's what Dinan does.

We can understand why BMW would be reluctant to offer an M3 with seriously stiffer suspension, lots of negative camber and whopping big front tires. A car with a harsher ride, shorter tire life and heavier steering is not going to appeal to a lot of people. But isn't that the point of offering a sportier version of an already sporty car, to appeal to the hardcore, Red Bull-swilling track-day fiend? Mitsubishi offers a circuit-ready car with the Evo and Porsche does it with the GT3, so why can't BMW?

What about the larger brakes, you ask, are they ready for track abuse? In a word, yes. Brake fade did not get added to our list of gripes for the day, but we would have appreciated a more confidence-inspiring pedal feel; it sure took a lot of pressure to get these binders to slow the car down.

That leaves us with the Competition Package's M Track mode. As you'd expect, M Track mode raises the threshold for stability control intervention, allowing for a good deal of yaw movement. The problem is that it doesn't like you quickly going from one kind of slide to another. It will help dig you out of a terminal understeer grave and catch a wayward rear end before it kisses the guardrail, but try and pivot the car on your own and the dash light starts flickering in protest. The M3 felt so much friskier and faster with the stability control fully disabled that we wondered why BMW even bothered with M Track mode.

If you're looking for a distinctive-looking M3 and aren't a Red Bull-swilling track-day fiend, this car will serve you very well. If the latter description applies, you're gonna need to get a competition package for your Competition Package.—*Eric Gustafson*

driven

BMW M3 CS

The best bits of the CSL for far less money

M3 CS has one of the world's most throttle-adjustable chassis, as the marks on the road show. You can feel the difference the lightweight 19in alloys make to handling

It'll be ancient history by the time you read this but I've just sat through the US Grand Prix. Not a great advert for the 'pinnacle of motorsport' in a country that already struggles to get excited about F1. Ferrari's victory was an empty one, but watching the onboard footage of Schuey flat to the boards through Indianapolis' banking, sitting at over 200mph and 18,000rpm for a full 20 seconds and then wiping off 130mph in just a few yards and peeling into Turn One is gobsmackingly, jaw-droppingly impressive.

What's that got to do with the new M3 CS? Well,

just like the Ferraris at the Brickyard, the M3 has little meaningful competition; and like those screaming F1 missiles the BMW is no less impressive because of it. The CS is essentially an M3 that's borrowed a few tasty bits from its exotic, expensive and now out-of-production CSL sibling. Bigger brake discs, the quicker steering rack, revised springs and those gorgeous 19in forged alloys.

Okay, they're not quite as light as the genuine CSL rims but they still look great, and if the newfound composure and ride quality are anything to go by they're definitely a whole heap lighter than the ubiquitous 19-inchers that regular M3s roll on. As well as the mechanical changes, the CS also gains the CSL's M-Track mode function, heightening the stability control's tolerance of slip angles and wheelspin to such an extent that even the very best drivers are equally quick around a track with the electronic safety net still in place.

The price of these mechanical, cosmetic and electronic tweaks is just £2400 over the standard £41,115 M3. This package has been sold in the US and Europe for some time as the Competition Package', but BMW GB was concerned that the optional upgrade may upset CSL owners, who have already been hit in the wallet. Now that CSL residuals are firming up and with the launch of the E90 3-series, BMW GB decided its 911-chaser needed a shot in the arm.

There's nothing to touch the CS at the money. The Monaro VXR is cheaper and more powerful, but it's a blunt instrument compared to the scalpel-sharp BMW. Audi's powerful new RS4 should be up to the fight, but prices start at £50K. So the CS's closet rival is, in fact, the standard M3.

And the good news is that the CS has a sharpness and accuracy that the M3 never quite attains. You'll notice the new steering rack first, with its meatier weighting and more immediate response. Then you'll realise that the ride seems flatter, less disturbed by sharp lumps and bumps passing beneath the wheels. Up the pace and this firm but pliant set-up just gets better and the M3's trademark pogo-ing motion never materialises.

What hasn't changed is that wonderful, free-revving 3.2-litre 338bhp straight-six; it may lack the CSL's snorting induction system but it's still a stunning accompaniment to the fluid, fleet-footed chassis. Wrung out past 8000rpm it has more than enough top-end fireworks to justify the street-racer stance.

The straight-six has too much power for the brakes to rein-in, despite bigger discs. They're overwhelmed by the engine's venom and quickly protest when used hard on the road, with expensive-sounding groans and a soft pedal. Even snicking down through the slightly long-winded manual 'box to help deceleration (SMG is an £2100 option) does little to halt the brakes' decline. Fortunately the CS is so entertaining through the turns that you're happy to drive around the weak brakes and instead revel in one of the most throttle-adjustable chassis in the world.

I can't think of another 300bhp+ car that feels so

benign when you tweak the tail wide and play out a slide than the M3 CS. There's a bit of understeer in steady-state cornering but the 255-section rear rubber is easily overwhelmed if you're of a mind, and from there it's simply a matter of balancing the opposite lock with power.

Of course, you can do the same in a standard M3, but the CS has tangible gains in feel and agility and quickly gives you confidence to use all of its potential. The CSL was always a great car with a crazy price-tag. The CS is just a great car, and if you're buying an M3 you'd be crazy not to pay out £2400 for the added bite, polish and aesthetic attitude that it brings.

Jethro Bovingdon

Specification

Engine	In-line 6-cyl, 3246cc, 24v
Max power	338bhp @ 7900rpm
Max torque	269lb ft @ 5000rpm
Top speed	155mph (limited)
0-62mph	5.1sec
Basic price	£43,555
On sale	Now

evo RATING ★★★★★

+ CSL dynamics at a realistic price
− Likely to be a common sight

>WORDS Ben B >PICS Jason C

THE FINAL FLING

The CS will be the last six-pot BMW M3. Be rude not to test it, really...

FIVE YEARS AGO THE E46 BMW M3 was unleashed and a legend was born. As fun as a Porsche 911 yet as practical as a, er, BMW 3-Series, the 343bhp monster was criticised for just two things – woolly steering and fade-prone stoppers.

Soon, though, the party will be over. In 2007 BMW will release an all-new V8 M3, forever changing the supercar-slayer's DNA.

So, like anyone who's been dumped, the M3 is putting on its glad rags, covering up the wrinkles and going on the razz. Re-branded as the M3 CS, it's on sale now for £43,555.

BMW's plan with the M3 CS is simple. Nick the brakes, steering and gorgeous 19s off the £58k (gulp!) M3 CSL, but leave that car's lightweight trickery, 20bhp extra and ludicrous price tag in place. The result looks like it could be the ultimate all-round M3.

The purpose of this test is to celebrate the life of the last six-pot M3 and answer three questions. Firstly, is the CS worth £2400 more than the regular M3? Back in the (almost) real world, we'll also ask if a five-year-old M3 is worth a credit-busting £18,000 loan. And thirdly, we'll find out if you can really hang its arse out easily like those motoring journos say.

Drooling over the CS for two seconds, I'm already tempted to tick the first box. Those rims, that Interlagos Blue paint, the gorgeous leather. Jesus, it's horny. But stare for longer and you realise that the M3 really is cast from the old-school BMW mould. The clocks, the switches, the bodyshell – all are familiar from the early '90s 3-Series.

On the road, though, it's still up with the best. Reckon the new steering and brakes are gimmicks? Think again. Even a year after my last M3 drive, it's obvious the CS steering is pleasingly chunkier and the brakes bite like a pitbull gnawing a postie.

> "PILES ON SPEED LIKE A FREE-FALLING PIANO"

With 343bhp, BMW have pushed the 3.2-litre lump to its limits. So, unlike the smooth 3.0-litre in my 1994 M3, there's a step in the delivery low down and an impatience to put on the rpm that's not there in the old car. The 'box is a tad notchier too.

The small sacrifice in refinement is worth it when you really nail it, mind. Pummel down your favourite B-road and the M3 CS piles on speed like a free-falling piano. There's the classic metallic rasp from around 3000 revs and a non-stop surge to over 7000rpm that's as addictive as popping bubble wrap.

Get to the corners and the M3 CS does the business too. Four-wheel drive? Bullshit Mr Evo. You've got all >

Arse out in public at every available opportunity. And that's just our 'Chelle...

One manoeuvre you won't find in the Highway Code

'Ben send smoke signal. He say M3 is good'

The Abi Titmus of engines: not the best to look at, but as naughty as you like

the grip you'll ever need here.

Feel like you're going too quick? Just accelerate and let the back end push you through. The CS is beautifully balanced but the suspension is very solid, so hold on tight when you ease into three figures.

That amazing balance and solid suspension comes together for the M3's party piece – powersliding. Traction off, roundabout ahead, power on and... understeer. Like all rear-drivers, the M3 firstly pushes on at the front if you're too eager. It's a safety feature that makes the car easier to control if you overcook it.

But keep your foot on the gas and the balance shifts. First to a gentle four-wheel drift, then to a full-on, tail-wagging tyre-roaster. The M3 will hang at barmy angles and we love it for that.

"YOU'VE GOT ALL THE GRIP HERE YOU'LL EVER NEED"

GET AN M3 FOR £18K

Looking like new cars but costing up to £25k less, 2001 M3s are well worth finding. We found several for under £20k and one for £18k with 89,000 miles. Pick of the bunch, though, was a spec'd 2002 car on 19s with full BMW service history and 16 months warranty. Yours for £19.5k.

If you're stretching yourself, left-hand-drive cars are well worth a look. Kevin from BMW tuners Birds UK prefers them, in fact. 'They're originally designed to be left hookers so those cars feel sweeter,' he says. Expect a few thou off the price.

As with all BMWs, M3s are offered with a mind-boggling number of options. The best are 19s, sat-nav, Harman Kardon stereo and a Tracker. If you're not buying from BMW, get it properly checked.

While largely bulletproof, 3.2-litre M3s do have a chink in their armour – the complex VANOS variable valve systems. So get one with the BMW warranty and keep it up to date. Finally, try and get a car that's just had its Inspection Two service. In theory, you should then be some 36,000 miles from any really big bills.

Suede and leather. Nice

MAX LIKES
- 24mpg
- Stupidly quick
- Tough looks
- Build quality
- Handling

MAX DISLIKES
- Looking old
- Engine and 'box not as smooth as 1990s M3
- Tricky sat-nav

Just lie down in the middle of the road and take a picture as we scream past, we told the snapper. Amazingly, he did

TECH SPEC

ENGINE 3246cc, 6-cylinder, 24-valve • double VANOS • quad exhaust pipes
TRANSMISSION 6-speed manual (SMG is optional) • rear-wheel-drive
SUSPENSION Front: single joint spring strut axle • rear: central-arm axle with longitudinal control arms and double track control arms
BRAKES Front: 345mm discs with single-pot calipers • rear: 328mm discs
WHEELS & TYRES Front: 8x19in CSL-style alloys with 225/40 ZR19 Continental SportContacts • rear: 9.5x19in rims with 255/35 ZR19 rubber
BODYWORK Two-door coupe with full M-spec bodykit, vented wings, bonnet bulge and flared arches • available in all M3 colours plus Interlagos Blue
INTERIOR Full M-spec leather
PERFORMANCE Max power – 343bhp • max speed – 155mph • 0-62mph – 5.2secs
PRICE £43,555

Double-barrelled pipes blow the opposition away

CAR TEST RESULTS

	PERFORMANCE	HANDLING	LOOKS	INTERIOR	VALUE FOR MONEY	MAX POTENTIAL	TOTAL/30
Nissan 350Z	4	5	5	3	5	4	26
BMW M3 CS	5	5	5	4	4	3	26
Nismo S 350Z	4	5	5	4	3	4	25
Focus ST	5	4	4	4	4	4	25
Impreza WRX STi UK	5	5	4	3	4	4	25
Mitsi Evo FQ-340	5	5	4	3	3	4	24
Mitsi Evo VIII 260	4	5	3	4	4	4	24
Civic Type-R	4	5	3	4	4	4	24
Clio Trophy	4	5	4	4	3	3	24
Vauxhall Astra VXR	5	4	4	3	4	3	23
Clio 182 Cup	4	5	3	3	5	3	23
VW Golf R32	5	4	3	4	3	4	23
Golf Mk5 GTi	4	4	3	4	4	3	22
Mazda RX-8	4	5	3	4	3	3	22
Mini Cooper S	4	5	3	4	3	3	22
Seat Leon Cupra R	4	3	3	4	5	3	22

THE REST: Mitsi Colt CZT, Megane 225, Peugeot 206 GTi, Toyota Celica VVTi – 21 • Ford Focus ST170 – 20 • Astra GSi, Citroën C2 VTS, Seat Ibiza 20V TFR, MG ZR 160, Citroën C1 – 19

The styling may be getting on, but we still love it

VERDICT

After a day grinning like Pete Burns on LSD, we've got our answers.

First up, yes, the M3 CS is worth an extra £2400 on a 'normal' M3. The new steering and brakes are that good.

Second, is a 2001 M3 worth £18,000? Yes. The model barely changed over its life, so Y-plates can pass for new cars. Expect prices to fall further when the V8 car comes out.

Then we'd fit AP six-piston brake calipers, upgrade to new LED lights, fit the CS steering rack and get a non-tacky personal plate. Just watch out for hefty insurance premiums. Adrian Flux (*adrianflux.co.uk*) wouldn't quote for a 19 or 22-year-old. The price for a 26-year-old? £1400.

Finally, does it hang the back end out? Oh yes indeed...

"PRICES WILL FALL WHEN THE NEW V8 M3 COMES OUT"

BMW M3

$49,595–$57,295

EPA FUEL ECONOMY:

16 mpg city >>> 24 mpg hwy

Compare To:

- Audi S4
- Chevrolet Corvette
- Porsche 911 Carrera

MODELS				
Model	MSRP	Eng	Tran	Seats
Coupe	$49,595	I-6	6M	5
Convertible	$57,295	I-6	6M	4

SPECIFICATIONS	
Layout	rwd
Wheelbase	107.5 in.
Track, f/r	59.4/60.0 in.
Length	176.9 in.
Width	70.1 in.
Height	54.0 in.
Curb weight	3415 lb
Base engine	3.2-liter dohc 24V I-6
Horsepower	333 bhp @ 7900 rpm
Torque	262 lb-ft @ 4900 rpm
Optional engines	none
Transmission	6M, 6SMG
Suspension, f/r	ind/ind
Brakes, f/r	disc/disc, ABS
Tires	225/45ZR-18 f, 255/40ZR-19 r
Luggage capacity	9.5 cu ft
Fuel capacity	16.6 gal.
Side airbags	std
Stability control	std

WARRANTY	
Bumper-to-bumper	4 years/50,000 miles
Powertrain	4 years/50,000 miles
Roadside assistance	avail.

www.bmwusa.com

As we await the new E90-based M3 (with its rumored 4.0-liter 400-bhp V-8), we have to make do with the current E46 coupe and convertible and potent 333-bhp 3.2-liter inline-6. Yeah, we'll be just fine in the meantime. Despite the fact there are basically no changes to the M3 for 2006, it remains one of the most revered cars on the road. It combines sports-car handling with an upright, sedan-based body. It's available with either a 6-speed manual or the 6-speed SMG paddle-shift system. The Competition package adds stiffer suspension calibration, a quicker steering ratio, larger front brakes, 19-in. wheels, an M Track mode for the DSC system and an Alcantara-wrapped steering wheel. Though we're looking forward to the new M3, we will surely miss this current car's inline-6—one of the sweetest engines ever built.

What's Hot

- Rev-happy inline-6
- Great shift linkage
- Competition package

What's Not

- Understeers at limit
- Strange exhaust note
- Subdued styling

What's New

- Leather interior standard
- Rear sunshade option
- Optional 19-in. wheels

G770

The new M3 is coming soon. But its predecessors make for a formidable warm-up act. By **Chris Chilton**

Photography Barry Hayden

THREE KINGS

M3 CSL

BACK TO BASICS
E46 CSL (left) was the perfect antidote to the cosseting, softer E36. No-one could argue with its intent... though few agreed with the CSL's £58k price tag

M3. NO CONFUSION, JUST INSTANT COMPREHENSION. THE BADGE, the name, is universally understood. One letter and one number that combined are as globally recognisable as Schuey's chin. As you've probably read on the preceding pages, there's a new one coming this year and BMW can't afford to get it wrong. Here are three reasons why: the three greatest M3s of their generation, an E30 Sport Evo, an E36 Evo saloon and an E46 CSL, made-in-metal reminders of everything the M3 stands for.

Yet the moniker has come to stand for something quite different to the original E30 that BMW first revealed at the '85 Frankfurt motor show. Like so many of the greatest road cars, the M3 started off on the circuit, only finding its way onto autobahns because 5000 road cars were required to satisfy homologation requirements.

That first M3, based on the E30 saloon, was an unqualified success in every respect. It dominated touring car championships here and abroad, fending off the attack of Sierra and Merc 190 Cosworths and was a commercial success too, developing a strong following worldwide, and particularly in Britain; this despite coming in left-hand drive only and carrying a lofty £23k price tag that made it appear, on paper at least, dubious value in the face of Ford's faster, cheaper and lairier Cossie.

But if a close look reveals just where that money went, a drive confirms that it was worth it. Much more than a tarted-up 325i Sport, the original E30 shares only the bonnet with its humbler siblings. Those fabulous arches are all steel and flared to allow the racing version to run big rubber, the rear windscreen is uniquely raked to help direct air towards the rear spoiler and both screens are bonded to the body rather than housed in old fashioned rubbers to improve aerodynamics which was probably ▸

THE DARK SIDE
Joining the E30 club means driving from the left – we're not talking sexual innuendo here – and acclimatising to a dog-leg 'box. Quirks are part of the appeal, though

like urinating on a bonfire given the cliff-face grille's ability to scythe through the air. If, like me, you remember Saturday afternoons glued to the TV while Steve Soper doorhandled his E30 around Brands, you will not fail to get goose bumps standing in the company of what, to most people, is just another square old BMW. Then if, like me, you're very lucky, you get given the keys and lose the plot altogether.

Maths was never my strongest suit but you don't need a degree in hard sums to realise that the original M3 is so much more than the total of those parts. It's not particularly quick, it doesn't sound that special, you have to sit on the left and from inside it looks and feels no better than the mouldy 318i that some thoughtless sod has abandoned in the layby down the road.

But by the first corner you've worked out that although the first to second change is a little slow, the dog-leg pattern 'box with first down and to the left is a breeze and that neither it nor the left-hand drive layout are remotely hindering your progress.

By the second corner you're convinced that the steering is almost everything everyone says about it. Light, full of feel and razor sharp, its only slight failing is longish gearing (3.7 between the stops) which means that it never turns in quite as quickly as you'd expect.

By the third corner your mind is focused on the incredible combination of ride comfort and body control, how light and alert the car feels, how great the visibility is thanks to those slim pillars, and you begin to fully understand why millionaires with garages full of exotica are beating a path to E30 M3 ownership in the hope of fulfilment.

But the last corner, well that's the most dangerous corner of all. By then you're reaching for the cheque book yourself.

Which in the case of this beautiful black, one-of-600 Sport Evo would mean shelling out £17k as opposed to the £11k a regular M3 would set you back. That extra money buys different spoilers front and rear; a special interior with some very '80s red seatbelts; lower suspension; thinner glass and a smaller petrol tank to reduce weight. The 2.3-litre four is also stretched to 2.5-litres and from around 200bhp and 176lb ft (depending on year and spec) to 237bhp and 177lb ft.

That equates to around 6.0sec to 60mph and 16sec to the ton – a healthy ▸

LEFT FOR DEAD Later E36 (blue car pictured) may leave the E30 Sport Evo behind like OJ Simpson fleeing a theoretical crime scene, but the old car's got it licked dynamically

E30: OUR CHOICE BMW M3 EVOLUTION 2

See a good Evo 2, buy it. Nearly 20 years old, they're getting rarer by the day

THE SPORT EVO IS A WASTE of money. There, I've said it. May the torrent of raging emails commence. Yes, the last E30 has bags of limited edition appeal with its larger capacity, bucket seats, adjustable spoilers and, erm, pinstripes. But around £15k for an old E30? Drive one and it feels ludicrously over-valued. The stretched 2.5-litre engine is coarser than the 2.3, but otherwise the driving experience is little different to any other E30 M3.

No, the ideal choice is 1988's Evo 2. To keep the E30 competitive during 1980s touring car races, BMW evolved the race car but regulations demanded 500 examples be made for the road. Homologation they called it.

Between March and May 1988, 501 Evo 2s were produced (although the numbered plaque points to 500) in either Macao Blue, Nogaro Silver or Misano Red. Externally, the cars looked identical to the Evo 1, though 16in rims were standard not optional. Under the bonnet lies the biggest clue: the plenum chamber and rocker cover are white and detailed in M colours. The engine itself is the most powerful 2.3-litre, making 220bhp thanks to new pistons, cams, Motronic ECU, higher compression ratio and a revised air intake. The flywheel is also lighter and the final drive taller, hence a higher top speed – 148mph plays 143mph.

Exterior mods were similarly hardcore: lighter boot lid, front/rear spoilers and bumper supports along with thinner glass. Inside, Evo 2 owners get part-leather chairs.

If you want something genuinely rare, properly usable and truly race-bred, look no further.

BEN BARRY

NEED TO KNOW

E30 BMW M3 EVOLUTION 2

Price 1988: £26,960
Engine: 2302cc 16V in-line four, 220bhp @ 6750rpm, 181lb ft @ 4750rpm
Transmission: Five-speed manual, limited-slip differential, rear-wheel drive
Performance: 0-60mph 6.6sec, 148mph
Weight: 1200kg
Made from: Steel
Price now: £9-13k

improvement on the 7.0sec/18sec of the standard car but little better than hot hatch performance these days. 'Too many people have got the wrong idea about the E30 M3 and come back from a drive disappointed,' says Tony Halse of premier BMW finders and fettlers Munich Legends. 'What you're buying is a brilliant chassis, but none of them is truly quick. If it's straight-line go you're after you're looking at the wrong car.'

But that's not to say the M3's big capacity short-stroke four isn't without soul. It's not hugely refined or even that pleasant to listen to, but it is purposeful, just about torquey enough to pull the 1200kg shell along happily at low revs, and leaps to the redline when pushed, seemingly coming on cam twice, first at 5000rpm and then again at 6000rpm for the final 1000rpm flourish. There are only five rather than six forward gears but they're well stacked and fifth is a direct drive rather than overdrive, the pedals are ideal for heel and toeing and, just like every other control, perfectly weighted. And despite sharing its semi-trailing arm rear end with the regular E30 whose tail happy waywardness is the stuff of legend, the limited-slip-equipped M3 seems perfectly planted, happy to indulge you when you wish but only at your bidding.

Frankly, this thing is a revelation, agile and communicative like an Elise but practical, comfortable and equipped with anti-lock brakes, air con and most of the other things we expect of modern grown up cars. Could you really happily spend £22k on a new VW Golf GTI when you ▸

THE BUSINESS E36 saloon brings M5-like refinements and understatement to the M3 party. Estoril Blue paint marks this as a 3.2-litre Evo car. VANOS unit should explode any second now

E36: OUR CHOICE BMW M3 GT

Where most M3 GTs live and, indeed, die – on the racetrack. Buy yours wisely

THE E36 M3 NEVER TRULY recovered from its initial press slating. But I adore them and have owned both a 3.0-litre coupé and 3.2-litre saloon – the former for five years and 50,000 miles.

The '90s yielded some great drivers' machines and the E36 is one of them, coming when technology bounded forward before electronic safety nets truly took hold. This is partly why the E46 weighs 1570kg while the E36 comes in at 1460kg – there's little in it at the traffic light grand prix.

If you're deciding between the 3.0-litre or 3.2-litre, don't. It's 3.0-litre every time. These engines and five-speeders are smoother and far more reliable, the 3.2-litre cars' VANOS system (variable valve timing) being a particular weak spot. My own 3.2 had two VANOS units in 80,000 miles, costing £1500 a time where my abused 3.0-litre carries on regardless.

The big E36 weakness is snappy handling (grip, grip, grip… ooh) and vague steering. Unfortunately the 3.2's revised settings are superior, but not improved enough to sway me.

Any 3.0-litre coupé is a great buy, but the pick is 1995's GT. A homologation special, it came with green paint, larger front and rear spoilers and five-spoke alloys. The engine was usefully upgraded with race-ready mods and the GT got lower, stiffer suspension.

If you crave a GT but can't find RHD, don't be afraid to sit on the left – these cars are more plentiful and lack the UK cars' jarring wood trim. Compared with the E30 Sport Evo, the rarer GT seems conspicuously under-valued.
BEN BARRY

NEED TO KNOW

E36 BMW M3 GT

Price 1995: £39,000
Engine: 2990cc 24V straight six, 295bhp @ 7000rpm, 238lb ft @ 3900rpm
Transmission: Five-speed manual, limited-slip differential, rear-wheel drive
Performance: 0-60mph 5.4sec, 155mph
Weight: 1460kg
Made from: Steel/aluminium doors
Price now: £9-12k

BACK TO BASICS
No leather-swathed pampering for M3 CSL pilots, the lightweight special is a true road racer. Special owners' handbook indulges trackday fantasies

could have a nice one of these for half as much? Your only problem might be finding one; those with good cars tend to hang on to them and the cheap stuff is a vortex waiting to swallow your wallet whole.

You'll have no such trouble finding the car that replaced it, the E36, although again, the cheap stuff is best avoided. If Halse is right and the chassis is the heart of an E30, then it's the engine that takes centre stage in its successor. The parallel with Carol Shelby's Mustangs 20 years earlier is uncanny. Like the first generation GT350s, the E30 was built as a road-going racer, but by the second generation the lure of the dollar had turned the cars into faster, softer, more usable machines.

There was even an M3 saloon, but don't overlook it based on the number of doors. The E36 M3 saloon is a forgotten gem. Marrying the 318i's soul of discretion exterior with the luxury of a 7-series and the wickedness of the M3 coupé's new six-cylinder motor, it's the perfect Q-car and much rarer than its M3 coupé or convertible stablemates.

And there's nothing remotely soft about the engine. Starting out as a sophisticated 3.0-litre straight six fitted with variable valve timing on the inlet side and producing 286bhp and 238lb ft of churn, it transformed the M3's performance, dropping the 60mph sprint into the high fives and making 150mph a reality.

In contemporary tests *CAR* said the early saloon's bespoke, softer suspension settings made it more satisfying than the coupé; later Evo saloons like the one we drove got the coupé's setup and its bigger 3.2-litre engine and corresponding increase in power: 321bhp and 258lb ft made the then-new Porsche 996 appear as undernourished as a Kenyan marathon runner.

Inevitably, with its priorities shifted so far from those of the E30 the E36 feels radically different to its predecessor today, just as it did to the puzzled journalists who first drove it in 1992. Objectively it isn't a bad car, but it's easy to understand why hacks pleaded with BMW to call it the 330i instead and give them a proper M3. The steering – heavier and deader than the E30's, though pleasingly shorter between the lockstops – doesn't fizz with feedback like the older car's, although Evo versions are better than the 3.0-litre cars in this respect, and you can certainly feel that extra 250kg of kerbweight with every degree of lock applied to the wheel and every ▸

IN THE GENES
No DNA tests required to verify genealogy here. CSL picks up where the fast-living Sport Evo E30 left off – driving pleasure comes before everything else

THE CSL IS GREAT FOR ADRENALINE-FUELLED BLASTS, BUT THE TRACKDAY VIBE WEARS THIN

E46: OUR CHOICE BMW M3 CS

THE E46 MODEL RANGE IS far less confusing than the previous two generations. There's no saloon this time, no capacity hikes and no homologation specials – though BMW did campaign a Porsche-slaying V8 M3 GTR in the American Le Mans series, only 10 road cars appeared as a sop. All are brilliant, though avoid the convertible – a 330 is good enough for poseurs.

Of the three variants that remain – coupé, CS and CSL – the CS is the pick of the bunch. Built as a last-of-the-line special edition to keep E46 interest alive, it features CSL extras without exposing you to that hardcore car's drawbacks. So you get CSL-style wheels, uprated brakes, a track-mode option – which reduces the role of electronic safety gizmos – and the CSL's sharper steering and suede-covered steering wheel.

Drive one and the improvements to steering are particularly noticeable, the rim intimately feeding back the car's relationship with the asphalt and feeling particularly right when utterly sideways. However, these later cars still command high prices, which perhaps puts them out of contention for many. If that's your story, the base M3 is still an excellent choice and is rapidly plunging into £15k territory.

And what of the CSL? An utter hooligan, it's like your party animal mate: great fun for adrenaline-fuelled blasts, but the trackday vibe – particularly the hard-as-nails ride and rigid seats – wears thin on a four-hour bumper-to-bumper trek round the M25 after a two-day photo shoot… Over-priced at nearly £60k when new, they're now great value at half that.
BEN BARRY

The CS looks like a CSL, steers like a CSL, but it doesn't cost like a CSL. We love them

NEED TO KNOW

E46 BMW M3
CS

Price 2005: £43,555
Engine: 3246cc 24V straight six, 343bhp @ 7900rpm, 269lb ft @ 4900rpm
Transmission: Six-speed manual or semi-auto, limited-slip diff, rear-wheel drive
Performance: 0-60mph 4.8sec, 155mph
Weight: 1570kg
Made from: Steel, carbon roof
Price now: £35-38k

IT'S A CAR THAT CAN STILL TEACH US SO MUCH; A SIMPLE, LIGHT, FUN REAR-DRIVER

FAMILY TREE
E30 looks on bewildered, wondering how it spawned the autobahn-slaying E36. But the old-timer sees itself in the trackday nutcase E46 CSL

bump that passes beneath the 17-inch rims. The control weights are a mess too, the Evo's six-speed gearbox isn't as slick as the 3.0-litre E36's five-speeder, the clutch requires serious legwork and the throttle is absurdly stiff. You jump into the E30 and everything clicks, but not here, not in the E36.

But it's no boat and certainly doesn't fall to pieces when you up the pace, remaining composed if hardly as sharp as the E30. And once you're accustomed to the greater physical effort required to drive quickly, you find the confidence to exploit the stronger brakes and better stiction on faster corners. You also feel increasingly confident to delve into the straight six's huge reserves of power through slower bends, creating the sort of controlled smokey slides the E30 has the balance but not the grunt to perform, at least not in the dry. And the 36's huge reserves of torque, greater refinement and bigger cabin make it a genuinely appealing everyday prospect, especially with prices stretching down so low.

This much performance for less than £10k is real bargain territory because you'd need something like the last of our trio, the E46 CSL, to outdo you in a straight sprint. But let's rewind to 2000 and the launch of the car on which the CSL was based, a car whose mission was to deliver the sales success of the E36 but reclaim some of that respect lost in the switch from E30.

The rear wheel arches bulged, the front wings gained gills from the '70s CSL and the exhaust sprouted an extra pair of pipes to further mark the differentiation between it and its more mundane coupé siblings. The engine continued in 3.2-litre guise, but power shot up to 343bhp, 60mph tumbled to five dead and rear tyres began to fear for their lives in the face of a new M-diff which could provide 100 percent lock up across the back axle; sideways showboating had never been easier. It was and still is a great, but the CSL is better; just not the £20k better BMW seemed to think when it set the price at close to £60,000 in 2003. Plenty of speculators lost their shirts and immaculate sub-10,000-mile cars are now changing hands for as little as half that, making them phenomenal used buys.

Despite the carbon roof and interior embellishments, the special alloys, lightweight bumpers and boot lid and extra 17bhp, Halse reckons most potential buyers just don't see the CSL as different enough from a newer, regular E46 at the same price to take the plunge. But it is a different experience, even shorn of the Michelin Cup tyres as this car was for our rainswept photoshoot. Curiously, steering feel just off centre seems better without the Cup tyres, removing that leap of faith feeling you got when first turning in on the silly rubber. Definitely more at home on the smooth stuff, the more hardcore springs and dampers can struggle on messy B-roads but there's a taste of E30 Sport Evo in its alertness. This is helped by the quicker steering rack and the 110kg that was lopped from the tubby standard car's 1570kg kerbweight.

But best of all, it sounds absolutely glorious, the huge carbon airbox complete with dinner plate-sized butterfly valve filling the cabin with an incredible demonic shriek as you work your way up to 8200rpm before grabbing the next of six ratios in the mandatory SMG paddle-shift 'box. Turn down the wick and you've got a respectable motorway cruiser.

Which would you have? Office opinion here leans in favour of the CSL but if pressed I'd take an E30 for its purity. It's a car that can still teach us so much, and one which surely has a place in 2007. A simple, light, fun rear-driver that can fit the family and do the trackday stuff; no-one makes anything comparable these days. An RX-8 is on the right lines but falls short. So what about it, Nissan?

Another thought occurs, however. For the likely £50k a properly-specced next generation E90 M3 will cost, you could easily afford one car from each of these three previous generations. Focused E30, usable E36 and bonkers E46 CSL: even by the standards of the do-it-all M3, that's one pretty formidable line-up.

Thanks to Munich Legends (01825 740456 or munichlegends.co.uk) and owners Craig Smith and Nick Roberts for the E30 and E36.